# THE
# COMMERCIAL DIVER'S
# HANDBOOK

## *Second Edition*

Surface-Supplied Diving, Decompression,
& Chamber Operations Field Guide

## HAL LOMAX

BEST
PUBLISHING
COMPANY

The opinions expressed in this work are those of the author(s) and do not reflect the opinions of Best Publishing Company or its Editors.

Information contained in this work has been obtained by Best Publishing Company from sources believed to be reliable. However, neither Best Publishing Company nor its authors guarantees the accuracy or completeness of any information published herein and neither Best Publishing Company nor its authors shall be responsible for any errors, omissions, or claims for damages, including exemplary damages, arising out of use, inability to use, or with regard to the accuracy or sufficiency of the information contained in this publication.

Neither the editor, authors, publisher, or any other party associated with the production of this Handbook accept responsibility for any accident or injury resulting from the use of materials contained herein. Diving is an activity that has inherent risks. An individual may experience injury that can result in disability or death. All persons who wish to engage in diving activities must receive professional instructions. This Handbook does not consti-tute legal, medical, or other professional advice. Information in this publication is current as of the date of the printing.

All photos and images provided by author unless noted in the text.

©2020 Best Publishing Company

ISBN: 978-1-947239-27-2
Library of Congress Control Number: 2020918746

Best Publishing Company
631 US Highway 1, Suite 307
North Palm Beach, FL 33408

# TABLE OF CONTENTS

# INTRODUCTION

This handbook is intended to be used only by fully trained, competent commercial divers and not as a training manual for divers. It is presented as a pocket guide for the use of the decompression tables included, a refresher for safe and proper chamber operations, and as a quick reference guide for the treatment of diving-related disorders with a hyperbaric chamber.

## BASIC DECOMPRESSION THEORY

It is an established fact that, by weight, ⅘ of the human body is liquid. It is also an established fact that at high partial pressures, gases are absorbed into liquids, until there is no longer a pressure gradient. Knowing both of these facts, we can understand that the deeper a diver descends, the more inert gas his/her body absorbs. This is due to the pressure gradient from the respiratory system to the circulatory system, which transfers the inert gas and oxygen to the body tissues, and the pressure gradient from the blood vessels to the body tissue. This gas absorption will continue up to the point of total saturation.

There are several different terms used for the process of the body taking on inert gas: gas uptake, taking on a gas load, and saturation. An inert gas takes the same amount of time to go into solution, regardless of the depth, but less goes into solution at shallower depths and more at deeper depths. In the same way that inert gas goes into solution as the diver descends, so it also must come out of solution as the diver ascends on return to the surface. The terms used for the elimination of inert gas are: decompression, off-gassing and desaturation.

For this inert gas to safely come out of solution, it has to happen at a controlled rate. If inert gas is allowed to come out of solution too quickly, bubbles are formed in the tissues and bloodstream. These bubbles, when in tissue, put pressure on the surrounding tissue, nerves, or organs, causing pain and damage. When they occur in the bloodstream, they block the flow of blood, causing tissue damage and tissue death. These conditions, regardless of the inert gas used and regardless of the body system affected, are known as decompression sickness or more commonly, "the bends."

Different tissues in the body take on a gas load and off-gas at different rates. Tissue with greater blood flow will absorb inert gas at a faster rate and also off-gas quicker. Denser tissue will take more time to absorb gas and off-gas. Some tissue will absorb more inert gas and will require more to get it to the point of saturation. Body fat absorbs five times as much inert gas as water does. Because of this, divers must keep the percentage of fat in the body to a minimum and maintain fitness to help reduce the chance of decompression sickness.

We can take other measures as well. Proper hydration is critical in gas transfer, as is maintaining the proper core temperature of the diver, so we must ensure thermal stress on the diver is kept to a minimum and that the diver does not become dehydrated. By taking these measures and ensuring that we use the decompression tables properly, we are giving the diver the best possible chance to avoid suffering from pressure-related illness.

## DEVELOPMENT OF DECOMPRESSION TABLES

To avoid decompression sickness, we follow decompression tables that set out specific times spent at specific depths during the ascent to allow the inert gas to be safely eliminated from all of the various body tissues. Every decompression table used, whether a standard air table, a mixed gas table, a surface decompression table, or a saturation table, is based on the gas laws. Every decompression table used is also based on work previously done by other researchers, going back to the early work done by Robert Boyle (of Boyle's Law fame) in the late 1600s.

This has created a growing body of knowledge of how the human body absorbs gas while under pressure, how it eliminates the absorbed gas on ascent, and the times and depths to allow this elimination to happen safely. The early tables were developed by trial and error (involving painful experiences for the test subjects), while the most modern tables were developed by tracking inert gas bubbles in the tissues and bloodstream using Doppler ultrasound.

## DECOMPRESSION TABLES PRESENTED

This handbook presents a selection of decompression tables representing those most commonly used worldwide by commercial divers at the time of publication. It is anticipated that in time, the contractors using the older US Navy (USN) tables will upgrade to Revision 7; a few have done so already. We have included the Rev. 7 tables in this edition because they are now starting to see usage. It is expected that within the next two years they will be used by many of the diving contractors. The tables commonly used by the larger contractors in the Gulf of Mexico are included again. These "Gulf of Mexico" tables were produced by taking the *USN Rev. 3* tables and building the "padding" in. They have a good track record, in that when followed sensibly and correctly, there is seldom an incident. In fact, when compared to *USN Rev. 6 or 7,* the Gulf of Mexico tables are quite similar. Also included are the Canadian Navy diving tables, commonly called the DCIEM tables. These tables have been in use for more than 25 years, during which there have been few, if indeed any, recorded incidents. Various diving contractors throughout the world are using these tables, and they appear to be gaining popularity every year as their reputation spreads.

## DIFFERENCES IN THE VARIOUS TABLES

Each individual table has its own characteristics: the no-decompression limits; the ascent rates; the allowed surface interval; the decompression stop depths; and the decompression times. For example, the *USN Rev. 7* tables have a standard ascent rate of 30 feet per minute (fpm), while the DCIEM tables have an ascent rate of 60 fpm. The 60-ft table in the *USN Rev. 7* shows a no-decompression (no-D) limit of 63 minutes, while the DCIEM manual has a no-D limit of just 50 minutes. Furthermore, the surface interval allowed in surface decompression dives is not the same in these two tables.

Due to the differences in the various tables, it is absolutely imperative that divers **do not utilize the elements of more than one diving table on any**

**given dive or series of repetitive dives.** The specified ascent rates, stop times, stop depths, surface intervals, or decompression details cannot be substituted among the various diving tables.

## UNIQUE FEATURES AND COMMON FEATURES

With each set of tables, the ascent rates, travel rates between stops, decompression stop times, allowed surface intervals, and other features unique to that particular table are provided. For clarity, all of the tables are presented in feet of seawater only. Some common features among all the tables are as follows:

- The diver's depth is determined by a calibrated pneumofathometer (pneumo) gauge.
- The pneumofathometer correction factor is applied to all readings.
- The deepest depth (with correction factor added) is utilized to determine the proper table.
- For depth of dive the pneumo reading is taken at or below the diver's ankle (when standing).
- For decompression stops the pneumo reading is taken at the diver's midchest.
- The table selected is always **at least** the next greater depth than the maximum depth of the dive.
- Bottom time runs from leaving surface to leaving bottom, rounded up to the next full minute.
- The table selected is always **at least** the next longer time than the actual bottom time.
- The next longer table again is used if the diver is exceptionally cold or performing strenuous work.

| Pneumofathometer Reading | Correction Factor |
| --- | --- |
| 0 fsw – 100 fsw | + 1 fsw |
| 101 fsw – 200 fsw | + 2 fsw |
| 201 fsw – 300 fsw | + 4 fsw |
| 301 fsw – 400 fsw | + 7 fsw |

Source: *US Navy Diving Manual*

## REPETITIVE DIVES AND ASCENT TO ALTITUDE

Even on no-decompression dives, the diver must deal with a gas load. Diving tables typically are developed with the ascent on a no-D dive calculated as the required decompression. But even with the timed ascent rate, the diver has nitrogen remaining in his/her body after no-D dives, with more of a gas load on the diver the closer he/she gets to the no-D limit. This is the reason that any dive that follows another within a 12-hour period (18 hours when using DCIEM) is considered a repetitive dive and requires calculation of the residual nitrogen in establishing the bottom time of the second dive and any other consecutive dives.

This handbook presents two different sets of repetitive diving tables: *USN Rev. 7* and DCIEM. These two systems, though using the same decompression theory, cannot be interchanged in any way.

## ASCENT TO ALTITUDE AFTER DIVING

Ascending to altitudes above sea level after diving may pose a problem to the diver even on no-D dives, depending upon the gas load carried and the altitude to which he/she ascends. This handbook includes a table from *USN Rev. 7* for surface intervals required before ascent to various altitudes above sea level.

## DIVING OPERATIONS AT ALTITUDE

This handbook also includes procedures for diving at altitude as used by the Canadian Navy and the depth corrections for diving at altitude table as found in the DCIEM manual.

## NITROX

The use of nitrox ($N_2O_2$) has become more common on the commercial diving job. This handbook contains a section on nitrox operations. The nitrox section has a brief description of nitrox theory, a formula for establishing equivalent air depth (EAD), quick reference tables for calculating EAD, an overview of nitrox blending methods, and basic instructions for partial pressure blending of nitrox.

## HELIUM-OXYGEN

Although surface-supplied helium-oxygen (surface gas) has been discontinued in some areas of the world, there are still a lot of areas where it is used. This handbook includes the DCIEM helium-oxygen tables, reckoned by most in the industry to be the safest mixed-gas tables available today.

## TREATMENT OF DIVING-RELATED DISORDERS

This handbook includes flowcharts and treatment tables from the *USN Rev. 7* and a section on diving medicine and treatment of diving disorders. Diving supervisors have been trained to select and run treatment tables, hyperbaric physicians have been trained in the management of diving disorders, and the DMT has been trained to attend to the stricken diver while consulting with the hyperbaric physician ashore when necessary.

This handbook is not intended to be a definitive text on diving medicine and treatment but rather a refresher, as well as a quick reference guide to give the diving crew information so that they can assist the DMT in his/her duties.

It is strongly recommended on every decompression diving operation that the diving crew have at least one fully trained, qualified DMT for every shift, more than one if one will be diving, and an on-call hyperbaric physician readily available for consultation. Furthermore, it is strongly recommended that, unless there is an operational hyperbaric chamber very close by, dives beyond the no-decompression limits be avoided.

The Diving Medical Advisory Committee (DMAC) is an international group of physicians that provide medical guidance on hyperbaric and diving-related matters. The DMAC Medical Kits (DMAC 15, Rev. 4) are required on most offshore projects today. For the user's convenience, we have included the contents list for the DMAC 15 (Rev. 4) Trauma Kit and Chamber Internal Medical Kit, plus the DMAC 15 (Rev. 4) list of recommended drugs. The lists may be found in the section on diving medicine.

# SECTION 1
## Using the *USN Revision 7* Decompression Tables

### MOVING ONWARD FROM REVISION 6 TO REVISION 7

The air decompression tables found in the *USN Rev. 6* represented the largest change seen in a new revision of the manual since publication of the first edition. The standard air and surface decompression tables, formerly separate, were all combined in one document. The practice of surface decompression using air was no longer accepted, and the tables gave the user the option of in-water oxygen decompression. The air decompression tables found in *USN Rev. 7* do not represent nearly as great a change, but they have changed somewhat. Procedures have remained the same, but there are some changes in no-decompression limits and decompression stop times.

**Users of these tables should be aware that in-water oxygen decompression requires special precautions, including oxygen cleaning of the diving equipment and the dive control panel.**

### REVISION 7

When comparing the *USN Rev. 7* diving tables presented in this handbook with those found in the *USN Rev. 7*, the user will notice a few slight changes. The tables presented in this handbook do not extend nearly as far into the "exceptional exposure" range as do those in the *USN Rev. 7*. The safety guidelines and regulations governing commercial diving allow "exceptional exposure" dives only in the event of an emergency, so the extremely long bottom times are not required. Sufficient "exceptional exposure" room is provided to allow for emergencies.

In addition, while *USN Rev. 7* provides tables up to and including 300 fsw, this manual only provides tables up to 250 fsw. Air diving is not commonly performed deeper than 170 fsw in commercial operations, but for the abort procedure in the treatment tables, air tables up to 250 fsw are required. The tables have also been highlighted for ease of use in the field. The lower row on each schedule is highlighted green to indicate in-water oxygen decompression stops. The $O_2$ breathing periods in the chamber are highlighted in green. In the tables provided, all values indicated, whether time or depth, are intended to be exactly as found in the *USN Rev. 7*.

Choosing the Proper Table: Once the diver has arrived on bottom, take the initial pneumofathometer reading, and apply the appropriate correction factor to establish the maximum depth. Use the table greater than the maximum depth. For example, a pneumo reading of 72 fsw is taken. With the correction factor applied, the maximum depth is 73 fsw, so choose the 80 fsw table or greater, depending on company procedure. In areas with extreme tidal ranges, pneumo readings must be taken at regular intervals throughout the dive, as the diver's depth may change significantly over the duration of the dive.

Descent Rate: Although not considered critical, the descent rate will be determined by the diver's ability to equalize, but it should not exceed 75 fsw per minute.

Bottom Time: The diver's bottom time starts as soon as the diver leaves surface and ends as soon as the diver leaves bottom and starts the ascent. Bottom time is always rounded up to the next full minute. Choose the next greater table or as specified in the company procedures.

Ascent Rate (No-D or In-Water D): The ascent rate is 30fsw per minute (20 seconds per 10 fsw), with variations between 20 fsw and 40 fsw per minute being acceptable. The same rate is used between water stops and between the last stop and the surface.

Ascent Rate (Surface D): The ascent rate for surface decompression is 30 fsw per minute from bottom and between stops and 40 fsw per minute from the last stop (40 fsw) to the surface. If no stops are required, the ascent rate changes from 30 fsw per minute to 40 fsw per minute at the 40 fsw level.

Stop Times (In-Water Air): Stop time at the first stop begins when the diver arrives at the stop depth and ends when the diver leaves. Subsequent stop times include the travel time between stops.

Stop Times (In-Water Air/$O_2$): If the first stop is an air stop, it begins when the diver arrives. If it is an oxygen stop, it begins when the diver is confirmed on oxygen (after the vent) and ends when the diver leaves.

First In-Water Oxygen Stop: The first oxygen breathing water stop (if using in-water $O_2$) is at 30 fsw.

Last Water Stop (In-Water D): The last water stop for in-water decompression is at 20 fsw.

Last Water Stop (Surface D): The last water stop for surface decompression (when required) is at 40 fsw.

## PROCEDURE FOR WATER STOPS (IN-WATER AIR/OXYGEN DECOMPRESSION)

If water stops are required deeper than 30 fsw, they are to be performed on air. The first oxygen breathing water stop is at 30 fsw. The time for travel from the 40 fsw air stop (if required) to the 30 fsw stop, including the shift over to oxygen breathing, should not exceed 3 minutes. If no 30 fsw stop is required, the first is 20 fsw. Stop time begins when the diver is confirmed on oxygen. The diver is confirmed on oxygen once the diver's breathing gas has been changed from air to oxygen, and he or she has ventilated the helmet for 20 seconds.

After every 30 minutes of continuous oxygen breathing, an air break of 5 minutes is required. Time on air does not count toward the diver's decompression commitment. The only exceptions on the air breaks is when the total decompression time on oxygen is less than 35 minutes or when the final oxygen breathing period is 35 minutes or less. In these two instances, the air break may be skipped.

Ascent from the 30 fsw stop to the 20 fsw stop is performed while breathing oxygen. Ascent from the 20 fsw stop to surface is performed while breathing oxygen. If the total time on decompression stops breathing air/oxygen exceeds 90 minutes, surface decompression using oxygen is recommended, due to the possibility of CNS oxygen toxicity.

## CORRECTING VARIATIONS IN ASCENT RATE

The following rules for correcting variations in ascent rate are provided by the US Navy and apply to the in-water air decompression, in-water oxygen decompression, and surface decompression tables from *USN Rev. 7* as found in this handbook. As stated previously, variations between 20 and 40 fsw per minute are considered acceptable and do not require correction.

Travel Rate Exceeded: If the ascent rate exceeds 40 fsw per minute, stop the ascent, allow the watches to catch up, and restart the ascent.

Early Arrival at the First Decompression Stop: If the first stop is on air, begin the stop time once the required travel time has elapsed.

If the first stop is on oxygen, put the diver on oxygen on arrival at the stop. With the diver confirmed on oxygen, begin the stop time once the required travel time has elapsed.

### Delays in Arriving at the First Decompression Stop

- Delays up to one minute: A delay of up to and including one minute in arriving at the first decompression stop may be ignored.

- Delays greater than one minute, deeper than 50 fsw: Round up the delay time to the next whole minute and add to the bottom time. Select correct bottom time increment on the table. If no change is required, continue with decompression. If a change in the schedule is required and there are stops deeper than the diver's current depth, perform any missed deeper stops at the diver's current depth. Do not send the diver deeper. Once completed, continue decompression from current depth.

- Delays greater than one minute, shallower than 50 fsw: Round up the delay time to the next whole minute and add it to the first stop time.

## Delays in Leaving a Stop or Between Stops

- Delay less than one minute leaving an air stop: Disregard a delay of less than one minute. Resume the decompression schedule when delay is finished.

- Delay less than one minute between air stops: Disregard delays of less than one minute between air stops.

- Delay greater than one minute leaving air stop or between stops deeper than 50 fsw: Add the delay to the bottom time and recalculate decompression. If a new schedule is required, enter the new schedule at present stop or subsequent stop if between stops. Ignore missed stops or times deeper than the depth of delay.

- Delay greater than one minute leaving air stop or between stops shallower than 50 fsw: Ignore delay. Resume schedule when delay is finished.

- Delay leaving 30fsw $O_2$ stop or between 30 fsw and 20 fsw $O_2$ stop: Subtract any delay leaving 30 fsw $O_2$ stop or traveling between 30 fsw and 20 fsw $O_2$ stop from the 20 fsw stop time. If delay causes time on $O_2$ deeper than 20 fsw to exceed 30 min, give diver an air break at 30 min. When problem is resolved, resume $O_2$ decompression. Time on air to be considered "dead time."

- Delay leaving 20 fsw $O_2$ stop: Delays in leaving 20 fsw stop may be ignored. If diver's time on $O_2$ reached 30 min, give an air break and remain on air until problem resolved, then surface on $O_2$.

- Delay in travel from 40 fsw or 40 fsw stop to surface (Sur D $O_2$): Disregard delay unless five-minute surface interval is exceeded. If SI is exceeded, see next item.

#### Exceeding Five-Minute Surface Interval (Sur-D-O₂)

- SI greater than 5 min, less than 7 min: If the surface exceeds 5 min but is less than or equal to 7 min, increase $O_2$ period at 50 fsw to 30 min and ascend to 40 fsw on air break. This penalty is considered normal surface decompression and not an emergency procedure.

- SI greater than 7 min: Take diver to 60 fsw in chamber on $O_2$. If original schedule called for two $O_2$ periods or less, treat on USN TT5. If original schedule called for two and a half $O_2$ periods or more, treat diver on USN TT6.

## STANDARD PROCEDURE FOR SURFACE DECOMPRESSION USING OXYGEN

Follow the top row across on the appropriate decompression table for depth and bottom time. Complete any decompression stops required 40 fsw or deeper. On completion of the 40 fsw water stop, bring the diver to the surface at 40fsw per minute. If a 40 fsw stop is not required, the diver ascends from bottom to 40 fsw at an ascent rate of 30 fsw per minute and from 40 fsw to the surface at 40 fsw per minute.

The surface interval starts when the diver leaves the 40 fsw stop or passes 40 fsw on ascent. The surface interval ends when the diver is at 50 fsw in the chamber, breathing oxygen. Oxygen breathing periods are 30 minutes; half-periods are 15 minutes. The first half-period is spent at 50 fsw. If only one half-period is required, the diver is brought from 50 fsw to surface at 30 fsw per minute. If one full period is required, the first half is at 50 fsw, and the second half is at 40fsw. Travel from 50 fsw to 40 fsw is performed on oxygen, at a rate of 30 fsw per minute.

Travel from 50 fsw to 40 fsw is included in the first oxygen period. Five-minute air breaks are given at the end of each oxygen breathing period. Travel from 40 fsw to surface is at 30 fsw per minute breathing air. If more than four oxygen periods are required, the remaining oxygen periods (beyond the fourth) are performed at 30 fsw. Travel from 40 fsw to 30 fsw is performed during the air break, and at 30 fsw per minute.

Travel from 30 fsw to surface is at 30 fsw per minute breathing air. Note: The practice of a "slow bleed" from final stop depth to surface on oxygen as is common offshore is acceptable.

## PROCEDURE FOR SURFACE DECOMPRESSION FROM 30 FSW AND 20 FSW WATER STOPS

The supervisor has the option to cut short the in-water phase of decompression (air or $O_2$) and shift to surface decompression using oxygen. This may be desirable in the case of rapidly deteriorating sea-state, if the diver becomes ill, or if other events arise that would impact the diver's in-water decompression. Should the supervisor decide to shift to surface decompression mode, there are two options: prescribing the full number of oxygen breathing periods indicated in the surface decompression schedule or giving the diver credit for time spent decompressing on air or oxygen in-water, thereby reducing the number of oxygen periods. The following procedure is used:

1. If surface decompression is elected before the diver has shifted to oxygen, use the full number of oxygen-breathing periods shown in the table.

2. If surface decompression is elected after the diver has shifted to oxygen, compute the number of chamber oxygen periods as follows: multiply remaining time on oxygen at stops by 1.1 and divide the total by 30. Round the result up to the nearest half-period. The minimum requirement is one-half oxygen breathing period at 50 fsw.

3. If surface decompression is elected while the diver is decompressing on air, first convert the remaining air stop time to the equivalent oxygen stop time as shown below, then compute required chamber oxygen periods as in #2 of this list.

### Converting Stop Time on Air to Equivalent Stop Time on Oxygen

- Diver at 30 fsw: Divide the 30 fsw air stop time shown in the table by the 30 fsw oxygen time. The result is the *air/oxygen trading ratio.* Divide the remaining air stop time at 30 fsw by the air/oxygen trading ratio. The result is the equivalent remaining oxygen time at 30 fsw. Add the oxygen stop time at 20 fsw shown in the table. Multiply the sum by 1.1 and divide the total by 30. Round up the result to the nearest half period. The minimum requirement is one half-period at 50 fsw.

- Diver at 20 fsw: Divide the 20 fsw air stop time shown in the table by the 20 fsw oxygen time to achieve the trading ratio. Divide the remaining air stop time at 20 fsw by the air/oxygen trading ratio to establish equivalent remaining oxygen time. Multiply this figure by 1.1 and divide the total by 30. Round up the result to the nearest half period. The minimum requirement is one half period at 50 fsw.

## SAFE WAY OUT PROCEDURE

If diver cannot equalize to reach the 50 fsw $O_2$ stop in the chamber, press diver as deep as he or she can initially equalize. Have the diver begin $O_2$ breathing at that depth. Continue attempting to press the diver deeper. If the in-water air or air/$O_2$ schedule for that depth and time called for only a 20 fsw stop, attempt to press to 20 fsw. If the schedule called for a 30 fsw stop, attempt to press to 30 fsw. Double the number of $O_2$ periods called for in the table and have the diver perform them at the deepest depth the diver can achieve. $O_2$ time begins when the diver initially starts on $O_2$. Insert a 15-minute air break every 60 min. Time on air is "dead time" and does not count toward the decompression commitment.

Once $O_2$ time is completed, surface the chamber at 30 fsw per minute. Once on surface, observe the diver closely for signs of decompression sickness (DCS). The safe way out is intended to be used only for divers with equalization problems and is not to be used as a substitute for normal surface decompression.

### Selecting the Mode of Decompression

In-Water Air: In-water air decompression is most suitable for dives requiring less than 15 minutes total decompression stop time.

In-Water Air/$O_2$: In-water air/oxygen is strongly recommended when more than 15 minutes total decompression stop time is required in water. It is a good alternative to surface decompression when a chamber is not available or site conditions such as decontamination after haz-mat will compromise the surface interval time.

Surface Decompression Using Oxygen: The preferred method and safest for the diver is surface decompression using oxygen. This mode reduces the time that the diver must remain in the water and allows for visual monitoring of the diver during the decompression phase.

## REPETITIVE DIVES

Any time that a second dive is performed less than 12 hours after the first dive, the second dive is considered a repetitive dive. Diving contractors today do not allow repetitive dives to be performed after a dive that required any decompression. Many diving contractors do not allow repetitive dives under any circumstances, regardless of depth or nature of the dive. Some, however, still allow repetitive dives following no-decompression dives, and some allow repetitive dives on shallow dives only.

Even with no-decompression dives, the diver still carries a gas load. Any gas load the diver carries is added in his or her bloodstream and tissue to the gas load he or she takes on while performing repetitive dives. It must be accounted for in subsequent decompression. The gas load the diver carries following a dive and any subsequent surface interval is reckoned as "residual nitrogen time" (RNT) and is expressed in minutes. The depth and bottom time of the first dive obviously determine the RNT, and the longer the surface interval, the more the RNT diminishes. Once calculated, the RNT is added to the bottom time of the second dive, becoming the equivalent single dive time (ESDT) of the second dive and is used to calculate any decompression requirement.

Tables 9-7 and 9-8 from *USN Rev. 7* are provided to determine RNT and thereby calculate the ESDT of the repetitive dive. Before performing repetitive dives, first ensure repetitive dives are allowed by the contractor or client. It is strongly recommended that repetitive dives not be performed following any dive that required decompression.

## ASCENT TO ALTITUDE AFTER DIVING

In the same way that an existing gas load on the diver must be considered before performing a second dive, it must also be considered before ascent to altitude, whether the ascent is due to driving over mountainous terrain or flying in an aircraft. Most diving contractors state a minimum time before flying in their corporate safety policy, but few address driving over mountains. Included in this handbook is a table that indicates the required surface interval before ascent to altitude.

## EMERGENCY PROCEDURES

### Bottom Time Exceeds Table

In the unlikely even that a diver becomes trapped or has a severely fouled umbilical, and the bottom time exceeds those contained in this handbook, consult *USN Rev. 7*. The tables in this handbook have been shortened considerably due to safety guidelines in the commercial diving industry. In the event that the bottom time still exceeds the table, read down through the deeper tables until a bottom time of sufficient length is located. The air decompression tables in *USN Rev. 7* have exceptionally long bottom times inserted at various depths specifically for this contingency.

### Loss of Oxygen Supply in the Water

If the diver cannot be shifted to oxygen at 30 fsw or 20 fsw:

1. Have the diver continue on air while the problem is investigated.

2. If the problem can be resolved quickly, have the diver vent as soon as the oxygen is online and continue with the oxygen decompression as called for in the table. Time on air is "dead time."

3. If the problem cannot be resolved quickly, choose either surface decompression or in-water air. If surface decompression is chosen, the surface interval begins once the diver leaves the water stop.

If the oxygen supply is lost after the diver has shifted to oxygen on the 30 fsw or 20 fsw stop:

1.    Shift the diver to air.

2.    If the problem can be resolved quickly, have the diver vent as soon as the oxygen is online, and continue with the oxygen decompression as called for in the table. Time on air is "dead time."

3.    If the problem cannot be resolved and a chamber is available and ready, multiply the remaining oxygen stop time by 1.1, divide the total by 30, and round up the result to the next highest half period of oxygen breathing.

4.    If the problem cannot be resolved and a chamber is not available and ready, continue in-water decompression on air. Compute the remaining stop time on air at the depth of loss by multiplying the remaining stop time on oxygen by the ratio of air stop time to oxygen stop time at that depth.

*Example:* Diver is on oxygen stop at 20 fsw with 10 minutes remaining and oxygen is lost. The table calls for 140min on air at 20 fsw or 34min on $O_2$ at 20 fsw. The ratio of air stop time to oxygen stop time is 140/34 = 4.12. The remaining time on air at 20 fsw is 10 x 4.12 = 41.2 minutes. Rounding up the result gives the diver 42 minutes at 20 fsw on air.

If the loss of oxygen occurs on the 30 fsw stop, compute the remaining stop time on air at 30 fsw as above, then use the entire 20 fsw air stop time as indicated by the in-water air table.

### CNS Oxygen Toxicity Symptoms (Nonconvulsive) Occurring on Water Stop

Most divers will easily tolerate the oxygen exposures presented in these tables. CNS oxygen toxicity symptoms, if they do develop, are most likely to occur near the end of the 20 fsw stop. Nausea is the most likely symptom.

If the diver develops CNS toxicity symptoms on the 30 fsw or 20 fsw stop, take the following action:

1. If a chamber is on site and ready, shift to surface decompression. Ventilate the diver with air as the diver travels to surface. Multiply the remaining water stop time by 1.1, and divide the result by 30. Round up to the nearest oxygen breathing half-period. The minimum required is one half-period at 50 fsw.

2. If no chamber is available and the event occurs on a 30 fsw stop, shift the diver to air and bring the diver to 20 fsw. Once at 20 fsw, have the diver ventilate. Complete decompression on air at 20 fsw. Compute air stop time as follows: multiply the missed 30 fsw stop time by the ratio of air to oxygen stop time to obtain the equivalent missed air stop time at 30 fsw. Add this to the 20 fsw air stop time indicated in the air decompression table.

3. If no chamber is available and the event occurs on a 20 fsw stop, shift the diver to air and ventilate the diver. Multiply the missed oxygen time by the ratio of air to oxygen stop time at 20 fsw to obtain the equivalent air stop time. Complete decompression on air.

### Oxygen Convulsion Occurring at the 30 fsw or 20 fsw Water Stop

If, despite the measures above, symptoms progress to an oxygen convulsion, or if a convulsion suddenly occurs, take the following action:

1. Immediately shift the diver to air (if not already done).

2. If using 2 divers, have the unaffected diver ventilate the stricken diver.

3. Immediately deploy the standby and have the standby ventilate the diver.

4. Hold the divers at depth until the tonic-clonic phase of the convulsion has subsided (typically 1 – 2 minutes).

5. As soon as the tonic-clonic phase subsides, confirm that the diver is breathing (via diver radio) and have standby reconfirm.

6. If the diver is not breathing, have standby ensure an open airway by tilting the diver's head back.

7. If the stricken diver does not start breathing again, or if it is not possible to determine if the diver is breathing, have the standby attempt to maintain the open airway and recover the diver to surface at 30 fsw per minute. As soon as the diver is on surface, give airway and breathing support as necessary and immediately treat for arterial gas embolism.

8. If the diver is breathing, hold the diver at depth until he or she is stable, then surface decompress. Multiply the remaining stop time by 1.1, divide by 30 and round up to the next half oxygen period. One half-period is the minimum requirement.

9. If surface decompression is not possible, continue in-water decompression on air. Compute air stop time at the depth of the incident by multiplying the remaining oxygen stop time by the ratio of air stop time to oxygen stop time at that depth. If the event occurred on the 30 fsw stop, complete the air stop time remaining for 30 fsw, then complete the full 20 fsw stop as directed by the air decompression table.

### Symptoms of Decompression Sickness (DCS) Occurring During the Surface Interval

If during surface decompression operations the diver presents symptoms of Type I DCS during the surface interval (SI) either in-water travel or dress-down, compress the diver to 50 fsw as normally done. Delay neuro exam until diver is confirmed on oxygen at 50 fsw. If Type I symptoms are relieved within 15 minutes at 50 fsw, there are no neurological signs noted, and the SI did not exceed 5 minutes, increase the 50fsw stop to 30 minutes, travel from 50 fsw to 40 fsw on an air break, and then follow the schedule for the normal surface decompression (see Figure 1).

If Type I symptoms do not resolve during the 15-minute 50 fsw stop, or if symptoms resolve but the 5 min SI was exceeded, compress the diver to 60 fsw on oxygen. If the original schedule required two or fewer oxygen periods, treat on a USN Treatment Table 5. If the schedule required 2.5 or more, treat on a USN Treatment Table 6. Treatment time begins when the diver reaches 60 fsw on either table.

Figure 1. USN Table 9-2.

| Surface Interval (Note 1) | Asymptomatic Diver | Symptomatic Diver (Type I DCS) |
|---|---|---|
| 5 min or less | Follow original schedule | Increase $O_2$ time at 50 fsw from 15 to 30 min (Note 2) |
| Greater than 5 min but less than or equal to 7 min | Increase $O_2$ time at 50 fsw from 15 to 30 min | Treatment Table 5 if 2 or fewer SurDO$_2$ periods |
| Greater than 7 min | Treatment Table 5 if 2 or fewer SurDO$_2$ periods<br><br>Treatment Table 6 if more than 2 SurDO$_2$ periods | Treatment Table 6 if more than 2 SurDO$_2$ periods |

Notes:
1. Surface interval is the time from leaving the 40-fsw water stop to arriving at the 50-fsw chamber stop.
2. Type I symptoms must completely resolve during the first 15 minutes at 50 fsw and a full neurological examination at 50 fsw must be normal. If symptoms do not resolve within 15 min, treat the diver on Treatment Tables 5 or 6 as indicated for surface intervals longer than 5 min.
3. If Type II symptoms are present at any time during the surface interval or the neurological examination at 50 fsw is abnormal, treat the diver on Treatment Table 6.

Source: *US Navy Diving Manual Revision 7*

If Type II symptoms present at any time during the surface interval or if the neurological exam performed at 50 fsw indicates "abnormal," compress the diver to 60 fsw on oxygen and treat on a USN Treatment Table 6. Treatment time begins as soon as the diver reaches 60 fsw.

### Loss of Oxygen Supply to the Chamber

Any time the oxygen supply to the chamber is interrupted, have the occupant immediately begin breathing chamber air. If the interruption is temporary, resume oxygen breathing as soon as it is restored, and count the time on air as "dead time."

If the interruption is permanent, complete the decompression on 50/50 nitrox (preferred, if possible) or on chamber air.

If 50/50 is available, multiply the remaining time on oxygen by two to establish time required. When breathing the 50/50, air breaks are not required. The occupant may, however, wish to remove the built-in breathing system (BIBS) mask to drink. In this case, time on air is considered "dead time."

If only chamber air is available, multiply the remaining time on oxygen by the ratio of in-water air stop times to in-water oxygen stop times at both 30 fsw and 20 fsw to get the equivalent chamber time on air. Have the occupant spend 10% of the 50/50 time or equivalent air time at 40 fsw, 20% of the time at 30 fsw, and the remaining 70% of the time at 20 fsw. If the loss occurred at 50 fsw, ascend to 40 fsw and begin the stop time as outlined above. If the loss occurs at 30 fsw, have the occupant spend 30% of the time at 30 fsw and the remaining 70% at 20 fsw. Upon completion of the 20 fsw stop, surface the diver.

### CNS Oxygen Toxicity Occurring in the Chamber

At the first sign of CNS oxygen toxicity, remove the BIBS mask, with the occupant breathing chamber air or the BIBS feed changed from oxygen to air if the BIBS has multiple feeds. Fifteen minutes after all toxicity symptoms have subsided, resume oxygen breathing at the point of interruption. If symptoms develop a second time, do the following:

1.  Remove BIBS mask (or change BIBS feed to air).

2.  After all symptoms have subsided, bring the chamber 10 feet up in depth at 1 fsw/min ascent rate.

3.  Resume oxygen breathing at the shallower depth at the point of interruption.

4.  If symptoms develop a third time, finish decompression on chamber air. Compute the chamber time breathing air as in the previous Loss of Oxygen section. If the diver is at 40 fsw, 10% of the time is spent at 40 fsw, 20% is spent at 30 fsw, and the remaining 70% is spent at 20 fsw. If the diver is at 30 fsw, 30% is spent at 30 fsw, and

70% of the time is spent at 20 fsw. Surface the diver after the 20 fsw stop time is completed.

## Asymptomatic Omitted Decompression

Omitted decompression must be dealt with quickly and in the proper manner, even when there are no symptoms of decompression sickness evident. The depth at which the omission occurs and the length of time the diver is on surface until action can be taken will determine the course of action taken (see Figure 2).

Figure 2. Management of Asymptomatic Omitted Decompression.

| Deepest Decompression Stop Omitted | Surface Interval (Note 1) | Action | |
|---|---|---|---|
| | | Chamber Available (Note 2) | No Chamber Available |
| None | Any | Observe on surface for 1 hour | |
| | Less than 1 min | Return to depth of stop. Increase stop time by 1 min. Resume decompression according to original schedule. | |
| 20 or 30 fsw | 1 to 7 min | Use Surface Decompression Procedure (Note 3) | Return to depth of stop. Multiply 30 and/or 20 fsw air or $O_2$ stop times by 1.5. |
| | Greater than 7 min | Treatment Table 5 if 2 or fewer SurDO$_2$ periods. Treatment Table 6 if more than 2 SurDO$_2$ periods | |
| Deeper than 30 fsw | Any | Treatment Table 6 (Note 4) | Descent to depth of first stop. Follow the schedule to 30 fsw. Switch to $O_2$ at 30 fsw if available. Multiply 30 and 20 fsw air or $O_2$ stops by 1.5. |

Notes:
1. For surface decompression, surface interval is the time from the stop to arriving at the depth in the chamber.
2. Using a recompression chamber is strongly preferred over in–water recompression for returning a diver to pressure.
3. For surface intervals greater than 5 minutes but less than or equal to 7 minutes, increase the oxygen time at 50 fsw from 15 to 30 minutes.
4. If a diver missed a stop deeper than 50fsw, compress to 165 fsw and start Treatment Table 6A.

Source: U.S. Navy

## No Stops Required

If a diver makes an uncontrolled ascent (faster than 30 fsw/minute) to the surface on a no-decompression dive, the diver should be observed on the surface for one hour. If the diver remains asymptomatic, recompression will not be necessary. If the diver shows any symptoms of DCS or arterial gas embolism (AGE), the diver must be treated immediately following the appropriate flowchart and treatment table.

## Omitted 30 fsw or 20 fsw Stop

If a diver omits any or all of the stop time at either or both of the 30 fsw or 20 fsw decompression stops, the following actions are to be taken:

1. If the diver is on surface for less than one minute, return the diver to the depth of the stop the diver left. Increase the time at that stop by one minute. Resume decompression as originally indicated.

2. If the diver is on surface between one and five minutes and a chamber is on site, put the diver in the chamber and complete the decompression using surface decompression. If the diver was on an oxygen water stop at the time of omission, multiply the remaining time on oxygen by 1.1, divide the total by 30, then round up to the next highest half period of chamber oxygen. If the diver was on an air water stop at the time of omission, convert the remaining air stop time to equivalent time on oxygen (see Procedure for Surface Decompression from 30 fsw and 20 fsw Water Stops). If the omission occurs at 30 fsw, add the remaining equivalent oxygen time at 30 fsw the time shown in the table at 20 fsw. Use the sum of these two figures to compute the number of chamber oxygen periods. If the omission occurs at 20 fsw, use the remaining equivalent oxygen time to compute the chamber oxygen time. In any and all cases, the minimum is to be one-half oxygen period (15 minutes) at 50 fsw in the chamber.

3. If the diver is on surface more than five minutes but less than or equal to seven minutes, and a chamber is ready and available, put

the diver in the chamber and finish the decompression as outlined in #2 above, increasing the time at 50 fsw from 15 to 30 minutes.

4.  If the diver is on surface for more than 7 minutes and the chamber is available, run on a Treatment Table 5 if the original schedule called for 2 oxygen periods or less. If the schedule called for 2.5 or more, run the diver on a Treatment Table 6.

5.  If the diver is on surface over 1 minute, and there is no chamber available on site, return the diver to the omitted stop depth. Finish decompression in water, but multiply the 30 fsw and 20 fsw stop times (whether air or oxygen) by 1.5.

## Omitted Decompression Stops Deeper Than 30 fsw

If a diver omits part or all of a decompression stop at 40 fsw or deeper and a chamber is ready and available, treat the diver on a Treatment Table 6. If a chamber is not available, return the diver to the depth of the first decompression stop on the schedule. Follow the original decompression schedule. At 30 fsw, shift the diver to oxygen if available. Multiply the 30 fsw and 20 fsw air or oxygen stops by 1.5 to complete decompression.

## Decompression Sickness Occurring in the Water

On rare occasions, decompression sickness occurs in water during prolonged decompression using air or air/oxygen. The most common symptom is joint pain, but numbness, weakness, hearing loss, and vertigo have been known to occur. Typically, this happens on the shallow stops, just prior to surfacing. The diver should be brought to surface, the surface interval should be kept less than five minutes and regardless what symptoms present, the diver should be treated for Type II on a Treatment Table 6. Following treatment, the diver should be observed for six hours, and any recurrence should be treated as a recurrence of Type II symptoms.

Figure 3. USN Table 9-7.
No-Decompression Limits and Repetitive Group Designators for No-Decompression Air Dives.

| Depth (fsw) | No-Stop Limit | Repetitive Group Designation | | | | | | | | | | | | | | | |
|---|---|---|---|---|---|---|---|---|---|---|---|---|---|---|---|---|---|
| | | A | B | C | D | E | F | G | H | I | J | K | L | M | N | O | Z |
| 10 | Unlimited | 57 | 101 | 158 | 245 | 426 | * | | | | | | | | | | | |
| 15 | Unlimited | 36 | 60 | 88 | 121 | 163 | 217 | 297 | 449 | * | | | | | | | | |
| 20 | Unlimited | 26 | 43 | 61 | 82 | 106 | 133 | 165 | 205 | 256 | 330 | 461 | * | | | | | |
| 25 | 1102 | 20 | 33 | 47 | 62 | 78 | 97 | 117 | 140 | 166 | 198 | 236 | 285 | 354 | 469 | 992 | 1102 |
| 30 | 371 | 17 | 27 | 38 | 50 | 62 | 76 | 91 | 107 | 125 | 145 | 167 | 193 | 223 | 260 | 307 | 371 |
| 35 | 232 | 14 | 23 | 32 | 42 | 52 | 63 | 74 | 87 | 100 | 115 | 131 | 148 | 168 | 190 | 215 | 232 |
| 40 | 163 | 12 | 20 | 27 | 36 | 44 | 53 | 63 | 73 | 84 | 95 | 108 | 121 | 135 | 151 | 163 | |
| 45 | 125 | 11 | 17 | 24 | 31 | 39 | 46 | 55 | 63 | 72 | 82 | 92 | 102 | 114 | 125 | | |
| 50 | 92 | 9 | 15 | 21 | 28 | 34 | 41 | 48 | 56 | 63 | 71 | 80 | 89 | 92 | | | |
| 55 | 74 | 8 | 14 | 19 | 25 | 31 | 37 | 43 | 50 | 56 | 63 | 71 | 74 | | | | |
| 60 | 63 | 7 | 12 | 17 | 22 | 28 | 33 | 39 | 45 | 51 | 57 | 63 | | | | | |
| 70 | 48 | 6 | 10 | 14 | 19 | 23 | 28 | 32 | 37 | 42 | 47 | 48 | | | | | |
| 80 | 39 | 5 | 9 | 12 | 16 | 20 | 24 | 28 | 32 | 36 | 39 | | | | | | |
| 90 | 33 | 4 | 7 | 11 | 14 | 17 | 21 | 24 | 28 | 31 | 33 | | | | | | |
| 100 | 25 | 4 | 6 | 9 | 12 | 15 | 18 | 21 | 25 | | | | | | | | |
| 110 | 20 | 3 | 6 | 8 | 11 | 14 | 16 | 19 | 20 | | | | | | | | |
| 120 | 15 | 3 | 5 | 7 | 10 | 12 | 15 | | | | | | | | | | |
| 130 | 12 | 2 | 4 | 6 | 9 | 11 | 12 | | | | | | | | | | |
| 140 | 10 | 2 | 4 | 6 | 8 | 10 | | | | | | | | | | | |
| 150 | 8 | | 3 | 5 | 7 | 8 | | | | | | | | | | | |
| 160 | 7 | | 3 | 5 | 6 | 7 | | | | | | | | | | | |
| 170 | 6 | | | 4 | 6 | | | | | | | | | | | | |
| 180 | 6 | | | 4 | 5 | 6 | | | | | | | | | | | |
| 190 | 5 | | | 3 | 5 | | | | | | | | | | | | |

* Highest repetitive group that can be achieved at this depth regardless of bottom time.

Source: *US Navy Diving Manual Revision 7*

## Figure 4. USN Table 9-8.
## Residual Nitrogen Time Table for Repetitive Air Dives.

Locate the diver's repetitive group designation from his previous dive along the diagonal line above the table. Read horizontally to the interval in which the diver's surface interval lies.

Next, read vertically downward to the new repetitive group designation. Continue downward in this same column to the row that represents the depth of the repetitive dive. The time given at the intersection is residual nitrogen time, in minutes, to be applied to the repetitive dive.

\* Dives following surface intervals longer than this are not repetitive dives. Use actual bottom times in the Air Decompression Tables to compute decompression for such dives.

Repetitive Group at Beginning of Surface Interval

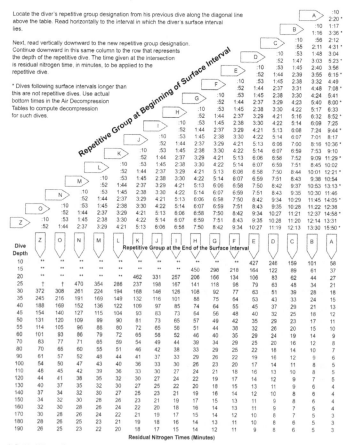

Residual Nitrogen Times (Minutes)

Repetitive Group at the End of the Surface Interval

| Dive Depth | Z | O | N | M | L | K | J | I | H | G | F | E | D | C | B | A |
|---|---|---|---|---|---|---|---|---|---|---|---|---|---|---|---|---|
| 10 | ** | ** | ** | ** | ** | ** | ** | ** | ** | ** | ** | 427 | 246 | 159 | 101 | 58 |
| 15 | ** | ** | ** | ** | ** | ** | ** | ** | 450 | 298 | 218 | 164 | 122 | 89 | 61 | 37 |
| 20 | ** | ** | ** | ** | ** | 462 | 331 | 257 | 206 | 166 | 134 | 106 | 83 | 62 | 44 | 27 |
| 25 | † | † | 470 | 354 | 286 | 237 | 198 | 167 | 141 | 118 | 98 | 79 | 63 | 48 | 34 | 21 |
| 30 | 372 | 308 | 261 | 224 | 194 | 168 | 146 | 126 | 108 | 92 | 77 | 63 | 51 | 39 | 28 | 18 |
| 35 | 245 | 216 | 191 | 169 | 149 | 132 | 116 | 101 | 88 | 75 | 64 | 53 | 43 | 33 | 24 | 15 |
| 40 | 188 | 169 | 152 | 136 | 122 | 109 | 97 | 85 | 74 | 64 | 55 | 45 | 37 | 29 | 21 | 13 |
| 45 | 154 | 140 | 127 | 115 | 104 | 93 | 83 | 73 | 64 | 56 | 48 | 40 | 32 | 25 | 18 | 12 |
| 50 | 131 | 120 | 109 | 99 | 90 | 81 | 73 | 65 | 57 | 49 | 42 | 35 | 29 | 23 | 17 | 11 |
| 55 | 114 | 105 | 96 | 88 | 80 | 72 | 65 | 58 | 51 | 44 | 38 | 32 | 26 | 20 | 15 | 10 |
| 60 | 101 | 93 | 86 | 79 | 72 | 65 | 58 | 52 | 46 | 40 | 35 | 29 | 24 | 19 | 14 | 9 |
| 70 | 83 | 77 | 71 | 65 | 59 | 54 | 49 | 44 | 39 | 34 | 29 | 25 | 20 | 16 | 12 | 8 |
| 80 | 70 | 65 | 60 | 55 | 51 | 46 | 42 | 38 | 33 | 29 | 25 | 22 | 18 | 14 | 10 | 7 |
| 90 | 61 | 57 | 52 | 48 | 44 | 41 | 37 | 33 | 29 | 26 | 22 | 19 | 16 | 12 | 9 | 6 |
| 100 | 54 | 50 | 47 | 43 | 40 | 36 | 33 | 30 | 26 | 23 | 20 | 17 | 14 | 11 | 8 | 5 |
| 110 | 48 | 45 | 42 | 39 | 36 | 33 | 30 | 27 | 24 | 21 | 18 | 16 | 13 | 10 | 8 | 5 |
| 120 | 44 | 41 | 38 | 35 | 32 | 30 | 27 | 24 | 22 | 19 | 17 | 14 | 12 | 9 | 7 | 5 |
| 130 | 40 | 37 | 35 | 32 | 30 | 27 | 25 | 22 | 20 | 18 | 15 | 13 | 11 | 9 | 6 | 4 |
| 140 | 37 | 34 | 32 | 30 | 27 | 25 | 23 | 21 | 19 | 16 | 14 | 12 | 10 | 8 | 6 | 4 |
| 150 | 34 | 32 | 30 | 28 | 26 | 23 | 21 | 19 | 17 | 15 | 13 | 11 | 9 | 8 | 6 | 4 |
| 160 | 32 | 30 | 28 | 26 | 24 | 22 | 20 | 18 | 16 | 14 | 13 | 11 | 9 | 7 | 5 | 4 |
| 170 | 30 | 28 | 26 | 24 | 22 | 21 | 19 | 17 | 15 | 14 | 12 | 10 | 8 | 7 | 5 | 3 |
| 180 | 28 | 26 | 25 | 23 | 21 | 19 | 18 | 16 | 14 | 13 | 11 | 10 | 8 | 6 | 5 | 3 |
| 190 | 26 | 25 | 23 | 22 | 20 | 18 | 17 | 15 | 14 | 12 | 11 | 9 | 8 | 6 | 5 | 3 |

\*\* Residual Nitrogen Time cannot be determined using this table (see paragraph 9-9.1 subparagraph 8 for instructions).

† Read vertically downward to the 30 fsw repetitive dive depth. Use the corresponding residual nitrogen times to compute the equivalent single dive time. Decompress using the 30 fsw air decompression table.

Source: *US Navy Diving Manual Revision 7*

Figure 5. Required Surface Interval Before Ascent to Altitude.

| Repet Group Designator | Increase in Altitude (feet) | | | | | | | | | |
|---|---|---|---|---|---|---|---|---|---|---|
| | 1000 | 2000 | 3000 | 4000 | 5000 | 6000 | 7000 | 8000 | 9000 | 10000 |
| A | 0:00 | 0:00 | 0:00 | 0:00 | 0:00 | 0:00 | 0:00 | 0:00 | 0:00 | 0:00 |
| B | 0:00 | 0:00 | 0:00 | 0:00 | 0:00 | 0:00 | 0:00 | 0:00 | 0:00 | 1:42 |
| C | 0:00 | 0:00 | 0:00 | 0:00 | 0:00 | 0:00 | 0:00 | 0:00 | 1:48 | 6:23 |
| D | 0:00 | 0:00 | 0:00 | 0:00 | 0:00 | 0:00 | 0:00 | 1:45 | 5:24 | 9:59 |
| E | 0:00 | 0:00 | 0:00 | 0:00 | 0:00 | 0:00 | 1:37 | 4:39 | 8:18 | 12:54 |
| F | 0:00 | 0:00 | 0:00 | 0:00 | 0:00 | 1:32 | 4:04 | 7:06 | 10:45 | 15:20 |
| G | 0:00 | 0:00 | 0:00 | 0:00 | 1:19 | 3:38 | 6:10 | 9:13 | 12:52 | 17:27 |
| H | 0:00 | 0:00 | 0:00 | 1:06 | 3:10 | 5:29 | 8:02 | 11:04 | 14:43 | 19:18 |
| I | 0:00 | 0:00 | 0:56 | 2:45 | 4:50 | 7:09 | 9:41 | 12:44 | 16:22 | 20:58 |
| J | 0:00 | 0:41 | 2:25 | 4:15 | 6:19 | 8:39 | 11:11 | 14:13 | 17:52 | 22:27 |
| K | 0:30 | 2:03 | 3:47 | 5:37 | 7:41 | 10:00 | 12:33 | 15:35 | 19:14 | 23:49 |
| L | 1:45 | 3:18 | 5:02 | 6:52 | 8:56 | 11:15 | 13:48 | 16:50 | 20:29 | 25:04 |
| M | 2:54 | 4:28 | 6:12 | 8:01 | 10:06 | 12:25 | 14:57 | 18:00 | 21:38 | 26:14 |
| N | 3:59 | 5:32 | 7:16 | 9:06 | 11:10 | 13:29 | 16:02 | 19:04 | 22:43 | 27:18 |
| O | 4:59 | 6:33 | 8:17 | 10:06 | 12:11 | 14:30 | 17:02 | 20:05 | 23:43 | 28:19 |
| Z | 5:56 | 7:29 | 9:13 | 11:03 | 13:07 | 15:26 | 17:59 | 21:01 | 24:40 | 29:15 |

NOTES:

All exceptional exposure dives require a 48-hour surface. Interval Before Ascent to Altitude

All treatments for decompression sickness or arterial gas embolism require a 72-hour surface interval before ascent to altitude.

When using this table, use the highest repetitive group factor obtained in the previous 24 hours.

Cabin pressures in commercial aircraft vary somewhat but typically are in the 8,000 ft range.

Surface $HeO_2$ dives require a 12-hour surface interval for no-decompression and 24 hours if the dive was beyond the no-decompression limit.

Source: Adapted from US Navy Diving Manual Rev. 7

# SECTION 2
# USN 30 fsw – 250 fsw Tables

The following air decompression tables are from the *US Navy Diving Manual Rev. 7* and have been modified for ease of use. The pale blue bar represents the bottom time limit set by the International Oil and Gas Producers Association in IOGP 411, the yellow bar represents that point at which surface decompression is required, and the red bar represents the exceptional exposure point. The green column to the right represents oxygen breathing periods in the deck chamber. Green highlight represents $O_2$ water stop time.

| US Navy Air Decompression Table | | | | | | | | | | | | | | |
|---|---|---|---|---|---|---|---|---|---|---|---|---|---|---|
| *As found in US Navy Diving Manual Revision 7* | | | | | | | | | | | | | | |
| **30 FSW** | **Time to First Stop** | **IN–WATER DECOMPRESSION STOPS (FSW)** Stop times expressed in minutes and include travel time to the stop except the first stop. Travel time is not included in the first stop time. | | | | | | | | | | **Total Ascent Time** | *US Navy Revision 7* | |
| **Bottom Time (min)** | **(M:S)** | **Gas** | **100** | **90** | **80** | **70** | **60** | **50** | **40** | **30** | **20** | **(M:S)** | **Chamber Oxygen Periods** | **Repet Group** |
| 371 | 1:00 | Air | | | | | | | | | 0 | 1:00 | 0 | Z |
| 380 | 0:20 | Air<br>Air/$O_2$ | | | | | | | | | 5<br>1 | 6:00<br>**2:00** | 0.5 | Z |
| **Surface Decompression Beyond This Point** | | | | | | | | | | | | | | |
| 420 | 0:20 | Air<br>Air/$O_2$ | | | | | | | | | 22<br>5 | 23:00<br>**6:00** | 0.5 | Z |
| **Exceptional Exposure – Emergency Use Only** | | | | | | | | | | | | | | |
| 480 | 0:20 | Air<br>Air/$O_2$ | | | | | | | | | 42<br>9 | 43:00<br>**10:00** | 1 | |
| 540 | 0:20 | Air<br>Air/$O_2$ | | | | | | | | | 71<br>14 | 72:00<br>**15:00** | 1.5 | |
| 600 | 0:20 | Air<br>Air/$O_2$ | | | | | | | | | 92<br>19 | 93:00<br>**20:00** | 1.5 | |

| US Navy Air Decompression Table |||||||||||||||
|---|---|---|---|---|---|---|---|---|---|---|---|---|---|---|
| *As found in US Navy Diving Manual Revision 7* |||||||||||||||

| 35 FSW | Time to First Stop | IN–WATER DECOMPRESSION STOPS (FSW) Stop times expressed in minutes and include travel time to the stop except the first stop. Travel time is not included in the first stop time. ||||||||| Total Ascent Time | US Navy Revision 7 ||
| --- | --- | --- | --- | --- | --- | --- | --- | --- | --- | --- | --- | --- | --- | --- |
| Bottom Time (min) | (M:S) | Gas | 100 | 90 | 80 | 70 | 60 | 50 | 40 | 30 | 20 | (M:S) | Chamber Oxygen Periods | Repet Group |
| 232 | 1:00 | Air | | | | | | | | | 0 | 1:10 | 0 | Z |
| 240 | 0:30 | Air Air/O$_2$ | | | | | | | | | 4 2 | 5:10 **3:10** | 0.5 | Z |
| **Surface Decompression Beyond This Point** |||||||||||||||
| **IOGP BOTTOM TIME LIMIT** |||||||||||||||
| 270 | 0:30 | Air Air/O$_2$ | | | | | | | | | 28 7 | 29:10 **8:10** | 0.5 | Z |
| 300 | 0:30 | Air Air/O$_2$ | | | | | | | | | 53 13 | 54:10 **14:10** | 0.5 | Z |
| 330 | 0:30 | Air Air/O$_2$ | | | | | | | | | 71 18 | 72:10 **19:10** | 1 | Z |
| **Exceptional Exposure – Emergency Use Only** |||||||||||||||
| 360 | 0:30 | Air Air/O$_2$ | | | | | | | | | 88 22 | 89:10 **23:10** | 1 | |
| 420 | 0:30 | Air Air/O$_2$ | | | | | | | | | 134 29 | 135:10 **30:10** | 1.5 | |
| 480 | 0:30 | Air Air/O$_2$ | | | | | | | | | 173 38 | 174:10 **44:10** | 1.5 | |

**US Navy Air Decompression Table**
*As found in US Navy Diving Manual Revision 7*

| 40 FSW | Time to First Stop | IN–WATER DECOMPRESSION STOPS (FSW) Stop times expressed in minutes and include travel time to the stop except the first stop. Travel time is not included in the first stop time. | | | | | | | | | | Total Ascent Time | US Navy Revision 7 | |
|---|---|---|---|---|---|---|---|---|---|---|---|---|---|---|---|
| Bottom Time (min) | (M:S) | Gas | 100 | 90 | 80 | 70 | 60 | 50 | 40 | 30 | 20 | (M:S) | Chamber Oxygen Periods | Repet Group |
| 163 | 1:20 | Air | | | | | | | | | 0 | 1:20 | 0 | 0 |
| 170 | 0:40 | Air | | | | | | | | | 6 | 7:20 | 0.5 | 0 |
| | | Air/O$_2$ | | | | | | | | | 2 | **3:20** | | |
| 180 | 0:40 | Air | | | | | | | | | 14 | 15:20 | 0.5 | Z |
| | | Air/O$_2$ | | | | | | | | | 5 | **6:20** | | |

**Surface Decompression Beyond This Point**

| 40 FSW | Time to First Stop | Gas | 100 | 90 | 80 | 70 | 60 | 50 | 40 | 30 | 20 | Total Ascent Time | Chamber Oxygen Periods | Repet Group |
|---|---|---|---|---|---|---|---|---|---|---|---|---|---|---|
| 190 | 0:40 | Air | | | | | | | | | 21 | 22:20 | 0.5 | Z |
| | | Air/O$_2$ | | | | | | | | | 7 | **8:20** | | |
| 200 | 0:40 | Air | | | | | | | | | 27 | 28:20 | 0.5 | Z |
| | | Air/O$_2$ | | | | | | | | | 9 | **10:20** | | |
| 210 | 0:40 | Air | | | | | | | | | 39 | 40:20 | 0.5 | Z |
| | | Air/O$_2$ | | | | | | | | | 11 | **12:20** | | |
| 220 | 0:40 | Air | | | | | | | | | 52 | 53:20 | 0.5 | Z |
| | | Air/O$_2$ | | | | | | | | | 12 | **13:20** | | |
| 230 | 0:40 | Air | | | | | | | | | 64 | 65:20 | 1 | Z |
| | | Air/O$_2$ | | | | | | | | | 16 | **17:20** | | |
| 240 | 0:40 | Air | | | | | | | | | 75 | 76:20 | 1 | Z |
| | | Air/O$_2$ | | | | | | | | | 19 | **20:20** | | |

**IOGP BOTTOM TIME LIMIT**

**Exceptional Exposure -- Emergency Use Only**

| 40 FSW | Time to First Stop | Gas | 100 | 90 | 80 | 70 | 60 | 50 | 40 | 30 | 20 | Total Ascent Time | Chamber Oxygen Periods | Repet Group |
|---|---|---|---|---|---|---|---|---|---|---|---|---|---|---|
| 270 | 0:40 | Air | | | | | | | | | 101 | 102:20 | 1 | Z |
| | | Air/O$_2$ | | | | | | | | | 26 | **27:20** | | |
| 300 | 0:40 | Air | | | | | | | | | 128 | 129:20 | 1.5 | |
| | | Air/O$_2$ | | | | | | | | | 33 | **34:20** | | |

## US Navy Air Decompression Table
*As found in US Navy Diving Manual Revision 7*

| 45 FSW | Time to First Stop | IN–WATER DECOMPRESSION STOPS (FSW) Stop times expressed in minutes and include travel time to the stop except the first stop. Travel time is not included in the first stop time. | | | | | | | | | | Total Ascent Time | US Navy Revision 7 | |
|---|---|---|---|---|---|---|---|---|---|---|---|---|---|---|
| Bottom Time (min) | (M:S) | Gas | 100 | 90 | 80 | 70 | 60 | 50 | 40 | 30 | 20 | (M:S) | Chamber Oxygen Periods | Repet Group |
| 125 | 1:30 | Air | | | | | | | | | 0 | 1:30 | 0 | N |
| 130 | 0:50 | Air<br>Air/O$_2$ | | | | | | | | | 2<br>1 | 3:30<br>2:30 | 0.5 | 0 |
| 140 | 0:50 | Air<br>Air/O$_2$ | | | | | | | | | 14<br>5 | 15:30<br>6:30 | 0.5 | 0 |
| **Surface Decompression Beyond This Point** | | | | | | | | | | | | | | |
| 150 | 0:50 | Air<br>Air/O$_2$ | | | | | | | | | 25<br>8 | 26:30<br>9:30 | 0.5 | Z |
| 160 | 0:50 | Air<br>Air/O$_2$ | | | | | | | | | 34<br>11 | 35:30<br>12:30 | 0.5 | Z |
| 170 | 0:50 | Air<br>Air/O$_2$ | | | | | | | | | 41<br>14 | 42:30<br>15:30 | 1 | Z |
| 180 | 0:50 | Air<br>Air/O$_2$ | | | | | | | | | 59<br>17 | 60:30<br>18:30 | 1 | Z |
| 190 | 0:50 | Air<br>Air/O$_2$ | | | | | | | | | 75<br>19 | 76:30<br>20:30 | 1 | Z |
| **IOGP BOTTOM TIME LIMIT** | | | | | | | | | | | | | | |
| **Exceptional Exposure – Emergency Use Only** | | | | | | | | | | | | | | |
| 200 | 0:50 | Air<br>Air/O$_2$ | | | | | | | | | 89<br>23 | 90:30<br>24:30 | 1 | Z |
| 210 | 0:50 | Air<br>Air/O$_2$ | | | | | | | | | 101<br>27 | 102:30<br>28:30 | 1 | Z |

## US Navy Air Decompression Table
*As found in US Navy Diving Manual Revision 7*

| 50 FSW | Time to First Stop | IN–WATER DECOMPRESSION STOPS (FSW) Stop times expressed in minutes and include travel time to the stop except the first stop. Travel time is not included in the first stop time. | | | | | | | | | | Total Ascent Time | US Navy Revision 7 | |
|---|---|---|---|---|---|---|---|---|---|---|---|---|---|---|
| Bottom Time (min) | (M:S) | Gas | 100 | 90 | 80 | 70 | 60 | 50 | 40 | 30 | 20 | (M:S) | Chamber Oxygen Periods | Repet Group |
| 92 | 1:40 | Air | | | | | | | | | 0 | 1:40 | 0 | M |
| 95 | 1:00 | Air Air/O$_2$ | | | | | | | | | 2 1 | 3:40 **2:40** | 0.5 | M |
| 100 | 1:00 | Air Air/O$_2$ | | | | | | | | | 4 2 | 5:40 **3:40** | 0.5 | N |
| 110 | 1:00 | Air Air/O$_2$ | | | | | | | | | 8 4 | 9:40 **5:40** | 0.5 | O |

**Surface Decompression Beyond This Point**

| | | | | | | | | | | | | | | | |
|---|---|---|---|---|---|---|---|---|---|---|---|---|---|---|
| 120 | 1:00 | Air Air/O$_2$ | | | | | | | | | 21 7 | 22:40 **8:40** | 0.5 | O |
| 130 | 1:00 | Air Air/O$_2$ | | | | | | | | | 34 12 | 35:40 **13:40** | 0.5 | Z |
| 140 | 1:00 | Air Air/O$_2$ | | | | | | | | | 45 16 | 46:40 **17:40** | 1 | Z |
| 150 | 1:00 | Air Air/O$_2$ | | | | | | | | | 56 19 | 57:40 **20:40** | 1 | Z |
| 160 | 1:00 | Air Air/O$_2$ | | | | | | | | | 78 23 | 79:40 **24:40** | 1 | Z |

**IOGP BOTTOM TIME LIMIT**

**Exceptional Exposure – Emergency Use Only**

| | | | | | | | | | | | | | | | |
|---|---|---|---|---|---|---|---|---|---|---|---|---|---|---|
| 170 | 1:00 | Air Air/O$_2$ | | | | | | | | | 96 26 | 97:40 **27:40** | 1 | Z |
| 180 | 1:00 | Air Air/O$_2$ | | | | | | | | | 111 30 | 112:40 **31:40** | 1.5 | Z |
| 190 | 1:00 | Air Air/O$_2$ | | | | | | | | | 125 35 | 126:40 **36:40** | 1.5 | Z |
| 200 | 1:00 | Air Air/O$_2$ | | | | | | | | | 136 39 | 137:40 **45:40** | 1.5 | Z |

| US Navy Air Decompression Table | | | | | | | | | | | | | | | |
| As found in US Navy Diving Manual Revision 7 | | | | | | | | | | | | | | | |

| **55 FSW** | **Time to First Stop** | **IN–WATER DECOMPRESSION STOPS (FSW)** Stop times expressed in minutes and include travel time to the stop except the first stop. Travel time is not included in the first stop time. | | | | | | | | | | **Total Ascent Time** | **US Navy Revision 7** | |
|---|---|---|---|---|---|---|---|---|---|---|---|---|---|---|---|
| **Bottom Time (min)** | **(M:S)** | **Gas** | **100** | **90** | **80** | **70** | **60** | **50** | **40** | **30** | **20** | **(M:S)** | **Chamber Oxygen Periods** | **Repet Group** |
| 74 | 1:50 | Air | | | | | | | | | 0 | 1:50 | 0 | L |
| 75 | 1:10 | Air | | | | | | | | | 1 | 2:50 | 0.5 | L |
|  |  | Air/O$_2$ | | | | | | | | | 1 | 2:50 |  |  |
| 80 | 1:10 | Air | | | | | | | | | 4 | 5:50 | 0.5 | M |
|  |  | Air/O$_2$ | | | | | | | | | 2 | 3:50 |  |  |
| 90 | 1:10 | Air | | | | | | | | | 10 | 11:50 | 0.5 | N |
|  |  | Air/O$_2$ | | | | | | | | | 5 | 6:50 |  |  |
| **Surface Decompression Beyond This Point** | | | | | | | | | | | | | | |
| 100 | 1:10 | Air | | | | | | | | | 17 | 18:50 | 0.5 | O |
|  |  | Air/O$_2$ | | | | | | | | | 5 | 9:50 |  |  |
| 110 | 1:10 | Air | | | | | | | | | 34 | 35:50 | 0.5 | O |
|  |  | Air/O$_2$ | | | | | | | | | 12 | 13:50 |  |  |
| 120 | 1:10 | Air | | | | | | | | | 48 | 49:50 | 1 | Z |
|  |  | Air/O$_2$ | | | | | | | | | 17 | 18:50 |  |  |
| **IOGP BOTTOM TIME LIMIT** | | | | | | | | | | | | | | |
| 130 | 1:10 | Air | | | | | | | | | 59 | 60:50 | 1 | Z |
|  |  | Air/O$_2$ | | | | | | | | | 22 | 23:50 |  |  |
| 140 | 1:10 | Air | | | | | | | | | 84 | 85:50 | 1 | Z |
|  |  | Air/O$_2$ | | | | | | | | | 26 | 27:50 |  |  |
| **Exceptional Exposure – Emergency Use Only** | | | | | | | | | | | | | | |
| 150 | 1:10 | Air | | | | | | | | | 105 | 106:50 | 1 | Z |
|  |  | Air/O$_2$ | | | | | | | | | 30 | 31:50 |  |  |
| 160 | 1:10 | Air | | | | | | | | | 123 | 124:50 | 1.5 | Z |
|  |  | Air/O$_2$ | | | | | | | | | 34 | 35:50 |  |  |

| US Navy Air Decompression Table | | | | | | | | | | | | | | |
| As found in US Navy Diving Manual Revision 7 | | | | | | | | | | | | | | |
| **60 FSW** | **Time to First Stop** | **IN–WATER DECOMPRESSION STOPS (FSW)** Stop times expressed in minutes and include travel time to the stop except the first stop. Travel time is not included in the first stop time. | | | | | | | | | | **Total Ascent Time** | **US Navy Revision 7** | |
| **Bottom Time (min)** | **(M:S)** | **Gas** | **100** | **90** | **80** | **70** | **60** | **50** | **40** | **30** | **20** | **(M:S)** | **Chamber Oxygen Periods** | **Repet Group** |
| 63 | 2:00 | Air | | | | | | | | | 0 | 2:00 | 0 | K |
| 65 | 1:20 | Air Air/O$_2$ | | | | | | | | | 2 1 | 4:00 3:00 | 0.5 | L |
| 70 | 1:20 | Air Air/O$_2$ | | | | | | | | | 7 4 | 9:00 6:00 | 0.5 | L |
| 80 | 1:20 | Air Air/O$_2$ | | | | | | | | | 14 7 | 16:00 9:00 | 0.5 | N |
| **Surface Decompression Beyond This Point** | | | | | | | | | | | | | | |
| 90 | 1:20 | Air Air/O$_2$ | | | | | | | | | 23 10 | 25:00 12:00 | 0.5 | 0 |
| 100 | 1:20 | Air Air/O$_2$ | | | | | | | | | 42 15 | 44:00 17:00 | 1 | Z |
| 110 | 1:20 | Air Air/O$_2$ | | | | | | | | | 57 21 | 59:00 23:00 | 1 | Z |
| 120 | 1:20 | Air Air/O$_2$ | | | | | | | | | 75 26 | 77:00 28:00 | 1 | Z |
| **IOGP BOTTOM TIME LIMIT** | | | | | | | | | | | | | | |
| **Exceptional Exposure – Emergency Use Only** | | | | | | | | | | | | | | |
| 130 | 1:20 | Air Air/O$_2$ | | | | | | | | | 102 31 | 104:00 33:00 | 1.5 | Z |
| 140 | 1:20 | Air Air/O$_2$ | | | | | | | | | 124 35 | 126:00 37:00 | 1.5 | Z |

# US Navy Air Decompression Table
*As found in US Navy Diving Manual Revision 7*

| 70 FSW | Time to First Stop | IN–WATER DECOMPRESSION STOPS (FSW) Stop times expressed in minutes and include travel time to the stop except the first stop. Travel time is not included in the first stop time. | | | | | | | | | | Total Ascent Time | US Navy Revision 7 | |
|---|---|---|---|---|---|---|---|---|---|---|---|---|---|---|
| Bottom Time (min) | (M:S) | Gas | 100 | 90 | 80 | 70 | 60 | 50 | 40 | 30 | 20 | (M:S) | Chamber Oxygen Periods | Repet Group |
| 48 | 2:20 | Air | | | | | | | | | 0 | 2:20 | 0 | K |
| 50 | 1:40 | Air | | | | | | | | | 2 | 4:20 | 0.5 | K |
|  |  | Air/$O_2$ | | | | | | | | | 1 | 3:20 | | |
| 55 | 1:40 | Air | | | | | | | | | 9 | 11:20 | 0.5 | L |
|  |  | Air/$O_2$ | | | | | | | | | 5 | 7:20 | | |
| 60 | 1:40 | Air | | | | | | | | | 14 | 16:20 | 0.5 | M |
|  |  | Air/$O_2$ | | | | | | | | | 8 | 10:20 | | |
| **Surface Decompression Beyond This Point** | | | | | | | | | | | | | | |
| 70 | 1:40 | Air | | | | | | | | | 24 | 26:20 | 0.5 | N |
|  |  | Air/$O_2$ | | | | | | | | | 13 | 15:20 | | |
| 80 | 1:40 | Air | | | | | | | | | 44 | 46:20 | 1 | O |
|  |  | Air/$O_2$ | | | | | | | | | 17 | 19:20 | | |
| 90 | 1:40 | Air | | | | | | | | | 64 | 66:20 | 1 | Z |
|  |  | Air/$O_2$ | | | | | | | | | 24 | 26:20 | | |
| **IOGP BOTTOM TIME LIMIT** | | | | | | | | | | | | | | |
| **Exceptional Exposure – Emergency Use Only** | | | | | | | | | | | | | | |
| 100 | 1:40 | Air | | | | | | | | | 88 | 90:20 | 1.5 | Z |
|  |  | Air/$O_2$ | | | | | | | | | 31 | 33:20 | | |
| 110 | 1:40 | Air | | | | | | | | | 120 | 122:20 | 1.5 | Z |
|  |  | Air/$O_2$ | | | | | | | | | 38 | 45:20 | | |
| 120 | 1:40 | Air | | | | | | | | | 145 | 147:20 | 2 | Z |
|  |  | Air/$O_2$ | | | | | | | | | 44 | 51:20 | | |

## US Navy Air Decompression Table
*As found in US Navy Diving Manual Revision 7*

| 80 FSW | Time to First Stop | IN–WATER DECOMPRESSION STOPS (FSW) Stop times expressed in minutes and include travel time to the stop except the first stop. Travel time is not included in the first stop time. | | | | | | | | | | Total Ascent Time | US Navy Revision 7 | |
|---|---|---|---|---|---|---|---|---|---|---|---|---|---|---|---|
| Bottom Time (min) | (M:S) | Gas | 100 | 90 | 80 | 70 | 60 | 50 | 40 | 30 | 20 | (M:S) | Chamber Oxygen Periods | Repet Group |
| 39 | 2:40 | Air | | | | | | | | | 0 | 2:40 | 0 | J |
| 40 | 2:00 | Air<br>Air/O₂ | | | | | | | | | 1<br>1 | 3:40<br>**3:40** | 0.5 | J |
| 45 | 2:00 | Air<br>Air/O₂ | | | | | | | | | 10<br>5 | 12:40<br>**7:40** | 0.5 | K |
| **Surface Decompression Beyond This Point** | | | | | | | | | | | | | | |
| 50 | 2:00 | Air<br>Air/O₂ | | | | | | | | | 17<br>9 | 19:40<br>**11:40** | 0.5 | M |
| 55 | 2:00 | Air<br>Air/O₂ | | | | | | | | | 24<br>13 | 26:40<br>**15:40** | 0.5 | M |
| 60 | 2:00 | Air<br>Air/O₂ | | | | | | | | | 30<br>16 | 32:40<br>**18:40** | 1 | N |
| 70 | 2:00 | Air<br>Air/O₂ | | | | | | | | | 54<br>22 | 56:40<br>**24:40** | 1 | O |
| **IOGP BOTTOM TIME LIMIT** | | | | | | | | | | | | | | |
| 80 | 2:00 | Air<br>Air/O₂ | | | | | | | | | 77<br>30 | 79:40<br>**32:40** | 1.5 | Z |
| **Exceptional Exposure – Emergency Use Only** | | | | | | | | | | | | | | |
| 90 | 2:00 | Air<br>Air/O₂ | | | | | | | | | 114<br>39 | 116:40<br>**46:40** | 1.5 | Z |
| 100 | 1:40 | Air<br>Air/O₂ | | | | | | | | 1<br>1 | 147<br>46 | 150:20<br>**54:20** | 2 | Z |
| 110 | 1:40 | Air<br>Air/O₂ | | | | | | | | 6<br>3 | 171<br>51 | 179:20<br>**61:20** | 2 | Z |

## US Navy Air Decompression Table
*As found in US Navy Diving Manual Revision 7*

| 90 FSW | Time to First Stop | Gas | IN–WATER DECOMPRESSION STOPS (FSW) Stop times expressed in minutes and include travel time to the stop except the first stop. Travel time is not included in the first stop time. | | | | | | | | | Total Ascent Time | US Navy Revision 7 | |
|---|---|---|---|---|---|---|---|---|---|---|---|---|---|---|
| Bottom Time (min) | (M:S) | Gas | 100 | 90 | 80 | 70 | 60 | 50 | 40 | 30 | 20 | (M:S) | Chamber Oxygen Periods | Repet Group |
| 33 | 3:00 | Air | | | | | | | | | 0 | 3:00 | 0 | J |
| 35 | 2:20 | Air / Air/O$_2$ | | | | | | | | | 4 / 2 | 7:00 / 5:00 | 0.5 | J |
| 40 | 2:20 | Air / Air/O$_2$ | | | | | | | | | 14 / 7 | 17:00 / 10:00 | 0.5 | L |
| **Surface Decompression Beyond This Point** | | | | | | | | | | | | | | |
| 45 | 2:20 | Air / Air/O$_2$ | | | | | | | | | 23 / 12 | 26:00 / 15:00 | 0.5 | M |
| 50 | 2:20 | Air / Air/O$_2$ | | | | | | | | | 31 / 17 | 34:00 / 20:00 | 1 | N |
| 55 | 2:20 | Air / Air/O$_2$ | | | | | | | | | 39 / 21 | 42:00 / 24:00 | 1 | O |
| 60 | 2:20 | Air / Air/O$_2$ | | | | | | | | | 56 / 24 | 59:00 / 27:00 | 1 | O |
| **IOGP BOTTOM TIME LIMIT** | | | | | | | | | | | | | | |
| 70 | 2:20 | Air / Air/O$_2$ | | | | | | | | | 83 / 32 | 86:00 / 35:00 | 1.5 | Z |
| **Exceptional Exposure – Emergency Use Only** | | | | | | | | | | | | | | |
| 80 | 2:00 | Air / Air/O$_2$ | | | | | | | | 5 / 3 | 125 / 40 | 132:40 / 50:40 | 2 | Z |
| 90 | 2:00 | Air / Air/O$_2$ | | | | | | | | 13 / 7 | 158 / 46 | 173:40 / 60:40 | 2 | Z |
| 100 | 2:00 | Air / Air/O$_2$ | | | | | | | | 19 / 10 | 185 / 53 | 206:40 / 70:40 | 2.5 | |

# US Navy Air Decompression Table
*As found in US Navy Diving Manual Revision 7*

| 100 FSW | Time to First Stop | IN–WATER DECOMPRESSION STOPS (FSW) Stop times expressed in minutes and include travel time to the stop except the first stop. Travel time is not included in the first stop time. | | | | | | | | | | Total Ascent Time | US Navy Revision 7 | |
|---|---|---|---|---|---|---|---|---|---|---|---|---|---|---|---|
| Bottom Time (min) | (M:S) | Gas | 100 | 90 | 80 | 70 | 60 | 50 | 40 | 30 | 20 | (M:S) | Chamber Oxygen Periods | Repet Group |
| 25 | 3:20 | Air | | | | | | | | | 0 | 3:20 | 0 | H |
| 30 | 2:40 | Air Air/O$_2$ | | | | | | | | | 3 2 | 6:20 **5:20** | 0.5 | J |
| 35 | 2:40 | Air Air/O$_2$ | | | | | | | | | 15 8 | 18:20 **11:20** | 0.5 | L |
| **Surface Decompression Beyond This Point** | | | | | | | | | | | | | | |
| 40 | 2:40 | Air Air/O$_2$ | | | | | | | | | 26 14 | 29:20 **17:20** | 1 | M |
| 45 | 2:40 | Air Air/O$_2$ | | | | | | | | | 36 19 | 39:20 **22:20** | 1 | N |
| 50 | 2:40 | Air Air/O$_2$ | | | | | | | | | 47 24 | 50:20 **27:20** | 1 | 0 |
| **IOGP BOTTOM TIME LIMIT** | | | | | | | | | | | | | | |
| 55 | 2:40 | Air Air/O$_2$ | | | | | | | | | 65 28 | 68:20 **31:20** | 1.5 | Z |
| 60 | 2:40 | Air Air/O$_2$ | | | | | | | | | 81 33 | 84:20 **36:20** | 1.5 | Z |
| **Exceptional Exposure – Emergency Use Only** | | | | | | | | | | | | | | |
| 70 | 2:20 | Air Air/O$_2$ | | | | | | | | 11 6 | 124 39 | 138:00 **53:00** | 2 | Z |
| 80 | 2:20 | Air Air/O$_2$ | | | | | | | | 21 11 | 160 45 | 184:00 **61:00** | 2.5 | Z |
| 90 | 2:00 | Air Air/O$_2$ | | | | | | | 2 2 | 28 14 | 196 53 | 228:40 **82:00** | 2.5 | |

| 110 FSW | Time to First Stop | IN–WATER DECOMPRESSION STOPS (FSW) Stop times expressed in minutes and include travel time to the stop except the first stop. Travel time is not included in the first stop time. | | | | | | | | | Total Ascent Time | US Navy Revision 7 | |
|---|---|---|---|---|---|---|---|---|---|---|---|---|---|---|
| Bottom Time (min) | (M:S) | Gas | 100 | 90 | 80 | 70 | 60 | 50 | 40 | 30 | 20 | (M:S) | Chamber Oxygen Periods | Repet Group |
| 20 | 3:40 | Air | | | | | | | | | 0 | 3:40 | 0 | H |
| 25 | 3:00 | Air Air/O$_2$ | | | | | | | | | 5 3 | 8:40 6:40 | 0.5 | I |
| 30 | 3:00 | Air Air/O$_2$ | | | | | | | | | 14 7 | 17:40 10:40 | 0.5 | K |
| **Surface Decompression Beyond This Point** | | | | | | | | | | | | | | |
| 35 | 3:00 | Air Air/O$_2$ | | | | | | | | | 27 14 | 30:40 17:40 | 1 | M |
| 40 | 3:00 | Air Air/O$_2$ | | | | | | | | | 39 20 | 42:40 23:40 | 1 | N |
| **IOGP BOTTOM TIME LIMIT** | | | | | | | | | | | | | | |
| 45 | 3:00 | Air Air/O$_2$ | | | | | | | | | 50 26 | 53:40 29:40 | 1 | O |
| 50 | 3:00 | Air Air/O$_2$ | | | | | | | | | 71 32 | 74:40 35:40 | 1.5 | Z |
| **Exceptional Exposure – Emergency Use Only** | | | | | | | | | | | | | | |
| 55 | 2:40 | Air Air/O$_2$ | | | | | | | | 5 3 | 85 33 | 93:20 44:20 | 1.5 | Z |
| 60 | 2:40 | Air Air/O$_2$ | | | | | | | | 13 7 | 111 36 | 127:20 51:20 | 2 | Z |
| 70 | 2:40 | Air Air/O$_2$ | | | | | | | | 26 14 | 155 42 | 184:20 64:20 | 2.5 | Z |

US Navy Air Decompression Table
As found in US Navy Diving Manual Revision 7

| US Navy Air Decompression Table | | | | | | | | | | | | | | | |
| As found in US Navy Diving Manual Revision 7 | | | | | | | | | | | | | | | |

| 120 FSW | Time to First Stop | IN–WATER DECOMPRESSION STOPS (FSW) Stop times expressed in minutes and include travel time to the stop except the first stop. Travel time is not included in the first stop time. | | | | | | | | | | Total Ascent Time | US Navy Revision 7 | |
|---|---|---|---|---|---|---|---|---|---|---|---|---|---|---|---|
| Bottom Time (min) | (M:S) | Gas | 100 | 90 | 80 | 70 | 60 | 50 | 40 | 30 | 20 | (M:S) | Chamber Oxygen Periods | Repet Group |
| 15 | 4:00 | Air | | | | | | | | | 0 | 4:00 | 0 | F |
| 20 | 3:20 | Air Air/O₂ | | | | | | | | | 4 2 | 8:00 6:00 | 0.5 | H |
| 25 | 3:20 | Air Air/O₂ | | | | | | | | | 9 5 | 13:00 9:00 | 0.5 | J |
| Surface Decompression Beyond This Point | | | | | | | | | | | | | | | |
| 30 | 3:20 | Air Air/O₂ | | | | | | | | | 24 13 | 28:00 17:00 | 0.5 | L |
| 35 | 3:20 | Air Air/O₂ | | | | | | | | | 38 20 | 42:00 24:00 | 1 | N |
| IOGP BOTTOM TIME LIMIT | | | | | | | | | | | | | | | |
| 40 | 3:00 | Air Air/O₂ | | | | | | | | 2 1 | 49 26 | 54:40 30:40 | 1 | O |
| 45 | 3:00 | Air Air/O₂ | | | | | | | | 3 2 | 71 31 | 77:40 36:40 | 1.5 | Z |
| Exceptional Exposure – Emergency Use Only | | | | | | | | | | | | | | | |
| 50 | 3:00 | Air Air/O₂ | | | | | | | | 10 5 | 84 33 | 98:40 46:40 | 1.5 | Z |
| 55 | 3:00 | Air Air/O₂ | | | | | | | | 19 10 | 116 35 | 138:40 53:40 | 2 | Z |
| 60 | 3:00 | Air Air/O₂ | | | | | | | | 27 14 | 142 39 | 172:40 61:40 | 2 | Z |

| US Navy Air Decompression Table | | | | | | | | | | | | | | |
| As found in US Navy Diving Manual Revision 7 | | | | | | | | | | | | | | |
| 130 FSW | Time to First Stop | IN–WATER DECOMPRESSION STOPS (FSW) Stop times expressed in minutes and include travel time to the stop except the first stop. Travel time is not included in the first stop time. | | | | | | | | | | Total Ascent Time | US Navy Revision 7 | |
| Bottom Time (min) | (M:S) | Gas | 100 | 90 | 80 | 70 | 60 | 50 | 40 | 30 | 20 | (M:S) | Chamber Oxygen Periods | Repet Group |
| 12 | 4:20 | Air | | | | | | | | | 0 | 4:20 | 0 | F |
| 15 | 3:40 | Air<br>Air/O₂ | | | | | | | | | 3<br>2 | 7:20<br>6:20 | 0.5 | G |
| 20 | 3:40 | Air<br>Air/O₂ | | | | | | | | | 8<br>5 | 12:20<br>9:20 | 0.5 | I |
| Surface Decompression Beyond This Point | | | | | | | | | | | | | | |
| 25 | 3:40 | Air<br>Air/O₂ | | | | | | | | | 17<br>9 | 21:20<br>13:20 | 0.5 | K |
| 30 | 3:20 | Air<br>Air/O₂ | | | | | | | | 2<br>1 | 32<br>17 | 38:00<br>22:00 | 1 | M |
| IOGP BOTTOM TIME LIMIT | | | | | | | | | | | | | | |
| 35 | 3:20 | Air<br>Air/O₂ | | | | | | | | 5<br>3 | 44<br>23 | 53:00<br>30:00 | 1 | O |
| 40 | 3:20 | Air<br>Air/O₂ | | | | | | | | 6<br>3 | 66<br>30 | 76:00<br>37:00 | 1.5 | Z |
| Exceptional Exposure – Emergency Use Only | | | | | | | | | | | | | | |
| 45 | 3:00 | Air<br>Air/O₂ | | | | | | | 1<br>1 | 11<br>6 | 84<br>33 | 99:40<br>49:00 | 1.5 | Z |
| 50 | 3:00 | Air<br>Air/O₂ | | | | | | | 2<br>2 | 20<br>10 | 118<br>36 | 143:40<br>57:00 | 2 | Z |
| 55 | 3:00 | Air<br>Air/O₂ | | | | | | | 4<br>4 | 28<br>14 | 146<br>40 | 181:40<br>67:00 | 2 | Z |

## US Navy Air Decompression Table
### As found in US Navy Diving Manual Revision 7

| 140 FSW | Time to First Stop | IN–WATER DECOMPRESSION STOPS (FSW) Stop times expressed in minutes and include travel time to the stop except the first stop. Travel time is not included in the first stop time. | | | | | | | | | | Total Ascent Time | US Navy Revision 7 | |
|---|---|---|---|---|---|---|---|---|---|---|---|---|---|---|
| Bottom Time (min) | (M:S) | Gas | 100 | 90 | 80 | 70 | 60 | 50 | 40 | 30 | 20 | (M:S) | Chamber Oxygen Periods | Repet Group |
| 10 | 4:40 | Air | | | | | | | | | 0 | 4:40 | 0 | E |
| 15 | 4:00 | Air | | | | | | | | | 5 | 9:40 | 0.5 | H |
| | | Air/O$_2$ | | | | | | | | | 3 | 7:40 | | |
| 20 | 4:00 | Air | | | | | | | | | 13 | 17:40 | 0.5 | J |
| | | Air/O$_2$ | | | | | | | | | 7 | 11:40 | | |
| **Surface Decompression Beyond This Point** | | | | | | | | | | | | | | |
| 25 | 3:40 | Air | | | | | | | | 3 | 24 | 31:20 | 1 | L |
| | | Air/O$_2$ | | | | | | | | 2 | 12 | 18:20 | | |
| 30 | 3:40 | Air | | | | | | | | 7 | 37 | 48:20 | 1 | N |
| | | Air/O$_2$ | | | | | | | | 4 | 19 | 27:20 | | |
| **IOGP BOTTOM TIME LIMIT** | | | | | | | | | | | | | | |
| 35 | 3:20 | Air | | | | | | | 2 | 7 | 49 | 71:00 | 1.5 | O |
| | | Air/O$_2$ | | | | | | | 2 | 4 | 26 | 36:20 | | |
| **Exceptional Exposure – Emergency Use Only** | | | | | | | | | | | | | | |
| 40 | 3:20 | Air | | | | | | | 4 | 7 | 82 | 97:00 | 1.5 | Z |
| | | Air/O$_2$ | | | | | | | 4 | 4 | 33 | 50:20 | | |
| 45 | 3:20 | Air | | | | | | | 5 | 18 | 116 | 141:00 | 2 | Z |
| | | Air/O$_2$ | | | | | | | 5 | 9 | 36 | 59:20 | | |
| 50 | 3:20 | Air | | | | | | | 8 | 27 | 142 | 184:00 | 2 | Z |
| | | Air/O$_2$ | | | | | | | 8 | 14 | 39 | 70:20 | | |

## US Navy Air Decompression Table
### As found in US Navy Diving Manual Revision 7

| 150 FSW | Time to First Stop | IN–WATER DECOMPRESSION STOPS (FSW) Stop times expressed in minutes and include travel time to the stop except the first stop. Travel time is not included in the first stop time. | | | | | | | | | Total Ascent Time | US Navy Revision 7 | |
|---|---|---|---|---|---|---|---|---|---|---|---|---|---|---|
| Bottom Time (min) | (M:S) | Gas | 100 | 90 | 80 | 70 | 60 | 50 | 40 | 30 | 20 | (M:S) | Chamber Oxygen Periods | Repet Group |
| 8 | 5:00 | Air | | | | | | | | | 0 | 5:00 | 0 | E |
| 10 | 4:20 | Air | | | | | | | | | 2 | 7:00 | 0.5 | F |
| | | Air/O$_2$ | | | | | | | | | 1 | 6:00 | | |
| 15 | 4:20 | Air | | | | | | | | | 8 | 13:00 | 0.5 | H |
| | | Air/O$_2$ | | | | | | | | | 5 | 10:00 | | |
| **Surface Decompression Beyond This Point** | | | | | | | | | | | | | | |
| 20 | 4:00 | Air | | | | | | | | 2 | 15 | 21:40 | 0.5 | K |
| | | Air/O$_2$ | | | | | | | | 1 | 8 | 13:40 | | |
| 25 | 4:00 | Air | | | | | | | | 7 | 29 | 40:40 | 1 | M |
| | | Air/O$_2$ | | | | | | | | 4 | 14 | 22:40 | | |
| **IOGP BOTTOM TIME LIMIT** | | | | | | | | | | | | | | |
| 30 | 3:40 | Air | | | | | | | 4 | 7 | 45 | 60:20 | 1.5 | O |
| | | Air/O$_2$ | | | | | | | 4 | 4 | 22 | 34:40 | | |
| **Exceptional Exposure – Emergency Use Only** | | | | | | | | | | | | | | |
| 35 | 3:40 | Air | | | | | | | 6 | 7 | 74 | 91:20 | 1.5 | Z |
| | | Air/O$_2$ | | | | | | | 6 | 4 | 30 | 44:40 | | |
| 40 | 3:20 | Air | | | | | | 2 | 8 | 14 | 106 | 132:00 | 2 | Z |
| | | Air/O$_2$ | | | | | | 2 | 8 | 7 | 35 | 59:20 | | |
| 45 | 3:20 | Air | | | | | | 3 | 8 | 24 | 142 | 181:00 | 2 | Z |
| | | Air/O$_2$ | | | | | | 3 | 8 | 12 | 40 | 72:20 | | |

## US Navy Air Decompression Table
*As found in US Navy Diving Manual Revision 7*

| 160 FSW | Time to First Stop | IN–WATER DECOMPRESSION STOPS (FSW) Stop times expressed in minutes and include travel time to the stop except the first stop. Travel time is not included in the first stop time. | | | | | | | | | | Total Ascent Time | US Navy Revision 7 | |
|---|---|---|---|---|---|---|---|---|---|---|---|---|---|---|
| Bottom Time (min) | (M:S) | Gas | 100 | 90 | 80 | 70 | 60 | 50 | 40 | 30 | 20 | (M:S) | Chamber Oxygen Periods | Repet Group |
| 7 | 5:20 | Air | | | | | | | | | 0 | 5:20 | 0 | E |
| 10 | 4:40 | Air | | | | | | | | | 4 | 9:20 | 0.5 | F |
|  |  | Air/O₂ | | | | | | | | | 2 | **7:20** |  |  |
| 15 | 4:20 | Air | | | | | | | | 2 | 10 | 17:00 | 0.5 | I |
|  |  | Air/O₂ | | | | | | | | 1 | 6 | **12:00** |  |  |
| **Surface Decompression Beyond This Point** | | | | | | | | | | | | | | |
| 20 | 4:00 | Air | | | | | | | 1 | 4 | 19 | 28:40 | 0.5 | L |
|  |  | Air/O₂ | | | | | | | 1 | 2 | 10 | **18:00** |  |  |
| 25 | 4:00 | Air | | | | | | | 4 | 7 | 35 | 50:40 | 1 | N |
|  |  | Air/O₂ | | | | | | | 4 | 4 | 17 | **30:00** |  |  |
| **IOGP BOTTOM TIME LIMIT** | | | | | | | | | | | | | | |
| 30 | 3:40 | Air | | | | | | 2 | 6 | 7 | 62 | 81:20 | 1.5 | Z |
|  |  | Air/O₂ | | | | | | 2 | 6 | 4 | 26 | **42:40** |  |  |
| **Exceptional Exposure – Emergency Use Only** | | | | | | | | | | | | | | |
| 35 | 3:40 | Air | | | | | | 4 | 6 | 8 | 89 | 111:20 | 1.5 | Z |
|  |  | Air/O₂ | | | | | | 4 | 6 | 4 | 34 | **57:40** |  |  |
| 40 | 3:20 | Air | | | | | | 6 | 6 | 21 | 134 | 171:20 | 2 | Z |
|  |  | Air/O₂ | | | | | | 6 | 6 | 11 | 38 | **70:40** |  |  |
| 45 | 3:20 | Air | | | | | 2 | 5 | 11 | 28 | 166 | 216:00 | 2.5 | Z |
|  |  | Air/O₂ | | | | | 2 | 5 | 11 | 14 | 45 | **86:20** |  |  |

## US Navy Air Decompression Table
### As found in US Navy Diving Manual Revision 7

| 170 FSW — Bottom Time (min) | Time to First Stop (M:S) | Gas | 100 | 90 | 80 | 70 | 60 | 50 | 40 | 30 | 20 | Total Ascent Time (M:S) | Chamber Oxygen Periods | Repet Group |
|---|---|---|---|---|---|---|---|---|---|---|---|---|---|---|
| 5 | 5:40 | Air | | | | | | | | | 0 | 5:40 | 0 | D |
| 10 | 5:00 | Air | | | | | | | | | 6 | 11:40 | 0.5 | G |
|  |  | Air/O₂ | | | | | | | | | 3 | 8:40 | | |

**Surface Decompression Beyond This Point**

| 170 FSW — Bottom Time (min) | Time to First Stop (M:S) | Gas | 100 | 90 | 80 | 70 | 60 | 50 | 40 | 30 | 20 | Total Ascent Time (M:S) | Chamber Oxygen Periods | Repet Group |
|---|---|---|---|---|---|---|---|---|---|---|---|---|---|---|
| 15 | 4:40 | Air | | | | | | | | 3 | 13 | 21:20 | 0.5 | J |
|  |  | Air/O₂ | | | | | | | | 2 | 6 | 13:20 | | |
| 20 | 4:20 | Air | | | | | | | 3 | 6 | 24 | 38:00 | 1 | M |
|  |  | Air/O₂ | | | | | | | 3 | 3 | 12 | 23:20 | | |

**IOGP BOTTOM TIME LIMIT**

| 170 FSW — Bottom Time (min) | Time to First Stop (M:S) | Gas | 100 | 90 | 80 | 70 | 60 | 50 | 40 | 30 | 20 | Total Ascent Time (M:S) | Chamber Oxygen Periods | Repet Group |
|---|---|---|---|---|---|---|---|---|---|---|---|---|---|---|
| 25 | 4:00 | Air | | | | | | 1 | 7 | 7 | 41 | 60:40 | 1 | O |
|  |  | Air/O₂ | | | | | | 1 | 7 | 4 | 20 | 37:00 | | |

**Exceptional Exposure – Emergency Use Only**

| 170 FSW — Bottom Time (min) | Time to First Stop (M:S) | Gas | 100 | 90 | 80 | 70 | 60 | 50 | 40 | 30 | 20 | Total Ascent Time (M:S) | Chamber Oxygen Periods | Repet Group |
|---|---|---|---|---|---|---|---|---|---|---|---|---|---|---|
| 30 | 4:00 | Air | | | | | | 5 | 7 | 7 | 77 | 100:40 | 1.5 | Z |
|  |  | Air/O₂ | | | | | | 5 | 7 | 3 | 30 | 50:00 | | |
| 35 | 3:40 | Air | | | | | 2 | 6 | 6 | 15 | 120 | 153:20 | 2 | Z |
|  |  | Air/O₂ | | | | | 2 | 6 | 6 | 8 | 37 | 68:40 | | |
| 40 | 3:40 | Air | | | | | 4 | 6 | 9 | 25 | 158 | 208:20 | 2.5 | Z |
|  |  | Air/O₂ | | | | | 4 | 6 | 9 | 12 | 44 | 84:40 | | |

*US Navy Revision 7*

*IN–WATER DECOMPRESSION STOPS (FSW) Stop times expressed in minutes and include travel time to the stop except the first stop. Travel time is not included in the first stop time.*

| US Navy Air Decompression Table | | | | | | | | | | | | | | |
|---|---|---|---|---|---|---|---|---|---|---|---|---|---|---|
| *As found in US Navy Diving Manual Revision 7* | | | | | | | | | | | | | | |

| 180 FSW | Time to First Stop | IN–WATER DECOMPRESSION STOPS (FSW) Stop times expressed in minutes and include travel time to the stop except the first stop. Travel time is not included in the first stop time. | | | | | | | | | | Total Ascent Time | US Navy Revision 7 | |
|---|---|---|---|---|---|---|---|---|---|---|---|---|---|---|
| Bottom Time (min) | (M:S) | Gas | 100 | 90 | 80 | 70 | 60 | 50 | 40 | 30 | 20 | (M:S) | Chamber Oxygen Periods | Repet Group |
| **PROHIBITED EXCEPT TO SAVE LIFE** | | | | | | | | | | | | | | |
| **Exceptional Exposure – Emergency Use Only** | | | | | | | | | | | | | | |
| **Surface Decompression Beyond This Point** | | | | | | | | | | | | | | |
| 6 | 6:00 | Air | | | | | | | | | 0 | 6:00 | 0 | E |
| 10 | 5:20 | Air | | | | | | | | | 8 | 14:00 | 0.5 | G |
|  |  | Air/O₂ | | | | | | | | | 4 | **10:00** | | |
| 15 | 4:40 | Air | | | | | | | 2 | 3 | 14 | 24:20 | 0.5 | K |
|  |  | Air/O₂ | | | | | | | 2 | 2 | 7 | **16:40** | | |
| 20 | 4:20 | Air | | | | | | 1 | 5 | 7 | 29 | 47:00 | 1 | M |
|  |  | Air/O₂ | | | | | | 1 | 5 | 3 | 15 | **29:20** | | |
| 25 | 4:20 | Air | | | | | | 5 | 6 | 7 | 57 | 80:00 | 1.5 | O |
|  |  | Air/O₂ | | | | | | 5 | 6 | 4 | 24 | **44:20** | | |
| 30 | 4:00 | Air | | | | | 3 | 6 | 6 | 7 | 95 | 121:40 | 1.5 | Z |
|  |  | Air/O₂ | | | | | 3 | 6 | 6 | 4 | 34 | **63:00** | | |
| 35 | 3:40 | Air | | | | 1 | 5 | 6 | 6 | 22 | 140 | 188:20 | 2 | Z |
|  |  | Air/O₂ | | | | 1 | 5 | 6 | 6 | 11 | 41 | **79:40** | | |

| 190 FSW | Time to First Stop | IN–WATER DECOMPRESSION STOPS (FSW) Stop times expressed in minutes and include travel time to the stop except the first stop. Travel time is not included in the first stop time. | | | | | | | | | | Total Ascent Time | US Navy Revision 7 | |
|---|---|---|---|---|---|---|---|---|---|---|---|---|---|---|
| Bottom Time (min) | (M:S) | Gas | 100 | 90 | 80 | 70 | 60 | 50 | 40 | 30 | 20 | (M:S) | Chamber Oxygen Periods | Repet Group |
| PROHIBITED EXCEPT TO SAVE LIFE | | | | | | | | | | | | | | |
| Exceptional Exposure – Emergency Use Only | | | | | | | | | | | | | | |
| Surface Decompression Beyond This Point | | | | | | | | | | | | | | |
| 5 | 6:20 | Air | | | | | | | | | 0 | 6:20 | 0 | D |
| 10 | 5:20 | Air | | | | | | | | 2 | 8 | 16:00 | 0.5 | H |
|    |      | Air/O₂ | | | | | | | | 1 | 4 | 11:00 | | |
| 15 | 4:40 | Air | | | | | | 1 | 3 | 3 | 16 | 28:20 | 0.5 | K |
|    |      | Air/O₂ | | | | | | 1 | 3 | 2 | 8 | 19:40 | | |
| 20 | 4:20 | Air | | | | | 1 | 2 | 6 | 7 | 34 | 55:00 | 1 | N |
|    |      | Air/O₂ | | | | | 1 | 2 | 6 | 4 | 17 | 35:20 | | |
| 25 | 4:20 | Air | | | | | 2 | 6 | 7 | 7 | 72 | 99:00 | 1.5 | Z |
|    |      | Air/O₂ | | | | | 2 | 6 | 7 | 3 | 28 | 51:20 | | |
| 30 | 4:00 | Air | | | | 1 | 6 | 5 | 7 | 13 | 122 | 158:40 | 2 | Z |
|    |      | Air/O₂ | | | | 1 | 6 | 5 | 7 | 7 | 38 | 74:00 | | |
| 35 | 4:00 | Air | | | | 4 | 5 | 6 | 8 | 26 | 165 | 218:40 | 2.5 | Z |
|    |      | Air/O₂ | | | | 4 | 5 | 6 | 8 | 13 | 45 | 91:00 | | |

The table title (spanning top): **US Navy Air Decompression Table** — *As found in US Navy Diving Manual Revision 7*

| US Navy Air Decompression Table | | | | | | | | | | | | | |
| As found in US Navy Diving Manual Revision 7 | | | | | | | | | | | | | |
| **200 FSW** | **Time to First Stop** | **IN−WATER DECOMPRESSION STOPS (FSW)** Stop times expressed in minutes and include travel time to the stop except the first stop. Travel time is not included in the first stop time. | | | | | | | | | | **Total Ascent Time** | **US Navy Revision 7** | |
| **Bottom Time (min)** | **(M:S)** | **Gas** | **100** | **90** | **80** | **70** | **60** | **50** | **40** | **30** | **20** | **(M:S)** | **Chamber Oxygen Periods** | **Repet Group** |
| PROHIBITED EXCEPT TO SAVE LIFE | | | | | | | | | | | | | | |
| Exceptional Exposure – Emergency Use Only | | | | | | | | | | | | | | |
| Surface Decompression Beyond This Point | | | | | | | | | | | | | | |
| 5 | 6:40 | Air | | | | | | | | | 0 | 6:40 | 0 | E |
| 10 | 5:40 | Air | | | | | | | | 3 | 8 | 17:20 | 0.5 | H |
|  |  | Air/O₂ | | | | | | | | 2 | 4 | **12:20** |  |  |
| 15 | 5:00 | Air | | | | | | 2 | 3 | 5 | 19 | 34:40 | 0.5 | L |
|  |  | Air/O₂ | | | | | | 2 | 3 | 3 | 8 | **23:00** |  |  |
| 20 | 4:40 | Air | | | | | 2 | 4 | 6 | 7 | 43 | 67:20 | 1 | O |
|  |  | Air/O₂ | | | | | 2 | 4 | 6 | 4 | 20 | **41:40** |  |  |
| 25 | 4:20 | Air | | | | 1 | 5 | 6 | 6 | 7 | 85 | 115:00 | 1.5 | Z |
|  |  | Air/O₂ | | | | 1 | 5 | 6 | 6 | 4 | 32 | **64:20** |  |  |
| 30 | 4:20 | Air | | | | 4 | 6 | 5 | 7 | 19 | 145 | 191:00 | 2 | Z |
|  |  | Air/O₂ | | | | 4 | 6 | 5 | 7 | 10 | 42 | **84:20** |  |  |
| 35 | 4:00 | Air | | | 2 | 5 | 5 | 6 | 13 | 28 | 188 | 251:40 | 2.5 | |
|  |  | Air/O₂ | | | 2 | 5 | 5 | 6 | 13 | 14 | 51 | **106:00** |  |  |

| 250 FSW | Time to First Stop | IN–WATER DECOMPRESSION STOPS (FSW) Stop times expressed in minutes and include travel time to the stop except the first stop. Travel time is not included in the first stop time. | | | | | | | | | | | Total Ascent Time | US Navy Revision 7 | |
|---|---|---|---|---|---|---|---|---|---|---|---|---|---|---|---|
| Bottom Time (min) | (M:S) | Gas | 110 | 100 | 90 | 80 | 70 | 60 | 50 | 40 | 30 | 20 | (M:S) | Chamber Oxygen Periods | Repet Group |
| **PROHIBITED EXCEPT TO SAVE LIFE** | | | | | | | | | | | | | | | |
| **Exceptional Exposure – Emergency Use Only** | | | | | | | | | | | | | | | |
| **Surface Decompression Beyond This Point** | | | | | | | | | | | | | | | |
| 4 | 7:40 | Air | | | | | | | | | | 4 | 12:20 | 0.5 | F |
| | | Air/O₂ | | | | | | | | | | 2 | **10:20** | | |
| 5 | 7:40 | Air | | | | | | | | | | 7 | 15:20 | 0.5 | G |
| | | Air/O₂ | | | | | | | | | | 4 | **12:20** | | |
| 10 | 6:20 | Air | | | | | | 2 | 2 | 4 | 3 | 15 | 33:00 | 0.5 | L |
| | | Air/O₂ | | | | | | 2 | 2 | 4 | 2 | 7 | **24:20** | | |
| 15 | 5:40 | Air | | | | 2 | 2 | 3 | 4 | 6 | 7 | 53 | 83:20 | 1 | O |
| | | Air/O₂ | | | | 2 | 2 | 3 | 4 | 6 | 4 | 22 | **49:40** | | |
| 20 | 5:20 | Air | | | 2 | 2 | 4 | 6 | 6 | 6 | 11 | 125 | 168:00 | 2 | Z |
| | | Air/O₂ | | | 2 | 2 | 4 | 6 | 6 | 6 | 6 | 39 | **82:20** | | |
| 25 | 5:00 | Air | | 1 | 4 | 4 | 5 | 6 | 6 | 10 | 28 | 189 | 258:40 | 2.5 | |
| | | Air/O₂ | | 1 | 4 | 4 | 5 | 6 | 6 | 10 | 14 | 51 | **112:00** | | |
| 30 | 4:40 | Air | 1 | 4 | 4 | 4 | 5 | 6 | 9 | 25 | 28 | 267 | 358:20 | 3.5 | |
| | | Air/O₂ | 1 | 4 | 4 | 4 | 5 | 6 | 9 | 25 | 15 | 72 | **160:40** | | |
| 35 | 4:40 | Air | 3 | 4 | 4 | 5 | 5 | 10 | 19 | 26 | 28 | 363 | 472:20 | 4 | |
| | | Air/O₂ | 3 | 4 | 4 | 5 | 5 | 10 | 19 | 26 | 14 | 93 | **204:40** | | |

# SECTION 3
# Instructions for Use:
# USN Modified Gulf of Mexico (GOM) Tables

The air decompression tables most commonly used offshore in the Gulf of Mexico are the modified USN or Gulf of Mexico tables. They have been known by several other names over the years because every major contractor has used them and inserted their name and corporate logo on the masthead. As the name modified USN suggests, these tables are based on the air decompression tables found in *US Navy Diving Manual Revision 3*, with modifications to make those tables safer for use through "padding."

## USING THE STANDARD AIR TABLE

The Standard Air Table has been modified in the following ways: the exceptional exposure dives start with significantly shorter bottom times than those found in the *US Navy Diving Manual Revision 3*; in-water decompression is performed with air or optional 50/50 $N_2O_2$; and times at decompression stops are significantly longer. Most contractors have their own depth/time addition rule, which can vary from 2 ft/2 min to 5 ft/5 min, and employees are required to adjust depth and bottom time accordingly. This applies to the surface decompression tables as well.

- Ascent Rate: The ascent rate on the standard air table is 60 feet per minute, to surface if no decompression required, or to the first decompression stop, and between in-water stops.

- Stop Times: The stop times on the standard air table begin when the diver arrives at stop depth and end when the diver begins travel to the next stop.

- Breathing Gas for Decompression: Air may be used for decompression, but 50/50 $N_2O_2$ is the preferred breathing gas. If the dive is deeper than 60 fsw, the diver is switched to 50/50 on ascent as the diver reaches the 60 fsw level, and the diver continues breathing 50/50 through the water stops to the surface. Decompression times are not modified when $N_2O_2$ is the breathing medium.

## USING THE SURFACE DECOMPRESSION WITH OXYGEN TABLE

The Sur-D-$O_2$ Table has been modified in the following ways: in-water stops may be performed with air or with 50/50 $N_2O_2$; a 10 min 50 fsw chamber stop (on oxygen) was added prior to the specified 40 fsw stop on oxygen; and the ascent (in chamber) from the 40 fsw stop to surface was changed from 1:20 to 10:00 minutes.

- Ascent Rate: The ascent rate on the surface decompression using the oxygen table is 25 feet per minute from bottom to the first in-water stop, one minute between water stops, and one minute from 30 fsw to surface.

- Stops (in-water): Stop times begin when the diver reaches the stop depth and end when the diver leaves. The final in-water stop is at 30 fsw.

- Surface Interval: The surface interval begins when the diver leaves the 30 fsw water stop and ends when the diver is at 50 fsw in the chamber. The diver should be on oxygen immediately at 50 fsw in the chamber, but up to three minutes is allowed. The total time allowed for the surface interval is five minutes. Exceeding the surface interval time requires treatment for omitted decompression.

- Stops (Chamber): The first chamber stop is at 50 fsw. Blow down time to 50 fsw is recommended to be 30 seconds. The diver breathes $O_2$ for 10 minutes at 50 fsw and then the diver is brought to 40 fsw in 1 minute. On arrival at 40 fsw, the diver has his or her first air break and then breathes oxygen on the 40 fsw stop. Travel time from 40 fsw to surface following decompression is 10 minutes while breathing oxygen. Maximum oxygen breathing periods are 20 minutes without a 5-minute air break.

- Breathing Gas for Decompression Air may be used for the in-water phase of decompression, but the option of using 50/50 exists, providing the water stops are 60 feet or shallower. Oxygen is the breathing gas used in the chamber, with air breaks inserted after every 20 minute oxygen period.

## EMERGENCY PROCEDURES FOR SURFACE DECOMPRESSION USING OXYGEN

### Safe-Way-Out Procedure

If the diver cannot equalize on the blow down to 50 fsw, take the following action:

- If the chamber is to a depth of at least 20 fsw, stop at 20 fsw.

- If the chamber is not to 20 fsw, gradually increase depth until 20 fsw is reached.

- The diver breathes oxygen at 20 fsw for twice the 50 fsw and 40 fsw times.

- Ascend to 10 fsw. The diver breathes oxygen at 10 fsw for twice the 50 fsw and 40 fsw times.

### Oxygen System Failure

In the event of an oxygen system failure, maintain the chamber at depth and start air breathing. If oxygen can be restored within 15 minutes, count time on air as "dead time," and resume decompression at the point of interruption. If oxygen cannot be restored within 15 minutes, finish the stop time as indicated on air, then ascend to 20 fsw. Repeat the 40 fsw stop time on air. Ascend to 10 fsw. Remain at 20 fsw breathing air for twice the 40 fsw stop time.

### CNS Oxygen Toxicity at 50 fsw Chamber Stop

In the event CNS oxygen toxicity occurs at the 50 fsw chamber stop and the first symptoms did not include a convulsion, the following actions should be taken:

- Remove BIBS from diver and have the diver breathe chamber air.

- Wait for all symptoms to subside, wait an additional 15 minutes, then travel to 40 fsw.

- Resume decompression at 40 fsw. Air breathing time is considered "dead time." Add any remaining time at 50 fsw to the 40 fsw stop time

### CNS Oxygen Toxicity at 40 fsw Chamber Stop

In the event CNS oxygen toxicity occurs at the 40 fsw chamber stop and the first symptoms did not include a convulsion, the following actions should be taken:

- Remove BIBS from diver and have the diver breathe chamber air.
- Wait for all symptoms to subside, wait an additional 15 minutes, then resume oxygen breathing.
- Resume decompression at the point of interruption. Time on air is considered "dead time."

### Oxygen Convulsion at 50 fsw or 40 fsw Chamber Stop

If the first symptom of CNS oxygen toxicity at either chamber stop is a convulsion, oxygen breathing must not be restarted. In this case, the following actions should be taken:

- Remove BIBS from the diver and have the diver breathe chamber air.
- Maintain chamber depth. Wait for convulsions to stop, ensuring that the diver has a clear airway and is breathing. Wait until the diver is fully conscious and all symptoms have resolved.
- If chamber is at 50 fsw, travel to 40 fsw. Combine 50 fsw and 40 fsw stop times. Finish combined stop times on air.
- If chamber is at 40 fsw, count all time at 40 fsw toward stop time. Complete any required stop time on chamber air
- Ascend to 20 fsw. Repeat combined 50 fsw and 40 fsw stop time on air
- Ascend to 10 fsw. Breathe air at 10 fsw for twice the combined 50 fsw and 40 fsw stop time.

### Omitted Decompression or Exceeded Surface Interval

If the diver is asymptomatic, press in chamber to 60 fsw and initiate a USN Treatment Table 5. If the diver presents signs or symptoms, press in chamber to 60 fsw and initiate a USN Treatment Table 6.

# SECTION 4
# USN Modified (Gulf of Mexico)
# Standard Air Tables

| US Navy Modified (Gulf of Mexico) Tables *Standard Air Tables* | | | | | | | | | | | | | |
|---|---|---|---|---|---|---|---|---|---|---|---|---|---|
| **40 ft** | **IN–WATER STOPS (MIN) AT DEPTHS (FSW)** Breathing medium is air with the option of 50/50 $N_2O_2$ at 60 fsw and shallower stops. | | | | | | | | | | | | |
| **Bottom Time (min)** | **Time to First Stop** | **100** | **90** | **80** | **70** | **60** | **50** | **40** | **30** | **20** | **10** | **Decomp Time (min)** | **Repet Group** |
| 200 | 0:00 | | | | | | | | | | 0 | 0:40 | * |
| 210 | 0:30 | | | | | | | | | | 2 | 2:40 | N |
| 230 | 0:30 | | | | | | | | | | 7 | 7:40 | N |
| 250 | 0:30 | | | | | | | | | | 11 | 11:40 | O |
| 270 | 0:30 | | | | | | | | | | 15 | 15:40 | O |
| **Standard Operational Depth/Time Limits** | | | | | | | | | | | | | |
| 300 | 0:30 | | | | | | | | | | 19 | 19:40 | Z |
| 360 | 0:30 | | | | | | | | | | 23 | 23:40 | |
| 480 | 0:30 | | | | | | | | | | 41 | 41:40 | |
| 720 | 0:30 | | | | | | | | | | 69 | 69:40 | |

IN-WATER PHASE:
Ascent rate is 60 fpm; stop time runs from arrival to leaving stop depth; travel time not included in stop time.

50/50 $N_2O_2$:
The 50/50 blend is not recommended for use in-water deeper than 60 fsw due to excessive $ppO_2$. Switch to blend at 60 fsw on ascent. $N_2O_2$ mix not to be routed through panel until diver is at 60 fsw. Umbilical to be thoroughly flushed with air and logged prior to each dive.

* Repetitive dives allowed only after a minimum surface interval of six hours, using only the modified GOM repet dive tables.

| US Navy Modified (Gulf of Mexico) Tables | | | | | | | | | | | | |
|:---:|:---:|:---:|:---:|:---:|:---:|:---:|:---:|:---:|:---:|:---:|:---:|:---:|
| *Standard Air Tables* | | | | | | | | | | | | |
| **50 ft** | **IN–WATER STOPS (MIN) AT DEPTHS (FSW)** Breathing medium is air with the option of 50/50 $N_2O_2$ at 60 fsw and shallower stops. | | | | | | | | | | | |
| **Bottom Time (min)** | **Time to First Stop** | **100** | **90** | **80** | **70** | **60** | **50** | **40** | **30** | **20** | **10** | **Decomp Time (min)** | **Repet Group** |
| 100 | 0:00 | | | | | | | | | | 0 | 0:50 | * |
| 110 | 0:40 | | | | | | | | | | 3 | 3:50 | L |
| 120 | 0:40 | | | | | | | | | | 5 | 5:50 | M |
| 140 | 0:40 | | | | | | | | | | 10 | 10:50 | M |
| 160 | 0:40 | | | | | | | | | | 21 | 21:50 | N |
| 180 | 0:40 | | | | | | | | | | 29 | 29:50 | O |
| 200 | 0:40 | | | | | | | | | | 35 | 35:50 | O |
| **Standard Operational Depth/Time Limits** | | | | | | | | | | | | | |
| 220 | 0:40 | | | | | | | | | | 40 | 40:50 | Z |
| 240 | 0:40 | | | | | | | | | | 47 | 47:50 | Z |

IN-WATER PHASE:
Ascent rate is 60 fpm; stop time runs from arrival to leaving stop depth; travel time not included in stop time.

50/50 $N_2O_2$:
The 50/50 blend is not recommended for use-water deeper than 60 fsw due to excessive $ppO_2$; switch to blend at 60 fsw on ascent; $N_2O_2$ mix not to be routed through panel until diver is at 60 fsw; umbilical to be thoroughly flushed with air and logged prior to each dive.

* Repetitive dives allowed only after a minimum surface interval of six hours, using only the modified GOM repet dive tables.

| | US Navy Modified (Gulf of Mexico) Tables<br>*Standard Air Tables* | | | | | | | | | | | | |
|---|---|---|---|---|---|---|---|---|---|---|---|---|---|
| **60 ft** | **IN–WATER STOPS (MIN) AT DEPTHS (FSW)**<br>Breathing medium is air with the option of 50/50 $N_2O_2$ at 60 fsw and shallower stops. | | | | | | | | | | | | |
| **Bottom Time (min)** | **Time to First Stop** | **100** | **90** | **80** | **70** | **60** | **50** | **40** | **30** | **20** | **10** | **Decomp Time (min)** | **Repet Group** |
| 60 | 0:00 | | | | | | | | | | 0 | 1:00 | * |
| 70 | 0:50 | | | | | | | | | | 2 | 3:00 | K |
| 80 | 0:50 | | | | | | | | | | 7 | 8:00 | L |
| 100 | 0:50 | | | | | | | | | | 14 | 15:00 | M |
| 120 | 0:50 | | | | | | | | | | 26 | 27:00 | N |
| 140 | 0:50 | | | | | | | | | | 39 | 40:00 | O |
| **Standard Operational Depth/Time Limits** | | | | | | | | | | | | | |
| 160 | 0:50 | | | | | | | | | | 48 | 49:00 | Z |
| 180 | 0:50 | | | | | | | | | | 56 | 57:00 | Z |
| 200 | 0:40 | | | | | | | | | 1 | 69 | 71:00 | Z |
| 240 | 0:40 | | | | | | | | | 2 | 79 | 82:00 | |
| 360 | 0:40 | | | | | | | | | 20 | 119 | 140:00 | |
| 480 | 0:40 | | | | | | | | | 44 | 148 | 193:00 | |
| 720 | 0:40 | | | | | | | | | 78 | 187 | 266:00 | |

IN-WATER PHASE:
Ascent rate is 60 fpm; stop time runs from arrival to leaving stop depth; travel time not included in stop time.

50/50 $N_2O_2$:
The 50/50 blend is not recommended for use in water deeper than 60 fsw due to excessive $ppO_2$; switch to blend at 60 fsw on ascent; $N_2O_2$ mix not to be routed through panel until diver is at 60 fsw; umbilical to be thoroughly flushed with air and logged prior to each dive.

* Repetitive dives allowed only after a minimum surface interval of six hours, using only the modified GOM repet dive tables.

| US Navy Modified (Gulf of Mexico) Tables | | | | | | | | | | | | | |
| --- | --- | --- | --- | --- | --- | --- | --- | --- | --- | --- | --- | --- | --- |
| Standard Air Tables | | | | | | | | | | | | | |

| 70 ft | IN–WATER STOPS (MIN) AT DEPTHS (FSW) Breathing medium is air with the option of 50/50 N₂O₂ at 60 fsw and shallower stops. | | | | | | | | | | | | |
| --- | --- | --- | --- | --- | --- | --- | --- | --- | --- | --- | --- | --- | --- |

| Bottom Time (min) | Time to First Stop | 100 | 90 | 80 | 70 | 60 | 50 | 40 | 30 | 20 | 10 | Decomp Time (min) | Repet Group |
| --- | --- | --- | --- | --- | --- | --- | --- | --- | --- | --- | --- | --- | --- |
| 50 | 0:00 | | | | | | | | | | 0 | 1:10 | * |
| 60 | 1:00 | | | | | | | | | | 8 | 9:10 | K |
| 70 | 1:00 | | | | | | | | | | 14 | 15:10 | L |
| 80 | 1:00 | | | | | | | | | | 18 | 19:10 | M |
| 90 | 1:00 | | | | | | | | | | 23 | 24:10 | N |
| 100 | 1:00 | | | | | | | | | | 33 | 34:10 | N |
| 110 | 0:50 | | | | | | | | | 2 | 41 | 44:10 | O |
| 120 | 0:50 | | | | | | | | | 4 | 47 | 52:10 | O |
| Standard Operational Depth/Time Limits | | | | | | | | | | | | | |
| 160 | 0:50 | | | | | | | | | 6 | 52 | 59:10 | O |
| 180 | 0:50 | | | | | | | | | 8 | 56 | 65:10 | Z |
| 200 | 0:50 | | | | | | | | | 9 | 61 | 71:10 | Z |
| 240 | 0:50 | | | | | | | | | 13 | 72 | 86:10 | Z |
| 360 | 0:50 | | | | | | | | | 19 | 79 | 99:10 | Z |

IN-WATER PHASE:
Ascent rate is 60 fpm; stop time runs from arrival to leaving stop depth; travel time not included in stop time.

50/50 N₂O₂:
The 50/50 blend is not recommended for use in water deeper than 60 fsw due to excessive ppO₂; switch to blend at 60 fsw on ascent; N₂O₂ mix not to be routed through panel until diver is at 60 fsw; umbilical to be thoroughly flushed with air and logged prior to each dive.

* Repetitive dives allowed only after a minimum surface interval of six hours, using only the modified GOM repet dive tables.

## US Navy Modified (Gulf of Mexico) Tables
### Standard Air Tables

| 80 ft | IN–WATER STOPS (MIN) AT DEPTHS (FSW) Breathing medium is air with the option of 50/50 N$_2$O$_2$ at 60 fsw and shallower stops. | | | | | | | | | | | | |
|---|---|---|---|---|---|---|---|---|---|---|---|---|---|
| Bottom Time (min) | Time to First Stop | 100 | 90 | 80 | 70 | 60 | 50 | 40 | 30 | 20 | 10 | Decomp Time (min) | Repet Group |
| 40 | 0:00 | | | | | | | | | | 0 | 1:20 | * |
| 50 | 1:10 | | | | | | | | | | 10 | 11:20 | K |
| 60 | 1:10 | | | | | | | | | | 17 | 18:10 | L |
| 70 | 1:10 | | | | | | | | | | 23 | 24:20 | M |
| 80 | 1:00 | | | | | | | | | 2 | 31 | 34:20 | N |
| 90 | 1:00 | | | | | | | | | 7 | 39 | 47:20 | N |
| 100 | 1:00 | | | | | | | | | 11 | 46 | 58:20 | O |
| 110 | 1:00 | | | | | | | | | 13 | 53 | 67:20 | O |
| Standard Operational Depth/Time Limits | | | | | | | | | | | | | |
| 120 | 1:00 | | | | | | | | | 17 | 56 | 74:20 | Z |
| 130 | 1:00 | | | | | | | | | 19 | 63 | 83:20 | Z |
| 140 | 1:00 | | | | | | | | | 26 | 69 | 96:20 | Z |
| 150 | 1:00 | | | | | | | | | 32 | 77 | 110:20 | Z |
| 180 | 1:00 | | | | | | | | | 35 | 85 | 121:20 | |

IN-WATER PHASE:
Ascent rate is 60 fpm; stop time runs from arrival to leaving stop depth; travel time not included in stop time.

50/50 N$_2$O$_2$:
The 50/50 blend is not recommended for use in-water deeper than 60 fsw due to excessive ppO$_2$. Switch to blend at 60 fsw on ascent. N$_x$O$_2$ mix not to be routed through panel until diver is at 60 fsw. Umbilical to be thoroughly flushed with air and logged prior to each dive.

* Repetitive dives allowed only after a minimum surface interval of six hours, using only the modified GOM repet dive tables.

| US Navy Modified (Gulf of Mexico) Tables<br>*Standard Air Tables* | | | | | | | | | | | | | |
|---|---|---|---|---|---|---|---|---|---|---|---|---|---|
| **90 ft** | **IN–WATER STOPS (MIN) AT DEPTHS (FSW)**<br>Breathing medium is air with the option of 50/50 $N_2O_2$ at 60 fsw and shallower stops. | | | | | | | | | | | | |
| Bottom Time (min) | Time to First Stop | 100 | 90 | 80 | 70 | 60 | 50 | 40 | 30 | 20 | 10 | Decomp Time (min) | Repet Group |
| 30 | 0:00 | | | | | | | | | | 0 | 1:30 | * |
| 40 | 1:20 | | | | | | | | | | 7 | 8:30 | J |
| 50 | 1:20 | | | | | | | | | | 18 | 19:30 | L |
| 60 | 1:20 | | | | | | | | | | 25 | 26:30 | M |
| 70 | 1:10 | | | | | | | | | 7 | 30 | 38:30 | N |
| 80 | 1:10 | | | | | | | | | 13 | 40 | 54:30 | N |
| 90 | 1:10 | | | | | | | | | 18 | 48 | 67:30 | O |
| **Standard Operational Depth/Time Limits** | | | | | | | | | | | | | |
| 100 | 1:10 | | | | | | | | | 21 | 54 | 76:30 | Z |
| 110 | 1:10 | | | | | | | | | 24 | 61 | 86:30 | Z |
| 120 | 1:10 | | | | | | | | | 32 | 68 | 101:30 | Z |
| 130 | 1:00 | | | | | | | | 5 | 36 | 74 | 116:30 | Z |

IN-WATER PHASE:
Ascent rate is 60 fpm; stop time runs from arrival to leaving stop depth; travel time not included in stop time.

50/50 $N_2O_2$:
The 50/50 blend is not recommended for use in-water deeper than 60 fsw due to excessive $ppO_2$. Switch to blend at 60 fsw on ascent. $N_2O_2$ mix not to be routed through panel until diver is at 60 fsw. Umbilical to be thoroughly flushed with air and logged prior to each dive.

* Repetitive dives allowed only after a minimum surface interval of six hours, using only the modified GOM repet dive tables.

| | US Navy Modified (Gulf of Mexico) Tables | | | | | | | | | | | | |
|---|---|---|---|---|---|---|---|---|---|---|---|---|---|
| | *Standard Air Tables* | | | | | | | | | | | | |
| **100 ft** | **IN–WATER STOPS (MIN) AT DEPTHS (FSW)** | | | | | | | | | | | | |
| | Breathing medium is air with the option of 50/50 $N_2O_2$ at 60 fsw and shallower stops. | | | | | | | | | | | | |
| Bottom Time (min) | Time to First Stop | 100 | 90 | 80 | 70 | 60 | 50 | 40 | 30 | 20 | 10 | Decomp Time (min) | Repet Group |
| 25 | 0:00 | | | | | | | | | | 0 | 1:40 | * |
| 30 | 1:30 | | | | | | | | | | 3 | 4:40 | I |
| 40 | 1:30 | | | | | | | | | | 15 | 16:40 | K |
| 50 | 1:20 | | | | | | | | | 2 | 24 | 27:40 | L |
| 60 | 1:20 | | | | | | | | | 9 | 28 | 38:40 | N |
| 70 | 1:20 | | | | | | | | | 17 | 39 | 57:40 | O |
| 80 | 1:20 | | | | | | | | | 23 | 48 | 72:40 | O |
| **Standard Operational Depth/Time Limits** | | | | | | | | | | | | | |
| 90 | 1:10 | | | | | | | | 3 | 23 | 57 | 84:40 | Z |
| 100 | 1:10 | | | | | | | | 7 | 23 | 66 | 97:40 | Z |
| 110 | 1:10 | | | | | | | | 10 | 34 | 72 | 117:40 | Z |
| 120 | 1:10 | | | | | | | | 12 | 41 | 78 | 132:40 | Z |
| 180 | 1:00 | | | | | | | 1 | 29 | 53 | 118 | 202:40 | |

IN-WATER PHASE:
Ascent rate is 60 fpm; stop time runs from arrival to leaving stop depth; travel time not included in stop time.

50/50 $N_2O_2$:
The 50/50 blend is not recommended for use in-water deeper than 60 fsw due to excessive $ppO_2$. Switch to blend at 60 fsw on ascent. $N_2O_2$ mix not to be routed through panel until diver is at 60 fsw. Umbilical to be thoroughly flushed with air and logged prior to each dive.

* Repetitive dives allowed only after a minimum surface interval of six hours, using only the modified GOM repet dive tables.

| US Navy Modified (Gulf of Mexico) Tables | | | | | | | | | | | | | |
| Standard Air Tables | | | | | | | | | | | | | |
| **110 ft** | **IN–WATER STOPS (MIN) AT DEPTHS (FSW)** | | | | | | | | | | | | |
| | Breathing medium is air with the option of 50/50 $N_2O_2$ at 60 fsw and shallower stops. | | | | | | | | | | | | |
| Bottom Time (min) | Time to First Stop | 100 | 90 | 80 | 70 | 60 | 50 | 40 | 30 | 20 | 10 | Decomp Time (min) | Repet Group |
|---|---|---|---|---|---|---|---|---|---|---|---|---|---|
| 20 | 0:00 | | | | | | | | | | 0 | 1:50 | * |
| 25 | 1:40 | | | | | | | | | | 3 | 4:50 | H |
| 30 | 1:40 | | | | | | | | | | 7 | 8:50 | J |
| 40 | 1:30 | | | | | | | | | 2 | 21 | 24:50 | L |
| 50 | 1:30 | | | | | | | | | 8 | 26 | 35:50 | M |
| 60 | 1:30 | | | | | | | | | 18 | 36 | 55:50 | N |
| 70 | 1:20 | | | | | | | | 1 | 23 | 48 | 73:50 | O |
| **Standard Operational Depth/Time Limits** | | | | | | | | | | | | | |
| 80 | 1:20 | | | | | | | | 7 | 23 | 57 | 88:50 | Z |
| 90 | 1:20 | | | | | | | | 12 | 30 | 64 | 107:50 | Z |
| 100 | 1:20 | | | | | | | | 15 | 37 | 72 | 125:50 | Z |

IN-WATER PHASE:
Ascent rate is 60 fpm; stop time runs from arrival to leaving stop depth; travel time not included in stop time.

50/50 $N_2O_2$:
The 50/50 blend is not recommended for use in-water deeper than 60 fsw due to excessive $ppO_2$. Switch to blend at 60 fsw on ascent. $N_2O_2$ mix not to be routed through panel until diver is at 60 fsw. Umbilical to be thoroughly flushed with air and logged prior to each dive.

* Repetitive dives allowed only after a minimum surface interval of six hours, using only the modified GOM repet dive tables.

| US Navy Modified (Gulf of Mexico) Tables |
|---|
| *Standard Air Tables* |

| 120 ft | **IN–WATER STOPS (MIN) AT DEPTHS (FSW)** Breathing medium is air with the option of 50/50 $N_2O_2$ at 60 fsw and shallower stops. | | | | | | | | | | | | |
|---|---|---|---|---|---|---|---|---|---|---|---|---|---|
| **Bottom Time (min)** | **Time to First Stop** | **100** | **90** | **80** | **70** | **60** | **50** | **40** | **30** | **20** | **10** | **Decomp Time (min)** | **Repet Group** |
| 15 | 0:00 | | | | | | | | | | 0 | 2:00 | * |
| 20 | 1:50 | | | | | | | | | | 2 | 4:00 | H |
| 25 | 1:50 | | | | | | | | | | 6 | 8:00 | I |
| 30 | 1:50 | | | | | | | | | | 14 | 16:00 | J |
| 40 | 1:40 | | | | | | | | | 5 | 25 | 32:00 | L |
| 50 | 1:40 | | | | | | | | | 15 | 31 | 48:00 | N |
| 60 | 1:30 | | | | | | | | 2 | 22 | 45 | 71:00 | O |
| 70 | 1:30 | | | | | | | | 9 | 23 | 55 | 89:00 | O |
| **Standard Operational Depth/Time Limits** | | | | | | | | | | | | | |
| 80 | 1:30 | | | | | | | | 15 | 27 | 63 | 107:00 | Z |
| 90 | 1:30 | | | | | | | | 19 | 37 | 74 | 132:00 | Z |
| 100 | 1:30 | | | | | | | | 23 | 45 | 80 | 150:00 | Z |

IN-WATER PHASE:
Ascent rate is 60 fpm; stop time runs from arrival to leaving stop depth; travel time not included in stop time.

50/50 $N_2O_2$:
The 50/50 blend is not recommended for use in-water deeper than 60 fsw due to excessive $ppO_2$. Switch to blend at 60 fsw on ascent. $N_2O_2$ mix not to be routed through panel until diver is at 60 fsw. Umbilical to be thoroughly flushed with air and logged prior to each dive.

* Repetitive dives allowed only after a minimum surface interval of six hours, using only the modified GOM repet dive tables.

| US Navy Modified (Gulf of Mexico) Tables | | | | | | | | | | | | | |
| :---: | :---: | :---: | :---: | :---: | :---: | :---: | :---: | :---: | :---: | :---: | :---: | :---: | :---: |
| *Standard Air Tables* | | | | | | | | | | | | | |

| 130 ft | IN-WATER STOPS (MIN) AT DEPTHS (FSW) Breathing medium is air with the option of 50/50 $N_2O_2$ at 60 fsw and shallower stops. | | | | | | | | | | | | |
| :---: | :---: | :---: | :---: | :---: | :---: | :---: | :---: | :---: | :---: | :---: | :---: | :---: |
| **Bottom Time (min)** | **Time to First Stop** | **100** | **90** | **80** | **70** | **60** | **50** | **40** | **30** | **20** | **10** | **Decomp Time (min)** | **Repet Group** |
| 10 | 0:00 | | | | | | | | | | 0 | 2:10 | * |
| 15 | 2:00 | | | | | | | | | | 1 | 3:10 | F |
| 20 | 2:00 | | | | | | | | | | 4 | 6:10 | H |
| 25 | 2:00 | | | | | | | | | | 10 | 12:10 | J |
| 30 | 1:50 | | | | | | | | | 3 | 18 | 23:10 | M |
| 40 | 1:50 | | | | | | | | | 10 | 25 | 37:10 | N |
| 50 | 1:40 | | | | | | | | 3 | 21 | 37 | 63:10 | O |
| **Standard Operational Depth/Time Limits** | | | | | | | | | | | | | |
| 60 | 1:40 | | | | | | | | 9 | 23 | 52 | 86:10 | Z |
| 70 | 1:40 | | | | | | | | 16 | 34 | 61 | 103:10 | Z |
| 80 | 1:30 | | | | | | | 3 | 19 | 35 | 72 | 131:10 | Z |
| 90 | 1:30 | | | | | | | 8 | 19 | 45 | 80 | 154:10 | Z |

IN-WATER PHASE:
Ascent rate is 60 fpm; stop time runs from arrival to leaving stop depth; travel time not included in stop time.

50/50 $N_2O_2$:
The 50/50 blend is not recommended for use in-water deeper than 60 fsw due to excessive $ppO_2$. Switch to blend at 60 fsw on ascent. $N_2O_2$ mix not to be routed through panel until diver is at 60 fsw. Umbilical to be thoroughly flushed with air and logged prior to each dive.

* Repetitive dives allowed only after a minimum surface interval of six hours, using only the modified GOM repet dive tables.

## US Navy Modified (Gulf of Mexico) Tables
### Standard Air Tables

**140 ft**

### IN–WATER STOPS (MIN) AT DEPTHS (FSW)
Breathing medium is air with the option of 50/50 $N_2O_2$ at 60 fsw and shallower stops.

| Bottom Time (min) | Time to First Stop | 100 | 90 | 80 | 70 | 60 | 50 | 40 | 30 | 20 | 10 | Decomp Time (min) | Repet Group |
|---|---|---|---|---|---|---|---|---|---|---|---|---|---|
| 10 | 0:00 | | | | | | | | | | 0 | 2:20 | * |
| 15 | 2:10 | | | | | | | | | | 2 | 4:20 | G |
| 20 | 2:10 | | | | | | | | | | 6 | 8:20 | I |
| 25 | 2:00 | | | | | | | | | 2 | 14 | 18:20 | J |
| 30 | 2:00 | | | | | | | | | 5 | 21 | 28:20 | K |
| 40 | 1:50 | | | | | | | | 2 | 16 | 26 | 46:20 | N |
| 50 | 1:50 | | | | | | | | 6 | 24 | 44 | 76:20 | O |
| **Standard Operational Depth/Time Limits** | | | | | | | | | | | | | |
| 60 | 1:50 | | | | | | | | 16 | 23 | 56 | 97:20 | Z |
| 70 | 1:40 | | | | | | | 4 | 19 | 32 | 68 | 125:20 | Z |
| 80 | 1:40 | | | | | | | 10 | 23 | 41 | 79 | 155:20 | Z |
| 90 | 1:30 | | | | | | 2 | 14 | 18 | 42 | 88 | 166:20 | |
| 120 | 1:30 | | | | | | 12 | 14 | 36 | 56 | 120 | 240:20 | |

IN-WATER PHASE:
Ascent rate is 60 fpm; stop time runs from arrival to leaving stop depth; travel time not included in stop time.

50/50 $N_2O_2$:
The 50/50 blend is not recommended for use in-water deeper than 60 fsw due to excessive pp$O_2$. Switch to blend at 60 fsw on ascent. $N_2O_2$ mix not to be routed through panel until diver is at 60 fsw. Umbilical to be thoroughly flushed with air and logged prior to each dive.

\* Repetitive dives allowed only after a minimum surface interval of six hours, using only the modified GOM repet dive tables.

| US Navy Modified (Gulf of Mexico) Tables |
| :---: |
| *Standard Air Tables* |

| 150 ft | IN–WATER STOPS (MIN) AT DEPTHS (FSW) |
| :---: | :--- |
| | Breathing medium is air with the option of 50/50 N$_2$O$_2$ at 60 fsw and shallower stops. |

| Bottom Time (min) | Time to First Stop | 100 | 90 | 80 | 70 | 60 | 50 | 40 | 30 | 20 | 10 | Decomp Time (min) | Repet Group |
| :---: | :---: | :---: | :---: | :---: | :---: | :---: | :---: | :---: | :---: | :---: | :---: | :---: | :---: |
| 5 | 0:00 | | | | | | | | | | 0 | 2:30 | C |
| 10 | 2:20 | | | | | | | | | | 1 | 3:30 | E |
| 15 | 2:20 | | | | | | | | | | 3 | 5:30 | G |
| 20 | 2:10 | | | | | | | | | 2 | 7 | 11:30 | H |
| 25 | 2:10 | | | | | | | | | 4 | 17 | 23:30 | K |
| 30 | 2:10 | | | | | | | | | 8 | 24 | 34:30 | L |
| 40 | 2:00 | | | | | | | | 5 | 19 | 33 | 59:30 | N |
| 50 | 2:00 | | | | | | | | 12 | 23 | 51 | 88:30 | O |
| **Standard Operational Depth/Time Limits** | | | | | | | | | | | | | |
| 60 | 1:50 | | | | | | | 3 | 19 | 26 | 62 | 112:30 | Z |
| 70 | 1:50 | | | | | | | 11 | 19 | 39 | 75 | 146:30 | Z |
| 80 | 1:40 | | | | | | 1 | 17 | 19 | 50 | 84 | 173:30 | Z |

IN-WATER PHASE:
Ascent rate is 60 fpm; stop time runs from arrival to leaving stop depth; travel time not included in stop time.

50/50 N$_2$O$_2$:
The 50/50 blend is not recommended for use in water deeper than 60 fsw due to excessive ppO$_2$; switch to blend at 60 fsw on ascent; N$_2$O$_2$ mix not to be routed through panel until diver is at 60 fsw; umbilical to be thoroughly flushed with air and logged prior to each dive.

* Repetitive dives allowed only after a minimum surface interval of six hours, using only the modified GOM repet dive tables.

## US Navy Modified (Gulf of Mexico) Tables
### Standard Air Tables

| 160 ft | IN–WATER STOPS (MIN) AT DEPTHS (FSW) Breathing medium is air with the option of 50/50 $N_2O_2$ at 60 fsw and shallower stops. | | | | | | | | | | | | |
|---|---|---|---|---|---|---|---|---|---|---|---|---|---|
| Bottom Time (min) | Time to First Stop | 100 | 90 | 80 | 70 | 60 | 50 | 40 | 30 | 20 | 10 | Decomp Time (min) | Repet Group |
| 5 | 0:00 | | | | | | | | | | 0 | 2:30 | D |
| 10 | 2:30 | | | | | | | | | | 1 | 3:30 | F |
| 15 | 2:20 | | | | | | | | | 1 | 4 | 5:30 | H |
| 20 | 2:20 | | | | | | | | | 3 | 11 | 11:30 | J |
| 25 | 2:20 | | | | | | | | | 7 | 20 | 23:30 | K |
| 30 | 2:10 | | | | | | | | 2 | 11 | 25 | 34:30 | M |
| 40 | 2:10 | | | | | | | | 7 | 23 | 39 | 59:30 | N |
| **Standard Operational Depth/Time Limits** | | | | | | | | | | | | | |
| 50 | 2:00 | | | | | | | 2 | 16 | 23 | 55 | 112:30 | Z |
| 60 | 2:00 | | | | | | | 9 | 19 | 33 | 69 | 146:30 | Z |
| 70 | 1:50 | | | | | | 1 | 17 | 22 | 44 | 80 | 173:30 | Z |

IN-WATER PHASE:
Ascent rate is 60 fpm; stop time runs from arrival to leaving stop depth; travel time not included in stop time.

50/50 $N_2O_2$:
The 50/50 blend is not recommended for use in water deeper than 60 fsw due to excessive $ppO_2$; switch to blend at 60 fsw on ascent; $N_2O_2$ mix not to be routed through panel until diver is at 60 fsw; umbilical to be thoroughly flushed with air and logged prior to each dive.

* Repetitive dives allowed only after a minimum surface interval of six hours, using only the modified GOM repet dive tables.

| US Navy Modified (Gulf of Mexico) Tables |
|---|
| Standard Air Tables |

| 170 ft | IN–WATER STOPS (MIN) AT DEPTHS (FSW) Breathing medium is air with the option of 50/50 $N_2O_2$ at 60 fsw and shallower stops. | | | | | | | | | | | | |
|---|---|---|---|---|---|---|---|---|---|---|---|---|---|
| Bottom Time (min) | Time to First Stop | 100 | 90 | 80 | 70 | 60 | 50 | 40 | 30 | 20 | 10 | Decomp Time (min) | Repet Group |
| 5 | 0:00 | | | | | | | | | | 0 | 2:50 | D |
| 10 | 2:40 | | | | | | | | | | 2 | 4:50 | F |
| 15 | 2:30 | | | | | | | | | 2 | 5 | 9:50 | H |
| 20 | 2:30 | | | | | | | | | 4 | 15 | 21:50 | J |
| 25 | 2:20 | | | | | | | | 2 | 7 | 23 | 34:50 | L |
| 30 | 2:20 | | | | | | | | 4 | 13 | 26 | 45:50 | M |
| 40 | 2:10 | | | | | | | 1 | 10 | 23 | 45 | 81:50 | 0 |
| Standard Operational Depth/Time Limits | | | | | | | | | | | | | |
| 50 | 2:10 | | | | | | | 5 | 18 | 23 | 61 | 109:50 | Z |
| 60 | 2:00 | | | | | | 2 | 15 | 22 | 37 | 74 | 152:50 | Z |
| 70 | 2:00 | | | | | | 8 | 17 | 19 | 51 | 86 | 183:50 | Z |
| 90 | 1:50 | | | | | 12 | 12 | 14 | 34 | 52 | 120 | 246:50 | |
| 120 | 1:30 | | | 2 | 10 | 12 | 18 | 32 | 42 | 82 | 156 | 356:50 | |

IN-WATER PHASE:
Ascent rate is 60 fpm; stop time runs from arrival to leaving stop depth; travel time not included in stop time.

50/50 $N_2O_2$:
The 50/50 blend is not recommended for use in water deeper than 60 fsw due to excessive $ppO_2$; switch to blend at 60 fsw on ascent; $N_2O_2$ mix not to be routed through panel until diver is at 60 fsw; umbilical to be thoroughly flushed with air and logged prior to each dive.

* Repetitive dives allowed only after a minimum surface interval of six hours, using only the modified GOM repet dive tables.

## US Navy Modified (Gulf of Mexico) Tables
*Standard Air Tables*

| | | | | | | | | | | | | | | |
|---|---|---|---|---|---|---|---|---|---|---|---|---|---|---|
| **180 ft** | **IN–WATER STOPS (MIN) AT DEPTHS (FSW)** Breathing medium is air with the option of 50/50 $N_2O_2$ at 60 fsw and shallower stops. | | | | | | | | | | | | | |
| **Bottom Time (min)** | **Time to First Stop** | **100** | **90** | **80** | **70** | **60** | **50** | **40** | **30** | **20** | **10** | **Decomp Time (min)** | **Repet Group** |
| 5 | 0:00 | | | | | | | | | | 0 | 3:00 | D |
| 10 | 2:50 | | | | | | | | | | 3 | 6:00 | F |
| 15 | 2:40 | | | | | | | | | 3 | 6 | 12:00 | I |
| 20 | 2:30 | | | | | | | | 1 | 5 | 17 | 26:00 | K |
| 25 | 2:30 | | | | | | | | 3 | 10 | 24 | 40:00 | L |
| 30 | 2:30 | | | | | | | | 6 | 17 | 27 | 53:00 | N |
| 40 | 2:20 | | | | | | | 3 | 14 | 23 | 50 | 93:00 | O |
| **Standard Operational Depth/Time Limits** | | | | | | | | | | | | | |
| 50 | 2:10 | | | | | | 2 | 9 | 19 | 30 | 65 | 128:00 | Z |
| 60 | 2:10 | | | | | | 5 | 16 | 19 | 44 | 81 | 168:00 | Z |

IN-WATER PHASE:
Ascent rate is 60 fpm; stop time runs from arrival to leaving stop depth; travel time not included in stop time.

50/50 $N_2O_2$:
The 50/50 blend is not recommended for use in water deeper than 60 fsw due to excessive $ppO_2$; switch to blend at 60 fsw on ascent; $N_2O_2$ mix not to be routed through panel until diver is at 60 fsw; umbilical to be thoroughly flushed with air and logged prior to each dive.

* Repetitive dives allowed only after a minimum surface interval of six hours, using only the modified GOM repet dive tables.

| US Navy Modified (Gulf of Mexico) Tables |||||||||||||| 
| Standard Air Tables |||||||||||||| 
| 190 ft | IN–WATER STOPS (MIN) AT DEPTHS (FSW) ||||||||||||| 
| | Breathing medium is air with the option of 50/50 N$_2$O$_2$ at 60 fsw and shallower stops. ||||||||||||| 
| Bottom Time (min) | Time to First Stop | 100 | 90 | 80 | 70 | 60 | 50 | 40 | 30 | 20 | 10 | Decomp Time (min) | Repet Group |
|---|---|---|---|---|---|---|---|---|---|---|---|---|---|
| 5 | 0:00 | | | | | | | | | | 0 | 3:10 | D |
| 10 | 2:50 | | | | | | | | | 1 | 3 | 7:10 | G |
| 15 | 2:50 | | | | | | | | | 4 | 7 | 14:10 | I |
| 20 | 2:40 | | | | | | | | 2 | 6 | 20 | 31:10 | K |
| 25 | 2:40 | | | | | | | | 5 | 11 | 25 | 44:10 | M |
| 30 | 2:30 | | | | | | | 1 | 8 | 19 | 32 | 63:10 | N |
| Standard Operational Depth/Time Limits |||||||||||||| 
| 40 | 2:30 | | | | | | | 8 | 14 | 23 | 55 | 103:10 | O |
| 50 | 2:20 | | | | | | 4 | 13 | 22 | 33 | 72 | 147:10 | Z |
| 60 | 2:20 | | | | | 10 | 17 | 19 | 50 | 84 | 183:10 | Z |

IN-WATER PHASE:
Ascent rate is 60 fpm; stop time runs from arrival to leaving stop depth; travel time not included in stop time.

50/50 N$_2$O$_2$:
The 50/50 blend is not recommended for use in water deeper than 60 fsw due to excessive ppO$_2$; switch to blend at 60 fsw on ascent; N$_2$O$_2$ mix not to be routed through panel until diver is at 60 fsw; umbilical to be thoroughly flushed with air and logged prior to each dive.

* Repetitive dives allowed only after a minimum surface interval of six hours, using only the modified GOM repet dive tables.

**US Navy Modified (Gulf of Mexico) Tables**
*Standard Air Tables*

| 200 ft | IN–WATER STOPS (MIN) AT DEPTHS (FSW) Breathing medium is air with the option of 50/50 $N_2O_2$ at 60 fsw and shallower stops. | | | | | | | | | | | | |
|---|---|---|---|---|---|---|---|---|---|---|---|---|---|
| Bottom Time (min) | Time to First Stop | 100 | 90 | 80 | 70 | 60 | 50 | 40 | 30 | 20 | 10 | Decomp Time (min) | Repet Group |
| 5 | 3:10 | | | | | | | | | | 1 | 4:20 | – |
| 10 | 3:00 | | | | | | | | | 1 | 4 | 8:20 | – |
| 15 | 2:50 | | | | | | | | 1 | 4 | 10 | 18:20 | – |
| 20 | 2:50 | | | | | | | | 3 | 7 | 27 | 40:20 | – |
| 25 | 2:50 | | | | | | | | 7 | 14 | 25 | 49:20 | – |
| 30 | 2:40 | | | | | | | 2 | 9 | 22 | 37 | 73:20 | – |
| **Standard Operational Depth/Time Limits** | | | | | | | | | | | | | |
| 40 | 2:30 | | | | | | 2 | 8 | 17 | 23 | 59 | 112:20 | – |
| 50 | 2:30 | | | | | | 6 | 16 | 22 | 39 | 75 | 161:20 | – |
| 60 | 2:20 | | | | | 2 | 13 | 17 | 24 | 51 | 89 | 199:20 | – |
| 90 | 1:50 | | 1 | 10 | 10 | 12 | 12 | 30 | 38 | 74 | 134 | 324:20 | – |

IN-WATER PHASE:
Ascent rate is 60 fpm; stop time runs from arrival to leaving stop depth; travel time not included in stop time.

50/50 $N_2O_2$:
The 50/50 blend is not recommended for use in water deeper than 60 fsw due to excessive $ppO_2$; switch to blend at 60 fsw on ascent; $N_2O_2$ mix not to be routed through panel until diver is at 60 fsw; umbilical to be thoroughly flushed with air and logged prior to each dive.

* Repetitive dives allowed only after a minimum surface interval of six hours, using only the modified GOM repet dive tables.

| | US Navy Modified (Gulf of Mexico) Tables | | | | | | | | | | | | |
| --- | --- | --- | --- | --- | --- | --- | --- | --- | --- | --- | --- | --- | --- |
| | *Standard Air Tables* | | | | | | | | | | | | |
| **210 ft** | **IN–WATER STOPS (MIN) AT DEPTHS (FSW)** Breathing medium is air with the option of 50/50 $N_2O_2$ at 60 fsw and shallower stops. | | | | | | | | | | | | |
| Bottom Time (min) | Time to First Stop | 100 | 90 | 80 | 70 | 60 | 50 | 40 | 30 | 20 | 10 | Decomp Time (min) | Repet Group |
| 5 | 3:20 | | | | | | | | | | 1 | 4:30 | – |
| 10 | 3:10 | | | | | | | | | 2 | 4 | 9:30 | – |
| 15 | 3:00 | | | | | | | | 1 | 5 | 13 | 22:30 | – |
| 20 | 3:00 | | | | | | | | 4 | 10 | 23 | 40:30 | – |
| 25 | 2:50 | | | | | | | 2 | 7 | 17 | 27 | 56:30 | – |
| 30 | 2:50 | | | | | | | 4 | 9 | 24 | 41 | 81:30 | – |
| **Standard Operational Depth/Time Limits** | | | | | | | | | | | | | |
| 40 | 2:40 | | | | | | 4 | 9 | 19 | 26 | 63 | 124:30 | – |
| 50 | 2:30 | | | | | 1 | 9 | 17 | 19 | 45 | 80 | 174:30 | – |

IN-WATER PHASE:
Ascent rate is 60 fpm; stop time runs from arrival to leaving stop depth; travel time not included in stop time.

50/50 $N_2O_2$:
The 50/50 blend is not recommended for use in water deeper than 60 fsw due to excessive $ppO_2$; switch to blend at 60 fsw on ascent; $N_2O_2$ mix not to be routed through panel until diver is at 60 fsw; umbilical to be thoroughly flushed with air and logged prior to each dive.

* Repetitive dives allowed only after a minimum surface interval of six hours, using only the modified GOM repet dive tables.

| 220 ft | — IN–WATER STOPS (MIN) AT DEPTHS (FSW) Breathing medium is air with the option of 50/50 $N_2O_2$ at 60 fsw and shallower stops. | | | | | | | | | | | |
|--------|---------|-----|-----|-----|-----|-----|-----|-----|-----|-----|-----|----------|--------|
| Bottom Time (min) | Time to First Stop | 100 | 90 | 80 | 70 | 60 | 50 | 40 | 30 | 20 | 10 | Decomp Time (min) | Repet Group |
| 5 | 3:30 | | | | | | | | | | 2 | 5:40 | – |
| 10 | 3:20 | | | | | | | | | 2 | 5 | 10:40 | – |
| 15 | 3:10 | | | | | | | | 2 | 5 | 16 | 26:40 | – |
| 20 | 3:00 | | | | | | | 1 | 3 | 11 | 24 | 42:40 | – |
| 25 | 3:00 | | | | | | | 3 | 8 | 19 | 33 | 66:40 | – |
| 30 | 2:50 | | | | | | 1 | 7 | 10 | 23 | 47 | 91:40 | – |
| **Standard Operational Depth/Time Limits** | | | | | | | | | | | | | |
| 40 | 2:50 | | | | | | 6 | 12 | 22 | 29 | 68 | 140:40 | – |
| 50 | 2:40 | | | | | 3 | 12 | 17 | 18 | 51 | 86 | 190:40 | – |

IN-WATER PHASE:
Ascent rate is 60 fpm; stop time runs from arrival to leaving stop depth; travel time not included in stop time.

50/50 $N_2O_2$:
The 50/50 blend is not recommended for use in water deeper than 60 fsw due to excessive $ppO_2$; switch to blend at 60 fsw on ascent; $N_2O_2$ mix not to be routed through panel until diver is at 60 fsw; umbilical to be thoroughly flushed with air and logged prior to each dive.

* Repetitive dives allowed only after a minimum surface interval of six hours, using only the modified GOM repet dive tables.

# SECTION 5
# USN Modified (Gulf of Mexico)
# Surface Decompression Air Tables

| US Navy Modified (Gulf of Mexico) Tables | | | | | | | | | | | | | |
|---|---|---|---|---|---|---|---|---|---|---|---|---|---|
| *Surface Decompression Air Tables* | | | | | | | | | | | | | |
| **70 FSW** | **SURFACE DECOMPRESSION USING OXYGEN** Air or 50/50 as breathing medium on in-water decompression stops. | | | | | | | | | | | | |
| Bottom Time (min) | Time to First Stop (min/sec) | Water Stops (in feet and minutes) | | | | | | Surface Interval | Chamber Stops (breathing O₂) | | 5 min Air Breaks | Ascent to Surf | Decomp Time (min) | Repet Group |
| | | 80 | 70 | 60 | 50 | 40 | 30 | | 50 | 40 | | | | |
| 52 | 1:36 | | | | | | 3 | Not to Exceed 5 min | – | – | | 10 minutes slow bleed on oxygen | 5:36 | K |
| 90 | 1:36 | | | | | | 3 | | 10 | 15 | 1 | | 50:36 | N |
| 120 | 1:36 | | | | | | 3 | | 10 | 23 | 2 | | 63:36 | O |
| **Standard Operational Depth/Time Limit** | | | | | | | | | | | | | |
| 150 | 1:36 | | | | | | 3 | Not to Exceed 5 min | 10 | 31 | 2 | 10 minutes slow bleed on oxygen | 71:36 | Z |
| 180 | 1:36 | | | | | | 3 | | 10 | 39 | 2 | | 79:36 | Z |

IN-WATER PHASE: Ascent rate is 25 fpm, time between water stops, and from 30-foot stop to surface is one minute. 50/50 may be used instead of air at 60 and shallower. The 50/50 is not to be routed through panel until diver is at 60 fsw. Umbilical to be flushed with air (and logged) after each dive if using 50/50.

CHAMBER PHASE: Diver is pressed from surface to 50 in chamber in 30 sec. SI ends when diver is at 50 in chamber. Diver has three min to begin O₂. After 50-foot stop, slide to 40 in 1 min (on O₂). First air break as soon as diver arrives at 40. Maximum O₂ time is 20 min without 5 min air break. Time on stop does not include air breaks.

REPET DIVES: Repetitive dives only performed after six-hour surface interval. Repet group not to exceed "O." Only modified USN GOM repet tables to be used.

| US Navy Modified (Gulf of Mexico) Tables | | | | | | | | | | | | | |
| --- | --- | --- | --- | --- | --- | --- | --- | --- | --- | --- | --- | --- | --- |
| *Surface Decompression Air Tables* | | | | | | | | | | | | | |
| **80 FSW** | **SURFACE DECOMPRESSION USING OXYGEN** Air or 50/50 as breathing medium on in–water decompression stops. | | | | | | | | | | | | |
| Bottom Time (min) | Time to First Stop (min/sec) | Water Stops (in feet and minutes) | | | | | | Surface Interval | Chamber Stops (breathing O₂) | | 5 min Air Breaks | Ascent to Surf | Decomp Time (min) | Repet Group |
| | | 80 | 70 | 60 | 50 | 40 | 30 | | 50 | 40 | | | | |
| 40 | 2:00 | | | | | | 3 | Not to Exceed 5 min | – | – | | 10 minutes slow bleed on oxygen | 6:00 | |
| 70 | 2:00 | | | | | | 3 | | 10 | 14 | 1 | | 50:00 | M |
| 85 | 2:00 | | | | | | 3 | | 10 | 20 | 2 | | 61:00 | N |
| 100 | 2:00 | | | | | | 3 | | 10 | 26 | 2 | | 67:00 | O |
| **Standard Operational Depth/Time Limit** | | | | | | | | | | | | | |
| 115 | 2:00 | | | | | | 3 | Not to Exceed 5 min | 10 | 31 | 2 | 10 minutes slow bleed on oxygen | 72:00 | Z |
| 130 | 2:00 | | | | | | 3 | | 10 | 37 | 2 | | 78:00 | Z |
| 150 | 2:00 | | | | | | 3 | | 10 | 44 | 3 | | 90:00 | Z |

IN-WATER PHASE: Ascent rate is 25 fpm, time between water stops, and from 30-foot stop to surface is one minute. 50/50 may be used instead of air at 60 and shallower. The 50/50 is not to be routed through panel until diver is at 60 fsw. Umbilical to be flushed with air (and logged) after each dive if using 50/50.

CHAMBER PHASE: Diver is pressed from surface to 50 in chamber in 30 sec. SI ends when diver is at 50 in chamber. Diver has three min to begin O₂. After 50-foot stop, slide to 40 in 1 min (on O₂). First air break as soon as diver arrives at 40. Maximum O₂ time is 20 min without 5 min air break. Time on stop does not include air breaks.

REPET DIVES: Repetitive dives only performed after six-hour surface interval. Repet group not to exceed "O." Only modified USN GOM repet tables to be used.

| 90 FSW | SURFACE DECOMPRESSION USING OXYGEN | | | | | | | | | | | | |
|---|---|---|---|---|---|---|---|---|---|---|---|---|---|
| | Air or 50/50 as breathing medium on in–water decompression stops. | | | | | | | | | | | | |

| Bottom Time (min) | Time to First Stop (min/sec) | Water Stops (in feet and minutes) | | | | | | Surface Interval | Chamber Stops (breathing O₂) | | 5 min Air Breaks | Ascent to Surf | Decomp Time (min) | Repet Group |
|---|---|---|---|---|---|---|---|---|---|---|---|---|---|---|
| | | 80 | 70 | 60 | 50 | 40 | 30 | | 50 | 40 | | | | |
| 32 | 2:24 | | | | | | 3 | Not to Exceed 5 min | – | – | | 10 minutes slow bleed on oxygen | 6:24 | J |
| 60 | 2:24 | | | | | | 3 | | 10 | 14 | 1 | | 50:24 | M |
| 70 | 2:24 | | | | | | 3 | | 10 | 20 | 2 | | 61:00 | N |
| 80 | 2:24 | | | | | | 3 | | 10 | 25 | 2 | | 66:00 | N |
| 90 | 2:24 | | | | | | 3 | | 10 | 30 | 2 | | 71:00 | O |
| Standard Operational Depth/Time Limit | | | | | | | | | | | | | | |
| 100 | 2:24 | | | | | | 3 | Not to Exceed 5 min | 10 | 34 | 2 | 10 minutes slow bleed on oxygen | 75:00 | Z |
| 110 | 2:24 | | | | | | 3 | | 10 | 39 | 2 | | 80:00 | Z |
| 120 | 2:24 | | | | | | 3 | | 10 | 43 | 3 | | 89:00 | Z |
| 130 | 2:24 | | | | | | 3 | | 10 | 48 | 3 | | 94:00 | Z |

IN-WATER PHASE: Ascent rate is 25 fpm, time between water stops, and from 30-foot stop to surface is one minute. 50/50 may be used instead of air at 60 and shallower. The 50/50 is not to be routed through panel until diver is at 60 fsw. Umbilical to be flushed with air (and logged) after each dive if using 50/50.

CHAMBER PHASE: Diver is pressed from surface to 50 in chamber in 30 sec. SI ends when diver is at 50 in chamber. Diver has three min to begin O₂. After 50-foot stop, slide to 40 in 1 min (on O₂). First air break as soon as diver arrives at 40. Maximum O₂ time is 20 min without 5 min air break. Time on stop does not include air breaks.

REPET DIVES: Repetitive dives only performed after six-hour surface interval. Repet group not to exceed "O." Only modified USN GOM repet tables to be used.

## US Navy Modified (Gulf of Mexico) Tables
*Surface Decompression Air Tables*

### 100 FSW — SURFACE DECOMPRESSION USING OXYGEN
Air or 50/50 as breathing medium on in–water decompression stops.

| Bottom Time (min) | Time to First Stop (min/sec) | Water Stops (in feet and minutes) | | | | | | Surface Interval | Chamber Stops (breathing $O_2$) | | 5 min Air Breaks | Ascent to Surf | Decomp Time (min) | Repet Group |
|---|---|---|---|---|---|---|---|---|---|---|---|---|---|---|
| | | 80 | 70 | 60 | 50 | 40 | 30 | | 50 | 40 | | | | |
| 26 | 2:48 | | | | | | 3 | Not to Exceed 5 min | – | – | | 10 minutes slow bleed on oxygen | 6:48 | I |
| 50 | 2:48 | | | | | | 3 | | 10 | 14 | 1 | | 50:48 | L |
| 60 | 2:48 | | | | | | 3 | | 10 | 20 | 2 | | 61:48 | N |
| 70 | 2:48 | | | | | | 3 | | 10 | 26 | 2 | | 67:48 | O |
| 80 | 2:48 | | | | | | 3 | | 10 | 32 | 2 | | 73:48 | O |
| **Standard Operational Depth/Time Limit** | | | | | | | | | | | | | | |
| 90 | 2:48 | | | | | | 3 | Not to Exceed 5 min | 10 | 38 | 2 | 10 minutes slow bleed on oxygen | 79:48 | Z |
| 100 | 2:48 | | | | | | 3 | | 10 | 44 | 3 | | 90:48 | Z |
| 110 | 2:48 | | | | | | 3 | | 10 | 49 | 3 | | 95:48 | Z |
| 120 | 2:24 | | | | | 2 | 4 | | 10 | 53 | 3 | | 103:24 | Z |

IN-WATER PHASE: Ascent rate is 25 fpm, time between water stops, and from 30-foot stop to surface is one minute. 50/50 may be used instead of air at 60 and shallower. The 50/50 is not to be routed through panel until diver is at 60 fsw. Umbilical to be flushed with air (and logged) after each dive if using 50/50.

CHAMBER PHASE: Diver is pressed from surface to 50 in chamber in 30 sec. SI ends when diver is at 50 in chamber. Diver has three min to begin $O_2$. After 50-foot stop, slide to 40 in 1 min (on $O_2$). First air break as soon as diver arrives at 40. Maximum $O_2$ time is 20 min without 5 min air break. Time on stop does not include air breaks.

REPET DIVES: Repetitive dives only performed after six-hour surface interval. Repet group not to exceed "O." Only modified USN GOM repet tables to be used.

| US Navy Modified (Gulf of Mexico) Tables | | | | | | | | | | | | |
|---|---|---|---|---|---|---|---|---|---|---|---|---|
| *Surface Decompression Air Tables* | | | | | | | | | | | | |

## 110 FSW — SURFACE DECOMPRESSION USING OXYGEN
### Air or 50/50 as breathing medium on in–water decompression stops.

| Bottom Time (min) | Time to First Stop (min/sec) | Water Stops (in feet and minutes) | | | | | | Surface Interval | Chamber Stops (breathing O₂) | | 5 min Air Breaks | Ascent to Surf | Decomp Time (min) | Repet Group |
|---|---|---|---|---|---|---|---|---|---|---|---|---|---|---|
| | | 80 | 70 | 60 | 50 | 40 | 30 | | 50 | 40 | | | | |
| 22 | 3:12 | | | | | | 3 | Not to Exceed 5 min | – | – | | 10 minutes slow bleed on oxygen | 7:12 | H |
| 40 | 3:12 | | | | | | 3 | | 10 | 12 | 1 | | 49:12 | L |
| 50 | 3:12 | | | | | | 3 | | 10 | 19 | 1 | | 56:12 | M |
| 60 | 3:12 | | | | | | 3 | | 10 | 26 | 2 | | 69:12 | N |
| 70 | 3:12 | | | | | | 3 | | 10 | 33 | 2 | | 75:12 | O |
| **Standard Operational Depth/Time Limit** | | | | | | | | | | | | | | |
| 80 | 2:48 | | | | | 2 | 3 | Not to Exceed 5 min | 10 | 40 | 3 | 10 minutes slow bleed on oxygen | 89:48 | Z |
| 90 | 2:48 | | | | | 2 | 4 | | 10 | 46 | 3 | | 96:48 | Z |
| 100 | 2:48 | | | | | 2 | 5 | | 10 | 51 | 3 | | 102:48 | Z |
| 110 | 2:48 | | | | | 2 | 12 | | 10 | 54 | 3 | | 112:48 | Z |

IN-WATER PHASE: Ascent rate is 25 fpm, time between water stops, and from 30-foot stop to surface is one minute. 50/50 may be used instead of air at 60 and shallower. The 50/50 is not to be routed through panel until diver is at 60 fsw. Umbilical to be flushed with air (and logged) after each dive if using 50/50.

CHAMBER PHASE: Diver is pressed from surface to 50 in chamber in 30 sec. SI ends when diver is at 50 in chamber. Diver has three min to begin O₂. After 50-foot stop, slide to 40 in 1 min (on O₂). First air break as soon as diver arrives at 40. Maximum O₂ time is 20 min without 5 min air break. Time on stop does not include air breaks.

REPET DIVES: Repetitive dives only performed after six-hour surface interval. Repet group not to exceed "O." Only modified USN GOM repet tables to be used.

| US Navy Modified (Gulf of Mexico) Tables | | | | | | | | | | | | | |
|---|---|---|---|---|---|---|---|---|---|---|---|---|---|
| Surface Decompression Air Tables | | | | | | | | | | | | | |

| 120 FSW | SURFACE DECOMPRESSION USING OXYGEN | | | | | | | | | | | | |
|---|---|---|---|---|---|---|---|---|---|---|---|---|---|
| | Air or 50/50 as breathing medium on in–water decompression stops. | | | | | | | | | | | | |

| Bottom Time (min) | Time to First Stop (min/sec) | Water Stops (in feet and minutes) | | | | | | Surface Interval | Chamber Stops (breathing O₂) | | 5 min Air Breaks | Ascent to Surf | Decomp Time (min) | Repet Group |
|---|---|---|---|---|---|---|---|---|---|---|---|---|---|---|
| | | 80 | 70 | 60 | 50 | 40 | 30 | | 50 | 40 | | | | |
| 18 | 3:36 | | | | | | 3 | Not to Exceed 5 min | – | – | | 10 minutes slow bleed on oxygen | 7:36 | H |
| 30 | 3:36 | | | | | | 3 | | 10 | 9 | 1 | | 46:36 | J |
| 40 | 3:36 | | | | | | 3 | | 10 | 16 | 1 | | 53:36 | L |
| 50 | 3:36 | | | | | | 3 | | 10 | 24 | 2 | | 66:36 | N |
| 60 | 3:12 | | | | | 2 | 3 | | 10 | 32 | 2 | | 77:12 | O |
| 70 | 3:12 | | | | | 2 | 4 | | 10 | 39 | 2 | | 85:12 | O |
| Standard Operational Depth/Time Limit | | | | | | | | | | | | | | |
| 80 | 3:12 | | | | | 2 | 5 | Not to Exceed 5 min | 10 | 46 | 3 | 10 min slow bleed on oxygen | 98:12 | Z |
| 90 | 3:12 | | | | | 4 | 8 | | 10 | 51 | 3 | | 108:12 | Z |

IN-WATER PHASE: Ascent rate is 25 fpm, time between water stops, and from 30-foot stop to surface is one minute. 50/50 may be used instead of air at 60 and shallower. The 50/50 is not to be routed through panel until diver is at 60 fsw. Umbilical to be flushed with air (and logged) after each dive if using 50/50.

CHAMBER PHASE: Diver is pressed from surface to 50 in chamber in 30 sec. SI ends when diver is at 50 in chamber. Diver has three min to begin O₂. After 50-foot stop, slide to 40 in 1 min (on O₂). First air break as soon as diver arrives at 40. Maximum O₂ time is 20 min without 5 min air break. Time on stop does not include air breaks.

REPET DIVES: Repetitive dives only performed after six-hour surface interval. Repet group not to exceed "O." Only modified USN GOM repet tables to be used.

| 130 FSW | SURFACE DECOMPRESSION USING OXYGEN<br>Air or 50/50 as breathing medium on in–water decompression stops. | | | | | | | | | | | | |

| Bottom Time (min) | Time to First Stop (min/sec) | Water Stops (in feet and minutes) | | | | | | Surface Interval | Chamber Stops (breathing O$_2$) | | 5 min Air Breaks | Ascent to Surf | Decomp Time (min) | Repet Group |
|---|---|---|---|---|---|---|---|---|---|---|---|---|---|---|
| | | 80 | 70 | 60 | 50 | 40 | 30 | | 50 | 40 | | | | |
| 15 | 4:00 | | | | | | 3 | Not to Exceed 5 min | – | – | | 10 minutes slow bleed on oxygen | 8:00 | F |
| 30 | 4:00 | | | | | | 3 | | 10 | 12 | 1 | | 50:00 | M |
| 40 | 4:00 | | | | | | 3 | | 10 | 21 | 2 | | 64:00 | N |
| 50 | 3:36 | | | | | 2 | 3 | | 10 | 29 | 2 | | 74:36 | O |
| **Standard Operational Depth/Time Limit** | | | | | | | | | | | | | | |
| 60 | 3:36 | | | | | 2 | 5 | Not to Exceed 5 min | 10 | 37 | 2 | 10 minutes slow bleed on oxygen | 84:36 | Z |
| 70 | 3:36 | | | | | 2 | 7 | | 10 | 45 | 3 | | 99:36 | Z |
| 80 | 3:36 | | | | | 6 | 10 | | 10 | 51 | 3 | | 112:36 | Z |
| 90 | 3:36 | | | | | 10 | 14 | | 10 | 56 | 3 | | 125:36 | Z |

IN-WATER PHASE: Ascent rate is 25 fpm, time between water stops, and from 30-foot stop to surface is one minute. 50/50 may be used instead of air at 60 and shallower. The 50/50 is not to be routed through panel until diver is at 60 fsw. Umbilical to be flushed with air (and logged) after each dive if using 50/50.

CHAMBER PHASE: Diver is pressed from surface to 50 in chamber in 30 sec. SI ends when diver is at 50 in chamber. Diver has three min to begin O$_2$. After 50-foot stop, slide to 40 in 1 min (on O$_2$). First air break as soon as diver arrives at 40. Maximum O$_2$ time is 20 min without 5 min air break. Time on stop does not include air breaks.

REPET DIVES: Repetitive dives only performed after six-hour surface interval. Repet group not to exceed "O." Only modified USN GOM repet tables to be used.

## US Navy Modified (Gulf of Mexico) Tables
*Surface Decompression Air Tables*

| 140 FSW | SURFACE DECOMPRESSION USING OXYGEN — Air or 50/50 as breathing medium on in–water decompression stops. | | | | | | | | | | | | |
|---|---|---|---|---|---|---|---|---|---|---|---|---|---|

| Bottom Time (min) | Time to First Stop (min/sec) | Water Stops (in feet and minutes) | | | | | | Surface Interval | Chamber Stops (breathing O₂) | | 5 min Air Breaks | Ascent to Surf | Decomp Time (min) | Repet Group |
|---|---|---|---|---|---|---|---|---|---|---|---|---|---|---|
| | | 80 | 70 | 60 | 50 | 40 | 30 | | 50 | 40 | | | | |
| 13 | 4:24 | | | | | | 3 | Not to Exceed 5 min | – | – | | 10 minutes slow bleed on oxygen | 8:24 | G |
| 25 | 4:24 | | | | | | 3 | | 10 | 11 | 1 | | 49:24 | J |
| 30 | 4:24 | | | | | | 3 | | 10 | 15 | 1 | | 53:24 | K |
| 35 | 4:24 | | | | | | 3 | | 10 | 20 | 2 | | 63:24 | N |
| 40 | 4:00 | | | | | 2 | 3 | | 10 | 24 | 2 | | 70:00 | N |
| 45 | 4:00 | | | | | 2 | 4 | | 10 | 29 | 2 | | 76:00 | O |
| 50 | 4:00 | | | | | 2 | 6 | | 10 | 33 | 2 | | 82:00 | O |
| **Standard Operational Depth/Time Limit** | | | | | | | | | | | | | | |
| 55 | 4:00 | | | | | 2 | 7 | Not to Exceed 5 min | 10 | 38 | 2 | 10 minutes slow bleed on oxygen | 88:00 | Z |
| 60 | 4:00 | | | | | 2 | 9 | | 10 | 43 | 3 | | 100:00 | Z |
| 65 | 4:00 | | | | | 4 | 11 | | 10 | 48 | 3 | | 109:00 | Z |
| 70 | 3:36 | | | | 2 | 7 | 13 | | 10 | 51 | 3 | | 119:36 | Z |

IN-WATER PHASE: Ascent rate is 25 fpm, time between water stops, and from 30-foot stop to surface is one minute. 50/50 may be used instead of air at 60 and shallower. The 50/50 is not to be routed through panel until diver is at 60 fsw. Umbilical to be flushed with air (and logged) after each dive if using 50/50.

CHAMBER PHASE: Diver is pressed from surface to 50 in chamber in 30 sec. SI ends when diver is at 50 in chamber. Diver has three min to begin O₂. After 50-foot stop, slide to 40 in 1 min (on O₂). First air break as soon as diver arrives at 40. Maximum O₂ time is 20 min without 5 min air break. Time on stop does not include air breaks.

REPET DIVES: Repetitive dives only performed after six-hour surface interval. Repet group not to exceed "O." Only modified USN GOM repet tables to be used.

## US Navy Modified (Gulf of Mexico) Tables
*Surface Decompression Air Tables*

| 150 FSW | SURFACE DECOMPRESSION USING OXYGEN Air or 50/50 as breathing medium on in–water decompression stops. | | | | | | | | | | | | |
|---|---|---|---|---|---|---|---|---|---|---|---|---|---|

| Bottom Time (min) | Time to First Stop (min/sec) | Water Stops (in feet and minutes) | | | | | | Surface Interval | Chamber Stops (breathing O₂) | | 5 min Air Breaks | Ascent to Surf | Decomp Time (min) | Repet Group |
|---|---|---|---|---|---|---|---|---|---|---|---|---|---|---|
| | | 80 | 70 | 60 | 50 | 40 | 30 | | 50 | 40 | | | | |
| 11 | 4:48 | | | | | | 3 | Not to Exceed 5 min | – | – | | 10 minutes slow bleed on oxygen | 8:48 | G |
| 25 | 4:48 | | | | | | 3 | | 10 | 13 | 1 | | 51:48 | K |
| 30 | 4:48 | | | | | | 3 | | 10 | 18 | 1 | | 56:48 | L |
| 35 | 4:24 | | | | | 2 | 4 | | 10 | 23 | 2 | | 70:24 | N |
| 40 | 4:24 | | | | | 5 | 7 | | 10 | 27 | 2 | | 80:24 | N |
| 45 | 4:24 | | | | | 6 | 9 | | 10 | 33 | 2 | | 89:24 | O |
| 50 | 4:00 | | | | 2 | 7 | 11 | | 10 | 38 | 2 | | 100:00 | O |
| **Standard Operational Depth/Time Limit** | | | | | | | | | | | | | | |
| 55 | 3:36 | | | 2 | 5 | 9 | 14 | | 10 | 44 | 3 | | 121:36 | Z |

IN-WATER PHASE: Ascent rate is 25 fpm, time between water stops, and from 30-foot stop to surface is one minute. 50/50 may be used instead of air at 60 and shallower. The 50/50 is not to be routed through panel until diver is at 60 fsw. Umbilical to be flushed with air (and logged) after each dive if using 50/50.

CHAMBER PHASE: Diver is pressed from surface to 50 in chamber in 30 sec. SI ends when diver is at 50 in chamber. Diver has three min to begin $O_2$. After 50-foot stop, slide to 40 in 1 min (on $O_2$). First air break as soon as diver arrives at 40. Maximum $O_2$ time is 20 min without 5 min air break. Time on stop does not include air breaks.

REPET DIVES: Repetitive dives only performed after six-hour surface interval. Repet group not to exceed "O." Only modified USN GOM repet tables to be used.

| | | US Navy Modified (Gulf of Mexico) Tables | | | | | | | | | | | |
|---|---|---|---|---|---|---|---|---|---|---|---|---|---|
| | | *Surface Decompression Air Tables* | | | | | | | | | | | |
| **160 FSW** | | **SURFACE DECOMPRESSION USING OXYGEN** | | | | | | | | | | | |
| | | Air or 50/50 as breathing medium on in–water decompression stops. | | | | | | | | | | | |

| Bottom Time (min) | Time to First Stop (min/sec) | Water Stops (in feet and minutes) | | | | | | Surface Interval | Chamber Stops (breathing O₂) | | 5 min Air Breaks | Ascent to Surf | Decomp Time (min) | Repet Group |
|---|---|---|---|---|---|---|---|---|---|---|---|---|---|---|
| | | 80 | 70 | 60 | 50 | 40 | 30 | | 50 | 40 | | | | |
| 9 | 5:12 | | | | | | 3 | Not to Exceed 5 min | – | – | | 10 minutes slow bleed on oxygen | 9:12 | F |
| 20 | 5:12 | | | | | | 3 | | 10 | 11 | 1 | | 50:12 | J |
| 25 | 5:12 | | | | | | 3 | | 10 | 16 | 1 | | 55:12 | K |
| 30 | 4:48 | | | | | 2 | 4 | | 10 | 21 | 2 | | 68:48 | M |
| 35 | 4:48 | | | | | 4 | 7 | | 10 | 26 | 2 | | 78:48 | N |
| 40 | 4:24 | | | | 3 | 6 | 9 | | 10 | 32 | 2 | | 92:24 | N |
| **Standard Operational Depth/Time Limit** | | | | | | | | | | | | | | |
| 45 | 4:00 | | | 3 | 4 | 8 | 12 | | 10 | 38 | 2 | | 108:00 | Z |

IN-WATER PHASE: Ascent rate is 25 fpm, time between water stops, and from 30-foot stop to surface is one minute. 50/50 may be used instead of air at 60 and shallower. The 50/50 is not to be routed through panel until diver is at 60 fsw. Umbilical to be flushed with air (and logged) after each dive if using 50/50.

CHAMBER PHASE: Diver is pressed from surface to 50 in chamber in 30 sec. SI ends when diver is at 50 in chamber. Diver has three min to begin $O_2$. After 50-foot stop, slide to 40 in 1 min (on $O_2$). First air break as soon as diver arrives at 40. Maximum $O_2$ time is 20 min without 5 min air break. Time on stop does not include air breaks.

REPET DIVES: Repetitive dives only performed after six-hour surface interval. Repet group not to exceed "O." Only modified USN GOM repet tables to be used.

## US Navy Modified (Gulf of Mexico) Tables
*Surface Decompression Air Tables*

| 170 FSW | **SURFACE DECOMPRESSION USING OXYGEN** Air or 50/50 as breathing medium on in–water decompression stops. | | | | | | | | | | | |
|---|---|---|---|---|---|---|---|---|---|---|---|---|

| Bottom Time (min) | Time to First Stop (min/sec) | Water Stops (in feet and minutes) | | | | | | Surface Interval | Chamber Stops (breathing O₂) | | 5 min Air Breaks | Ascent to Surf | Decomp Time (min) | Repet Group |
|---|---|---|---|---|---|---|---|---|---|---|---|---|---|---|
| | | 80 | 70 | 60 | 50 | 40 | 30 | | 50 | 40 | | | | |
| 7 | 5:36 | | | | | | 3 | Not to Exceed 5 min | -- | -- | | 10 minutes slow bleed on oxygen | 9:36 | F |
| 20 | 5:36 | | | | | | 3 | | 10 | 13 | 1 | | 52:36 | J |
| 25 | 5:36 | | | | | | 3 | | 10 | 19 | 1 | | 58:36 | L |
| 30 | 5:12 | | | | | 5 | 7 | | 10 | 23 | 2 | | 77:12 | M |
| 35 | 4:48 | | | | 4 | 6 | 9 | | 10 | 29 | 2 | | 90:48 | O |
| **Standard Operational Depth/Time Limit** | | | | | | | | | | | | | | |
| 40 | 4:24 | | | 4 | 4 | 8 | 13 | | 10 | 36 | 2 | | 108:24 | O |

IN-WATER PHASE: Ascent rate is 25 fpm, time between water stops, and from 30-foot stop to surface is one minute. 50/50 may be used instead of air at 60 and shallower. The 50/50 is not to be routed through panel until diver is at 60 fsw. Umbilical to be flushed with air (and logged) after each dive if using 50/50.

CHAMBER PHASE: Diver is pressed from surface to 50 in chamber in 30 sec. SI ends when diver is at 50 in chamber. Diver has three min to begin O₂. After 50-foot stop, slide to 40 in 1 min (on O₂). First air break as soon as diver arrives at 40. Maximum O₂ time is 20 min without 5 min air break. Time on stop does not include air breaks.

REPET DIVES: Repetitive dives only performed after six-hour surface interval. Repet group not to exceed "O." Only modified USN GOM repet tables to be used.

| US Navy Modified (Gulf of Mexico) Tables |
|---|
| *Surface Decompression Air Tables* |

| **180 FSW** | **SURFACE DECOMPRESSION USING OXYGEN** Air or 50/50 as breathing medium on in–water decompression stops. |
|---|---|

| Bottom Time (min) | Time to First Stop (min/sec) | Water Stops (in feet and minutes) | | | | | | Surface Interval | Chamber Stops (breathing O₂) | | 5 min Air Breaks | Ascent to Surf | Decomp Time (min) | Repet Group |
|---|---|---|---|---|---|---|---|---|---|---|---|---|---|---|
| | | 80 | 70 | 60 | 50 | 40 | 30 | | 50 | 40 | | | | |
| 15 | 5:36 | | | | | 4 | 6 | Not to Exceed 5 min | 10 | 20 | 2 | 10 min slow bleed on oxygen | 72:36 | |
| 30 | 4:48 | | | 2 | 3 | 5 | 10 | | 10 | 40 | 3 | | 108:48 | |
| **Standard Operational Depth/Time Limit** | | | | | | | | | | | | | | |
| 45 | 4:00 | 2 | | 4 | 6 | 12 | 18 | | 10 | 50 | 3 | | 142:00 | |

IN-WATER PHASE: Ascent rate is 25 fpm, time between water stops, and from 30-foot stop to surface is one minute. 50/50 may be used instead of air at 60 and shallower. The 50/50 is not to be routed through panel until diver is at 60 fsw. Umbilical to be flushed with air (and logged) after each dive if using 50/50.

CHAMBER PHASE: Diver is pressed from surface to 50 in chamber in 30 sec. SI ends when diver is at 50 in chamber. Diver has three min to begin $O_2$. After 50-foot stop, slide to 40 in 1 min (on $O_2$). First air break as soon as diver arrives at 40. Maximum $O_2$ time is 20 min without 5 min air break. Time on stop does not include air breaks.

REPET DIVES: Repetitive dives only performed after six-hour surface interval. Repet group not to exceed "O." Only modified USN GOM repet tables to be used.

| US Navy Modified (Gulf of Mexico) Tables |||||||||||||||
|:---:|:---:|:---:|:---:|:---:|:---:|:---:|:---:|:---:|:---:|:---:|:---:|:---:|:---:|:---:|
| *Surface Decompression Air Tables* |||||||||||||||
| **190 FSW** | **SURFACE DECOMPRESSION USING OXYGEN** <br> Air or 50/50 as breathing medium on in–water decompression stops. |||||||||||||||
| **Bottom Time (min)** | **Time to First Stop (min/sec)** | **Water Stops** <br> (in feet and minutes) |||||| **Surface Interval** | **Chamber Stops** <br> (breathing O₂) || **5 min Air Breaks** | **Ascent to Surf** | **Decomp Time (min)** | **Repet Group** |
| | | **80** | **70** | **60** | **50** | **40** | **30** | | **50** | **40** | | | | |
| 15 | 5:36 | | | | 2 | 4 | 6 | Not to Exceed 5 min | 10 | 20 | 2 | 10 min slow bleed on oxygen | 75:36 | |
| 30 | 5:12 | | | 3 | 5 | 8 | 12 | | 10 | 50 | 3 | | 127:12 | |
| **Standard Operational Depth/Time Limit** |||||||||||||||
| 45 | 4:24 | 2 | | 5 | 10 | 18 | 26 | | 10 | 60 | 4 | | 176:24 | |

IN-WATER PHASE: Ascent rate is 25 fpm, time between water stops, and from 30-foot stop to surface is one minute. 50/50 may be used instead of air at 60 and shallower. The 50/50 is not to be routed through panel until diver is at 60 fsw. Umbilical to be flushed with air (and logged) after each dive if using 50/50.

CHAMBER PHASE: Diver is pressed from surface to 50 in chamber in 30 sec. SI ends when diver is at 50 in chamber. Diver has three min to begin O₂. After 50-foot stop, slide to 40 in 1 min (on O₂). First air break as soon as diver arrives at 40. Maximum O₂ time is 20 min without 5 min air break. Time on stop does not include air breaks.

REPET DIVES: Repetitive dives only performed after six-hour surface interval. Repet group not to exceed "O." Only modified USN GOM repet tables to be used.

| 200 FSW | | | | | | | SURFACE DECOMPRESSION USING OXYGEN<br>Air or 50/50 as breathing medium on in–water decompression stops. | | | | | | |
|---|---|---|---|---|---|---|---|---|---|---|---|---|---|

**US Navy Modified (Gulf of Mexico) Tables**
*Surface Decompression Air Tables*

| Bottom Time (min) | Time to First Stop (min/sec) | Water Stops (in feet and minutes) | | | | | | Surface Interval | Chamber Stops (breathing O₂) | | 5 min Air Breaks | Ascent to Surf | Decomp Time (min) | Repet Group |
|---|---|---|---|---|---|---|---|---|---|---|---|---|---|---|
| | | 80 | 70 | 60 | 50 | 40 | 30 | | 50 | 40 | | | | |
| 15 | 6:00 | | | | 2 | 5 | 7 | Not to Exceed 5 min | 10 | 20 | 2 | 10 min slow bleed on oxygen | 78:00 | |
| 30 | 4:48 | 2 | | 4 | 6 | 10 | 16 | | 10 | 50 | 3 | | 138:48 | |
| **Standard Operational Depth/Time Limit** | | | | | | | | | | | | | | |
| 45 | 4:48 | 2 | | 5 | 12 | 20 | 30 | | 10 | 70 | 4 | | 194:48 | |

IN-WATER PHASE: Ascent rate is 25 fpm, time between water stops, and from 30-foot stop to surface is one minute. 50/50 may be used instead of air at 60 and shallower. The 50/50 is not to be routed through panel until diver is at 60 fsw. Umbilical to be flushed with air (and logged) after each dive if using 50/50.

CHAMBER PHASE: Diver is pressed from surface to 50 in chamber in 30 sec. SI ends when diver is at 50 in chamber. Diver has three min to begin O₂. After 50-foot stop, slide to 40 in 1 min (on O₂). First air break as soon as diver arrives at 40. Maximum O₂ time is 20 min without 5 min air break. Time on stop does not include air breaks.

REPET DIVES: Repetitive dives only performed after six-hour surface interval. Repet group not to exceed "O." Only modified USN GOM repet tables to be used.

## US Navy Modified (Gulf of Mexico) Tables
*Surface Decompression Air Tables*

| 210 FSW | SURFACE DECOMPRESSION USING OXYGEN — Air or 50/50 as breathing medium on in–water decompression stops. | | | | | | | | | | | | |
|---|---|---|---|---|---|---|---|---|---|---|---|---|---|
| Bottom Time (min) | Time to First Stop (min/sec) | Water Stops (in feet and minutes) | | | | | | Surface Interval | Chamber Stops (breathing O₂) | | 5 min Air Breaks | Ascent to Surf | Decomp Time (min) | Repet Group |
| | | 80 | 70 | 60 | 50 | 40 | 30 | | 50 | 40 | | | | |
| 15 | 6:24 | | | | 3 | 4 | 8 | Not to Exceed 5 min | 10 | 20 | 2 | 10 min slow bleed on oxygen | 79:24 | |
| 30 | 5:12 | 2 | | 4 | 7 | 12 | 18 | | 10 | 60 | 4 | | 159:12 | |
| Standard Operational Depth/Time Limit | | | | | | | | | | | | | | |
| 45 | 5:12 | 2 | | 6 | 14 | 24 | 36 | | 10 | 70 | 4 | | 208:12 | |

IN-WATER PHASE: Ascent rate is 25 fpm, time between water stops, and from 30-foot stop to surface is one minute. 50/50 may be used instead of air at 60 and shallower. The 50/50 is not to be routed through panel until diver is at 60 fsw. Umbilical to be flushed with air (and logged) after each dive if using 50/50.

CHAMBER PHASE: Diver is pressed from surface to 50 in chamber in 30 sec. SI ends when diver is at 50 in chamber. Diver has three min to begin O₂. After 50-foot stop, slide to 40 in 1 min (on O₂). First air break as soon as diver arrives at 40. Maximum O₂ time is 20 min without 5 min air break. Time on stop does not include air breaks.

REPET DIVES: Repetitive dives only performed after six-hour surface interval. Repet group not to exceed "O." Only modified USN GOM repet tables to be used.

| US Navy Modified (Gulf of Mexico) Tables | | | | | | | | | | | | | |
| *Surface Decompression Air Tables* | | | | | | | | | | | | | |

| 220 FSW | SURFACE DECOMPRESSION USING OXYGEN Air or 50/50 as breathing medium on in–water decompression stops. | | | | | | | | | | | | |
|---|---|---|---|---|---|---|---|---|---|---|---|---|---|
| Bottom Time (min) | Time to First Stop (min/sec) | Water Stops (in feet and minutes) | | | | | | Surface Interval | Chamber Stops (breathing O₂) | | 5 min Air Breaks | Ascent to Surf | Decomp Time (min) | Repet Group |
| | | 80 | 70 | 60 | 50 | 40 | 30 | | 50 | 40 | | | | |
| 15 | 6:24 | | | 2 | 4 | 5 | 10 | Not to Exceed 5 min | 10 | 40 | 3 | 10 min slow bleed on oxygen | 111:24 | |
| 30 | 5:36 | 2 | | 5 | 9 | 14 | 20 | | 10 | 60 | 4 | | 166:36 | |
| **Standard Operational Depth/Time Limit** | | | | | | | | | | | | | | |
| 45 | 5:36 | 2 | | 6 | 16 | 30 | 42 | | 10 | 70 | 4 | | 222:36 | |

IN-WATER PHASE: Ascent rate is 25 fpm, time between water stops, and from 30-foot stop to surface is one minute. 50/50 may be used instead of air at 60 and shallower. The 50/50 is not to be routed through panel until diver is at 60 fsw. Umbilical to be flushed with air (and logged) after each dive if using 50/50.

CHAMBER PHASE: Diver is pressed from surface to 50 in chamber in 30 sec. SI ends when diver is at 50 in chamber. Diver has three min to begin O₂. After 50-foot stop, slide to 40 in 1 min (on O₂). First air break as soon as diver arrives at 40. Maximum O₂ time is 20 min without 5 min air break. Time on stop does not include air breaks.

REPET DIVES: Repetitive dives only performed after six-hour surface interval. Repet group not to exceed "O." Only modified USN GOM repet tables to be used.

# SECTION 6
# Using the DCIEM (Canadian Navy) Tables

The Canadian Navy tables were developed between 1962 and 1983 by the Experimental Diving Unit of the Defence and Civil Institute of Environmental Medicine (DCIEM). After years of testing using both the Doppler ultrasonic bubble detection system and field trials, the tables were first released for use by civilian divers in 1992. In over twenty-five years of constant usage, there have been few, if any, recorded incidents when these tables are properly used. These tables are somewhat more conservative than those found in the latest version of the *US Navy Manual Rev. 7*.

Included in this handbook are the following DCIEM air tables: Table 1 (Standard Air) (see Section 7), Table 3 (Surface Decompression Using Oxygen) (see Sections 9 and 10), Table 4 (Repetitive Factors/Surface Intervals and No-D Repetitive Dives) (see Section 8), and Table 5 (Depth Corrections for Diving at Altitude) (see Section 11). In the unlikely event that recompression treatment is required after using these tables, the user is directed to the flowcharts and treatment tables as found in the *US Navy Manual, Rev. 7*.

## CHOOSING THE PROPER DECOMPRESSION TABLE
Once the diver has reached bottom (or the underwater job site), a pneumofathometer reading is taken. The correction factor is added to establish the maximum depth. The next greater depth table is selected (unless further padding is required by the employer). Once the bottom time is established, the schedule with the next greater bottom time is selected.

### Descent Rate
The descent when using these tables will be determined by the diver's ability to equalize; however, the maximum rate should be 60 fsw/min.

### Bottom Time
Bottom time begins when the diver leaves surface and ends when the diver begins ascent, rounded up to the next full minute.

### Ascent Rate

The ascent rate is 60 fsw per minute, with an allowed variance of +10 fsw per minute. This rate is used from bottom to the first stop, between subsequent stops, and from the final stop to the surface.

### Stop Time (Air Stops)

Decompression stop time includes the travel time to the stop. Stop time ends when the diver begins ascent to the next stop, or to the surface.

### Stop Time (Oxygen Stops)

Decompression stop time starts once the diver is confirmed on oxygen (after 20-second vent).

### Surface Interval (Repetitive Dive)

The surface interval (SI) begins when the diver surfaces from the first dive and ends when the diver leaves surface for the second dive.

### Surface Interval (Surface Decompression)

The surface interval begins when the diver leaves the 30 fsw water stop (or bottom when no stops required) and ends when the diver reaches the 40 fsw chamber stop. The maximum surface interval is seven minutes.

### Effective Bottom Time (EBT)

On repetitive dives, EBT is the bottom time of the repetitive dive adjusted to allow for the residual nitrogen of the first dive(s) for decompression purposes.

### Repetitive Factor (RF)

An RF is a figure used for repetitive dive calculations, determined by the repetitive group and the surface interval.

### Repetitive Group (RG)

An RG is a letter relating to the amount of residual nitrogen carried by the diver immediately upon surfacing from a dive (used in calculating RF for repetitive dives).

## CORRECTING VARIATIONS IN ASCENT RATE

As was stated previously, the ascent rate is 60 fsw per minute, with anything between 50 fsw and 70 fsw per minute being deemed acceptable. The following rules apply to variations in ascent rate that exceed those parameters.

### Ascent Rate Too Slow:

1.  If the delay starts deeper than half the maximum depth of the dive, the delay is added to the bottom time, and the diver is decompressed according to the new bottom time.

2.  If the delay starts shallower than half the maximum depth, the delay is added to the stop time of the next decompression stop. If no stops are required, stop the diver a 10 fsw for the time of delay.

### Ascent Rate Too Fast:

1.  If stops are required, no correction is required as stop time includes travel time to the stop

2.  If no stops required, observe the diver for signs of DCS for at least one hour.

### Omitted Decompression

In the event that the diver surfaces without completing the required decompression, the following actions are to be taken:

1.  If the 30 fsw stop or deeper stops were not completed, treat as follows: (a) if less than 30 minutes missed, see Treatment Table 5; (b) if more than 30 minutes missed, see Treatment Table 6.

2.  If the 30 fsw stop and all previous stops were completed, place diver in chamber on $O_2$ and decompress according to the appropriate Surface Decompression Using Oxygen Table.

### Flying After Diving

Following a no-decompression dive, enough surface interval must pass to allow the RF to diminish to 1.0 before flying. Following a decompression dive, a minimum of 24 hours is required before flying.

# SECTION 7
# DCIEM Standard Air Tables

| DCIEM Standard Air Decompression | | | | | | | | | | |
|---|---|---|---|---|---|---|---|---|---|---|
| **20 FSW** | **DECOMPRESSION STOP TIMES (in minutes)** | | | | | | | | **Decom. Time (min)** | **Repet Group** |
| **Bottom Time (min)** | **80** | **70** | **60** | **50** | **40** | **30** | **20** | **10** | | |
| 30 | | | | | | | | | 1 | A |
| 60 | | | | | | | | | 1 | B |
| 90 | | | | | | | | | 1 | C |
| 120 | | | | | | | | | 1 | D |
| 150 | | | | | | | | | 1 | E |
| 180 | | | | | | | | | 1 | F |
| 240 | | | | | | | | | 1 | G |
| 300 | | | | | | | | | 1 | H |
| 360 | | | | | | | | | 1 | I |
| 420 | | | | | | | | | 1 | J |
| 480 | | | | | | | | | 1 | K |
| 600 | | | | | | | | | 1 | L |
| 720 | | | | | | | | | 1 | M |

| DCIEM Standard Air Decompression | | | | | | | | | | |
|---|---|---|---|---|---|---|---|---|---|---|
| **30 FSW** | **DECOMPRESSION STOP TIMES (in minutes)** | | | | | | | | **Decom. Time (min)** | **Repet Group** |
| **Bottom Time (min)** | **80** | **70** | **60** | **50** | **40** | **30** | **20** | **10** | | |
| 30 | | | | | | | | | 1 | A |
| 60 | | | | | | | | | 1 | C |
| 90 | | | | | | | | | 1 | D |
| 120 | | | | | | | | | 1 | F |
| 150 | | | | | | | | | 1 | G |
| 180 | | | | | | | | | 1 | H |
| 210 | | | | | | | | | 1 | J |
| 240 | | | | | | | | | 1 | K |
| 270 | | | | | | | | | 1 | L |
| 300 | | | | | | | | | 1 | M |
| 330 | | | | | | | | 3 | 3 | N |
| 360 | | | | | | | | 5 | 5 | O |
| **Exceptional Exposures Beyond this Point – Surface Decompression Using Oxygen Recommended** | | | | | | | | | | |
| 390 | | | | | | | | 7 | 7 | |
| 400 | | | | | | | | 10 | 10 | |
| 420 | | | | | | | | 14 | 14 | |
| 450 | | | | | | | | 19 | 19 | |
| 480 | | | | | | | | 23 | 23 | |

| DCIEM Standard Air Decompression | | | | | | | | | | |
|---|---|---|---|---|---|---|---|---|---|---|
| **40 FSW** | **DECOMPRESSION STOP TIMES (in minutes)** | | | | | | | | **Decom. Time (min)** | **Repet Group** |
| **Bottom Time (min)** | **80** | **70** | **60** | **50** | **40** | **30** | **20** | **10** | | |
| 20 | | | | | | | | | 1 | A |
| 30 | | | | | | | | | 1 | B |
| 60 | | | | | | | | | 1 | D |
| 90 | | | | | | | | | 1 | G |
| 120 | | | | | | | | | 1 | H |
| 150 | | | | | | | | | 1 | J |
| 160 | | | | | | | | 3 | 3 | K |
| 170 | | | | | | | | 5 | 5 | L |
| 180 | | | | | | | | 8 | 8 | M |
| **Exceptional Exposures Beyond This Point – Surface Decompression Using Oxygen Recommended** | | | | | | | | | | |
| 190 | | | | | | | | 10 | 10 | |
| 200 | | | | | | | | 14 | 14 | |
| 210 | | | | | | | | 18 | 18 | |
| 240 | | | | | | | | 28 | 28 | |
| 270 | | | | | | | | 38 | 38 | |
| 300 | | | | | | | | 48 | 48 | |
| 330 | | | | | | | | 57 | 57 | |
| 360 | | | | | | | | 66 | 66 | |

| DCIEM Standard Air Decompression | | | | | | | | | | |
|---|---|---|---|---|---|---|---|---|---|---|
| **50 FSW** | DECOMPRESSION STOP TIMES (in minutes) | | | | | | | | Decom. Time (min) | Repet Group |
| Bottom Time (min) | 80 | 70 | 60 | 50 | 40 | 30 | 20 | 10 | | |
| 10 | | | | | | | | | 1 | A |
| 20 | | | | | | | | | 1 | B |
| 30 | | | | | | | | | 1 | C |
| 40 | | | | | | | | | 1 | D |
| 50 | | | | | | | | | 1 | E |
| 60 | | | | | | | | | 1 | F |
| 75 | | | | | | | | | 1 | G |
| 100 | | | | | | | | 6 | 6 | I |
| 120 | | | | | | | | 12 | 12 | K |
| 130 | | | | | | | | 18 | 18 | L |
| 140 | | | | | | | | 24 | 24 | M |
| **Exceptional Exposures Beyond This Point – Surface Decompression Using Oxygen Recommended** | | | | | | | | | | |
| 150 | | | | | | | | 29 | 29 | |
| 160 | | | | | | | | 33 | 33 | |
| 170 | | | | | | | | 38 | 38 | |
| 180 | | | | | | | | 43 | 43 | |
| 200 | | | | | | | | 53 | 53 | |
| 220 | | | | | | | | 63 | 63 | |
| 240 | | | | | | | | 74 | 74 | |

| DCIEM Standard Air Decompression | | | | | | | | | | |
|---|---|---|---|---|---|---|---|---|---|---|
| **60 FSW** | DECOMPRESSION STOP TIMES (in minutes) | | | | | | | | Decom. Time (min) | Repet Group |
| Bottom Time (min) | 80 | 70 | 60 | 50 | 40 | 30 | 20 | 10 | | |
| 10 | | | | | | | | | 1 | A |
| 20 | | | | | | | | | 1 | B |
| 30 | | | | | | | | | 1 | D |
| 40 | | | | | | | | | 1 | E |
| 50 | | | | | | | | | 1 | F |
| 60 | | | | | | | | 5 | 5 | G |
| 80 | | | | | | | | 10 | 10 | I |
| 90 | | | | | | | | 19 | 19 | J |
| 100 | | | | | | | | 26 | 26 | K |
| 110 | | | | | | | | 32 | 32 | L |
| 120 | | | | | | | 2 | 37 | 39 | M |
| **Exceptional Exposures Beyond This Point – Surface Decompression Using Oxygen Recommended** | | | | | | | | | | |
| 130 | | | | | | | 2 | 43 | 45 | |
| 140 | | | | | | | 3 | 49 | 52 | |
| 150 | | | | | | | 3 | 55 | 58 | |
| 160 | | | | | | | 4 | 62 | 66 | |
| 170 | | | | | | | 4 | 70 | 74 | |
| 180 | | | | | | | 5 | 77 | 82 | |
| 190 | | | | | | | 5 | 85 | 90 | |

| DCIEM Standard Air Decompression | | | | | | | | | | |
|---|---|---|---|---|---|---|---|---|---|---|
| **70 FSW** | **DECOMPRESSION STOP TIMES (in minutes)** | | | | | | | | **Decom. Time (min)** | **Repet Group** |
| **Bottom Time (min)** | **80** | **70** | **60** | **50** | **40** | **30** | **20** | **10** | | |
| 10 | | | | | | | | | 1 | A |
| 20 | | | | | | | | | 1 | C |
| 25 | | | | | | | | | 1 | D |
| 35 | | | | | | | | | 1 | E |
| 40 | | | | | | | | 5 | 5 | F |
| 50 | | | | | | | | 10 | 10 | G |
| 60 | | | | | | | 2 | 11 | 13 | H |
| 70 | | | | | | | 3 | 19 | 22 | J |
| 80 | | | | | | | 4 | 27 | 31 | K |
| 90 | | | | | | | 5 | 34 | 39 | M |
| 100 | | | | | | | 6 | 41 | 47 | N |
| **Exceptional Exposures Beyond This Point – Surface Decompression Using Oxygen Recommended** | | | | | | | | | | |
| 110 | | | | | | | 7 | 48 | 55 | |
| 120 | | | | | | | 8 | 56 | 64 | |
| 130 | | | | | | | 9 | 65 | 74 | |
| 140 | | | | | | | 11 | 74 | 85 | |
| 150 | | | | | | | 17 | 81 | 98 | |
| 160 | | | | | | | 22 | 89 | 111 | |
| 170 | | | | | | | 27 | 98 | 125 | |
| 180 | | | | | | | 31 | 107 | 138 | |

| DCIEM Standard Air Decompression | | | | | | | | | | |
|---|---|---|---|---|---|---|---|---|---|---|
| **80 FSW** | **DECOMPRESSION STOP TIMES (in minutes)** | | | | | | | | **Decom. Time (min)** | **Repet Group** |
| **Bottom Time (min)** | **80** | **70** | **60** | **50** | **40** | **30** | **20** | **10** | | |
| 10 | | | | | | | | | 2 | A |
| 15 | | | | | | | | | 2 | C |
| 20 | | | | | | | | | 2 | D |
| 25 | | | | | | | | | 2 | E |
| 30 | | | | | | | | 6 | 6 | F |
| 40 | | | | | | | 2 | 10 | 12 | G |
| 50 | | | | | | | 4 | 12 | 16 | H |
| 55 | | | | | | | 5 | 17 | 22 | I |
| 60 | | | | | | | 6 | 22 | 28 | J |
| 65 | | | | | | | 7 | 27 | 34 | J |
| 70 | | | | | | | 8 | 31 | 39 | K |
| 75 | | | | | | | 9 | 35 | 44 | L |
| 80 | | | | | | | 9 | 40 | 49 | M |
| **Exceptional Exposures Beyond This Point – Surface Decompression Using Oxygen Recommended** | | | | | | | | | | |
| 85 | | | | | | | 10 | 44 | 54 | |
| 90 | | | | | | | 11 | 48 | 59 | |
| 95 | | | | | | | 11 | 53 | 64 | |
| 100 | | | | | | 2 | 10 | 58 | 70 | |
| 110 | | | | | | 3 | 14 | 66 | 83 | |
| 120 | | | | | | 3 | 20 | 76 | 99 | |
| 130 | | | | | | 4 | 24 | 87 | 115 | |
| 140 | | | | | | 5 | 29 | 98 | 132 | |

| DCIEM Standard Air Decompression | | | | | | | | | | |
|---|---|---|---|---|---|---|---|---|---|---|
| **90 FSW** | DECOMPRESSION STOP TIMES (in minutes) | | | | | | | | Decom. Time (min) | Repet Group |
| Bottom Time (min) | 80 | 70 | 60 | 50 | 40 | 30 | 20 | 10 | | |
| 5 | | | | | | | | | 2 | A |
| 10 | | | | | | | | | 2 | B |
| 15 | | | | | | | | | 2 | C |
| 20 | | | | | | | | | 2 | D |
| 25 | | | | | | | | 8 | 8 | E |
| 30 | | | | | | | 3 | 9 | 12 | F |
| 40 | | | | | | | 6 | 11 | 17 | H |
| 45 | | | | | | | 7 | 16 | 23 | I |
| 50 | | | | | | | 9 | 21 | 30 | J |
| 55 | | | | | | | 10 | 27 | 37 | K |
| 60 | | | | | | 2 | 9 | 32 | 43 | L |
| **Exceptional Exposures Beyond This Point – Surface Decompression Using Oxygen Recommended** | | | | | | | | | | |
| 65 | | | | | | 3 | 9 | 37 | 49 | |
| 70 | | | | | | 4 | 9 | 42 | 55 | |
| 75 | | | | | | 4 | 10 | 47 | 61 | |
| 80 | | | | | | 5 | 10 | 53 | 68 | |
| 85 | | | | | | 5 | 11 | 59 | 75 | |
| 90 | | | | | | 6 | 15 | 62 | 83 | |
| 95 | | | | | | 6 | 18 | 68 | 92 | |
| 100 | | | | | | 7 | 21 | 73 | 101 | |

| DCIEM Standard Air Decompression | | | | | | | | | | |
|---|---|---|---|---|---|---|---|---|---|---|
| **100 FSW** | DECOMPRESSION STOP TIMES (in minutes) | | | | | | | | Decom. Time (min) | Repet Group |
| Bottom Time (min) | 80 | 70 | 60 | 50 | 40 | 30 | 20 | 10 | | |
| 5 | | | | | | | | | 2 | A |
| 10 | | | | | | | | | 2 | B |
| 15 | | | | | | | | | 2 | D |
| 20 | | | | | | | | 8 | 2 | E |
| 25 | | | | | | | 3 | 10 | 8 | F |
| 30 | | | | | | | 6 | 10 | 12 | G |
| 35 | | | | | | | 8 | 11 | 17 | H |
| 40 | | | | | | | 9 | 18 | 23 | I |
| 45 | | | | | | 3 | 8 | 25 | 30 | J |
| 50 | | | | | | 4 | 9 | 30 | 37 | K |
| 55 | | | | | | 5 | 9 | 37 | 43 | L |
| **Exceptional Exposures Beyond This Point – Surface Decompression Using Oxygen Recommended** | | | | | | | | | | |
| 60 | | | | | | 6 | 9 | 43 | 58 | |
| 65 | | | | | | 7 | 10 | 48 | 65 | |
| 70 | | | | | | 8 | 10 | 55 | 73 | |
| 75 | | | | | | 8 | 15 | 59 | 82 | |
| 80 | | | | | | 9 | 18 | 65 | 92 | |
| 85 | | | | | 2 | 8 | 22 | 71 | 103 | |
| 90 | | | | | 2 | 8 | 25 | 79 | 114 | |
| 95 | | | | | 3 | 8 | 29 | 87 | 127 | |

| DCIEM Standard Air Decompression | | | | | | | | | | |
|---|---|---|---|---|---|---|---|---|---|---|
| **110 FSW** | **DECOMPRESSION STOP TIMES (in minutes)** | | | | | | | | **Decom. Time (min)** | **Repet Group** |
| **Bottom Time (min)** | **80** | **70** | **60** | **50** | **40** | **30** | **20** | **10** | | |
| 5 | | | | | | | | | 2 | A |
| 10 | | | | | | | | | 2 | B |
| 12 | | | | | | | | | 2 | C |
| 15 | | | | | | | | 5 | 5 | D |
| 20 | | | | | | | 3 | 9 | 12 | F |
| 25 | | | | | | | 6 | 10 | 16 | G |
| 30 | | | | | | | 9 | 11 | 20 | H |
| 35 | | | | | | 4 | 7 | 19 | 30 | I |
| 40 | | | | | | 5 | 8 | 26 | 39 | J |
| 45 | | | | | | 6 | 9 | 33 | 48 | K |
| 50 | | | | | | 8 | 9 | 39 | 56 | M |
| 55 | | | | | | 9 | 9 | 46 | 64 | N |
| **Exceptional Exposures Beyond This Point – Surface Decompression Using Oxygen Recommended** | | | | | | | | | | |
| 60 | | | | | 3 | 7 | 11 | 53 | 74 | |
| 65 | | | | | 3 | 8 | 16 | 58 | 85 | |
| 70 | | | | | 4 | 8 | 20 | 64 | 96 | |
| 75 | | | | | 5 | 8 | 23 | 73 | 109 | |
| 80 | | | | | 5 | 8 | 28 | 81 | 122 | |
| 85 | | | | | 6 | 8 | 32 | 91 | 137 | |
| 90 | | | | | 6 | 9 | 35 | 101 | 151 | |
| 95 | | | | | 7 | 9 | 40 | 111 | 167 | |

| DCIEM Standard Air Decompression | | | | | | | | | | |
|---|---|---|---|---|---|---|---|---|---|---|
| **120 FSW** | **DECOMPRESSION STOP TIMES (in minutes)** | | | | | | | | **Decom. Time (min)** | **Repet Group** |
| **Bottom Time (min)** | **80** | **70** | **60** | **50** | **40** | **30** | **20** | **10** | | |
| 5 | | | | | | | | | 2 | A |
| 10 | | | | | | | | | 2 | C |
| 15 | | | | | | | | 10 | 10 | E |
| 20 | | | | | | | 5 | 10 | 15 | F |
| 25 | | | | | | | 9 | 11 | 20 | G |
| 30 | | | | | | 5 | 7 | 17 | 29 | I |
| 35 | | | | | | 6 | 9 | 25 | 40 | J |
| 40 | | | | | | 8 | 9 | 33 | 50 | K |
| 45 | | | | | 3 | 7 | 9 | 41 | 60 | M |
| 50 | | | | | 4 | 7 | 10 | 49 | 70 | N |
| **Exceptional Exposures Beyond This Point – Surface Decompression Using Oxygen Recommended** | | | | | | | | | | |
| 55 | | | | | 5 | 7 | 15 | 54 | 81 | |
| 60 | | | | | 6 | 8 | 19 | 61 | 94 | |
| 65 | | | | | 7 | 8 | 23 | 70 | 108 | |
| 70 | | | | | 7 | 9 | 27 | 80 | 123 | |
| 75 | | | | 2 | 6 | 9 | 32 | 91 | 140 | |
| 80 | | | | 3 | 6 | 9 | 37 | 103 | 158 | |
| 85 | | | | 3 | 7 | 10 | 41 | 114 | 175 | |
| 90 | | | | 3 | 7 | 14 | 44 | 124 | 192 | |
| 95 | | | | 4 | 7 | 16 | 49 | 134 | 210 | |

| DCIEM Standard Air Decompression | | | | | | | | | | |
|---|---|---|---|---|---|---|---|---|---|---|
| **130 FSW** | DECOMPRESSION STOP TIMES (in minutes) | | | | | | | | Decom. Time (min) | Repet Group |
| Bottom Time (min) | 80 | 70 | 60 | 50 | 40 | 30 | 20 | 10 | | |
| 5 | | | | | | | | | 2 | A |
| 8 | | | | | | | | | 2 | B |
| 10 | | | | | | | | 5 | 5 | C |
| 15 | | | | | | | 4 | 9 | 13 | E |
| 20 | | | | | | | 8 | 10 | 18 | G |
| 25 | | | | | | 5 | 7 | 12 | 24 | H |
| 30 | | | | | | 7 | 8 | 23 | 38 | J |
| 35 | | | | | 3 | 6 | 9 | 32 | 50 | K |
| 40 | | | | | 5 | 6 | 10 | 40 | 61 | M |
| 45 | | | | | 6 | 7 | 10 | 50 | 73 | N |
| **Exceptional Exposures Beyond This Point – Surface Decompression Using Oxygen Recommended** | | | | | | | | | | |
| 50 | | | | | 7 | 8 | 16 | 55 | 86 | |
| 55 | | | | 2 | 6 | 8 | 21 | 64 | 101 | |
| 60 | | | | 3 | 6 | 8 | 26 | 75 | 118 | |
| 65 | | | | 4 | 6 | 9 | 31 | 86 | 136 | |
| 70 | | | | 5 | 6 | 9 | 36 | 100 | 156 | |
| 75 | | | | 5 | 7 | 11 | 40 | 113 | 176 | |
| 80 | | | | 6 | 7 | 15 | 44 | 125 | 197 | |
| 85 | | | | 6 | 7 | 18 | 49 | 135 | 215 | |
| 90 | | | | 7 | 7 | 22 | 54 | 144 | 234 | |

| DCIEM Standard Air Decompression | | | | | | | | | | |
|---|---|---|---|---|---|---|---|---|---|---|
| **140 FSW** | **DECOMPRESSION STOP TIMES (in minutes)** | | | | | | | | **Decom. Time (min)** | **Repet Group** |
| **Bottom Time (min)** | **80** | **70** | **60** | **50** | **40** | **30** | **20** | **10** | | |
| 7 | | | | | | | | | 2 | B |
| 10 | | | | | | | | 7 | 7 | D |
| 15 | | | | | | | 6 | 9 | 15 | F |
| 20 | | | | | | 4 | 7 | 11 | 22 | G |
| 25 | | | | | | 7 | 8 | 19 | 34 | I |
| 30 | | | | | 4 | 6 | 9 | 29 | 48 | K |
| 35 | | | | | 6 | 6 | 10 | 39 | 61 | L |
| 40 | | | | | 7 | 7 | 10 | 49 | 73 | N |
| 45 | | | | 3 | 6 | 7 | 17 | 56 | 89 | O |
| **Exceptional Exposures Beyond This Point – Surface Decompression Using Oxygen Recommended** | | | | | | | | | | |
| 50 | | | | 4 | 6 | 8 | 22 | 65 | 105 | |
| 55 | | | | 5 | 6 | 9 | 27 | 78 | 125 | |
| 60 | | | | 6 | 6 | 9 | 33 | 91 | 145 | |
| 65 | | | | 7 | 6 | 11 | 38 | 106 | 168 | |
| 70 | | | 2 | 5 | 7 | 15 | 42 | 120 | 191 | |
| 75 | | | 3 | 5 | 8 | 18 | 47 | 133 | 214 | |
| 80 | | | 3 | 6 | 8 | 21 | 54 | 143 | 235 | |
| 85 | | | 4 | 6 | 8 | 25 | 61 | 151 | 255 | |
| 90 | | | 4 | 6 | 8 | 30 | 68 | 157 | 273 | |

| DCIEM Standard Air Decompression | | | | | | | | | | |
|---|---|---|---|---|---|---|---|---|---|---|
| **150 FSW** | DECOMPRESSION STOP TIMES (in minutes) | | | | | | | | Decom. Time (min) | Repet Group |
| Bottom Time (min) | 80 | 70 | 60 | 50 | 40 | 30 | 20 | 10 | | |
| 6 | | | | | | | | | 3 | B |
| 10 | | | | | | | | 9 | 9 | D |
| 15 | | | | | | | 8 | 10 | 18 | F |
| 20 | | | | | | 6 | 8 | 11 | 25 | H |
| 25 | | | | | 4 | 6 | 8 | 25 | 43 | J |
| 30 | | | | | 6 | 7 | 9 | 35 | 57 | K |
| 35 | | | | 3 | 5 | 7 | 10 | 46 | 71 | M |
| 40 | | | | 4 | 6 | 8 | 16 | 54 | 88 | O |
| **Exceptional Exposures Beyond This Point – Surface Decompression Using Oxygen Recommended** | | | | | | | | | | |
| 45 | | | | 6 | 6 | 8 | 22 | 65 | 107 | |
| 50 | | | | 7 | 6 | 9 | 28 | 78 | 128 | |
| 55 | | | 3 | 5 | 6 | 10 | 34 | 94 | 152 | |
| 60 | | | 4 | 5 | 7 | 13 | 39 | 110 | 178 | |
| 65 | | | 4 | 6 | 7 | 17 | 44 | 125 | 203 | |
| 70 | | | 5 | 6 | 7 | 21 | 50 | 139 | 228 | |
| 75 | | | 6 | 5 | 8 | 25 | 58 | 148 | 250 | |
| 80 | | | 6 | 6 | 8 | 29 | 67 | 155 | 271 | |

| DCIEM Standard Air Decompression | | | | | | | | | | |
|---|---|---|---|---|---|---|---|---|---|---|
| **160 FSW** | **DECOMPRESSION STOP TIMES (in minutes)** | | | | | | | | **Decom. Time (min)** | **Repet Group** |
| **Bottom Time (min)** | **80** | **70** | **60** | **50** | **40** | **30** | **20** | **10** | | |
| 6 | | | | | | | | | 3 | B |
| 10 | | | | | | | 3 | 9 | 12 | D |
| 15 | | | | | | 4 | 7 | 10 | 21 | G |
| 20 | | | | | 3 | 5 | 8 | 16 | 32 | H |
| 25 | | | | | 6 | 6 | 9 | 30 | 51 | K |
| 30 | | | | 4 | 5 | 6 | 10 | 42 | 67 | M |
| 35 | | | | 5 | 6 | 7 | 14 | 52 | 84 | N |
| **Exceptional Exposures Beyond This Point – Surface Decompression Using Oxygen Recommended** | | | | | | | | | | |
| 40 | | | | 7 | 6 | 8 | 21 | 62 | 104 | |
| 45 | | | 3 | 5 | 6 | 9 | 28 | 76 | 127 | |
| 50 | | | 4 | 5 | 7 | 9 | 35 | 93 | 153 | |
| 55 | | | 5 | 6 | 7 | 14 | 39 | 112 | 183 | |
| 60 | | | 6 | 6 | 7 | 18 | 45 | 129 | 211 | |
| 65 | | 3 | 4 | 6 | 8 | 22 | 53 | 142 | 238 | |
| 70 | | 3 | 5 | 6 | 8 | 27 | 62 | 152 | 263 | |

| DCIEM Standard Air Decompression | | | | | | | | | | |
|---|---|---|---|---|---|---|---|---|---|---|
| **170 FSW** | DECOMPRESSION STOP TIMES (in minutes) | | | | | | | | Decom. Time (min) | Repet Group |
| Bottom Time (min) | 80 | 70 | 60 | 50 | 40 | 30 | 20 | 10 | | |
| 5 | | | | | | | | | 3 | B |
| 10 | | | | | | | 5 | 9 | 14 | D |
| 15 | | | | | | 6 | 7 | 10 | 23 | G |
| 20 | | | | | 5 | 6 | 8 | 22 | 41 | I |
| 25 | | | | 3 | 5 | 6 | 10 | 35 | 59 | K |
| 30 | | | | 6 | 5 | 7 | 11 | 48 | 77 | M |
| 35 | | | 3 | 4 | 6 | 8 | 19 | 58 | 98 | O |
| **Exceptional Exposures Beyond This Point – Surface Decompression Using Oxygen Recommended** | | | | | | | | | | |
| 40 | | | 4 | 5 | 6 | 9 | 26 | 72 | 122 | |
| 45 | | | 6 | 5 | 6 | 10 | 34 | 91 | 152 | |
| 50 | | 3 | 4 | 5 | 7 | 14 | 39 | 111 | 183 | |
| 55 | | 3 | 5 | 5 | 8 | 19 | 45 | 129 | 214 | |
| 60 | | 4 | 5 | 6 | 8 | 23 | 54 | 144 | 244 | |
| 65 | | 5 | 5 | 6 | 8 | 29 | 64 | 154 | 271 | |
| 70 | | 5 | 5 | 7 | 12 | 31 | 76 | 160 | 296 | |

| DCIEM Standard Air Decompression | | | | | | | | | | |
|---|---|---|---|---|---|---|---|---|---|---|
| **180 FSW** | **DECOMPRESSION STOP TIMES (in minutes)** | | | | | | | | **Decom. Time (min)** | **Repet Group** |
| **Bottom Time (min)** | **80** | **70** | **60** | **50** | **40** | **30** | **20** | **10** | | |
| 5 | | | | | | | | | 3 | B |
| 10 | | | | | | | 7 | 9 | 16 | E |
| 15 | | | | | | 8 | 7 | 11 | 26 | H |
| 20 | | | | | 7 | 6 | 8 | 27 | 48 | J |
| 25 | | | | 5 | 5 | 7 | 10 | 40 | 67 | M |
| 30 | | | 3 | 5 | 5 | 8 | 15 | 53 | 89 | O |
| **Exceptional Exposures Beyond This Point – Surface Decompression Using Oxygen Recommended** | | | | | | | | | | |
| 35 | | | 5 | 5 | 6 | 8 | 24 | 66 | 114 | |
| 40 | | 3 | 4 | 5 | 6 | 9 | 32 | 85 | 144 | |
| 45 | | 4 | 4 | 5 | 7 | 14 | 38 | 107 | 179 | |
| 50 | | 5 | 4 | 6 | 7 | 19 | 45 | 127 | 213 | |
| 55 | | 5 | 5 | 6 | 8 | 24 | 53 | 144 | 245 | |
| 60 | 3 | 3 | 5 | 7 | 9 | 29 | 65 | 155 | 276 | |

# SECTION 8
# Repetitive Dives Using the DCIEM Tables

After the completion of every dive (including no-decompression dives), there is still nitrogen remaining in solution in the bloodstream and tissues of the diver. This residual nitrogen is eliminated gradually to a point that, after approximately 18 hours, the nitrogen level in the diver's body is at the normal level. Any time that a second dive is planned while the diver carries a residual gas load (within 18 hours), this residual nitrogen has to be factored in when planning the second dive.

Included in this handbook are the DCIEM standard air tables. (See Section 7). These tables have repetitive group designations for the various depths and bottom times to allow for repetitive dive planning. **The repetitive group designations found in the DCIEM tables are to be used with the DCIEM repetitive diving procedures only.** They **MUST NOT** be interchanged with any other repetitive diving procedures or diving tables.

## REPETITIVE DIVING PROCEDURES

Every dive that falls within the normal air diving range found in the standard air table has a repetitive group (RG) letter to use for repetitive dive calculations. Repetitive dives do not follow exceptional exposure dives. Although the surface decompression using oxygen table has RG letters provided, standard practice offshore is that repetitive dives are not performed after decompression.

## SI Less than 15 Minutes

Multiple dives with a surface interval of less than 15 minutes are not considered repetitive dives but combined single dives. When both dives are to the same depth, bottom times are simply added together to establish the effective bottom time (EBT) of the dive, and decompression, if required, is carried out according to the EBT.

Example:

| | |
|---|---|
| First Dive: 50 fsw/35 min | RG = D SI = 8 min |
| Second Dive: 50 fsw/60 min | EBT = 35 + 60 = 95 min |
| Decompression required | 50 fsw/100 min; 6 min at 10 fsw |

When the dives are to different depths, we find the bottom time at the second dive depth that carries the same RG letter as the first dive. Then we add this bottom time to the intended bottom time for the second dive and obtain the EBT for the second dive.

Example:

| | |
|---|---|
| First Dive: 100 fsw/15 min | RG = D(Table 1S) |
| Surface Interval | 10 min |
| Second Dive Depth = 55 fsw | Group D at 60 fsw; Bottom Time = 30 min |
| Second Dive Bottom Time = 30 min | EBT = 30 + 30 = 60 min |
| Decompression required | 60 fsw/60 min; 5 min at 10 fsw |

## SI Greater than 18 Hours
Multiple dives with a surface interval greater than 18 hours are not considered repetitive dives, as the residual nitrogen carried by the diver from the first dive would have been eliminated. They are conducted as single dives.

## Using the DCIEM Repetitive Dive Tables
From the standard air or short standard air table, establish the repetitive group (RG) of the dive, based on the bottom time and depth of the dive. In Table 4A: Repetitive Factors/Surface Intervals, find the matching RG in the far left column. Follow the same line horizontally to the appropriate SI. The box at the intersection of the RG and the SI has a number, which is the repetitive factor (RF). In Table 4B: No-Decompression Repetitive Diving find the applicable RF column and follow it down to the depth of the planned second dive. The box at the intersection contains a number,

which is the no-decompression limit for the dive. The number is the actual bottom time and not the EBT.

## DCIEM TABLE 4 (REPETITIVE DIVING)

### TABLE (4A) REPETITIVE FACTORS / SURFACE INTERVALS

| Repetitive Group (RG) | Repetitive Factors (RF) for Surface Intervals (SI) stated in hours and minutes | | | | | | | | | | |
|---|---|---|---|---|---|---|---|---|---|---|---|
| | 0:15→0:29 | 0:30→0:59 | 1:00→1:29 | 1:30→1:59 | 2:00→2:59 | 3:00→3:59 | 4:00→5:59 | 6:00→8:59 | 9:00→11:59 | 12:00→14:59 | 15:00→18:00 |
| A | 1.4 | 1.2 | 1.1 | 1.1 | 1.1 | 1.1 | 1.1 | 1.1 | 1.0 | 1.0 | 1.0 |
| B | 1.5 | 1.3 | 1.2 | 1.2 | 1.2 | 1.1 | 1.1 | 1.1 | 1.1 | 1.0 | 1.0 |
| C | 1.6 | 1.4 | 1.3 | 1.2 | 1.2 | 1.2 | 1.1 | 1.1 | 1.1 | 1.0 | 1.0 |
| D | 1.8 | 1.5 | 1.4 | 1.3 | 1.3 | 1.2 | 1.2 | 1.1 | 1.1 | 1.1 | 1.0 |
| E | 1.9 | 1.6 | 1.5 | 1.4 | 1.3 | 1.3 | 1.2 | 1.2 | 1.1 | 1.1 | 1.0 |
| F | 2.0 | 1.7 | 1.6 | 1.5 | 1.4 | 1.3 | 1.3 | 1.2 | 1.1 | 1.1 | 1.0 |
| G | | 1.9 | 1.7 | 1.6 | 1.5 | 1.4 | 1.3 | 1.2 | 1.1 | 1.1 | 1.0 |
| H | | | 1.8 | 1.7 | 1.6 | 1.5 | 1.4 | 1.3 | 1.1 | 1.1 | 1.1 |
| I | | | 1.9 | 1.8 | 1.7 | 1.6 | 1.4 | 1.3 | 1.1 | 1.1 | 1.1 |
| J | | | 2.0 | 1.9 | 1.8 | 1.7 | 1.5 | 1.3 | 1.2 | 1.1 | 1.1 |
| K | | | | 2.0 | 1.9 | 1.8 | 1.5 | 1.3 | 1.2 | 1.1 | 1.1 |
| L | | | | | 2.0 | 1.9 | 1.6 | 1.4 | 1.2 | 1.1 | 1.1 |
| M | | | | | | 2.0 | 1.6 | 1.4 | 1.2 | 1.1 | 1.1 |
| N | | | | | | | 1.7 | 1.4 | 1.2 | 1.1 | 1.1 |
| O | | | | | | | 1.7 | 1.4 | 1.2 | 1.1 | 1.1 |

### TABLE 4B NO-DECOMPRESSION REPETITIVE DIVING

| Depth (fsw) | Allowable No-Decompression Limits (in minutes) for Repetitive Factors (RF) | | | | | | | | | |
|---|---|---|---|---|---|---|---|---|---|---|
| | 1.1 | 1.2 | 1.3 | 1.4 | 1.5 | 1.6 | 1.7 | 1.8 | 1.9 | 2.0 |
| 30 | 272 | 250 | 230 | 214 | 200 | 187 | 176 | 166 | 157 | 150 |
| 40 | 136 | 125 | 115 | 107 | 100 | 93 | 88 | 83 | 78 | 75 |
| 50 | 60 | 55 | 50 | 45 | 41 | 38 | 36 | 34 | 32 | 31 |
| 60 | 40 | 35 | 31 | 29 | 27 | 26 | 24 | 23 | 22 | 21 |
| 70 | 30 | 25 | 21 | 19 | 18 | 17 | 16 | 15 | 14 | 13 |
| 80 | 20 | 18 | 16 | 15 | 14 | 13 | 12 | 12 | 11 | 11 |
| 90 | 16 | 14 | 12 | 11 | 11 | 10 | 9 | 9 | 8 | 8 |
| 100 | 13 | 11 | 10 | 9 | 9 | 8 | 8 | 7 | 7 | 7 |
| 110 | 10 | 9 | 8 | 8 | 7 | 7 | 6 | 6 | 6 | 6 |
| 120 | 8 | 7 | 7 | 6 | 6 | 6 | 5 | 5 | 5 | 5 |
| 130 | 7 | 6 | 6 | 5 | 5 | 5 | 4 | 4 | 4 | 4 |
| 140 | 6 | 5 | 5 | 5 | 4 | 4 | 4 | 3 | 3 | 3 |
| 150 | 5 | 5 | 4 | 4 | 4 | 3 | 3 | 3 | 3 | 3 |

## Repetitive Dives Not Requiring Decompression

If according to Table 4B the actual bottom time of the second dive is equal to or less than the no-decompression limit, the second dive will not require decompression.

If the actual bottom time of the second dive is within the no-decompression limit, the actual bottom time is multiplied by the RF to obtain the EBT of the second dive. Using the EBT and the recorded depth, the RG is then obtained from the decompression table used, and another repetitive dive may be performed (see the following paragraph on multiple repetitive dives).

## Multiple Repetitive Dives

If the RG of the just-completed dive is greater than the RG of the previous dive and the SI until the next dive is under 6 hours, no adjustment of the RG will be required. If the RG is lower than, or equal to the RG of the previous dive, the RG of the just-completed dive is adjusted upward so that it is equal to the RG of the previous dive plus one letter. For example, if the first dive had an RG of C, and the second dive has an RG of B, the RG of the second dive would be adjusted to D. If the SI between the second and third dive exceeds 6 hours, no adjustment is required to the RG of the second dive.

## Repetitive Dives Requiring Decompression

When the actual bottom time of the repetitive dive exceeds the no-decompression limit as found in Table 4B, decompression will be required. The actual bottom time is multiplied by the RF to obtain the EBT. The depth and EBT are then used to determine the required decompression using Table 1, 1S, or 3. (See Sections 7 and 10.)

If the actual bottom time of the repetitive dive exceeds the no-decompression limit as found in Table 4B, but the EBT is less than the no-decompression limit found in Table 1 or 1S, a 5-minute stop at 10 fsw is required. The no-D limits in Tables 1, 1S, and 3 are for single dives only.

## Sample Repetitive Dive Sheet for DCIEM Diving Tables

| Diver | Location | Date |
|-------|----------|------|
|       |          |      |

## Dive #1

| Leave Surface | Leave Bottom | Bottom Time | Arrive Surface |
|---------------|--------------|-------------|----------------|
| Depth | Table Used | Repetitive Group | Comments |

## Dive #2

| Surface Interval | Repetitive Factor (4A) | Depth | Table Used |
|------------------|------------------------|-------|------------|
| No D Limit (4B) | Planned BT | EBT (RF x BT) | Decomp. Required? |
| Leave Surface | Leave Bottom | Bottom Time | Stop 1 __fsw____min<br>On stop:<br>Leave stop: |
| Stop 2<br>____fsw____min<br>On stop:<br>Leave stop: | Stop 3<br>____fsw____min<br>On stop:<br>Leave stop: | Stop 4<br>____fsw____min<br>On stop:<br>Leave stop: | Arrive Surface |
| Standby Diver | Tender | Tender | Supervisor |

If the bottom time exceeds the no-D limit in 4B, but the EBT does not exceed the no-D limit in Table 1S, diver must perform a 5-minute water stop at 10 fsw.

# DCIEM SHORT STANDARD AIR TABLE (TABLE 1S)

| Depth (fsw) | No-Decompression Bottom Times (minutes) | Decompression Required Bottom Times (minutes) | | | | | | | | | 400 | 420 | 450 |
|---|---|---|---|---|---|---|---|---|---|---|---|---|---|
| 20 | 30 A   60 B   90 C   120 D | 150 E   180 F   240 G   300 H | 360 I   420 J   480 K   600 L | 720 M ∞ | | | | | | | | | |
| 30 | 30 A   45 B   60 C   90 D | 100 E   120 F   150 G   180 H | 190 I   210 J   240 K   270 L | 300 M | 330 N   360 O | | | | | | 180 M / 190 | 200 | 215 |
| 40 | 22 A   30 B   40 C | 60 D   70 E   80 F | 90 G   120 H   130 I | 150 J | 160 K / 170 L | | | | | | 105 J / 115 K | 124 L | 132 M |
| 50 | 18 A   25 B | 30 C   40 D | 50 E   60 F | 75 G | 85 H   95 I | | | | | | 70 H / 80 I | 85 J | 92 K |
| 60 | 14 A   20 B | 25 C   30 D | 40 E | | 60 G | | | | | | | | |

### Decompression Time (in minutes) at 10 fsw

| Depth (fsw) | No-Decompression Bottom Times (minutes) | Decompression Required Bottom Times (minutes) | | | | | | | | | 400 | 420 | 450 |
|---|---|---|---|---|---|---|---|---|---|---|---|---|---|
| 70 | 12 A   15 B | 20 C | 25 D | 35 E | 40 F | | | | | 5 | 10 | 15 | 20 / 66 J |
| 80 | 10 A   13 B | 15 C | 20 D | 25 E | 29 F | | | | | | 50 G | 48 H | 52 I |
| 90 | 9 A | 12 B | | | 35 G | | | | | | 35 G | | 43 I |
| 100 | 7 A | 10 B | 15 C | 20 D | 23 E | | | | | | 27 F / 21 E | 29 G | 36 H |
| 110 | | 6 A | 12 C | 15 D | 18 D | | | | | | 18 E / 15 E | 22 F | 30 H |
| 120 | | 6 A | 10 B | 12 C | 15 D | | | | | | 15 E / 13 D | 19 F | 25 G |
| 130 | | | 8 B | 8 B | 10 C | | | | | | 13 D / 11 D | 16 F | 21 G |
| 140 | | | 5 A | 7 B | | | | | | | 10 D | 14 F | 18 G |
| 150 | | | 5 A | 6 B | | | | | | | | 12 E | 15 F |

### Decompression Time (in minutes) at:

| | | | | | | | | | | | | 400 | 420 | 450 |
|---|---|---|---|---|---|---|---|---|---|---|---|---|---|---|
| 20 fsw | | | | | | | | | | | | - | 5 | 10 |
| 10 fsw | | | | | | | | | | | | 10 | 10 | 10 |

# SECTION 9
# Using the DCIEM
# Surface Decompression Tables

The procedure for surface decompression using oxygen with the DCIEM tables is quite similar to the older US Navy procedure, in that the final water stop is at 30 fsw and the entire time on oxygen in the chamber is spent at 40 feet. It differs, however, in that the allowed surface interval is longer, and the chamber times are significantly longer. On close examination, you will notice that at any given depth and bottom time, the water stops on the Standard Air Table and those on the Surface Decompression Using Oxygen Table are identical up to and including the 30 fsw stop. After completion of the 30-foot stop, the standard air table continues with in-water decompression, while the surface decompression table finishes on deck in the chamber on oxygen. Procedural details are as follows:

- **Ascent Rate:** The ascent rate is the same as the other DCIEM tables at 60 feet per minute + 10 feet per minute.

- **Water Stop Time:** The time for in-water stops includes the travel time to the stop, from the last stop or from bottom.

- **Last Water Stop:** The last water stop utilized in DCIEM Surface Decompression Using Oxygen is at 30 feet.

- **Surface Interval:** The maximum surface interval from the 30-foot stop to 40 feet in the chamber, or from bottom to 40 feet in the chamber if no water stops are required, is 7 minutes. Although extensive experimentation has proven the 7-minute surface interval to be safe, it is recommended that the surface interval be kept to a minimum. In the surface decompression tables, the "total decompression time" as shown includes 7 minutes for the surface interval.

## Pressurization (Blow Down)

The diver breathes oxygen by BIBS as soon as he or she enters the chamber, and the descent rate is as fast as the diver can equalize.

## Oxygen Breathing

The diver should not exceed 30 minutes of continuous oxygen breathing without a 5-minute air break. At the supervisor's discretion, the periods between air breaks may be shortened to 20 minutes. Oxygen is breathed from the time the diver begins pressurization until he or she reaches surface at the completion of the required decompression.

## EMERGENCY PROCEDURES

### Exceeding the Seven-Minute Surface Interval (Diver Asymptomatic)

Provided the diver is under pressure by minute 7, allow up to 10 minutes to arrive at 40 fsw before considering treatment. This allows for problems the diver may encounter in equalizing. If the diver is not under pressure by minute 7, the following actions are to be taken:

- If less than 30 minutes are required on chamber stops, use USN Treatment Table 5.

- If 30 minutes or more are required on chamber stops, use USN Treatment Table 6.

### Symptoms of Decompression Sickness Occurring During Surface Interval

Testing has indicated that when signs and symptoms occur during the surface interval, they are typically very mild, and they occur very late in the surface interval. When they occur, take the following action:

- When all signs and symptoms have completely resolved by the time the diver has been confirmed on oxygen at 40 feet in the chamber, continue decompression as planned.

- When all signs and symptoms have not completely resolved by the time the diver has been confirmed on oxygen at 40 feet, press the chamber to 60 feet, and initiate a Treatment Table 6.

## Loss of Oxygen to the Chamber

In the event of a loss of oxygen supply to the BIBS, the following actions apply:

- Maintain the diver at depth breathing chamber air.

- If the oxygen supply can be restored within 15 minutes, count time breathing air as "dead time" and continue the decompression at the point of interruption.

- If the oxygen supply cannot be restored, switch to the standard air table with the same depth and bottom time and decompress in the chamber on air. Time breathing oxygen is subtracted from the first air stop performed in the chamber.

## Minor Symptoms of Oxygen Toxicity

Symptoms of oxygen toxicity occurring in the chamber that do not include convulsions are treated as follows:

1. Remove BIBS from diver.

2. Once all symptoms have subsided either leave diver breathing air for an additional 15 minutes and resume $O_2$ from the point of interruption or decompress diver according to Standard Air Table.

3. If $O_2$ breathing is resumed and symptoms recur, decompress diver on Standard Air Table as above.

## Serious Symptoms of CNS Oxygen Toxicity (Including Convulsions)

More serious symptoms of CNS oxygen toxicity occurring in the chamber including convulsions are treated as follows:

- Remove BIBS from diver.

- Stabilize the diver—**do not change chamber depth during convulsions.**

- Decompress diver on air according to the appropriate Standard Air Table.

# SECTION 10
## DCIEM SurDO$_2$ Tables

| | | | | | | | | | | | |
|---|---|---|---|---|---|---|---|---|---|---|---|
| | **DCIEM Surface Decompression Using Oxygen** | | | | | | | | | | |
| **60 FSW** | **STOP TIMES (minutes) AT DIFFERENT DEPTHS (fsw)** | | | | | | | | | | |
| **Bottom Time (min)** | **In-Water Stops Breathing Air** | | | | | | **Surface Interval** | **Chamber on Oxygen** | **Total Decomp Time (min)** | **Repet Group** |
| | 80 | 70 | 60 | 50 | 40 | 30 | | **40** | | |
| 50 | | | | | | | | - | 1 | F |
| 70 | | | | | | | | 10 | 18 | H |
| 80 | | | | | | | Time from leaving 30 fsw stop (or bottom if no water stops required) to reaching the 40 fsw stop in chamber must not exceed 7 minutes. | 16 | 24 | H |
| 90 | | | | | | | | 20 | 28 | I |
| 100 | | | | | | | | 24 | 32 | J |
| 110 | | | | | | | | 28 | 36 | K |
| 120 | | | | | | | | 30 | 38 | K |
| **Exceptional Exposure: Emergency Use Only** | | | | | | | | | | |
| 130 | | | | | | | | 33* | 46 | |
| 140 | | | | | | | | 38* | 51 | |
| 150 | | | | | | | | 43* | 56 | |
| 160 | | | | | | | | 47* | 60 | |
| 170 | | | | | | | | 50* | 63 | |
| 180 | | | | | | | | 54* | 67 | |
| 190 | | | | | | | | 57* | 70 | |
| 200 | | | | | | | | 60** | 78 | |
| Number of 5-minute air breaks in chamber are indicated by asterisk (*). | | | | | | | | | | |

| DCIEM Surface Decompression Using Oxygen |||||||||||
|---|---|---|---|---|---|---|---|---|---|---|
| **70 FSW** | **STOP TIMES (minutes) AT DIFFERENT DEPTHS (fsw)** |||||||||| 
| **Bottom Time (min)** | **In-Water Stops Breathing Air** |||||| **Surface Interval** | **Chamber on Oxygen** | **Total Decomp Time (min)** | **Repet Group** |
| | 80 | 70 | 60 | 50 | 40 | 30 | | 40 | | |
| 35 | | | | | | | | - | 1 | E |
| 50 | | | | | | | | 6 | 14 | H |
| 60 | | | | | | | | 15 | 23 | H |
| 70 | | | | | | | | 21 | 29 | I |
| 80 | | | | | | | | 26 | 34 | J |
| 90 | | | | | | | | 30 | 38 | K |
| 100 | | | | | | | | 34* | 47 | K |
| **Exceptional Exposure: For Emergency Use Only** ||||||| | | | |
| 110 | | | | | | | | 40* | 53 | |
| 120 | | | | | | | | 46* | 59 | |
| 130 | | | | | | | | 50* | 63 | |
| 140 | | | | | | | | 55* | 68 | |
| 150 | | | | | | | | 60* | 73 | |
| 160 | | | | | | | | 64** | 82 | |
| 170 | | | | | | | | 71** | 89 | |
| 180 | | | | | | | | 76** | 94 | |

Surface Interval column note: Time from leaving 30 fsw stop (or bottom if no water stops required) to reaching the 40 fsw stop in chamber must not exceed 7 minutes.

Number of 5-minute air breaks in chamber are indicated by asterisk (*).

| DCIEM Surface Decompression Using Oxygen | | | | | | | | | | |
|---|---|---|---|---|---|---|---|---|---|---|
| **80 FSW** | STOP TIMES (minutes) AT DIFFERENT DEPTHS (fsw) | | | | | | | | | |
| Bottom Time (min) | In-Water Stops Breathing Air | | | | | | Surface Interval | Chamber on Oxygen 40 | Total Decomp Time (min) | Repet Group |
| | 80 | 70 | 60 | 50 | 40 | 30 | | | | |
| 25 | | | | | | | | – | 2 | E |
| 45 | | | | | | | | 12 | 20 | H |
| 50 | | | | | | | | 17 | 25 | H |
| 55 | | | | | | | | 21 | 29 | H |
| 60 | | | | | | | | 24 | 32 | I |
| 70 | | | | | | | | 30 | 38 | J |
| 80 | | | | | | | | 35* | 48 | K |
| **Exceptional Exposure: For Emergency Use Only** | | | | | | | Time from leaving 30 fsw stop (or bottom if no water stops required) to reaching the 40 fsw stop in chamber must not exceed 7 minutes. | | | |
| 90 | | | | | | 1 | | 41* | 55 | |
| 100 | | | | | | 2 | | 47* | 62 | |
| 110 | | | | | | 3 | | 53* | 69 | |
| 120 | | | | | | 3 | | 59* | 75 | |
| 130 | | | | | | 4 | | 63** | 85 | |
| 140 | | | | | | 5 | | 72** | 95 | |
| 150 | | | | | | 5 | | 79** | 102 | |
| 160 | | | | | | 6 | | 84** | 108 | |
| Number of 5-minute air breaks in chamber are indicated by asterisk (*). | | | | | | | | | | |

| DCIEM Surface Decompression Using Oxygen | | | | | | | | | | |
|---|---|---|---|---|---|---|---|---|---|---|
| **90 FSW** | STOP TIMES (minutes) AT DIFFERENT DEPTHS (fsw) | | | | | | | | | |
| **Bottom Time (min)** | **In-Water Stops Breathing Air** | | | | | | **Surface Interval** | **Chamber on Oxygen** | **Total Decomp Time (min)** | **Repet Group** |
| | **80** | **70** | **60** | **50** | **40** | **30** | | **40** | | |
| 20 | | | | | | | Time from leaving 30 fsw stop (or bottom if no water stops required) to reaching the 40 fsw stop in chamber must not exceed 7 minutes. | - | 2 | D |
| 35 | | | | | | | | 8 | 16 | G |
| 40 | | | | | | | | 16 | 24 | G |
| 45 | | | | | | | | 21 | 29 | H |
| 50 | | | | | | | | 25 | 33 | H |
| 55 | | | | | | 1 | | 28 | 37 | I |
| 60 | | | | | | 2 | | 30* | 45 | J |
| **Exceptional Exposure: For Emergency Use Only** | | | | | | | | | | |
| 70 | | | | | | 4 | | 37* | 54 | |
| 80 | | | | | | 5 | | 45* | 63 | |
| 90 | | | | | | 6 | | 52* | 71 | |
| 100 | | | | | | 7 | | 58* | 78 | |
| 110 | | | | | | 8 | | 65** | 91 | |
| 120 | | | | | | 8 | | 75** | 101 | |
| Number of 5-minute air breaks in chamber are indicated by asterisk (*). | | | | | | | | | | |

| DCIEM Surface Decompression Using Oxygen | | | | | | | | | | |
|---|---|---|---|---|---|---|---|---|---|---|
| **100 FSW** | **STOP TIMES (minutes) AT DIFFERENT DEPTHS (fsw)** | | | | | | | | | |
| **Bottom Time (min)** | **In-Water Stops Breathing Air** | | | | | | **Surface Interval** | **Chamber on Oxygen** | **Total Decomp Time (min)** | **Repet Group** |
| | **80** | **70** | **60** | **50** | **40** | **30** | | **40** | | |
| 15 | | | | | | | Time from leaving 30 fsw stop (or bottom if no water stops required) to reaching the 40 fsw stop in chamber must not exceed 7 minutes. | - | 2 | D |
| 30 | | | | | | | | 8 | 16 | G |
| 35 | | | | | | | | 17 | 25 | G |
| 40 | | | | | | 2 | | 22 | 32 | H |
| 45 | | | | | | 3 | | 27 | 38 | I |
| 50 | | | | | | 4 | | 30 | 42 | I |
| 55 | | | | | | 5 | | 31* | 49 | J |
| **Exceptional Exposure: For Emergency Use Only** | | | | | | | | | | |
| 60 | | | | | | 6 | | 37* | 56 | |
| 70 | | | | | | 8 | | 46* | 67 | |
| 80 | | | | | | 9 | | 54* | 76 | |
| 90 | | | | | 2 | 8 | | 60* | 83 | |
| 100 | | | | | 3 | 9 | | 72** | 102 | |
| 110 | | | | | 4 | 9 | | 81** | 112 | |
| Number of 5-minute air breaks in chamber are indicated by asterisk (*). | | | | | | | | | | |

| DCIEM Surface Decompression Using Oxygen | | | | | | | | | |
|---|---|---|---|---|---|---|---|---|---|
| **110 FSW** | STOP TIMES (minutes) AT DIFFERENT DEPTHS (fsw) | | | | | | | | |
| Bottom Time (min) | In-Water Stops Breathing Air | | | | | | Surface Interval | Chamber on Oxygen 40 | Total Decomp Time (min) | Repet Group |
| | 80 | 70 | 60 | 50 | 40 | 30 | | | | |
| 12 | | | | | | | | - | 2 | C |
| 25 | | | | | | | | 7 | 15 | G |
| 30 | | | | | | 2 | | 16 | 26 | G |
| 35 | | | | | | 4 | | 22 | 34 | H |
| 40 | | | | | | 5 | Time from leaving 30 fsw stop (or bottom if no water stops required) to reaching the 40 fsw stop in chamber must not exceed 7 minutes. | 27 | 40 | I |
| 45 | | | | | | 6 | | 30* | 49 | J |
| 50 | | | | | | 8 | | 34* | 55 | K |
| 55 | | | | | | 9 | | 40* | 62 | K |
| Exceptional Exposure: For Emergency Use Only | | | | | | | | | | |
| 60 | | | | | 3 | 7 | | 45* | 66 | |
| 65 | | | | | 3 | 8 | | 50* | 74 | |
| 70 | | | | | 4 | 8 | | 54* | 79 | |
| 75 | | | | | 5 | 8 | | 59* | 85 | |
| 80 | | | | | 5 | 8 | | 61** | 92 | |
| 85 | | | | | 6 | 8 | | 70** | 102 | |
| 90 | | | | | 6 | 9 | | 76** | 109 | |
| 95 | | | | | 7 | 9 | | 81** | 115 | |
| 100 | | | | | 7 | 10 | | 86** | 121 | |
| 105 | | | | | 8 | 13 | | 90** | 129 | |
| 110 | | | | | 8 | 16 | | 95*** | 142 | |

Number of 5-minute air breaks in chamber are indicated by asterisk (*).

| DCIEM Surface Decompression Using Oxygen | | | | | | | | | | |
|---|---|---|---|---|---|---|---|---|---|---|
| **120 FSW** | **STOP TIMES (minutes) AT DIFFERENT DEPTHS (fsw)** | | | | | | | | | |
| Bottom Time (min) | In-Water Stops Breathing Air | | | | | | Surface Interval | Chamber on Oxygen | Total Decomp Time (min) | Repet Group |
| | 80 | 70 | 60 | 50 | 40 | 30 | | 40 | | |
| 10 | | | | | | | | - | 2 | C |
| 20 | | | | | | | | 7 | 15 | F |
| 25 | | | | | | 2 | | 13 | 23 | G |
| 30 | | | | | | 5 | | 21 | 34 | G |
| 35 | | | | | | 6 | | 27 | 41 | H |
| 40 | | | | | | 8 | | 30* | 51 | I |
| 45 | | | | | 3 | 7 | | 36* | 59 | J |
| 50 | | | | | 4 | 7 | | 42* | 66 | K |
| **Exceptional Exposure: For Emergency Use Only** | | | | | | | Time from leaving 30 fsw stop (or bottom if no water stops required) to reaching the 40 fsw stop in chamber must not exceed 7 minutes. | | | |
| 55 | | | | | 5 | 7 | | 48* | 73 | |
| 60 | | | | | 6 | 8 | | 53* | 80 | |
| 65 | | | | | 7 | 8 | | 58* | 86 | |
| 70 | | | | | 7 | 9 | | 60** | 94 | |
| 75 | | | | 2 | 6 | 9 | | 70** | 105 | |
| 80 | | | | 3 | 6 | 9 | | 77** | 113 | |
| 85 | | | | 3 | 7 | 10 | | 83** | 121 | |
| 90 | | | | 3 | 7 | 14 | | 87** | 129 | |
| 95 | | | | 4 | 7 | 16 | | 90** | 135 | |
| 100 | | | | 4 | 7 | 20 | | 100*** | 154 | |
| Number of 5-minute air breaks in chamber are indicated by asterisk (*). | | | | | | | | | | |

## DCIEM Surface Decompression Using Oxygen

### 130 FSW

| Bottom Time (min) | In-Water Stops Breathing Air 80 | 70 | 60 | 50 | 40 | 30 | Surface Interval | Chamber on Oxygen 40 | Total Decomp Time (min) | Repet Group |
|---|---|---|---|---|---|---|---|---|---|---|
| 8 | | | | | | | | - | 2 | B |
| 20 | | | | | | | | 9 | 17 | G |
| 25 | | | | | | 5 | | 18 | 31 | G |
| 30 | | | | | | 7 | | 26 | 41 | H |
| 35 | | | | | 3 | 6 | | 30* | 52 | I |
| 40 | | | | | 5 | 6 | | 36* | 60 | J |
| 45 | | | | | 6 | 7 | | 43* | 69 | K |
| **Exceptional Exposure: For Emergency Use Only** | | | | | | | Time from leaving 30 fsw stop (or bottom if no water stops required) to reaching the 40 fsw stop in chamber must not exceed 7 minutes. | | | |
| 50 | | | | | 7 | 8 | | 49* | 77 | |
| 55 | | | | 2 | 6 | 8 | | 55* | 84 | |
| 60 | | | | 3 | 6 | 8 | | 60** | 95 | |
| 65 | | | | 4 | 6 | 9 | | 68** | 105 | |
| 70 | | | | 5 | 6 | 9 | | 76** | 114 | |
| 75 | | | | 5 | 7 | 11 | | 82** | 123 | |
| 80 | | | | 6 | 7 | 15 | | 87** | 133 | |
| 85 | | | | 6 | 7 | 18 | | 90*** | 144 | |
| 90 | | | | 7 | 7 | 22 | | 102*** | 161 | |

Number of 5-minute air breaks in chamber are indicated by asterisk (*).

| DCIEM Surface Decompression Using Oxygen | | | | | | | | | | |
|---|---|---|---|---|---|---|---|---|---|---|
| **140 FSW** | **STOP TIMES (minutes) AT DIFFERENT DEPTHS (fsw)** | | | | | | | | | |
| Bottom Time (min) | In-Water Stops Breathing Air | | | | | | Surface Interval | Chamber on Oxygen 40 | Total Decomp Time (min) | Repet Group |
| | 80 | 70 | 60 | 50 | 40 | 30 | | | | |
| 7 | | | | | | | | - | 3 | B |
| 15 | | | | | | | | 7 | 15 | F |
| 20 | | | | | | 4 | | 12 | 24 | G |
| 25 | | | | | | 7 | | 23 | 38 | H |
| 30 | | | | | 4 | 6 | | 30 | 48 | I |
| 35 | | | | | 6 | 6 | | 34* | 59 | J |
| 40 | | | | | 7 | 7 | | 42* | 69 | K |
| 45 | | | | 3 | 6 | 7 | | 49* | 78 | M |
| **Exceptional Exposure: For Emergency Use Only** | | | | | | | | | | |
| 50 | | | | 4 | 6 | 8 | | 56* | 87 | |
| 55 | | | | 5 | 6 | 9 | | 60** | 98 | |
| 60 | | | | 6 | 6 | 9 | | 71** | 110 | |
| 65 | | | | 7 | 6 | 11 | | 79** | 121 | |
| 70 | | | 2 | 5 | 7 | 15 | | 85** | 132 | |
| 75 | | | 3 | 5 | 8 | 18 | | 90** | 142 | |
| 80 | | | 3 | 6 | 8 | 21 | | 101*** | 162 | |
| 85 | | | 4 | 6 | 8 | 25 | | 108*** | 174 | |
| 90 | | | 4 | 6 | 8 | 30 | | 113*** | 184 | |
| Number of 5-minute air breaks in chamber are indicated by asterisk (*). | | | | | | | | | | |

*Surface Interval column note:* Time from leaving 30 fsw stop (or bottom if no water stops required) to reaching the 40 fsw stop in chamber must not exceed 7 minutes.

| DCIEM Surface Decompression Using Oxygen | | | | | | | | | | |
|---|---|---|---|---|---|---|---|---|---|---|
| **150 FSW** | STOP TIMES (minutes) AT DIFFERENT DEPTHS (fsw) | | | | | | | | | |
| Bottom Time (min) | In-Water Stops Breathing Air | | | | | | Surface Interval | Chamber on Oxygen 40 | Total Decomp Time (min) | Repet Group |
| | 80 | 70 | 60 | 50 | 40 | 30 | | | | |
| 6 | | | | | | | Time from leaving 30 fsw stop (or bottom if no water stops required) to reaching the 40 fsw stop in chamber must not exceed 7 minutes. | - | 3 | B |
| 15 | | | | | | | | 8 | 16 | G |
| 20 | | | | | | 6 | | 17 | 31 | G |
| 25 | | | | | 4 | 6 | | 26 | 44 | H |
| 30 | | | | | 6 | 7 | | 30* | 56 | I |
| 35 | | | | 3 | 5 | 7 | | 40* | 68 | K |
| 40 | | | | 4 | 6 | 8 | | 48* | 79 | M |
| **Exceptional Exposure: For Emergency Use Only** | | | | | | | | | | |
| 45 | | | | 6 | 6 | 8 | | 55* | 88 | |
| 50 | | | | 7 | 6 | 9 | | 60** | 100 | |
| 55 | | | 3 | 5 | 6 | 10 | | 73** | 115 | |
| 60 | | | 4 | 5 | 7 | 13 | | 81** | 128 | |
| 65 | | | 4 | 6 | 7 | 17 | | 87** | 139 | |
| 70 | | | 5 | 6 | 7 | 21 | | 97*** | 159 | |
| 75 | | | 6 | 5 | 8 | 25 | | 106*** | 173 | |
| 80 | | | 6 | 6 | 8 | 29 | | 112*** | 184 | |

Number of 5-minute air breaks in chamber are indicated by asterisk (*).

| DCIEM Surface Decompression Using Oxygen | | | | | | | | | | |
|---|---|---|---|---|---|---|---|---|---|---|
| **160 FSW** | STOP TIMES (minutes) AT DIFFERENT DEPTHS (fsw) | | | | | | | | | |
| Bottom Time (min) | In-Water Stops Breathing Air | | | | | | Surface Interval | Chamber on Oxygen **40** | Total Decomp Time (min) | Repet Group |
| | 80 | 70 | 60 | 50 | 40 | 30 | | | | |
| 6 | | | | | | | | - | 3 | B |
| 15 | | | | | | 4 | | 7 | 19 | G |
| 20 | | | | | 3 | 5 | | 21 | 37 | G |
| 25 | | | | | 6 | 6 | | 30 | 50 | I |
| 30 | | | | 4 | 5 | 6 | | 37* | 65 | J |
| 35 | | | | 5 | 6 | 7 | | 46* | 77 | L |
| **Exceptional Exposure: For Emergency Use Only** | | | | | | | | | | |
| 40 | | | | 7 | 6 | 8 | | 54* | 88 | |
| 45 | | | 3 | 5 | 6 | 9 | | 60* | 96 | |
| 50 | | | 4 | 5 | 7 | 9 | | 73** | 116 | |
| 55 | | | 5 | 6 | 7 | 14 | | 81** | 131 | |
| 60 | | | 6 | 6 | 7 | 18 | | 89** | 144 | |
| 65 | | 3 | 4 | 6 | 8 | 22 | | 101*** | 167 | |
| 70 | | 3 | 5 | 6 | 8 | 27 | | 109*** | 181 | |

Surface Interval column note: Time from leaving 30 fsw stop (or bottom if no water stops required) to reaching the 40 fsw stop in chamber must not exceed 7 minutes.

Number of 5-minute air breaks in chamber are indicated by asterisk (*).

| DCIEM Surface Decompression Using Oxygen | | | | | | | | | | |
|---|---|---|---|---|---|---|---|---|---|---|
| **170 FSW** | STOP TIMES (minutes) AT DIFFERENT DEPTHS (fsw) | | | | | | | | | |
| Bottom Time (min) | In-Water Stops Breathing Air | | | | | | Surface Interval | Chamber on Oxygen | Total Decomp Time (min) | Repet Group |
| | 80 | 70 | 60 | 50 | 40 | 30 | | 40 | | |
| 5 | | | | | | | Time from leaving 30 fsw stop (or bottom if no water stops required) to reaching the 40 fsw stop in chamber must not exceed 7 minutes. | - | 3 | B |
| 10 | | | | | | | | 6 | 14 | D |
| 15 | | | | | | 6 | | 11 | 25 | G |
| 20 | | | | | 5 | 6 | | 25 | 44 | H |
| 25 | | | | 3 | 5 | 6 | | 30* | 57 | J |
| 30 | | | | 6 | 5 | 7 | | 42* | 73 | K |
| 35 | | | 3 | 4 | 6 | 8 | | 51* | 85 | M |
| **Exceptional Exposure: For Emergency Use Only** | | | | | | | | | | |
| 40 | | | 4 | 5 | 6 | 9 | | 60* | 97 | |
| 45 | | | 6 | 5 | 6 | 10 | | 71** | 116 | |
| 50 | | 3 | 4 | 5 | 7 | 14 | | 81** | 132 | |
| 55 | | 3 | 5 | 5 | 8 | 19 | | 89** | 147 | |
| 60 | | 4 | 5 | 6 | 8 | 23 | | 102*** | 171 | |
| 65 | | 5 | 5 | 6 | 8 | 29 | | 111*** | 187 | |
| 70 | | 5 | 5 | 7 | 12 | 31 | | 118*** | 201 | |
| Number of 5-minute air breaks in chamber are indicated by asterisk (*). | | | | | | | | | | |

## DCIEM Surface Decompression Using Oxygen

**180 FSW** — STOP TIMES (minutes) AT DIFFERENT DEPTHS (fsw)

| Bottom Time (min) | In-Water Stops Breathing Air | | | | | | Surface Interval | Chamber on Oxygen 40 | Total Decomp Time (min) | Repet Group |
|---|---|---|---|---|---|---|---|---|---|---|
| | 80 | 70 | 60 | 50 | 40 | 30 | | | | |
| 5 | | | | | | | | - | 3 | B |
| 10 | | | | | | | | 7 | 15 | E |
| 15 | | | | | | 8 | | 15 | 31 | G |
| 20 | | | | | 7 | 6 | | 28 | 49 | H |
| 25 | | | | 5 | 5 | 7 | | 36* | 66 | J |
| 30 | | | 3 | 5 | 5 | 8 | | 47* | 81 | M |

**Exceptional Exposure: For Emergency Use Only**

| Bottom Time (min) | 80 | 70 | 60 | 50 | 40 | 30 | Surface Interval | Chamber on Oxygen 40 | Total Decomp Time (min) | Repet Group |
|---|---|---|---|---|---|---|---|---|---|---|
| 35 | | | 5 | 5 | 6 | 8 | | 57* | 94 | |
| 40 | | 3 | 4 | 5 | 6 | 9 | | 68** | 113 | |
| 45 | | 4 | 4 | 5 | 7 | 14 | | 79** | 131 | |
| 50 | | 5 | 4 | 6 | 7 | 19 | | 88** | 147 | |
| 55 | | 5 | 5 | 6 | 8 | 24 | | 102*** | 173 | |
| 60 | 3 | 3 | 5 | 7 | 9 | 29 | | 111*** | 190 | |

Surface Interval note: Time from leaving 30 fsw stop (or bottom if no water stops required) to reaching the 40 fsw stop in chamber must not exceed 7 minutes.

Number of 5-minute air breaks in chamber are indicated by asterisk (*).

| DCIEM Surface Decompression Using Oxygen | | | | | | | | | | |
|---|---|---|---|---|---|---|---|---|---|---|
| **190 FSW** | STOP TIMES (minutes) AT DIFFERENT DEPTHS (fsw) | | | | | | | | | |
| Bottom Time (min) | In-Water Stops Breathing Air | | | | | | Surface Interval | Chamber on Oxygen 40 | Total Decomp Time (min) | Repet Group |
| | 80 | 70 | 60 | 50 | 40 | 30 | | | | |
| Exceptional Exposure: For Emergency Use Only | | | | | | | | | | |
| 5 | | | | | | | Time from leaving 30 fsw stop (or bottom if no water stops required) to reaching the 40 fsw stop in chamber must not exceed 7 minutes. | - | 3 | - |
| 10 | | | | | | | | 8 | 16 | - |
| 15 | | | | | 4 | 5 | | 19 | 36 | - |
| 20 | | | | 4 | 5 | 6 | | 30 | 53 | - |
| 25 | | | 3 | 4 | 5 | 7 | | 41* | 73 | - |
| 30 | | | 5 | 5 | 5 | 8 | | 52* | 88 | - |
| 35 | | 3 | 4 | 5 | 6 | 9 | | 60* | 100 | - |
| 40 | | 5 | 4 | 5 | 7 | 12 | | 76** | 127 | - |
| 45 | | 6 | 4 | 6 | 7 | 18 | | 86** | 145 | - |
| 50 | 3 | 4 | 4 | 6 | 8 | 24 | | 100*** | 172 | - |
| 55 | 4 | 4 | 5 | 6 | 10 | 28 | | 111*** | 191 | - |
| X | - | - | - | - | - | - | | | - | - |
| X | - | - | - | - | - | - | | | - | - |
| Number of 5-minute air breaks in chamber are indicated by asterisk (*). | | | | | | | | | | |

| DCIEM Surface Decompression Using Oxygen | | | | | | | | | | |
|---|---|---|---|---|---|---|---|---|---|---|
| **200 FSW** | STOP TIMES (minutes) AT DIFFERENT DEPTHS (fsw) | | | | | | | | | |
| Bottom Time (min) | In-Water Stops Breathing Air | | | | | | Surface Interval | Chamber on Oxygen | Total Decomp Time (min) | Repet Group |
| | 80 | 70 | 60 | 50 | 40 | 30 | | 40 | | |
| Exceptional Exposure: For Emergency Use Only | | | | | | | Time from leaving 30 fsw stop (or bottom if no water stops required) to reaching the 40 fsw stop in chamber must not exceed 7 minutes. | | | |
| 10 | | | | | | | | 10 | 18 | - |
| 15 | | | | | 6 | 5 | | 22 | 41 | - |
| 20 | | | | 6 | 4 | 7 | | 31* | 61 | - |
| 25 | | | 5 | 4 | 5 | 8 | | 45* | 80 | - |
| 30 | | 3 | 4 | 5 | 6 | 8 | | 57* | 96 | - |
| 35 | | 5 | 4 | 5 | 7 | 9 | | 70** | 118 | - |
| 40 | 3 | 3 | 5 | 5 | 8 | 16 | | 83** | 141 | - |
| 45 | 4 | 4 | 4 | 6 | 8 | 22 | | 95*** | 166 | - |
| 50 | 5 | 4 | 5 | 6 | 10 | 27 | | 109*** | 189 | - |
| X | - | - | - | - | - | - | | | - | - |
| X | - | - | - | - | - | - | | | - | - |
| X | - | - | - | - | - | - | | | - | - |
| X | - | - | - | - | - | - | | | - | - |
| Number of 5-minute air breaks in chamber are indicated by asterisk (*). | | | | | | | | | | |

# SECTION 11
# Diving at Altitude Using DCIEM Tables

When at altitude, the atmospheric pressure is lower than at sea level; the higher the altitude, the lower the atmospheric pressure. Since the pressure at the water surface is lower, the absolute pressure at depth is also lower. Decompression tables and procedures are designed to allow the diver to safely off-gas at sea level and not at the reduced pressures encountered at altitude. The reduced atmospheric pressures at altitude cause dives at altitude to be the equivalent to deeper dives at sea level.

Dive depths and decompression stop depths must be corrected when performing dives at altitude. Table 5 provides corrections for dive depths at altitudes between 300 and 10,000 feet above sea level. Table 5 is designed to be used in conjunction with the DCIEM tables. **Do not** use this correction table with any other diving tables.

NOTE: Depth gauges and pneumofathometers are not reliable nor considered to be accurate above sea level. Depth of dive must be established by hard measurement (shot line).

### PROCEDURE FOR DIVING AT ALTITUDE:
- Establish the altitude of the dive site above sea level.
- Establish the actual depth of dive by measurement.
- In Table 5, find the depth correction for the actual depth.
- Add the depth correction to the actual depth to determine effective depth (ED).
- Using the normal diving tables, determine the decompression schedule using the effective depth and the proposed actual bottom time.
- Substitute the altitude stop depths from Table 5 for the normal stop depths (time does not change).

- Decompress using the altitude stop depths and the times from the normal diving table.

- Ascent and travel are 60 fpm at altitudes between 300 and 50,00 feet.

- Ascent and travel are 50 fpm at altitudes between 5000 and 10,000 feet.

## ACCLIMATIZATION TO ALTITUDE

When planning to dive at altitude, divers must acclimatize for 24 hours prior to performing a dive. Table 5 is based on the diver being acclimatized. If dives are performed less than 24 hours after arrival at altitude, an additional 10 feet must be added to the actual depths for Table 5.

| ALTITUDE DIVING WORKSHEET | |
|---|---|
| Altitude of Dive Site | feet above sea level |
| Actual Depth of Dive (measured) | feet sea water |
| Dive Depth Correction | feet sea water |
| Effective Depth (actual + correction) | feet sea water |
| Bottom Time | minutes |
| Table and Schedule Used Table: | Schedule: fsw / min |

| Altitude Decompression Schedule | | |
|---|---|---|
| Sea Level Stop Depth | Corrected Stop Depth | Stop Time |
| 50 fsw | fsw | minutes |
| 40 fsw | fsw | minutes |
| 30 fsw | fsw | minutes |
| 20 fsw | fsw | minutes |
| 10 fsw | fsw | minutes |

Source: Author

## DCIEM DEPTH CORRECTIONS FOR ALTITUDE (TABLE 5)

| Actual Depth (in feet) | Depth Corrections at Altitude (feet) | | | | | | | | |
|---|---|---|---|---|---|---|---|---|---|
| | 300 →999 | 1000 →1999 | 2000 →2999 | 3000 →3999 | 4000 →4999 | 5000 →5999 | 6000 →6999 | 7000 →7999 | 8000 →10000 |
| 30 | +0 | +10 | +10 | +10 | +10 | +10 | +10 | +20 | +20 |
| 40 | +0 | +10 | +10 | +10 | +10 | +10 | +20 | +20 | +20 |
| 50 | +0 | +10 | +10 | +10 | +10 | +20 | +20 | +20 | +20 |
| 60 | +0 | +10 | +10 | +10 | +20 | +20 | +20 | +20 | +30 |
| 70 | +0 | +10 | +10 | +10 | +20 | +20 | +20 | +30 | +30 |
| 80 | +0 | +10 | +10 | +20 | +20 | +20 | +30 | +30 | +40 |
| 90 | +0 | +10 | +10 | +20 | +20 | +20 | +30 | +30 | +40 |
| 100 | +0 | +10 | +10 | +20 | +20 | +30 | +30 | +30 | +40 |
| 110 | +0 | +10 | +20 | +20 | +20 | +30 | +30 | +30 | +50 |
| 120 | +0 | +10 | +20 | +20 | +30 | +30 | +30 | +40 | +50 |
| 130 | +0 | +10 | +20 | +20 | +30 | +30 | +40 | +40 | +50 |
| 140 | +0 | +10 | +20 | +20 | +30 | +30 | +40 | +40 | +60 |
| 150 | +10 | +10 | +20 | +20 | +30 | +40 | +40 | +50 | +60 |
| 160 | +10 | +20 | +20 | +30 | +30 | +40 | +40 | +50 | +60 |
| 170 | +10 | +20 | +20 | +30 | +30 | +40 | +50 | +50 | +70 |
| 180 | +10 | +20 | +20 | +30 | +40 | +40 | +50 | +50 | |
| 190 | +10 | +20 | +20 | +30 | +40 | +40 | +50 | | |
| 200 | +10 | +20 | +20 | +30 | +40 | +40 | | | |
| 210 | +10 | +20 | +20 | +30 | | | | | |
| 220 | +10 | +20 | +20 | | | | | | |
| 230 | +10 | | | | | | | | |

| | Actual Decompression Stop Depth at Altitude (feet) | | | | | | | | |
|---|---|---|---|---|---|---|---|---|---|
| Normal Stop Depth | 300 →999 | 1000 →1999 | 2000 →2999 | 3000 →3999 | 4000 →4999 | 5000 →5999 | 6000 →6999 | 7000 →7999 | 8000 →10000 |
| 10 | 10 | 10 | 10 | 9 | 9 | 9 | 8 | 8 | 8 |
| 20 | 20 | 20 | 19 | 18 | 18 | 17 | 16 | 16 | 15 |
| 30 | 30 | 29 | 28 | 27 | 26 | 25 | 24 | 24 | 23 |
| 40 | 40 | 39 | 38 | 36 | 35 | 34 | 32 | 31 | 30 |
| 50 | 50 | 49 | 47 | 45 | 44 | 42 | 40 | 39 | 38 |
| 60 | 59 | 58 | 56 | 54 | 52 | 50 | 48 | 47 | 45 |
| 70 | 69 | 68 | 66 | 63 | 61 | 59 | 56 | 54 | 52 |
| 80 | 79 | 77 | 75 | 72 | 70 | 67 | 64 | 62 | 60 |
| 90 | 89 | 87 | 84 | 81 | 78 | 75 | 72 | 70 | 67 |

# SECTION 12
## Diving Medicine

Since the majority of diving projects occur in remote locations and also since hyperbaric treatment facilities are not found in most hospitals, divers have traditionally treated their own as far as pressure-related illness and injury is concerned. This has been true especially with those incidents requiring hyperbaric treatment.

In the past, every diver on the crew was expected to know the basics of diving medicine, and usually every crew had one person who kept up on all of the latest as far as the treatments, medical procedures, and medical equipment needed. Just a few years ago, it was not an easy task to find a hyperbaric physician (even in larger population centers) and the training for and designation of a diving medical technician (DMT) did not yet exist.

The diving crew of today has more hyperbaric physicians available, better communications with the hyperbaric physicians ashore, and a DMT typically administers on-site care. We have more modern medical equipment, better chambers, more up-to-date treatment protocols, but even with all of this, the prevention, diagnosis, and on-site treatment of diving-related injury and illness still involves the diving crew. How we perform these duties at the dive site will determine whether the stricken diver will be able to work in the water again, and in some cases, whether the diver will live or die.

As stated in the introduction to this book, the diver has been previously trained in the basics of diving medicine, and the DMT has had considerably more in-depth medical training. The intent of this section is threefold: 1) To provide a refresher for the diving crew; 2) To be a pocket reference guide; and 3) To provide the most up-to-date diagnosis and treatment information available to the industry. This book is not meant to be an exhaustive volume on diving medicine.

In the event of an incident, the DMT will require assistance. The DMT will not expect you to insert a catheter or start an intravenous drip, but the DMT most likely will ask you to stay with and monitor the casualty provided that the diver is stable at some point during treatment. The DMT may even ask your help with an extremity strength test or in performing a neurological test. If the casualty is not ambulatory, the DMT will expect your help in getting the Stokes litter from the deck to the chamber. The better understanding that the diving crew has of diving medicine, the more help they can be to the DMT and ultimately to themselves.

The divers and supervisors would be well advised to read through the diving medicine section of the current *US Navy Diving Manual* at least once per year. While the DMT has to take a refresher course at regular intervals, the DMT should read about diving medicine periodically. Changes frequently occur in our industry and with diving medicine. There will probably be a few slight changes in diving medicine while reading this handbook.

One change is a common cutaneous (skin) symptom of decompression sickness—cutis marmorata—often called marbling, where the skin of the torso takes on that dark-bluish marble look. It is now considered a Type II symptom and is treated as such. Previously, all skin symptoms were considered to fit into the Type I DCS category. Also, examination and autopsies of cadavers has revealed that in cases of pulmonary overinflation syndrome, an actual tear does not have to occur in the alveoli of the lung. Gas can be forced to pass through the alveolar membrane without rupturing the membrane in an overinflation incident.

We need to stay ready. Holding practice drills on weather days is probably the best way to keep the diving crew sharp. Unconscious diver recovery drills, injured diver recovery drills, man down drills, standby deployment drills, and mock treatments all will pay off when the day comes that it happens in real time. Let's hope it never happens, but if it does, let's do our absolute best to be ready to act and know exactly what our role is.

## THERMOREGULATION

A huge issue in diving operations is exposure to cold water, and, increasingly more so, exposure to hot water. The human body is designed to operate at 98.6°F (37°C). There is a very narrow range in which the body's core temperature can fluctuate, and outside of this range, the body cannot function normally. To minimize thermal stress, proper protective equipment must be used or exposure must be limited.

Water has far greater thermal conductivity than air does, and because of this, heat transfer occurs at a much higher rate when the body is immersed in water than when surrounded by air. An air temperature of 72°F is comfortable for a person at rest, but water temperature must be at 91°F for a person not to have significant heat loss if the person is not wearing a suit of some sort. Lower water temperatures will cause hypothermia; higher temperatures cause hyperthermia. Either one of these conditions will affect the elimination of inert gas from the diver and in extreme cases, will result in death.

## HYPERTHERMIA

Typically, when divers think of thermoregulation, they think of hypothermia issues arising from cold water. In the past few years, however, hot water and hyperthermia have become more common. The human body actually generates enough heat every hour to warm two liters of ice-cold water up to body temperature; while performing heavy work, the body can generate up to ten times that amount of heat. If the heat generated was not transferred and allowed to build up within the body, in a very short time the temperature would pass 105°F (41°C), the point at which damage is being done to the body's cells.

The heat generated within the body is transferred by the blood and cooled using two organs: the lungs and the skin. Some of this heat is carried by the bloodstream to the lungs and discharged with exhaled breath. The majority of the heat transferred, however, is carried to the capillaries beneath the surface of the skin. The sweat glands release moisture, and with the evaporation of this moisture, the skin is cooled, which in turn cools the blood.

Any water above 80°F poses a risk of hyperthermia to divers. Shortening bottom times will help, but if the water is warmer than 95°F, a hot water suit with cool water running through the system is the only safe solution. Hyperthermia is a threat to surface crew as well as divers. A supply of cold drinking water or high electrolyte drink should be readily available to the crew. If the air temperature exceeds 100°F, the crew should operate in shifts to minimize individual exposures. Depending on the temperature and the work involved, the crew may need salt tablets. Hyperthermia is also an issue to decompression chamber occupants. Internal temperature of deck decompression chambers should never exceed 85°F.

**Symptoms of Hyperthermia in Order of Appearance**

| Initial onset | Excessive sweating, excessive thirst |
|---|---|
| Mild hyperthermia | Unquenchable thirst, fatigue, lethargy, muscle weakness, elevated pulse rate |
| Severe hyperthermia | Muscle tremors, muscle cramps, nausea, vomiting, shock, rapid shallow breathing, unconsciousness, cardiac arrest |

Diving supervisors and personnel should be aware that hyperthermia can occur both underwater in warm water, and on surface. Symptoms must not be ignored as initial onset symptoms will rapidly progress to severe in some individuals, depending on metabolism.

### Treatment of Hyperthermia

Patients with initial onset symptoms should be removed to a cooler area and hydrated with high electrolyte drinks such as Gatorade. Patients with mild symptoms should be removed to a cooler area, and may be cooled by immersion in a cool (not cold) bath or shower. Immersion in cold water may cause vasoconstriction which will slow the cooling process. They should also be hydrated with high electrolyte drinks.

Patients with severe symptoms must be cooled as quickly as possible and hydrated with high-electrolyte fluids, while vital signs are monitored. Ice packs in the armpit, groin, and sides of the neck will help with cooling. Unconscious patients will require intravenous rehydration. Resuscitation may be required. Medical attention (in a hospital) will be necessary for all patients presenting severe symptoms because muscle, liver, or kidney damage is possible.

## HYPOTHERMIA

Immersion hypothermia is a potential problem for the diver in almost every natural body of water on the planet, depending on the duration of the dive and the level of protection that the suit provides.

**Thermal Protection for Divers**

| Water Temp (°F) | Type of Suit |
| --- | --- |
| 80 – 75 | 3 – 5 mil wetsuit |
| 75 – 65 | 5 – 7 mil wetsuit |
| 65 – 35 | variable volume dry suit (thinsulate underwear for colder temps) |
| below 40 | hot water suit |

The above chart is only intended for a guideline; divers can work below 40°F in a dry suit, but extended bottom times at temperatures below this will require a hot-water suit to keep the diver's core temperature up sufficiently. Even a slight drop in the core temperature is an issue in deep diving, since metabolic rates change, affecting the rate that the body will take on a gas load and the rate that it off-gases. A chilled diver, particularly while decompressing, is much more susceptible to decompression sickness.

The task that the diver is performing seems to have some effect on the onset of hypothermia symptoms. Tasks such as welding, where the diver has to remain very still, seem to be worse than tasks involving heavier work; however, long durations of arduous work will increase the inert gas uptake.

## Symptoms of Hypothermia in Order of Appearance

| Initial onset | Chills, slight shivering |
|---|---|
| Mild hypothermia | Metabolism increases, uncontrolled shivering |
| Moderate hypothermia | Impaired mental function, slurred speech, enunciation problems |
| Serious hypothermia | Decreased shivering, muscle and joint rigidity, jerky movements |

## Patients with Symptoms Below Must Be Handled with Care to Avoid Damage to Internal Organs

| Severe hypothermia | Irrational behavior, confusion, stupor, joint and muscular rigidity, decreased pulse and respiration |
|---|---|
| Critical hypothermia | Unconsciousness, lack of response to pain stimuli, loss of reflex, pupils fixed and dilated, ventricular fibrillation, cardiac and respiratory failure, death |

The diving supervisor should be aware of any changes in the speech patterns of the diver, as well as an inability to perform simple tasks. Shivering does not occur in all cases of hypothermia. The dive should be aborted as soon as any hypothermia symptoms are noted.

### Treatment of Hypothermia

Patients with mild, moderate, serious, or severe hypothermia symptoms must not be rewarmed too quickly because blood circulation through cold tissue may cause "after drop," a condition in which the core temperature drops further after rewarming begins. Do not use direct heat to rewarm the casualty. Do not use hot baths, hot showers, or chemical hot packs. Do not rub extremities to encourage circulation. Place the casualty in a warm room and use blankets or sleeping bags and direct body contact. Continue to monitor pulse, respiration, and blood pressure until core temperature is back within the normal range. Provide 100% oxygen, warmed if possible. Conscious patients should be given warm drinks (water or sweetened juice) but diuretics such as caffeinated or alcoholic drinks should be avoided.

Patients with critical hypothermia symptoms should be rewarmed only on the advice of a physician, or in the absence of a physician, a DMT. If there is no pulse or respiration present, **do not assume death**. Hypothermia victims with no detectable vital signs have been rewarmed and made full recoveries even after hours with no apparent vital signs. It is believed that in some cases, after the initial rise in the metabolic rate, the metabolism slows (when the core temperature drops to a certain level), and the body goes into a near hibernation state. Do not start CPR unless it can be continued throughout the rewarming process under the advice of a physician or a DMT.

## RESPIRATORY PROBLEMS IN DIVING

Respiratory problems can occur on the surface, but these problems are increased in both severity and consequence because of the environment in which the diver works. If a person were to lose consciousness on the surface, the most serious consequence may be falling to the ground. In the underwater environment, losing consciousness can lead to death or a serious pressure-related injury.

Normal breathing is more difficult at depth due to the density of the breathing gas. As depth increases, gas density increases as well. Air is four times as dense at 100 fsw as it is on the surface. This difficulty in breathing, known as increased breathing resistance or increased work of breathing, dramatically reduces the ability to perform heavy work. On modern-demand diving helmets, there is a knob that allows the second stage regulator to be adjusted to overcome breathing resistance, but the diver has to make the adjustments. Increased pressure at depth means higher partial pressures of the gases making up the breathing gas mixtures. These higher partial pressures increase the severity of various respiratory problems. Percentages of various gases and contaminants that would not be a concern at surface pressure can be lethal at depth (Dalton's Law).

## HYPOXIA

Although the term hypoxia may apply to any situation where the body's cells are not able to receive sufficient oxygen to function normally, in diving operations, hypoxia is taken to mean "insufficient oxygen available in the diver's breathing gas." Hypoxia may occur due to using improper gas mixtures (bottom mix used at surface with less than 16% $O_2$), equipment problems (rust in high-pressure cylinders), medical problems (near drowning, carbon monoxide poisoning), or by entering a confined space with poor air quality. Regardless of the reason, hypoxia is deadly serious. The brain uses 20% of the oxygen the body absorbs, and the brain will only survive for between four and six minutes without oxygen before it dies.

### Signs and Symptoms
- Frequently no signs or symptoms (the diver may suddenly lose consciousness)
- Mental changes similar to alcohol intoxication
- Confusion, clumsiness, slowed responses
- Inappropriate or foolish behavior
- Cyanosis (blue lips, nail beds, skin)
- Breathing ceases

### Treatment
- Get casualty to surface or into fresh air.
- If casualty is conscious, administer 100% oxygen.
- If casualty is unconscious, treat as for gas embolism.
- Monitor ABCs, and administer CPR, if necessary.

## HYPERCAPNIA

The most common respiratory problem encountered in diving operations is hypercapnia, which is excessive carbon dioxide in the body tissues. This buildup of carbon dioxide can be caused by the following: inadequate ventilation of the helmet; failure of a carbon dioxide scrubber; excessive carbon dioxide in the breathing gas due to filtration failure; or by "skip breathing." Diving equipment always has dead air space, which can trap exhaled carbon dioxide and lead to hypercapnia. It is imperative to ventilate the diving helmet on a regular basis. Skip breathing is a dangerous practice. Carbon dioxide poisoning occasionally produces no symptoms until after the diver has resurfaced. The most common observed symptom is a headache, shortness of breath, and slight dizziness.

### Signs and Symptoms
- Overwhelming urge to breathe (air starvation)
- Headache (usually after surfacing), confusion
- Dizziness, nausea, perspiration, flushed skin
- Muscle weakness, clumsiness, slowed responses
- Muscle twitching, convulsions, unconsciousness (severe cases)

### Treatment
- Ventilate helmet immediately.
- If headache or other symptoms occur in water, surface as soon as possible.
- Administer fresh air or 100% oxygen, depending on severity of symptoms.
- Do not physically restrain a convulsing casualty.
- Place unconscious casualties in the recovery position and monitor circulation, airway, and breathing.

## CARBON MONOXIDE POISONING
The most dangerous respiratory problem a diver can encounter is carbon monoxide (CO) poisoning. Carbon monoxide is produced by the incomplete combustion of hydrocarbon fuels in internal combustion engines

and by burned lubricating oils, such as those used in compressors. Internal combustion engines produce carbon monoxide in high enough concentrations that exhaust fumes picked up by an intake and delivered to the diver can have dire consequences. CO has no odor, taste, or smell, and it cannot be seen in the air. This makes the presence of CO very difficult to detect, but worse still is the fact that often there are not any symptoms of poisoning prior to the casualty losing consciousness.

That is not the only bad news about CO. The hemoglobin (the red protein that bonds to oxygen) in the blood bonds with carbon monoxide about 300 times more readily than it does with oxygen. This stops the hemoglobin from bonding to both the oxygen and the carbon dioxide. CO bonds with myoglobin (the protein in muscle that stores and transports oxygen) and with the respiratory enzymes (they permit oxygen use in the cells). This basically stops all of the cellular functions in the body. Oxygen uptake, transport, and utilization are disrupted. CO poisoning is, in effect, hypoxia caused by CO, and the body starves for oxygen.

### Carboxyhemoglobin (HbCO) Relative to CO Exposure

| Continuous Exposure Level of CO | HbCO in Blood |
|---|---|
| 50 ppm | 8.4% |
| 40 ppm | 6.7% |
| 30 ppm | 5.0% |
| 20 ppm | 3.3% |
| 10 ppm | 1.7% |

The toxic effects of CO exposure increase as the depth increases. Once the CO has bonded with the hemoglobin creating carboxyhemoglobin, it then is difficult to eliminate it from the body. CO elimination is in half-times, in the same way that nitrogen elimination occurs. Breathing sea level air, it takes 5.5 hours for the first half of the CO to leave, 5.5

hours for half of the remainder to leave, 5.5 hours for half of that to leave, and so on. By breathing 100% oxygen at the surface, the half-time is cut to 1.5 hours. At 3 atmospheres absolute (ATA) in the chamber on $O_2$, the half-time for CO elimination is reduced to about 23 minutes.

### Signs and Symptoms

- Often no symptoms present before unconsciousness

- Headache, nausea, dizziness, muscle weakness, numbness in lips

- Cherry-red lips (once considered the classic symptom)

### Treatment

- Fresh air and oxygen if available; hyperbaric oxygen preferred

- Hyperbaric oxygen-USN TT5; TT6 recommended for acute CO poisoning

- Unconscious casualties will require treatment with hyperbaric oxygen.

## EXCESSIVE BREATHING RESISTANCE

The human body, because of its construction, requires a certain amount of effort in order to breathe. Effort is required to lift the rib cage and expand the intercostals (the muscles of the chest) when inhaling. This effort is known as "work of breathing." When the work of breathing becomes too great due to excessive breathing resistance, the body does not get the breathing gas exchange required to exhale enough carbon dioxide or to inhale enough breathing gas. The carbon dioxide levels build to the point of hypercapnia. This has been established as the probable cause in past diving accidents.

### Causes of Excessive Breathing Resistance

- Inadequate delivery pressure on breathing gas

- Regulator not adjusted for depth (increased gas density)

- Poorly tuned regulator in helmet (bent horseshoe yoke)

- Diving hose with too small bore

- Diving hose with dirt or debris inside bore

- Partially closed main supply valve on the air supply system

- Tight-fitting suit that constricts chest

### Prevention

- Use free-flow adjustment (dial-a-breath) as you descend.

- Maintain helmet regulators on a regular basis.

- Use the proper umbilical, and cap off or tape ends when not in use.

- Ensure that supply valves are properly opened during operations.

- Wear only proper-fitting suits and equipment.

## LIPOID PNEUMONIA

If a diver breathes air or breathing gas with suspended particles of petroleum vapor, he or she will contract lipoid pneumonia. When petroleum particles reach the lung, they prevent the lung from properly exchanging gases, in the same way that bacterial and viral pneumonia do. The difference is; with the proper medication, the other pneumonias are often cured. Lipoid pneumonia remains as long as the petroleum particles do, and that usually is a period of many years. This condition has often been called "black lung."

### Prevention

- Use only approved breathable compressor oil.

- Use clean filters on the downstream end of the system.

- Do not allow petroleum products around life support gear.

## OXYGEN TOXICITY

Oxygen is the one gas that we cannot survive without, yet at high partial pressures it becomes toxic. Divers are affected by two different types of oxygen toxicity: central nervous system (CNS) toxicity, and pulmonary (involving the rest of the body, particularly the lungs).

### CNS $O_2$ Toxicity

CNS oxygen toxicity can occur on the high end of the partial pressure levels with even a very short exposure. With a partial pressure above 1.6 atmospheric pressure (ATM), it can occur in as little as 5 minutes. CNS oxygen toxicity can lead to sudden unconsciousness with no warning. It can lead to seizures as well. The most common signs and symptoms can be remembered by using the acronym CONVENTID: convulsions, ears ringing, nausea, tingling and twitching of face and lips, irritability and restlessness, dyspnea and dizziness. These can present in any order. In fact, the most common is the twitching of lips and facial muscles that is often seen during surface decompression and hyperbaric oxygen treatments.

### Pulmonary and "Whole Body" Toxicity

Lower partial pressures of oxygen over longer periods of time will cause oxygen toxicity to develop, affecting other parts of the body, particularly the lungs. Even though partial pressures are not high enough to bring on CNS toxicity, the lungs show symptoms often after as little as half an hour of exposure. Symptoms of lung and whole-body toxicity include the following: chest pain, pain or coughing on deep breaths, fluid in the lungs, skin numbness, itching, headache, dizziness, nausea, vision problems, and reduction of aerobic capacity and pulmonary function.

### Individual Tolerance

Different individuals show different susceptibility to oxygen toxicity. In addition, any one individual may be more susceptible at one time than at another. The exact reason for these variations is not presently known, but it is suspected that temperature, physical exertion, immersion, breathing gas density, and elevated levels of $CO_2$ all increase susceptibility to $O_2$

toxicity. In the past, divers were required to have an "oxygen tolerance test" prior to employment as a diver. Due to the variations in susceptibility mentioned above, the test is seldom, if ever, used today as it has little, if any, predictive value.

## Prevention of Oxygen Toxicity

Decompression and treatment tables that use 100% oxygen administered in the chamber have "air breaks" built in to help prevent oxygen toxicity from affecting the occupant. By having a 5-minute air break between 30-minute oxygen breathing periods, the risk of both types of oxygen toxicity are reduced greatly. Even with air breaks, chamber operators must constantly watch for signs of CNS oxygen toxicity.

## Effects of Various Partial Pressures of Oxygen

| ppO (atm) | Effect and Where Encountered |
|---|---|
| <0.08 | Coma, death |
| <0.08 – 0.10 | Unconsciousness in most humans |
| 0.09 – 0.10 | Serious signs and symptoms of hypoxia |
| 0.14 – 0.16 | Initial signs and symptoms of hypoxia |
| 0.21 | Normal oxygen level in sea level air |
| 0.35 – 0.40 | Oxygen level in normal saturation diving operation |
| 0.50 | Threshold for whole body effects, maximum saturation diving exposure |
| 1.6 | NOAA limit for maximum exposure for a working diver |
| 2.2 | Oxygen level on 100% in chamber at 40 fsw (surface decompression) |
| 2.4 | 60/40 nitrox treatment gas at 6 ATA (165 fsw) |
| 2.8 | 100% oxygen at 2.8 ATA(60 fsw) as in USN TT5, TT6, and TT6A |
| 3.0 | 50/50 nitrox treatment gas at 6 ATA (165 fsw) |

## INERT GAS NARCOSIS

Inert gas narcosis occurs when the high partial pressure of inert gas dissolved in the body tissues causes the diver to display symptoms similar to intoxication. The most common inert gas narcosis encountered is nitrogen narcosis. Although named the "Rapture of the Deep" by Cousteau, there is nothing particularly "rapturous" about nitrogen narcosis, especially when it occurs in fast-moving, dark, or very cold water.

Nitrogen narcosis is dangerous to the diver because it increases the risk of getting into trouble, while reducing the diver's ability to get out of trouble.

The inert gases that cause narcosis, unless breathed at elevated partial pressures, have no narcotic effect. High pressure causes the gas to dissolve in the protein coverings of the nerve cells, and this, in turn, interferes with the ability of the nerve cells to respond to stimulus and to transmit the proper signals to the brain. The higher the partial pressure, the more inert gas is dissolved, and the more it affects the normal function of the nervous system (Henry's Law).

## Narcotic Effects of Nitrogen in Air Diving

| Depth in fsw | Effect on diver |
|---|---|
| 60 – 100 | Mild impairment of performance, mild euphoria |
| 100 | Reasoning and memory affected, delayed response to visual and auditory stimuli |
| 100 – 165 | Inappropriate laughter (may be overcome by self–control), idea fixation and overconfidence, errors in calculation. |
| 165 | Sleepiness, hallucinations, impaired judgment. |
| 165 – 230 | Party atmosphere, terror reaction in some, talkative, dizziness, uncontrollable laughter approaching hysteria in some divers |
| 230 – 300 | Exaggerated delay in response to stimuli, lack of concentration, mental confusion, increased auditory sensitivity (sounds seem louder) |
| 300 | Stupefaction, severe impairment of practical activity and judgment, mental abnormalities, memory loss, euphoria, hallucinations similar to those caused by hallucinogenic drugs |

This chart was developed through testing performed by the US Navy Experimental Diving Unit. As you can see, the effects of narcosis increase as the depth increases. Nitrogen is not the only inert gas that causes narcosis. Helium does not appear to have any narcotic effects, nor does neon, but argon is also narcotic, although at far deeper depths than nitrogen.

It appears that divers can become acclimatized, to a point, to the effects of narcosis. With repeated dives to deeper depths on air, many divers are less susceptible to nitrogen narcosis. It is thought that narcosis plays a large part in diving-related hypothermia, as the ability to perceive cold is reduced. Susceptibility to nitrogen narcosis is affected by the diver's diet, whether the diver drinks alcohol, and by the partial pressure of carbon dioxide. Having the diver vent the helmet well as the diver reaches bottom often will dramatically reduce the effects. Often, divers will not recall any of the effects of nitrogen narcosis after surfacing.

### Signs and Symptoms

- Lack of judgment, loss of practical skills
- A false sense of well being, regardless of circumstances
- Lack of concern for the job at hand or for personal safety
- Inappropriate laughter, euphoria
- Inability to remember or carry out instructions

### Prevention and Treatment

- Have divers eat healthy and cut fat intake.
- Have divers refrain from alcohol if diving the following day.
- Have divers ventilate the helmet well as they are nearing bottom.
- Reduce the diver's depth until symptoms subside.
- Gradually work the diver to deeper depths, over a period of time.

## BAROTRAUMA

The term barotrauma means "pressure injury." As the diver descends, the pressure on the outside of the body increases. Body tissues that are solid, or cavities that are liquid-filled, are not compressed. Any cavity in the body that is gas-filled, however, compresses and must be equalized. Failure to equalize, either on descent or ascent, causes the tissue in and around these cavities to be injured (suffer barotrauma). The most common areas to suffer barotrauma are the ear and the sinus cavities.

### The Ear

The human ear serves two main purposes: the sense of hearing and the sense of balance. The ear is divided into three sections: the outer ear, the middle ear, and the inner ear. The outer ear consists of the external ear and the ear canal. The middle ear consists of the eardrum, the small bones connecting the eardrum to the inner ear, and the Eustachian tube. The inner ear has the cochlea and the vestibular apparatus (balance center).

As the diver descends, pressure increases on the outside of the eardrum. To avoid injury, this pressure must be equalized. This may be done by swallowing, moving the jaw, or by the Valsalva maneuver. The Valsalva involves pressurizing the nose and mouth with the nostrils blocked. This forces gas into the Eustachian tube, equalizing the pressure on the outside of the eardrum. Divers should always clear their ears as they descend and avoid excessive pressure on the eardrum. Failure to clear the ears will result in barotrauma (ear squeeze), which can cause various conditions including tinnitus (ringing in the ears), vertigo, and ruptured eardrum.

### Ear Squeeze

Divers usually encounter problems clearing the ears due to inflammation and swelling of the Eustachian tube. This inflammation may be caused by cold or flu viruses, allergies, or by smoking. When the diver is unable to equalize the pressure within the middle ear on descent, a painful ear squeeze develops. If swallowing, moving the jaw, or performing the Valsalva maneuver does not alleviate the squeeze, the diver should stop descending, ascend slightly, and then try again. It is not recommended that the diver force his or her way beyond the pain. If the condition persists, the dive should be aborted.

Ear squeezes occurring on ascent are known as reverse squeezes. Decongestants and antihistamines will often reduce the swelling, allowing the Eustachian tube to open. Divers **should not** use these drugs prior to diving, however, for two reasons: they often alter other body functions (heart rhythm and temperature control), and they can wear off during the dive, resulting in a reverse squeeze. A better option is snuffing clean salt water up the nostrils.

### Vertigo

The inner ear performs two separate functions. The cochlea is the hearing sense organ, and the vestibular apparatus (including the semicircular canals) is the organ that senses motion and regulates the body's balance. If the balance mechanism is disrupted, the result is vertigo. Vertigo is not the same as dizziness. When experiencing vertigo, often the diver will see the horizon shift abruptly, and his environment will begin spinning very fast. If the victim is walking, often he will stumble and fall. Loss of balance, nausea, and vomiting are the typical symptoms. There are three different types of vertigo that commonly effect divers: alternobaric vertigo, caloric vertigo, and vertigo caused by disbaric illness, such as Type II decompression sickness or arterial gas embolism. All three types involve either the inner ear or the vestibular nerve that runs from the inner ear to the brain.

- Alternobaric vertigo. This condition results from overpressuring the middle ear due to repeated attempts to clear the ears. It also results when, during ascent, a reverse squeeze occurs, causing the middle ear to be overpressurized. Vertigo is often preceded by pain in the involved ear. The vertigo usually does not last long, but it is often very intense and may be incapacitating to the diver. If the pressure damages the round or oval window or other structures of the inner ear, ear surgery may be required.

- Caloric vertigo. This condition results from cold water stimulating the balance center (vestibular apparatus) in the inner ear. It may be caused simply by cold water entering one ear canal and not the other or by a ruptured eardrum allowing cold water to enter one of the middle ears. Caloric vertigo can be incapacitating to the diver, but the symptoms typically will pass as soon as the water in the middle ear warms up to body temperature.

- Vertigo caused by disbaric illness. This condition typically does not involve the inner ear or the vestibular apparatus but usually involves the vestibular nerve. The condition is a result of inert gas being released too quickly by body tissue and forming bubbles. The bubbles place pressure on the nerve, causing improper signals to be sent to the brain. Bubbles can also form in the inner ear itself, putting pressure on the vestibular apparatus. This can occur in Type II (CNS) decompression sickness or in arterial gas embolism. Regardless of the cause, the only way to correct this type of vertigo is through recompression treatment, appropriate to the cause.

### Eardrum Rupture

Ear squeeze, particularly a reverse squeeze, may result in eardrum rupture. Intense pain in the outer and middle ear area is felt at first, followed by almost immediate relief. Then immediately following the pain relief, vertigo and nausea are felt, often to the point of vomiting. Typically, there is partial or total hearing loss in the affected ear. If eardrum rupture is suspected, the patient must see a hyperbaric physician. No medications are to be administered into the ear canal without consultation with an ear, nose, and throat physician.

### Sinus Squeeze

The nasal sinuses are located in hollow cavities in the skull bones. They are lined with mucus membranes identical to those in the nose. The sinuses have air pockets in them that are joined to the nasal cavity by very small passages. The sinuses must be equalized as the diver descends and ascends, or a painful sinus squeeze will result. The sinus passages are susceptible to inflammation and swelling in the same way as the Eustachian tube. The sinuses will often hemorrhage, leading to a bloody discharge out of the nose after a dive. Sinus squeezes can be extremely painful, and a diver that pushes past the initial pain can get into the position that he or she can neither descend nor ascend without extreme pain. Head colds, allergies, and air pollution can cause the sinus passages to become inflamed. Divers must not dive with a head cold.

### Tooth Squeeze

When a tooth is decaying, it gives off gas. When compressed, a small pocket of this gas in a tooth will often suck the surrounding pulp into the cavity, creating pain. Poorly fitting or cracked dental fillings also may allow gas to leak in, around, and under them. If the gas exits the tooth as easily as it enters, there is no problem. If it does not, the tooth can crack, or in extreme cases, explode.

Wet welding and burning involve the diver being exposed to electrical current while immersed. This current usually will cause electrolysis in metals exposed to it. Metallic fillings in teeth that are metallic will corrode and disappear when this happens. Worse still, if this process allows gas to enter a tooth under pressure, it may not vent out of the tooth on ascent quickly enough to avoid an exploded tooth. Divers should have metallic fillings replaced with epoxy fillings whenever possible. Divers should maintain good dental health.

### Lung Squeeze

This condition is the result of diving to depth without adding any air to the lungs, a practice normally carried out by breath-hold or freedivers. When air is not added to the lungs as the diver descends, blood and tissue start to fill the areas normally filled with air, and eventually the chest collapses, bringing death. This could conceivably happen to a working diver, if the diver was heavily weighted and fell rapidly to the bottom.

### Body Squeeze

If a diver is using a constant volume dry suit or does not inflate a variable volume dry suit as he or she descends, the suit will collapse around the body, and folds in the suit will pinch the diver's body, creating purple welts and bruises. This is known as suit squeeze. Although a severe case looks bad, it is only painful for a short while, if at all. With surface-supplied diving gear, if the umbilical is cut off at the surface, the only thing preventing the diver from being squeezed up into his or her helmet is the presence of the nonreturn valve. For this reason, these nonreturn valves must be checked for proper function every time the helmets are installed online.

### Reverse Squeeze of the Stomach and Intestines

Gas produced in the gastrointestinal tract during digestion can cause problems for divers. If this gas is generated while the diver is under pressure, it will expand on ascent, causing pain in the abdomen. In most cases, the gas will pass harmlessly out through the mouth or anus. In an extreme case it could conceivably cause a rupture of these organs, although there have been no cases recorded to date. Each diver should know what foods cause gas to be produced and avoid eating gas-producing foods prior to pressurization. In addition, divers should avoid diving with an upset stomach or bowels.

## PULMONARY OVERINFLATION SYNDROMES

According to Boyle's Law, gas in the diver's lungs at depth will expand as the diver ascends. If the lung is full, and air is not exhaled, the result will be pulmonary overinflation. This condition is sometimes called "ruptured lung" or "burst lung syndrome," but this is very misleading. In an overinflation incident, the lungs do not have to actually rupture in order for an arterial gas embolism to occur. Breathing gas may, in fact, be forced through the alveolar membrane and into the capillary, causing an embolism without a "rupture" of the lung. A pressure differential of between 1.5 and 2.0 psi is sufficient to lead to pulmonary overinflation syndrome.

Excessive internal pressure on the lungs may be caused by deliberately holding the breath in a rapid ascent (panic); blocked airway (unconscious diver) in an uncontrolled ascent; a medical problem (diver with pneumonia or chest cold); or by a regulator failure occurring while the diver is inhaling. The possible consequences of pulmonary overinflation include mediastinal emphysema, subcutaneous emphysema, simple pneumothorax, tension pneumothorax, and arterial gas embolism. In each of these, gas escapes from the lung and causes various problems in other parts of the body. More than one of these conditions can occur simultaneously, and since some require recompression and some do not, accurate diagnosis is extremely important.

## MEDIASTINAL EMPHYSEMA

In mediastinal emphysema, gas from the lung escapes into the tissues around the heart, the major blood vessels, and the trachea.

Mediastinal Emphysema
(around heart & blood vessels)

### Signs and Symptoms

- Pain under breastbone, in neck, shoulder

- Shortness of breath, difficulty breathing

- Shock, cyanosis of skin or nailbeds

- Deviated Adam's apple, swollen neck

- Cough, voice changes

### Treatment

- Monitor ABCs, monitor for shock.

- Administer 100% oxygen.

- Watch for signs of other pulmonary barotraumas.
- Transport to the nearest medical facility.

## SUBCUTANEOUS EMPHYSEMA

In subcutaneous emphysema, gas from the lung is forced under the skin of the neck. It sometimes occurs along with mediastinal emphysema.

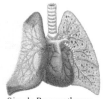

Subcutaneous Emphysema
(under tissues of the neck)

### Signs and Symptoms
- Full feeling in neck, change in voice
- Swelling around neck and upper chest
- Crackling under skin (rice-crispy neck)
- Cough

### Treatment
- Give oxygen. If breathing is impaired, see a doctor.
- Watch for signs of other pulmonary barotraumas.
- Recompression only necessary if symptoms of embolism are present.

## SIMPLE PNEUMOTHORAX

A simple pneumothorax is when gas released by a torn alveoli gets between the lung and the chest wall. This area has a two-layered membrane called the pleura. Gas gets between these layers, forming a bubble that expands on ascent, causing the lung to par-tially collapse. Symptoms clear up in time.

Simple Pneumothorax
(air between lung and chest wall)

### Signs and Symptoms
- Chest, shoulder, or upper back pain (aggravated by deep breathing)
- Casualty leans toward the affected side

- Hypotension, rapid shallow breathing
- Decreased lung sounds on affected side
- Symptoms not worsening

### Treatment
- Monitor closely for signs of tension pneumothorax.
- Monitor ABCs, administer 100% oxygen.
- Transport to nearest hospital.

## TENSION PNEUMOTHORAX

The difference between the tension and simple pneumothorax is that the tension pneumothorax gets worse with every breath. Each breath allows more gas to escape, collapsing the lung, and even pushing the heart out of place in some cases.

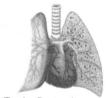

Tension Pneumothorax
(air between chest wall and lung)

### Signs and Symptoms
- Severe chest pain (during breathing)
- Leaning toward affected side
- Absence of lung sounds on affected side
- Dyspnea, hypotension, cyanosis, shock
- Symptoms steadily worsening with each breath

### Treatment
- Place casualty injured side down, monitoring ABCs.
- Treat casualty for shock and administer 100% oxygen.
- Ventilate gas from chest cavity with large bore catheter or chest tube.
- Transport immediately to hospital.

Divers recompressed for treatment of arterial gas embolism or decompression sickness also having a pneumothorax will experience relief of symptoms at depth. Any time a diver's condition deteriorates rapidly on ascent from treatment or from a dive and symptoms presenting involve the respiratory system, you should suspect a tension pneumothorax.

## ARTERIAL GAS EMBOLISM

The most serious of the pulmonary overinflation consequences is the arterial gas embolism. In the past, it was thought that an embolism occurred only with torn alveoli. It has been proven lately that gas pressure, if too high inside the alveoli, can force the gas through the membrane into the capillaries. The abbreviation AGE is commonly used. If there is brain involvement, it is referred

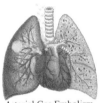

Arterial Gas Embolism
(air bubbles in arteries)

to as a cerebral arterial gas embolism or CAGE. The bubbles (emboli) in the arteries expand on ascent, blocking blood flow, resulting in the death of the affected tissues or organs. Onset of symptoms is usually sudden and dramatic, typically upon surfacing or within seconds of surfacing. It is critical that diagnosis and subsequent treatment happen very quickly. Any or all of the signs or symptoms in the list found below may be present in AGE or CAGE.

### Signs and Symptoms

- Chest pain, severe headache, cough, shortness of breath

- Bloody sputum, bloody froth around nose and/or mouth (not present in all cases)

- Impaired or distorted vision, blindness (partial or complete)

- Hearing abnormalities (ringing, roaring, hearing impairment)

- Large areas with abnormal sensation, numbness, tingling

- Loss of control of bodily functions, convulsions, tremors

- Weakness or paralysis, extreme fatigue, poor coordination

- Dizziness, confusion, difficulty in thinking, personality changes

- Sudden unconsciousness (usually immediately after surfacing)

- Respiratory arrest, irregular heart rhythm, death

**Treatment**
- Closely monitor ABCs; start CPR if necessary.

- Administer 100% oxygen with the casualty in the recovery position.

- Immediate recompression to depth of relief (not less than 60 fsw).

- Perform neurological examination on the casualty as soon as possible (at depth).

In the past, symptoms of arterial gas embolism required that the casualty be blown down to 165 fsw. This has changed in the past few years. In many cases, recovery/relief is achieved at 60 fsw, so the casualty is taken to 60 fsw and a neurological exam is performed. If there is significant relief within 20 minutes, a USN Treatment Table 6 is entered at that point. If significant relief is not achieved at 60 fsw, the casualty is taken down in increments, usually of 20 or 30 fsw, pausing 10 minutes to evaluate, until significant improvement or relief is achieved but not exceeding 165 fsw. Once the final depth is established, Treatment Table 6A is entered at that depth.

IMPORTANT NOTE: Type II decompression sickness and AGE often present the same or similar signs and symptoms. Typically, Type II symptoms are displayed after the casualty has been on the surface for 10 minutes, and symptoms of AGE or CAGE often are presented immediately upon surfacing, certainly in less than 10 minutes. **Casualties presenting any neurological symptoms less than 5 minutes after surfacing must be treated for arterial gas embolism.** If there is a medical facility in the immediate area with hyperbaric treatment capability, the casualty should be transported immediately to the facility. If not, recompress onsite, and get a physician to the chamber ASAP. Any delay in recompression will dramatically reduce the casualty's chances of recovery.

PREVENTION: Never hold your breath underwater; do not dive with a chest cold, bronchitis, or pneumonia; ascend at the prescribed ascent rate for the table; on an uncontrolled ascent – EXHALE.

## DECOMPRESSION SICKNESS

In order for a DCS diagnosis to be made, the casualty must have been either breathing gas under pressure or exposed to high altitude. Although some safety regulations require that divers carry a copy of their dive record (dive sheet) after decompression dives, the depth and duration are not relevant to treatment. Treatment is always based on symptoms presented. A diagnosis of DCS does not require the diver to have exceeded the no-decompression limits or improperly followed decompression tables. DCS can and has occurred in divers who were well within the no-decompression limits and followed decompression tables exactly as they were designed.

The only way to treat DCS is through recompression. When the diver is recompressed in the chamber, bubbles of inert gas are compressed back down and return to solution in the tissues and blood. Then through the treatment, inert gas is allowed to come out of solution slowly (without bubbling) and be exhaled by the diver. By using different treatment gases as the diver's breathing media, the inert gas partial pressure is kept low in both the respiratory system and arterial side of the circulatory system, while the pressure on the diver's body is high enough to keep the gas in the tissues and blood from bubbling as the diver off-gases. This is the same technique used in surface decompression using oxygen. Different treatment gases may be used: medical oxygen, nitrox, and various helium/oxygen mixes. Medical oxygen is the most common treatment gas used. It is important to use the exact treatment gas prescribed for the treatment table used.

**Symptoms of Decompression Sickness and the Percentage of Cases in Which They Occur**

| Decompression Sickness Symptom | Percentage |
|---|---|
| Localized joint pain (30% in arm, 70% in leg) | 58% |
| Motor or sensory impairment | 10% |
| Skin bends (marbling, welts, rash, or itching) | 10% |
| Dizziness, balance problems | 9% |
| Lymph node swelling and/or pain | 6% |
| Extreme fatigue, altered mental state, collapse | 5% |
| Cardiopulmonary involvement (chokes) | 2% |

Source: US Navy

DCS symptoms usually occur shortly after the diver surfaces. Type I symptoms often occur within 5 minutes of surfacing, while Type II symptoms often are not seen for at least 10 minutes. The following figures are provided by the US Navy:

- 42% of cases of DCS occurred within 1 hour

- 60% of cases of DCS occurred within 3 hours

- 83% of cases of DCS occurred within 8 hours

- 98% occurred within 24 hours

Decompression sickness (DCS) is categorized, assessed, and treated as Type I or Type II by symptoms.


### Type I Symptoms
- Joint or muscle pain—a dull ache that does not move and is present at rest.

- Lymph nodes—swelling and pain in the lymph nodes and surrounding tissue.

- Skin symptoms—purple welts, rash (most often on the torso), itching.

## Type II Symptoms

- Unusual extreme fatigue, numbness, tingling, muscle weakness, paralysis.

- Rapidly developing severe skin itching, bluish marble pattern on skin

- Vertigo, dizziness, hearing loss, ringing in the ears, vision problems, blindness.

- Disrupted motor performance, lack of coordination, disrupted mental status.

- Difficulty walking, balance problems, difficulty urinating

- Cardiorespiratory symptoms (chokes)—chest pain, cough, rapid shallow breaths.

## Time Before Treatment

Divers presenting Type I symptoms initially, when not given timely treatment, have progressed to Type II symptoms. This would indicate that a pain-only incident, when not treated immediately, may progress to a CNS incident. The frequency of this happening is not known, but several cases have been recorded to date. It is important to treat symptoms of either type of decompression sickness as soon as possible. The chance of complete recovery diminishes as the length of time before treatment increases.

## Extremity Pain Symptoms (Fixed, Not Radiating)

Pain from a sprain, strained muscle, or bruise occasionally may be mistaken for Type I DCS pain. Two ways to avoid this are to make notes if the diver mentions a soft tissue injury while in the water and to watch the diver walk and move as soon as the diver comes out of the water. Type I pain is always localized. It does not move around, and it does not radiate. The best way to describe Type I pain in a joint is that it feels like someone has a crowbar in your joint, gently prying it apart. Type I pain may be felt in the muscle as well, but not nearly as often as in the joints. If there is any question as to whether extremity pain is a DCS symptom or the result of a soft tissue injury, always treat for DCS Type I.

### Skin Symptoms

Skin (cutaneous) symptoms may be either Type I or Type II, depending on the manifestation. The most common of these is itching. Itching itself or if accompanied by a faint rash does not require recompression. Welts (purple raised areas resembling hives) are considered a Type I symptom and are treated as such. Marbling or mottling of the skin often precedes more serious Type II symptoms and is therefore treated as Type II. Marbling typically starts as intense itching, progresses to redness, then to a dark bluish discoloration resembling a marble pattern on the skin.

### Lymphatic Symptoms

Lymphatic symptoms (pain in lymph nodes and swelling of surrounding tissue) is considered a Type I DCS symptom. Pain is usually relieved very quickly on recompression. The swelling is sometimes present at the completion of treatment but dissipates over time.

### Torso and Radiating Extremity Pain Symptoms

Girdling pain, abdominal or thorax pain (not associated with breathing), pain that shoots down an arm or leg, or pain that moves from one location to another are considered to be a symptom of Type II, indicating spinal cord involvement. Any pain in the back which can not be linked to pain in a hip or shoulder should be considered a Type II symptom.

### Neurological Symptoms

Any neurological symptom occurring after a dive should be considered a symptom of Type II DCS or AGE. If there is any question whether it is AGE or DCS, always treat for AGE.

Fatigue is listed as a symptom of Type II DCS. Normal fatigue as occurring after a strenuous dive should not be considered a symptom, but if the diver is unusually fatigued after a dive that was not strenuous, perform a complete neurological examination and an extremity strength test to eliminate the possibility of Type II DCS. It is more common to notice problems in the extremity strength tests than it is in the neurological examination, but a deficit in either should be considered a Type II symptom.

Abnormal skin sensation (numbness, tingling, pins and needles, or electric-shock sensations), muscle weakness or paralysis, and mental status or motor-performance problems are considered the most common neurological Type II symptoms. Post-dive difficulty in urination is considered symptomatic of lower spinal cord involvement.

### Inner Ear Symptoms (The Staggers)

Inner ear symptoms (the staggers) include tinnitus (ringing), hearing loss, vertigo, dizziness, nausea, and vomiting. These may indicate inner ear barotrauma, but they also can indicate vestibular nerve problems or a bubble in the inner ear, which are symptoms of Type II DCS. The staggers can occur after an air dive but are seen most often in decompression after helium-oxygen dives, when the diver has switched from $HeO_2$ back to air. This condition is called the staggers due to the stricken diver's difficulty in walking.

### Pulmonary Symptoms (The Chokes)

Pulmonary Type II symptoms (the chokes) are an indicator of profuse intravascular bubbling causing circulation congestion in the capillaries of the lungs. The chokes often present first as chest pain aggravated by breathing or as an irritating, persistent cough. Breathing becomes more rapid, and symptoms of lung congestion progress rapidly. If not treated immediately, unconsciousness, complete collapse of the circulatory system, and death will result.

### Extremity Strength Testing and Neurological Assessment

There is a standard extremity strength test and a standard neurological assessment that must be performed on casualties presenting Type II and CAGE symptoms to determine deficit in either area. Due to the time it takes to perform these, they are best done after the casualty arrives at 60 fsw. There are, however, ways to get an initial indication of deficit that do not take much time and can be performed on the way to the chamber.

An easy way to see if there are extremity strength or balance problems is to have the diver walk while you watch closely. If the diver is having problems in either area, his or her gait will seem awkward and unsteady. Looking closely at the diver's eyes will often tell you a lot, as well. Unequal-sized pupils are an indication of neurological problems, while a squint may indicate vision or neurological problems.

Talking to the diver will obviously allow the diver to tell you if he or she has pain or altered sensation, but you can also observe indications of memory problems or other mental deficits through the diver's talk; this can be done while walking the diver to the chamber.

This handbook contains both the standard neurological and extremity strength test as used by the US Navy and the Rapid Neuro used by the Canadian Navy.

### PREPAREDNESS FOR MEDICAL EMERGENCIES
#### Personnel

There is no substitute for training and practice, so the DMT needs to keep his or her certification current and read regularly about diving medicine. Divers also need to keep current on basic diving medicine and renew their emergency first aid and CPR training as required. As stated earlier, practice drills are extremely important in maintaining readiness and discovering what will and will not work in real life. There should be at least one trained DMT on every shift on every diving crew.

## Medical Equipment

First aid kits, the diving medical advisory committee (DMAC) trauma kit, and the DMAC internal chamber kit must be regularly inventoried, making sure that not only all of the listed supplies are in the kits but also that any drugs and solutions with a shelf-life are current. Stretchers and Stokes litters (including lifting spreaders) must be regularly inspected, in good condition, and clean. The chamber must be kept clean and in a constant state of readiness, with primary, standby, and treatment gas supplies at the ready.

## Emergency Contact List

The emergency contact list must have 24-hour contact numbers for the on-call hyperbaric physician, the nearest hyperbaric treatment facility, the nearest hospital with a 24-hour emergency room, and the on-board contact number for the person who orders helicopters or crew boats. The contact list must be kept current and displayed in a prominent location in both the dive control van and the chamber van.

## *DMAC 15* Medical Kits

Two medical kits should be maintained for performing hyperbaric treatments; these are in addition to the normal first aid kits used by the diving crew. The chamber internal medical kit contains items that will be required to be in the chamber for every treatment, so it typically goes into the chamber with the DMT and the casualty and stays for the duration of the treatment. The trauma kit contains items that the DMT may require during a trauma event or a more complicated hyperbaric treatment . . . IV equipment, chest drains, syringes , etc, These items may be locked in through the medical or entrance lock when required, so the trauma kit stays outside of the chamber.

This handbook provides contents lists for both medical kits as well as a specified drug list provided by the International Marine Contractors Association (IMCA) Diving Medical Advisory Committee in *DMAC 15,*

*Revision 4.* Both kits must remain fully stocked at all times, with drugs and solutions in date and must be checked on a regular basis by the DMT.

### DMAC 15 (Rev 4) Trauma Kit Contents

| No. | SPECIFIED ITEM (Common Name) | No. Req'd |
|-----|------------------------------|-----------|
| | **DIAGNOSTIC EQUIPMENT** | |
| 1 | Pencil torch (penlight) | 1 |
| 2 | Electronic thermometer | 1 |
| 3 | Rectal thermometer – low range | 1 |
| 4 | Stethoscope | 1 |
| 5 | Aneroid sphygmomanometer (BP cuff) | 1 |
| 6 | Reflex hammer | 1 |
| 7 | Tape measure | 1 |
| 8 | Tuning fork – 128 Hz and 256 Hz | 2 |
| 9 | Pins for sensation test in neuro exam | 1 |
| 10 | Blood sugar testing equipment | 1 |
| 11 | Tongue depressors | 1 |
| 12 | Urine test strips | 1 set |
| 13 | Otoscope c/w spare bulb, batteries, ends | 1 |
| | **THORACENTESIS (CHEST DRAIN) EQUIPMENT** | |
| 1 | Intercostal drainage kit – flexible inducer | 2 |
| 2 | Emergency needle thoracentesis device | 4 |
| 3 | Heimlich valves | 2 |
| 4 | Straps or tape to secure chest drain | Set |
| | **URINARY CATHETERISATION EQUIPMENT** | |
| 1 | Nonlatex urinary catheters – size 16, 18 | 2 |
| 2 | Urine collection bags | 2 |

| No. | SPECIFIED ITEM (Common Name) | No. Req'd |
|-----|------------------------------|-----------|
| 3 | Catheter spigot valves | 2 |
| 4 | Sterile water in 20ml | 2 |
| 5 | Urethral anesthetic gel | 2 |
| 6 | Straps or tape to secure catheter system | Set |
| | **INTRAVENOUS ACCESS EQUIPMENT** | |
| 1 | Giving set (IV infusion set) | 3 |
| 2 | IV cannulae 16g | 4 |
| 3 | IV cannulae 18g | 4 |
| 4 | Butterfly infusion set 19g – optional | 4 |
| 5 | Magnetic hooks for IV bags | 2 |
| 6 | 3–way IV taps | 4 |
| 7 | Intraosseous infusion device | 2 |
| | **STERILE DRESSINGS** | |
| 1 | Gauze square pads 10 cm X 10 cm | 10 packs |
| 2 | Cotton wool balls | 5 packs |
| 3 | Triangular bandages | 4 |
| 4 | Trauma bandages (ambulance dressing) | 4 |
| 5 | Safety pins | 12 |
| 6 | Adhesive bandage 75mm X 3m | 2 |
| 7 | Adhesive bandage 25mm X 3m | 2 |
| 8 | Crepe bandage 6 inch | 2 |
| 9 | Crepe bandage 3 inch | 2 |
| 10 | Large dressing | 2 |
| 11 | Medium dressing | 2 |
| 12 | Adhesive plasters | 40 |

| No. | SPECIFIED ITEM (Common Name) | No. Req'd |
|-----|------------------------------|-----------|
| 13 | Dressing bowls – stainless | 2 |
| 14 | Eye pads | 4 |
| 15 | Eye wash kit | 1 |
| 16 | Soft silicone primary dressing 8 x 10 cm | 5 |
| 17 | SAM splint or equivalent for broken limbs | 1 |
| | **STERILE SUPPLIES – GENERAL** | |
| 1 | Universal containers | 4 |
| 2 | Medical drapes 60 X 90 cm | 2 |
| 3 | Alcohol swaps (sterile alcohol wipes) | 10 |
| 4 | Sterile gloves various sizes | 10 pair |
| 5 | Non–resorbable sutures – 2/0 and 3/0 | 6 |
| 6 | Sharps container, medium size | 1 |
| 7 | Resorbable sutures – 2/0 and 3/0 | 2 |
| 8 | 20 ml syringe | 5 |
| 9 | 10 ml syringe | 5 |
| 10 | 2 ml syringe | 5 |
| 11 | 18 g needle | 10 |
| 12 | 21 g needle | 10 |
| 13 | Antiseptic cream | 1 |
| | **STERILE SUPPLIES – SPECIFIC** | |
| 1 | Kidney bowl | 1 |
| 2 | Graduated bowl 60 – 100 ml | 1 |
| 3 | Skin disinfectant | 10 packs |
| 4 | 10 X 7.5 cm lint–free cotton swabs | 2 packs |
| 5 | Tissue backed surgical drapes 60 x 90 cm | 2 |

| No. | SPECIFIED ITEM (Common Name) | No. Req'd |
|-----|------------------------------|-----------|
| 6 | Yellow disposal bag | 1 |
| **STERILE INSTRUMENTS** | | |
| 1 | Spencer Wells forceps – 5 inch | 2 |
| 2 | Mosquito forceps | 1 |
| 3 | Dressing forceps | 1 |
| 4 | Fine toothed forceps | 1 |
| 5 | Disposable scalpels | 2 |
| 6 | Dressing scissors | 1 |
| 7 | Fine point scissors | 1 |
| 8 | Stainless steel ring cutter | 1 |
| **RESUSCITATION EQUIPMENT AND SUPPLIES** | | |
| 1 | Bag resuscitator with BIBS connection | 1 |
| 2 | Masks for above – various sizes | 3 |
| 3 | Pocket resuscitator with non–return | 1 |
| 4 | Supraglottic airways – size 3,4,5 | 3 |
| 5 | Automated external defibrillator | 1 |
| 6 | Oropharyngeal airways – size 3 and 4 | 2 |
| 7 | Foot powered suction device | 1 |
| 8 | Tourniquet to aid in venous access | 1 |
| 9 | Endotracheal suction catheter | 2 |
| 10 | Wide bore sucker | 2 |
| 11 | Nasopharyngeal airway – size 6 and 7 | 2 |

## DMAC 15 (Rev 4) Chamber Internal Medical Kit Contents

| No. | SPECIFIED ITEM (Common Name) | No. Req'd |
|-----|------------------------------|-----------|
| 1 | Arterial tourniquet | 1 |
| 2 | Polyethylene plastic bags | 3 |
| 3 | Pocket resuscitation mask with non–return | 1 |
| 4 | Oropharyngeal airways, size 3 and 4 | 2 |
| 5 | Tuff cut scissors (angled scissors) | 1 |
| 6 | Large dressing | 1 |
| 7 | Medium dressing | 1 |
| 8 | Triangular bandage | 2 |
| 9 | Adhesive tape 1 inch | 1 roll |
| 10 | Crepe bandages 3 inch | 2 |
| 11 | Hand operated suction pump | 1 |
| 12 | Suction catheter | 1 |
| 13 | Watertight bag | 1 |
| 14 | Cervical collar – adult, adjustable | 1 |
| 15 | Non–sterile gloves | 2 pair |
| 16 | Space blankets (foil blankets) | 2 |

## Required Medical Equipment Not Listed in DMAC 15 (Rev 4)

| No. | SPECIFIED ITEM (Common Name) | No. Req'd |
|-----|------------------------------|-----------|
| 1 | Stokes litter (basket stretcher) – must fit through chamber manway | 1 |
| 2 | Head restraint kit for Stokes litter | 1 |
| 3 | Backboard for spinal injuries | 1 |
| 4 | Portable oxygen administration kit | 1 |
| 5 | Workplace first–aid kit – may be required to treat non diving personnel | 1 |

# Drugs Required for *DMAC 15 (Rev 4)*

| # | Drug Name/Description | Medical Indication |
|---|---|---|
| **Anesthesia** | | |
| 1 | Lidocaine (injection) 10 ml | Local anaesthetic (up to 20 percent) |
| **Analgesia** | | |
| 2 | Aspirin (tablets) 3–500 mg | Mild/moderate pain–chest pain (cardiac) |
| 3 | Paracetamol / Tylenol (tablets) 500 mg | Mild/moderate pain–fever |
| 4 | Codeine (tablets) 25–30mg | Moderate to severe pain |
| 5 | Tramadol (injection) 100mg | Moderate to severe pain |
| 6 | Naloxone 0.4mg/ml | Opioid (morphine) overdose |
| 7 | Morphine (injection) 10mg | Severe and acute pain |
| **Resuscitation Drugs** | | |
| 8 | Adrenaline/epinephrine (injection) 10ml | Emergency Treatment for cardiopulmonary resuscitation |
| 9 | Amiodarone injection 150mg | Arrhythmias during CPR |
| 10 | Furosemide injection 40mg/20mg | Oedema, pulmonary oedema, resistant hypertension |
| **Nausea and Vomiting** | | |
| 11 | Fentiazin or Prochlorperazine (injection) or(oral) 25mg,5mg,3mg | Severe nausea, vomiting, vertigo, labyrinthine disorders |
| 12 | Hyoscine hydrobromide 300ug | Short acting drug for sea sickness |
| **Allergic Reactions** | | |
| 13 | Antihistamine for injection (chlorpheniramine) 10mg, 5mg | Symptomatic release of allergy. Urticarial–raised, often itchy |
| 14 | Oral antihistamine (centrizine dihydrochloride) 10mg | Symptomatic release of allergy. Non–sedating |
| 15 | Corticosteroid for injection. 100mg | Hypersensitivity reaction e.g anaphylaxis |
| 16 | Adrenaline/epinephrine autoinjector 0.3mg of 1 in 1000(1mg/ml) | Emergency treatment for acute anaphylaxis |

| # | Drug Name/Description | Medical Indication |
|---|---|---|
| **Drugs (Various)** | | |
| 17 | Atropine injection 4x1ml (600ug/ml) | For treating asystole, bradycardia |
| 18 | Glucose injection 2x500mg/ml 50ml | Management of Hypoglycemia |
| 19 | Glyceryl trinitrate sublingual tablets | Cardiac chest pain – Acute coronary syndromes |
| 20 | Intravenous fluids. (crystalloid infusion) 6 litres – NaCl 0.9% or Ringers | For intravenous hydration |
| 21 | Antipsychotic drug for injection | Relief of acute symptoms, schizophrenia |
| 22 | Anxiolytics for injection 10mg/2ml | Anxiety or insomnia, status epilepticus(convulsion) and for muscle relaxant where indicated |
| 23 | Anxiolytics for oral use (tablets)5mg | Short–term use in anxiety or insomnia, status epilepticus(convulsion) |
| 24 | Anxiolytics for rectal use 5mg suppositories | Short–term use in status epilepticus |
| **Burn Treatment** | | |
| 25 | Sulphonamides for topical use (skin) | Prophylaxis and treatment of infection in burns, treatment of abrasions, fingertip injuries |
| **Antibiotics** | | |
| 26 | Broad spectrum for oral use<br>* Co–amoxiclav, 21x625mg tablets<br>* A quinodole (Dicloxacilline) | Broad spectrum antibiotic.<br>useful in the treatment of gram negative bacterial infection |
| 27 | Macrolide antibiotic for oral use; Clarithromycin 250mg tablets | Susceptible infections in patients with penicillin hypersensitivity. |
| 28 | Antibiotics and corticosteroid ear drops. Sofradex (framycetin sulphate or dexamethasone/gramicidin) | Ear and eye infection 2–3 drops, 3–4 times daily |
| **Antifungal** | | |
| 29 | Antifungal drug (Clotrimazole) | For fungal skin infections |

The DMAC 15 (Rev 4) specified medical equipment and drugs are nearly identical to those listed in the *US Navy Diving Manual Revision 7*. Most offshore projects now follow IMCA Guidelines, so the decision was made to include the DMAC 15 (Rev 4) lists.

# SECTION 13
# Hyperbaric Treatment

Hyperbaric oxygen treatment is regularly used to treat pressure-related illness such as Type I and II decompression sickness and arterial gas embolism. It is also used therapeutically in nondiving related incidents to treat carbon monoxide poisoning, radiation burns, gangrene, and necrotizing fasciitis. The guidelines for hyperbaric oxygen therapy (HBOT) are as indicated in the following table:

### Guidelines for Conducting Hyperbaric Oxygen Therapy

| Indication | Treatment Table | Minimum # Treatments | Maximum # Treatments |
|---|---|---|---|
| Carbon Monoxide Poisoning, acute | Treatment Table 5 or Table 6 as recommended by the UMO | 1-3 | 3 |
| Gas Gangrene (Clostridial Myonecrosis) | Treatment Table 5 | 3 times in 24 hours 2 times per day for the next 2-5 days | 10 |
| Crush Injury, Compartment Syndrome, and other Acute Traumatic Ischemia | Treatment Table 9 | 2 times per day for 2-7 days | 14 |
| Central Retinal Artery Occlusion | Treatment Table 6 | 2 times daily to clinical plateau (typically < 1 week) plus 3 days | 3 days after clinical plateau |
| Diabetic Foot Ulcer | Treatment Table 9 | Daily for 3-4 weeks, based on healing response | 30 |
| Healing of Other Problem Wounds | Treatment Table 9 | Daily for 3-4 weeks, based on healing response | 60 |
| Severe Anemia | Treatment Table 5 or Table 9 as recommended by UMO | 3-4 times per day until blood replacement by transfusion or regrowth | variable, guided by clinical response |
| Intracranial Abscess | Treatment Table 9 | 1-2 times daily for up to 3 weeks | 20 |
| Necrotizing Soft Tissue Infection | Treatment Table 9 | 2 times daily until stabilization | 30 |
| Refractory Osteomyelitis | Treatment Table 5 or Table 9 as recommended by UMO | 20-40 treatments | 40 |
| Delayed Radiation Injury, Soft Tissue Necrosis, Bony Necrosis | Treatment Table 9 | For radiation injury: 30-60 treatments For prophylaxis: 20 treatments before surgery in radiated field; 10 sessions after surgery | 60 |
| Compromised Grafts and Flaps | Treatment Table 9 | 2 times daily up to 30 treatments | 20 |
| Acute Thermal Burn Injury | Treatment Table 9 | 2 times daily up to 30 treatments | 30 |
| Idiopathic Sudden Sensori-neural Hearing Loss | Treatment Table 9 | 10-20 treatments | 20 |

Source: *US Navy Diving Manual Revision 7*

The above table has been included primarily for information only; the treatments listed (with the possible exception of carbon monoxide poisoning) will be performed onshore and not on the offshore dive site. The primary focus of this handbook is commercial diving; therefore, the focus of this section will be on the treatment of diving-related disorders.

## LIFE SUPPORT CONSIDERATIONS DURING TREATMENTS

The shorter treatment tables (Treatment Tables 5, 6, 6A, 9, and Air Treatment Tables 1A and 2A) are short enough in duration that they will only involve one crew, and should not be too hard on the gas supplies and equipment. The longer treatment tables (Treatment Tables 3, 4, 7, and 8) will require additional crew and will be very hard on the gas supplies, consumables, and equipment. The good news is that the longer tables are seldom used. Due to the duration of the treatment tables (considerably longer than surface decompression) and the fact that they are an emergency medical treatment, issues such as manning, patient monitoring, and chamber environmental control come to the forefront.

### Manning Requirements for Treatments

The following are the minimum crew that will be required onsite to perform a treatment:

- Supervisor: Supervision of the treatment, chamber operations, time keeping for the occupants

- Outside Tender: Monitoring gas supplies, assisting occupants with entry and exit from chamber.

- DMT: Performing emergency medical procedures as required; acting as liaison with the on-call hyperbaric physician regarding the treatment.

- Inside Tender (optional): Monitoring the casualty as required, eliminating the need to keep the DMT inside the chamber throughout the entire treatment.

Although the minimum crew specified above will suffice in most cases, it is better to have a second outside tender to operate the chamber, freeing up the supervisor. Additional inside tenders will be required in incidents where CPR or assisted breathing is necessary. Additional inside tenders are required for longer treatments. The extremely long tables will require at least one crew change, possibly more, depending on the point in the original shift that the treatment was initiated.

## Temperature Control

The internal chamber temperature becomes more important on the treatment tables, since the patient is in the chamber environment for a much longer period of time, and the patient is undergoing an emergency medical treatment that is temperature sensitive. Although the table below shows maximum tolerance times for various temperatures up to 104°F, it is strongly recommended that the internal temperature of the chamber be kept below 85°F for all applications, whether regular surface decompression or performing a treatment.

When treating for arterial gas embolism and neurological symptoms in DCS, the patient's core temperature must be kept as close as possible to the normal range. This becomes more difficult when the chamber is too warm. In addition, temperature significantly affects the patient's ability to tolerate hyperbaric oxygen. The best way to maintain optimum internal temperature is to have the chamber inside a climate-controlled compartment or sea container. Other methods of dropping internal temperature include using a heater/chiller, venting the chamber, shading the chamber, and placing water-soaked blankets or burlap on the top of the chamber.

**Maximum Permissible Recompression Chamber Exposure Times
at Various Internal Chamber Temperatures**

| Internal Temperature | Maximum Tolerance Time | Permissible Treatment Tables |
|---|---|---|
| Over 104°F (40°C) | Intolerable | No treatments |
| 95–104°F (34.4–40°C) | 2 hours | Table 5, 9 |
| 85–94°F (29–34.4°C) | 6 hours | Tables 5, 6, 6A, 1A, 9 |
| Under 85°F (29°C) | Unlimited | All treatments |

NOTE:
Internal chamber temperature can be kept considerably below ambient by venting or by using an installed chiller unit. Internal chamber temperature can be measured using electronic, bimetallic, alcohol, or liquid crystal thermometers. Never use a mercury thermometer in or around hyperbaric chambers. Since chamber ventilation will produce temperature swings during ventilation, the above limits should be used as averages when controlling temperature by ventilation. Always shade chamber from direct sunlight.

*Source: US Navy Diving Manual Revision 7*

Also important is the minimum internal temperature. Although chamber blankets are normally provided, the internal temperature should not be allowed to drop below 70°F. Lower temperatures for extended periods will affect the metabolism, and gas elimination will not occur at the proper rate, either in normal surface decompression or in hyperbaric treatment.

### Oxygen Levels in the Chamber

Most chambers today are equipped with an oxygen monitor, so it is relatively easy to maintain the proper oxygen level in the chamber environment during treatments. The level must not be allowed to climb too high, thereby presenting a risk of fire; but with inside tenders typically breathing air, it must not be allowed to drop too low. Oxygen levels should be maintained in the 20-22% range, never being permitted to drop below 19% or climbing above 25%. Venting the chamber (while maintaining depth) will help in both cases.

### Carbon Dioxide Levels in the Chamber

Carbon dioxide must be maintained below 1.5% in the chamber environment. This is best accomplished when the chamber has a $CO_2$ monitor. Most $CO_2$ monitors are installed on the surface side of the exhaust line, so the maximum $CO_2$ reading should be 0.78% when the chamber is at 30 fsw, 0.53% when at 60 fsw, and 0.25% when at 165 fsw to maintain 1.5% at pressure. $CO_2$ monitors that take their reading internally need not be corrected. Although many newer chambers have $CO_2$ scrubbers, when there is work being performed by more than one person (CPR), ventilation will also be required to maintain the $CO_2$ level. If the chamber has neither a $CO_2$ monitor nor a scrubber, the standard rates of ventilation will apply: 3 standard cubic feet per minute (scfm) per occupant at rest; 6 scfm per occupant at work (CPR).

The formula to calculate ventilation rates is:

$$R = \frac{V \times 18}{T \times \frac{(P + 33)}{33}}$$

Where: R = ventilation rate in actual cubic feet per minute
V = chamber volume stated in cubic feet
T = time (seconds) to change chamber depth by 10 fsw
P = chamber gauge pressure in feet of seawater

When in doubt, ventilate two out of every five minutes with occupants resting and four out of every five minutes with occupants performing strenuous work.

Scrubbers do not necessarily eliminate the need for ventilation. With multiple occupants, particularly if they are working strenuously, ventilation will be required even with a $CO_2$ scrubber. Scrubber absorbent should be changed prior to the partial pressure of carbon dioxide reaching 1.5%.


### Patient Hydration

Successful treatment of DCS depends on adequate hydration of the patient. Thirst is an unreliable indicator of necessary water intake, particularly if the chamber occupants are sweating heavily. At temperatures above 85°F, patients and tenders should drink at least one liter of water per hour; below 85°F, they should drink one half liter of water per hour.

Only fully conscious patients may be given fluids by mouth. Water, juice, or noncarbonated drinks may be given by mouth.

Semiconscious and unconscious patients should be started on intravenous fluids immediately, using Ringer's lactate or normal saline at a rate of 75–100 cc per hour until specific IV instructions can be issued by a hyperbaric physician. Do not use glucose or dextrose solutions if brain or spinal cord involvement is suspected. Patients presenting Type II or AGE symptoms should be considered for IV hydration, even if conscious. The patient's ability to void the bladder should be assessed as soon as possible. If the patient cannot empty a full bladder, a urinary catheter must be inserted as soon as possible. Urine output at or above 0.5 cc/kg/hr is a reliable indication of adequate hydration; however clear colorless urine in both the patient and the tender is the best indicator.

### Breathing Gas

Any time the chamber is pressed deeper than 45 fsw, at least one occupant (inside tender) will be breathing air. At depths of less than 45 fsw, the inside tender may breathe oxygen but should not strap on a BIBS mask. The treatment tables that follow have instructions for tender oxygen breathing. High oxygen treatment gases are now being utilized deeper than 60 fsw, since a high partial pressure of oxygen offers a significant therapeutic advantage over air. The target zone is typically a partial pressure of 1.5 to 3.0 ATA of oxygen at treatment depth. This is best achieved using either $N_2O_2$ or $HeO_2$ at depths up to 165 fsw and at depths beyond 165 fsw with $HeO_2$ only.

| Depth (fsw) | Breathing Gas | O Percentage | ppO |
|---|---|---|---|
| 0 – 60 | Oxygen | 100% | 1.00 – 2.82 |
| 61–165 | NO or HeO | 50% | 1.42 – 3.00 |
| 166 – 225 | Helium/Oxygen Mix | 36% | 2.17 – 2.81 |

Decompression sickness following helium dives may be treated with either $N_2O_2$ or $HeO_2$. For treatment requiring depths beyond 165 fsw, $HeO_2$ is strongly recommended to avoid nitrogen narcosis. For treatment of decompression sickness following air or $N_2O_2$ dives, avoid helium mixtures as the breathing medium: studies have indicated that in these cases, helium may do more harm than good.

In cases where the patient cannot tolerate 100% oxygen at 60 fsw or shallower (CNS toxicity) high oxygen treatment gases are often a very good alternative, since they keep the $ppO_2$ significantly higher than air.

## OXYGEN TOXICITY OCCURING DURING TREATMENT

Acute CNS oxygen toxicity may develop on any oxygen treatment table. Pulmonary oxygen toxicity may develop on Treatment Tables 4, 7, or 8 during prolonged treatments or on a Treatment Table 6 if repeat treatments are required.

### CNS Toxicity

On oxygen treatment tables, the chamber operator and the inside tender or DMT must continually watch for initial signs and symptoms of CNS oxygen toxicity. The acronym CON-VENTID will help to remember the signs and symptoms: convulsions, vision, ears, nausea, twitching/tingling, irritability, dyspnea, and dizziness. At the first sign of CNS toxicity, the BIBS mask must be removed. Unfortunately, convulsions do occur sometimes with no other warning signs. CNS toxicity is unlikely to occur in a resting individual at 50 fsw and shallower and highly unlikely to occur at 30 fsw and shallower, even when active. Patients with AGE or severe Type II DCS may be more susceptible to CNS $O_2$ toxicity and seizures occurring as a result of these conditions may be hard to distinguish from convulsions due to CNS $O_2$ toxicity.

### Procedures for CNS Oxygen Toxicity During Treatment

At the first sign of oxygen toxicity, the patient must be removed from oxygen and allowed to breathe chamber air. Fifteen minutes after the last symptom has subsided, resume oxygen breathing. For Tables 5, 6, and 6A, resume oxygen breathing at the point of interruption. For Tables 4, 7, and 8, no lengthening of the table is required due to the interruption. If oxygen toxicity symptoms develop again, or if the first symptom is a convulsion, take the actions detailed below:

When using Treatment Table 5, 6, or 6A:

- Remove the BIBS mask from the patient.

- Wait for all symptoms to completely subside, then ascend 10 fsw at a rate of 1 fsw per minute. For convulsions, travel after the patient is fully relaxed and breathing normally.

- Resume oxygen breathing at the shallower depth at the point of interruption.

- If another toxicity symptom occurs after ascending 10 fsw, consult the on-call hyperbaric physician about modifications to the treatment

When using Treatment Table 4, 7, or 8

- Remove the BIBS mask from the patient.

- Consult the on-call hyperbaric physician before resuming oxygen breathing. No lengthening of the tables will be required to compensate for the interruption.

### Pulmonary Oxygen Toxicity

When using Treatment Tables 5, 6, or 6A, pulmonary oxygen toxicity is highly unlikely. When using Treatment Table 4, 7, or 8, or with repeated uses of TT5, 6, or 6A (particularly with extensions), the long periods of oxygen breathing may result in pulmonary toxicity. Patients will present end-inspiratory discomfort, which may progress to substantial burning and severe pain on inspiration.

If a patient shows a good response to treatment but complains of substernal burning, discontinue oxygen and consult with the hyperbaric physician. If, however, neurological deficit remains and improvement is noted (or if condition deteriorates when oxygen is stopped), oxygen should be continued as long as is considered beneficial or until pain limits inspiration. If oxygen breathing must be continued beyond the onset of substernal burning, or if the 2-hour air breaks found in TT4, 7, or 8 cannot be used due to deterioration in patient condition on the discontinuance of oxygen, the $O_2$ breathing periods should be changed to 20 minutes on $O_2$ followed by a 10-minute air break. Alternatively, a treatment gas with a lower percentage of oxygen may be used. The on-call hyperbaric physician will ultimately decide on the course of action.

### Loss of Oxygen During Treatment

The loss of oxygen to the BIBS during a treatment should be handled as indicated below:

If oxygen supply can be restored within 15 minutes:

- Maintain depth until oxygen is restored.

- Once oxygen is restored, resume treatment at the point of interruption.

If oxygen supply can be restored after 15 minutes but before 2 hours (table selected TT5, 6, or 6A):

- Maintain depth until oxygen is restored.

- Once oxygen is restored, complete treatment with maximum number of $O_2$ extensions.

If oxygen supply can be restored after 15 minutes but before 2 hours (table selected TT4, 7, or 8):

- Continue decompression as with oxygen, changing back to oxygen when it is restored.

- If the patient has worsening symptoms without oxygen, the decompression must be stopped. Once oxygen is restored, continue treatment from point where it was stopped.

If oxygen supply cannot be restored within 2 hours, switch to the comparable air treatment table at the current depth if at 60 fsw or shallower. The ascent rate must not exceed 1 fsw per minute between stops. If it becomes apparent that symptoms are worsening and a depth deeper than 60 fsw is needed, use Treatment Table 4.

## POST-TREATMENT CONSIDERATIONS

Inside tenders on Treatment Table 5, 6, 6A, 1A, 2A, or 3 will require a minimum 18-hour surface interval prior to performing no-decompression dives and a minimum 24-hour surface interval prior to decompression dives. Inside tenders on Treatment Table 4, 7, and 8 will require a minimum 48-hour surface interval prior to performing any dive.

### Observation Period

Patients treated on a Treatment Table 5 who have had complete relief must remain near the chamber for two hours. Patients treated for Type II DCS symptoms or patients treated on a Treatment Table 6 for Type I DCS symptoms who have had complete relief must remain near the chamber for six hours. Any patient treated on a TT6, 6A, 4, 7, 8, or 9 is likely to require at least some hospitalization. The hyperbaric physician will determine whether hospitalization is required and the length of observation time. Regardless, all patients undergoing treatment should remain within 1-hour travel time from the chamber for 24 hours and be accompanied for that period by a person able to recognize the recurrence of symptoms.

Inside tenders should remain near the chamber for 1 hour after a treatment. If they were inside tender on a TT4, 7, or 8, they should remain within 1-hour travel of the chamber for 24 hours.

## Flying After Treatment

Patients presenting any residual symptoms must not fly without first consulting with a hyperbaric physician. Patients experiencing complete relief after treatment for AGE or DCS must not fly for a minimum 72 hours after treatment.

Inside tenders on Treatment Table 5, 6, 6A, 1A, 2A or 3 must not fly for at least 24 hours. Inside tenders on Treatment Table 4, 7, or 8 must not fly for at least 72 hours.

## Air Evacuation

Occasionally patients will require air evacuation to a shore-based medical or treatment facility immediately upon the completion of treatment, and they will not meet the surface-interval requirements. These evacuations should be done only on the advice of the on-call hyperbaric physician. Aircraft with a cabin pressurized to 1 ATA should be used, if possible, or if it is an unpressurized cabin, the aircraft must stay below 1,000 feet above sea level. The patient should be maintained on 100% oxygen during transit. If available, load the patient into a hyperbaric stretcher for the evacuation, and maintain the pressure at 1 ATA.

## Residual Symptoms

After treatment, if a complete medical evaluation indicates that Type II DCS symptoms remain, the hyperbaric physician will most likely prescribe additional treatments. These will be better performed at a shore-based facility, since most offshore sites do not have the capacity to maintain daily treatments along with the day-to-day operations of the diving crew. Sometimes the physician will allow the patient to return home if there is a treatment facility nearby. If the patient is ambulatory and is travelling home or to a treatment facility, the patient must be escorted by someone who can assist, if required. The person escorting the patient should have a basic knowledge of diving medicine, and be familiar with the patient's case.

### Returning to Diving After Treatment

Divers presenting Type I DCS symptoms and meeting all the criteria for a Treatment Table 5 who have had complete relief may return to diving 48 hours after completion of treatment, providing there was no doubt about the presence or absence of Type II DCS symptoms. If there was some doubt about Type II symptoms, the diver will be required to consult with the hyperbaric physician before resumption of diving.

Divers presenting Type I symptoms but requiring treatment on TT6 who have had complete relief of all symptoms may return to diving after seven days.

Divers presenting symptoms and diagnosed with Type II DCS or AGE may be cleared to dive 30 days after treatment by the hyperbaric physician, provided no evidence of neurological deficit exists.

## NONSTANDARD TREATMENTS

All treatment recommendations presented in this handbook are as found in the *US Navy Diving Manual* Revision 7. They should be followed as closely as possible unless it becomes evident that they are not working. Only a hyperbaric physician may recommend changes to the treatment protocols, and any changes should then be approved by the corporate diving manager. The treatment tables found in this handbook are considered the minimum required and should in no case be shortened, except when either the patient is declared dead or the vessel on which the chamber is located is afire or in danger of sinking. In these cases, the abort procedures should be followed.

## TREATMENT ABORT PROCEDURES

All treatments must be followed through to the end unless the patient is declared dead or a condition arises that puts the chamber occupants and operators in mortal danger.

## Death During Treatment

If it appears that a diver undergoing treatment has died, the on-call hyperbaric physician must make the decision to abort. Once the decision to abort has been made, there are different options available for decompressing the inside tender(s), depending on the depth and the profile of the treatment table.

- If death occurs following initial recompression to 60, 165, or 225 on Treatment Tables 6, 6A, 4, or 8, decompress on the air/oxygen schedule in the air decompression table having the next deeper depth and next longer time than those achieved in the treatment. Even if $N_2O_2$ or $HeO_2$ were the breathing medium, the air/oxygen schedule still may be used.

- If death occurs after leaving initial treatment depth on a TT6 or 6A, decompress at 30 fsw per minute to 30 fsw, then begin oxygen breathing at 30 fsw for the time indicated in the table on the next page. Once oxygen breathing at 30 fsw is completed, ascend to surface breathing oxygen at a rate of 1 fsw per minute.

- If death occurs after leaving the initial treatment depth on TT4 or 8 or after beginning treatment on TT7 at 60 fsw, decompress by continuing the table as written. Alternatively, follow the table as written to 60 fsw. At 60 fsw, have tender breathe oxygen for three 30-minute periods, separated by 5-minute air breaks. Ascend at 30 fpm to 50 fsw. Perform two 30-minute $O_2$ periods separated by a 5-minute air break. Ascend at 30 fpm to 40 fsw. Perform a 60-minute $O_2$ period with a 15-minute air break at the end. Ascend at 30 fpm to 30 fsw. Perform a 60-minute $O_2$ period followed by a 15-minute air break. Ascend at 30 fpm to 20 fsw. Perform two 60-minute $O_2$ periods, separated by a 15-minute air break. After the final $O_2$ period at 20 fsw, ascend to surface at 30 fpm. Observe for signs of DCS.

## INSIDE TENDER OXYGEN BREATHING REQUIREMENTS

| Treatment Table Utilized | O Time (min) |
|---|---|
| TT5 with or without extension @ 30 fsw | :00 |
| TT6 with up to one extension @ either 60 fsw or 30 fsw | :30 |
| TT6 with more than one extension | :60 |
| TT6A with up to one extension @ either 60 fsw or 30 fsw | :60 |
| TT6A with more than one extension | :90 |

Note 1:Tender O breathing times are at 30 fsw, and tenders breathe O on ascent from 30 fsw to the surface.

Note 2: If tender has had hyperbaric exposure within the previous 18 hours, use the following guidance:
- For TT5, add an additional 20–minute O period to the times in the table
- For TT6 or TT6A, add an additional 60–minute O period to the times in the table.

Source: US Navy

### Abort due to Impending Disaster

If an impending disaster (vessel in danger of sinking, catastrophic mechanical failure, fire on board) forces the treatment to be aborted, the previous abort procedure above (Death during Treatment) may be used for all occupants. If there is insufficient time available, the following actions may be followed:

1. If deeper than 60 feet when deciding to abort, start travel immediately to 60 feet.

2. Once at 60 feet, put all chamber occupants on oxygen. Select the air/oxygen schedule in the air decompression table that corresponds to the deepest depth and total time attained in treatment.

3. If at 60 feet when deciding to abort, put all chamber occupants on $O_2$ for a period of time equal to all decompression stops 60 feet and deeper according to the air/oxygen schedule, then continue decompression according to the air/oxygen schedule. Complete as much of the oxygen breathing as possible.

4.  When no more time is available, surface the chamber (without exceeding 10 fpm if possible) and try to keep all occupants on oxygen during evacuation.

5.  Evacuate all chamber occupants to the nearest hyperbaric facility, and treat according to Treatment for Arterial Gas Embolism or Serious Decompression Sickness Flowchart. If no symptoms presented between abort and arrival at the facility, follow TT6.

### Rules for Recompression Treatment

**ALWAYS:**

1.  Follow the treatment tables accurately, unless modified by a Undersea Medical Officer with concurrence of the Commanding Officer or Officer-in-Charge (OIC).
2.  Have a qualified tender in the chamber at all times during treatment.
3.  Maintain the normal descent and ascent rates as much as possible.
4.  Examine the patient thoroughly at depth of relief or treatment depth.
5.  Treat an unconscious patient for arterial gas embolism or serious decompression sickness unless the possibility of such a condition can be ruled out without question.
6.  Use air treatment tables only if oxygen is unavailable.
7.  Be alert for warning signs of oxygen toxicity if oxygen is used.
8.  In the event of an oxygen convulsion, remove the oxygen mask and keep the patient from self-harm. Do not force the mouth open during a convulsion.
9.  Maintain oxygen usage within the time and depth limitations prescribed by the treatment table.
10. Check the patient's condition and vital signs periodically. Check frequently if the patient's condition is changing rapidly or the vital signs are unstable.
11. Observe patient after treatment for recurrence of symptoms. Observe 2 hours for pain-only symptoms, 6 hours for serious symptoms. Do not release patient without consulting a UMO.
12. Maintain accurate timekeeping and recording.
13. Maintain a well-stocked Primary and Secondary Emergency Kit.

**NEVER:**

1.  Permit any shortening or other alteration of the tables, except under the direction of a Undersea Medical Officer.
2.  Wait for a bag resuscitator. Use mouth-to-mouth resuscitation with a barrier device immediately if breathing ceases.
3.  Interrupt chest compressions for longer than 10 seconds.
4.  Permit the use of 100 percent oxygen below 60 feet in cases of DCS or AGE.
5.  Fail to treat doubtful cases.
6.  Allow personnel in the chamber to assume a cramped position that might interfere with complete blood circulation.

Source: *US Navy Diving Manual Revision 7*

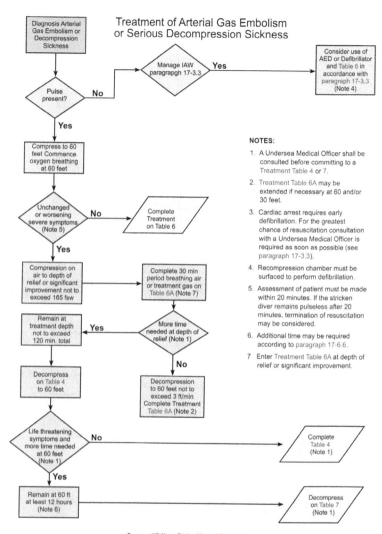

## Treatment of Arterial Gas Embolism or Serious Decompression Sickness

Diagnosis Arterial Gas Embolism or Decompression Sickness

Pulse present?

**No** → Manage IAW paragraph 17-3.3 → **Yes** → Consider use of AED or Defibrillator and Table 6 in accordance with paragraph 17-3.3 (Note 4)

**Yes**

Compress to 60 feet Commence oxygen breathing at 60 feet

Unchanged or worsening severe symptoms (Note 5) → **No** → Complete Treatment on Table 6

**Yes**

Compression on air to depth of relief or significant improvement not to exceed 165 fsw → Complete 30 min period breathing air or treatment gas on Table 6A (Note 7) → More time needed at depth of relief (Note 1)

**Yes** → Remain at treatment depth not to exceed 120 min. total

**No** → Decompression to 60 feet not to exceed 3 ft/min Complete Treatment Table 6A (Note 2)

Decompress on Table 4 to 60 feet

Life threatening symptoms and more time needed at 60 feet (Note 1) → **No** → Complete Table 4 (Note 1)

**Yes**

Remain at 60 ft at least 12 hours (Note 6) → Decompress on Table 7 (Note 1)

**NOTES:**

1. A Undersea Medical Officer shall be consulted before committing to a Treatment Table 4 or 7.

2. Treatment Table 6A may be extended if necessary at 60 and/or 30 feet.

3. Cardiac arrest requires early defibrillation. For the greatest chance of resuscitation consultation with a Undersea Medical Officer is required as soon as possible (see paragraph 17-3.3).

4. Recompression chamber must be surfaced to perform defibrillation.

5. Assessment of patient must be made within 20 minutes. If the stricken diver remains pulseless after 20 minutes, termination of resuscitation may be considered.

6. Additional time may be required according to paragraph 17-6.6.

7. Enter Treatment Table 6A at depth of relief or significant improvement.

Source: *US Navy Diving Manual Revision 7*

# Treatment of Type I Decompression Sickness

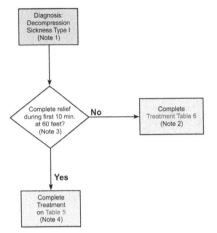

**NOTES:**

1. If a complete neurological exam was not completed before recompression, treat as a Type II symptom.

2. Treatment Table 6 may be extended up to four additional oxygen-breathing periods, two at 30 feet and/or two at 60 feet.

3. Diving Supervisor may elect to treat on Treatment Table 6.

4. Treatment Table 5 may be extended two oxygen-breathing periods at 30 fsw.

Source: *US Navy Diving Manual Revision 7*

## Two Schools of Thought on Treatment of TYPE I DCS

There are two schools of thought on the treatment of Type I DCS: those who stick exactly to the US Navy treatment protocol and use a Treatment Table 5 for pain only (Type I) and a Treatment Table 6 only if there is neurological deficit or other Type II signs or symptoms; and those who say all cases of decompression sickness should be treated on a Treatment Table 6. If the diving supervisor feels more at ease having the diver treated on a Table 6 for Type I symptoms, it is fine. If the supervisor is comfortable in using a Table 5 for Type I symptoms that is also fine. In all DCS cases, a thorough neurological exam must be performed even if it appears the stricken diver is only presenting Type I symptoms; using a Table 6 for a pain-only incident does not remove the need for a neuro exam.

# Treatment of Symptom Recurrence

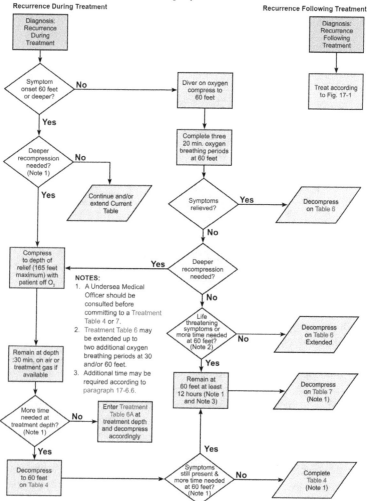

**Recurrence During Treatment**

**Recurrence Following Treatment**

Diagnosis: Recurrence During Treatment

Symptom onset 60 feet or deeper? — **No** → Diver on oxygen compress to 60 feet

**Yes**

Deeper recompression needed? (Note 1) — **No** → Continue and/or extend Current Table

**Yes**

Compress to depth of relief (165 feet maximum) with patient off O₂

Remain at depth :30 min. on air or treatment gas if available

More time needed at treatment depth? (Note 1) — **No** → Enter Treatment Table 6A at treatment depth and decompress accordingly

**Yes**

Decompress to 60 feet on Table 4

---

Diver on oxygen compress to 60 feet

Complete three 20 min. oxygen breathing periods at 60 feet

Symptoms relieved? — **Yes** → Decompress on Table 6

**No**

Deeper recompression needed? — **Yes** → Compress to depth of relief (165 feet maximum) with patient off O₂

**No**

Life threatening symptoms or more time needed at 60 feet? (Note 2) — **No** → Decompress on Table 6 Extended

**Yes**

Remain at 60 feet at least 12 hours (Note 1 and Note 3) → Decompress on Table 7 (Note 1)

**Yes**

Symptoms still present & more time needed at 60 feet? (Note 1) — **No** → Complete Table 4 (Note 1)

---

Diagnosis: Recurrence Following Treatment

Treat according to Fig. 17-1

---

**NOTES:**
1. A Undersea Medical Officer should be consulted before committing to a Treatment Table 4 or 7.
2. Treatment Table 6 may be extended up to two additional oxygen breathing periods at 30 and/or 60 feet.
3. Additional time may be required according to paragraph 17-6.6.

# Treatment Table 5

1. Descent rate - 20 ft/min.

2. Ascent rate - Not to exceed 1 ft/min. Do not compensate for slower ascent rates. Compensate for faster rates by halting the ascent.

3. Time on oxygen begins on arrival at 60 feet.

4. If oxygen breathing must be interrupted because of CNS Oxygen Toxicity, allow 15 minutes after the reaction has entirely subsided and resume schedule at point of interruption (see paragraph 17-8.10.1.1)

5. Treatment Table may be extended two oxygen-breathing periods at the 30-foot stop. No air break required between oxygen-breathing periods or prior to ascent.

6. Tender breathes 100 percent $O_2$ during ascent from the 30-foot stop to the surface. If the tender had a previous hyperbaric exposure in the previous 18 hours, an additional 20 minutes of oxygen breathing is required prior to ascent.

## Treatment Table 5 Depth/Time Profile

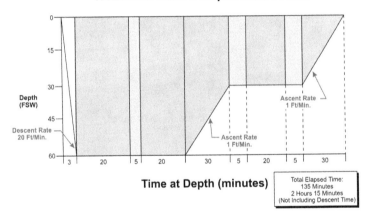

## Treatment Table 6

1. Descent rate - 20 ft/min.

2. Ascent rate - Not to exceed 1 ft/min. Do not compensate for slower ascent rates. Compensate for faster rates by halting the ascent.

3. Time on oxygen begins on arrival at 60 feet.

4. If oxygen breathing must be interrupted because of CNS Oxygen Toxicity, allow 15 minutes after the reaction has entirely subsided and resume schedule at point of interruption (see paragraph 17-8.10.1.1).

5. Table 6 can be lengthened up to 2 additional 25-minute periods at 60 feet (20 minutes on oxygen and 5 minutes on air), or up to 2 additional 75-minute periods at 30 feet (15 minutes on air and 60 minutes on oxygen), or both.

6. Tender breathes 100 percent $O_2$ during the last 30 min. at 30 fsw and during ascent to the surface for an unmodified table or where there has been only a single extension at 30 or 60 feet. If there has been more than one extension, the $O_2$ breathing at 30 feet is increased to 60 minutes. If the tender had a hyperbaric exposure within the past 18 hours an additional 60-minute $O_2$ period is taken at 30 feet.

## Treatment Table 6 Depth/Time Profile

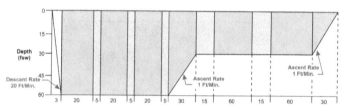

**Time at Depth (minutes)**

Total Elapsed Time:
285 Minutes
4 Hours 45 Minutes
(Not Including Descent Time)

# Treatment Table 6A

1. Descent rate - 20 ft/min.

2. Ascent rate - 165 fsw to 60 fsw not to exceed 3 ft/min, 60 fsw and shallower, not to exceed 1 ft/min. Do not compensate for slower ascent rates. Compensate for faster rates by halting the ascent.

3. Time at treatment depth does not include compression time.

4. Table begins with initial compression to depth of 60 fsw. If initial treatment was at 60 feet, up to 20 minutes may be spent at 60 feet before compression to 165 fsw. Contact a Undersea Medical Officer.

5. If a chamber is equipped with a high-O₂ treatment gas, it may be administered at 165 fsw and shallower, not to exceed 3.0 ata O₂ in accordance with paragraph 17-8.9. Treatment gas is administered for 25 minutes interrupted by 5 minutes of air. Treatment gas is breathed during ascent from the treatment depth to 60 fsw.

6. Deeper than 60 feet, if treatment gas must be interrupted because of CNS oxygen toxicity, allow 15 minutes after the reaction has entirely subsided before resuming treatment gas. The time off treatment gas is counted as part of the time at treatment depth. If at 60 feet or shallower and oxygen breathing must be interrupted because of CNS oxygen toxicity, allow 15 minutes after the reaction has entirely subsided and resume schedule at point of interruption (see paragraph 17-8.10.1.1).

7. Table 6A can be lengthened up to 2 additional 25-minute periods at 60 feet (20 minutes on oxygen and 5 minutes on air), or up to 2 additional 75-minute periods at 30 feet (60 minutes on oxygen and 15 minutes on air), or both.

8. Tender breathes 100 percent O₂ during the last 60 minutes at 30 fsw and during ascent to the surface for an unmodified table or where there has been only a single extension at 30 or 60 fsw. If there has been more than one extension, the O₂ breathing at 30 fsw is increased to 90 minutes. If the tender had a hyperbaric exposure within the past 18 hours, an additional 60 minute O₂ breathing period is taken at 30 fsw.

9. If significant improvement is not obtained within 30 minutes at 165 feet, consult with a Undersea Medical Officer before switching to Treatment Table 4.

## Treatment Table 6A Depth/Time Profile

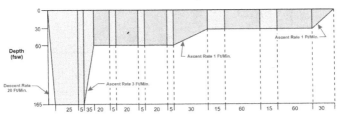

**Time at Depth (minutes)**

Total Elapsed Time:
350 Minutes
5 Hours 50 Minutes
(Not Including Descent Time)

# Treatment Table 4

1. Descent rate - 20 ft/min.

2. Ascent rate - 1 ft/min.

3. Time at 165 feet includes compression.

4. If only air is available, decompress on air. If oxygen is available, patient begins oxygen breathing upon arrival at 60 feet with appropriate air breaks. Both tender and patient breathe oxygen beginning 2 hours before leaving 30 feet. (see paragraph 17-6.5).

5. Ensure life-support considerations can be met before committing to a Table 4. (see paragraph 17-8.3) Internal chamber temperature should be below 85° F.

6. If oxygen breathing is interrupted, no compensatory lengthening of the table is required.

7. If switching from Treatment Table 6A or 3 at 165 feet, stay a maximum of 2 hours at 165 feet before decompressing.

8. If the chamber is equipped with a high-$O_2$ treatment gas, it may be administered at 165 fsw, not to exceed 3.0 ata $O_2$. Treatment gas is administered for 25 minutes interrupted by 5 minutes of air.

## Treatment Table 4 Depth/Time Profile

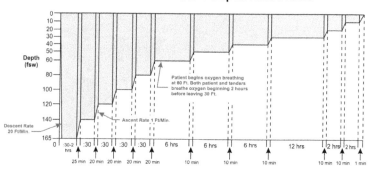

**Time at Depth**

Total Elapsed Time:
39 Hours 6 Minutes
(30 Minutes at 165 fsw) to
40 Hours 36 Minutes
(2 Hours at 165 fsw)

# Treatment Table 7

1. Table begins upon arrival at 60 feet. Arrival at 60 feet is accomplished by initial treatment on Table 6, 6A or 4. If initial treatment has progressed to a depth shallower than 60 feet, compress to 60 feet at 20 ft/min to begin Table 7.

2. Maximum duration at 60 feet is unlimited. Remain at 60 feet a minimum of 12 hours unless overriding circumstances dictate earlier decompression.

3. Patient begins oxygen breathing periods at 60 feet. Tender need breathe only chamber atmosphere throughout. If oxygen breathing is interrupted, no lengthening of the table is required.

4. Minimum chamber $O_2$ concentration is 19 percent. Maximum $CO_2$ concentration is 1.5 percent SEV (11.4 mmHg). Maximum chamber internal temperature is 85°F (paragraph 17-8.3).

5. Decompression starts with a 2-foot upward excursion from 60 to 58 feet. Decompress with stops every 2 feet for times shown in profile below. Ascent time between stops is approximately 30 seconds. Stop time begins with ascent from deeper to next shallower step. Stop at 4 feet for 4 hours and then ascend to the surface at 1 ft/min.

6. Ensure chamber life-support requirements can be met before committing to a Treatment Table 7.

7. A Undersea Medical Officer should be consulted before committing to this treatment table.

## Treatment Table 7 Depth/Time Profile

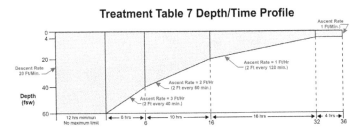

### Time at Depth (hours)

# Treatment Table 8

1. Enter the table at the depth which is exactly equal to or next greater than the deepest depth attained in the recompression. The descent rate is as fast as tolerable.

2. The maximum time that can be spent at the deepest depth is shown in the second column. The maximum time for 225 fsw is 30 minutes; for 165 fsw, 3 hours. For an asymptomatic diver, the maximum time at depth is 30 minutes for depths exceeding 165 fsw and 2 hours for depths equal to or shallower than 165 fsw.

3. Decompression is begun with a 2-fsw reduction in pressure if the depth is an even number. Decompression is begun with a 3-fsw reduction in pressure if the depth is an odd number. Subsequent stops are carried out every 2 fsw. Stop times are given in column three. The stop time begins when leaving the previous depth. Ascend to the next stop in approximately 30 seconds.

4. Stop times apply to all stops within the band up to the next quoted depth. For example, for ascent from 165 fsw, stops for 12 minutes are made at 162 fsw and at every two-foot interval to 140 fsw. At 140 fsw, the stop time becomes 15 minutes. When traveling from 225 fsw, the 166-foot stop is 5 minutes; the 164-foot stop is 12 minutes. Once begun, decompression is continuous. For example, when decompressing from 225 feet, ascent is not halted at 165 fsw for 3 hours. However, ascent may be halted at 60 fsw and shallower for any desired period of time.

5. While deeper than 165 fsw, a helium-oxygen mixture with 16-36 percent oxygen may be breathed by mask to reduce narcosis. A 64/36 helium-oxygen mixture is the preferred treatment gas. At 165 fsw and shallower, a $HeO_2$ or $N_2O_2$ mix with a $ppO_2$ not to exceed 3.0 ata may be given to the diver as a treatment gas. At 60 fsw and shallower, pure oxygen may be given to the divers as a treatment gas. For all treatment gases ($HeO_2$, $N_2O_2$, and $O_2$), a schedule of 25 minutes on gas and 5 minutes on chamber air should be followed for a total of four cycles. Additional oxygen may be given at 60 fsw after a 2-hour interval of chamber air. See Treatment Table 7 for guidance. If high $O_2$ breathing is interrupted, no lengthening of the table is required.

6. To avoid loss of the chamber seal, ascent may be halted at 4 fsw and the total remaining stop time of 240 minutes taken at this depth. Ascend directly to the surface upon completion of the required time.

7. Total ascent time from 225 fsw is 56 hours, 29 minutes. For a 165-fsw recompression, total ascent time is 53 hours, 52 minutes, and for a 60-fsw recompression, 36 hours, 0 minutes.

| Depth (fsw) | Max Time at Initial Treatment Depth (hours) | 2-fsw Stop Times (minutes) |
|---|---|---|
| 225 | 0.5 | 5 |
| 165 | 3 | 12 |
| 140 | 5 | 15 |
| 120 | 8 | 20 |
| 100 | 11 | 25 |
| 80 | 15 | 30 |
| 60 | Unlimited | 40 |
| 40 | Unlimited | 60 |
| 20 | Unlimited | 120 |

# Treatment Table 9

1. Descent rate - 20 ft/min.

2. Ascent rate - 20 ft/min. Rate may be slowed to 1 ft/min depending upon the patient's medical condition.

3. Time at 45 feet begins on arrival at 45 feet.

4. If oxygen breathing must be interrupted because of CNS Oxygen Toxicity, oxygen breathing may be restarted 15 minutes after all symptoms have subsided. Resume schedule at point of interruption (see paragraph 17-8.10.1.1).

5. Tender breathes 100 percent $O_2$ during last 15 minutes at 45 feet and during ascent to the surface regardless of ascent rate used.

6. Patient may breathe air or oxygen during ascent.

7. If patient cannot tolerate oxygen at 45 feet, this table can be modified to allow a treatment depth of 30 feet. The oxygen breathing time can be extended to a maximum of 3 to 4 hours.

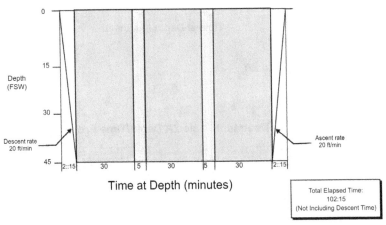

Treatment Table 9 Depth/Time Profile

Depth (FSW)

Descent rate 20 ft/min

Ascent rate 20 ft/min

Time at Depth (minutes)

Total Elapsed Time:
102:15
(Not Including Descent Time)

## Air Treatment Table 1A

1. Descent rate - 20 ft/min.
2. Ascent rate - 1 ft/min.
3. Time at 100 feet includes time from the surface.

### Treatment Table 1A Depth/Time Profile

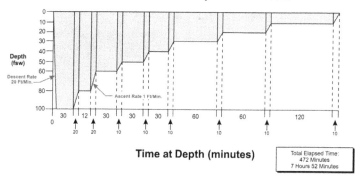

**Time at Depth (minutes)**

Total Elapsed Time:
472 Minutes
7 Hours 52 Minutes

## Air Treatment Table 2A

1. Descent rate - 20 ft/min.
2. Ascent rate - 1 ft/min.
3. Time at 165 feet includes time from the surface.

### Treatment Table 2A Depth/Time Profile

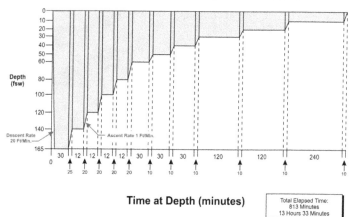

**Time at Depth (minutes)**

Total Elapsed Time:
813 Minutes
13 Hours 33 Minutes

# Air Treatment Table 3

1. Descent rate - 20 ft/min.

2. Ascent rate - 1 ft/min.

3. Time at 165 feet-includes time from the surface.

## Treatment Table 3 Depth/Time Profile

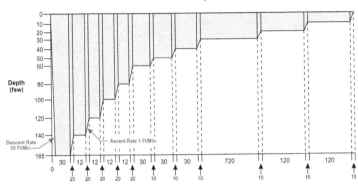

**Time at Depth (minutes)**

Total Elapsed Time:
1293 Minutes
21 Hours 33 Minutes

# SECTION 14
# Neurological Examination
# and Extremity Strength Testing

The neurological exam and extremity strength test are the primary methods we use to determine whether neurological deficit exists in a diver stricken with DCS or AGE. While nearly 60% of DCS cases are considered Type I with no neurological involvement, we must have a method to definitively state there is no neuro-involvement in the Type I cases and to identify and locate any deficit found in Type II cases. Typically, a deficit is more likely to be noticed in the extremity strength test than the neurological exam. Evidence of deficit in either requires that the stricken diver be treated for Type II DCS or AGE and establishes a baseline to determine the degree of improvement during treatment.

A debate has been ongoing for years as to the need for patient history (including the dive profile) in regards to hyperbaric treatment of pressure-related illness. Treatment for pressure-related illness is symptom-based, but there are cases in which the history can help to explain the patient's response to a given treatment protocol or even explain residual symptoms. Most hyperbaric physicians will want to see the patient's history, so even if you are inclined to disagree with the need, record it.

Treatment is not delayed for a neurological exam, but the initial assessment can take place while the crew is mustering and readying the chamber and medical equipment. The initial assessment will usually indicate the nature of the problem (whether Type I or Type II DCS). In the case of AGE, there is usually no question, and no time for an initial assessment. In other cases, for the initial assessment, the stricken diver is questioned about his or her symptoms. The DMT or other diving crew member assessing the diver should watch closely (while the diver is questioned and while the diver walks to the chamber) for the following:

- Is the diver having difficulty understanding questions, concentrating or remembering?

- Does the diver appear to be unusually irritable or moody?

- Are the diver's pupils equally sized? Do they track smoothly?

- Is the diver having difficulty with speech or enunciating words?

- Is there evidence of hearing difficulty or vision problems? (look for a squint)

- Is the diver experiencing balance problems? (unsteady on feet, stumbling gait)

The above observations are an excellent initial check for neurological problems. They will give a good indication of the following: mental status, balance/coordination, motor coordination, and sensory ability. The only information not gained here is regarding the reflexes. Make careful note of any and all deficiencies. The following questions should be asked while the above observations are made:

*If pain is the only symptom presenting, determine the following:*

1. Describe the pain (sharp, dull, throbbing).

2. In what area of the body is the pain?

3. Is the pain localized or hard to pinpoint?

4. Is the pain fixed or radiating?

5. When did the diver first notice the pain (prior to, during, or after the dive)?

*If symptoms other than localized pain are presenting, determine the following:*

1. Describe the symptoms (dizziness, vertigo, radiating pain, abnormal sensation, nausea, etc).

2. Is the diver feeling unusually fatigued for the amount of effort expended on the dive?

3. How long after the dive were the symptoms first noticed?

If the symptom was first noticed during the dive, determine if it was during descent, on bottom, during the ascent, or on decompression stops. Are the symptoms remaining the same or worsening with passing time? Are any additional symptoms developing? Has the diver ever experienced similar symptoms? Does the diver have any underlying medical conditions that might explain the symptoms? Has the diver ever suffered from DCS or AGE in the past?

If any symptoms other than localized pain presented, or if the initial assessment indicated any deficit, the remainder of the neuro exam and extremity strength test should be performed once the diver has been recompressed to 60 fsw. Details of the dive (depth, bottom time, profile) will be obtained from the dive control and may be recorded after blow down. The following forms may be used to record the results of the neurological exam and extremity strength test.

## NEUROLOGICAL EXAMINATION CHECKLIST

(Sheet 1 of 2)

(See text of Appendix 5A for examination procedures and definitions of terms.)

Patient's Name: _____ Date/Time: _____

Describe pain/numbness: _____

_____

### HISTORY

Type of dive last performed: _____ Depth: _____ How long: _____

Number of dives in last 24 hours: _____

Was symptom noticed before, during or after the dive? _____

If during, was it while descending, on the bottom or ascending? _____

Has symptom increased or decreased since it was first noticed? _____

Have any other symptoms occurred since the first one was noticed? _____

Describe: _____

Has patient ever had a similar symptom before? _____ When: _____

_____

### MENTAL STATUS/STATE OF CONSCIOUSNESS

_____

_____

**COORDINATION**

Walk: _____

Heel-to Toe: _____

Romberg: _____

Finger-to-Nose: _____

Heel Shin Slide: _____

Rapid Movement: _____

**CRANIAL NERVES**

Sense of Smell (I): _____

Vision/Visual Fld (II): _____

Eye Movements, Pupils (III, IV, VI): _____

Facial Sensation, Chewing (V): _____

Facial Expression Muscles (VII): _____

Hearing (VIII): _____

Upper Mouth, Throat Sensation (IX): _____

Gag & Voice (X): _____

Shoulder Shrug (XI): _____

Tongue (XII): _____

**STRENGTH (Grade 0 to 5)**

**UPPER BODY**

| | | |
|---|---|---|
| Deltoids | L _____ | R _____ |
| Latissimus | L _____ | R _____ |
| Biceps | L _____ | R _____ |
| Triceps | L _____ | R _____ |
| Forearms | L _____ | R _____ |
| Hand | L _____ | R _____ |

**LOWER BODY**

**HIPS**

| | | |
|---|---|---|
| Flexion | L _____ | R _____ |
| Extension | L _____ | R _____ |
| Abduction | L _____ | R _____ |
| Adduction | L _____ | R _____ |

**KNEES**

| | | |
|---|---|---|
| Flexion | L _____ | R _____ |
| Extension | L _____ | R _____ |

**ANKLES**

| | | |
|---|---|---|
| Dorsiflexion | L _____ | R _____ |
| Plantarflexion | L _____ | R _____ |

**TOES**

L _____ R _____

**Figure 5A-1a.** Neurological Examination Checklist (sheet 1 of 2).

Source: *U.S. Navy Diving Manual Revision 7*

# NEUROLOGICAL EXAMINATION CHECKLIST

(Sheet 2 of 2)

**REFLEXES**

(Grade: Normal, Hypoactive, Hyperactive, Absent)

| | | |
|---|---|---|
| Biceps | L _____ | R _____ |
| Triceps | L _____ | R _____ |
| Knees | L _____ | R _____ |
| Ankles | L _____ | R _____ |

Sensory Examination for Skin Sensation
(Use diagram to record location of sensory abnormalities – numbness, tingling, etc.)

**LOCATION**

Indicate results
as follows:

||| Painful
Area

≡ Decreased
Sensation

**COMMENTS**

_____
_____
_____
_____
_____
_____
_____
_____
_____

Examination Performed by: _____

**Figure 5A-1b.** Neurological Examination Checklist (sheet 2 of 2).

Source: *U.S. Navy Diving Manual Revision 7*

**Table 5A-1.** *Extremity Strength Tests.*

| Test | Procedure |
|------|-----------|
| Deltoid Muscles | The patient raises his arm to the side at the shoulder joint. The examiner places a hand on the patient's wrist and exerts a downward force that the patient resists. |
| Latissimus Group | The patient raises his arm to the side. The examiner places a hand on the underside of the patient's wrist and resists the patient's attempt to lower his arm. |
| Biceps | The patient bends his arm at the elbow, toward his chest. The examiner then grasps the patient's wrist and exerts a force to straighten the patient's arm. |
| Triceps | The patient bends his arm at the elbow, toward his chest. The examiner then places his hand on the patient's forearm and the patient tries to straighten his arm. |
| Forearm Muscles | The patient makes a fist. The examiner grips the patient's fist and resists while the patient tries to bend his wrist upward and downward. |
| Hand Muscles | • The patient strongly grips the examiner's extended fingers.<br>• The patient extends his hand with the fingers widespread. The examiner grips two of the extended fingers with two of his own fingers and tries to squeeze the patient's two fingers together, noting the patient's strength of resistance. |
| Lower Extremity Strength | • The patient walks on his heels for a short distance. The patient then turns around and walks back on his toes.<br>• The patient walks while squatting (duck walk).<br><br>These tests adequately assesses lower extremity strength as well as balance and coordination. If a more detailed examination of lower extremity strength is desired, testing should be accomplished at each joint as in the upper arm. |

***In the following tests, the patient sits on a solid surface such as a desk, with feet off the floor.***

| Test | Procedure |
|------|-----------|
| Hip Flexion | The examiner places his hand on the patient's thigh to resist as the patient tries to raise his thigh. |
| Hip Extension | The examiner places his hand on the underside of the patient's thigh to resist as the patient tries to lower his thigh. |
| Hip Abduction | The patients sits as above, with knees together. The examiner places a hand on the outside of each of the patient's knees to provide resistance. The patient tries to open his knees. |
| Hip Adduction | The patient sits as above, with knees apart. The examiner places a hand on the inside of each of the patient's knees to provide resistance. The patient tries to bring his knees together. |
| Knee Extension | The examiner places a hand on the patient's shin to resist as the patient tries to straighten his leg. |
| Knee Flexion | The examiner places a hand on the back of the patient's lower leg to resist as the patient tries to pull his lower leg to the rear by flexing his knee. |
| Ankle Dorsiflexion (ability to flex the foot toward the rear) | The examiner places a hand on top of the patient's foot to resist as the patient tries to raise his foot by flexing it at the ankle. |
| Ankle Plantarflexion (ability to flex the foot downward) | The examiner places a hand on the bottom of the patient's foot to resist as the patient tries to lower his foot by flexing it at the ankle. |
| Toes | • The patient stands on tiptoes for 15 seconds<br>• The patient flexes his toes with resistance provided by the examiner. |

Source: *U.S. Navy Diving Manual Revision 7*

# FORM FOR EXTREMITY STRENGTH TEST

| EXTREMITY STRENGTH TEST RESULTS | | | | |
|---|---|---|---|---|
| Test Performed | Left Side Normal /Abnormal | | Right Side Normal/Abnormal | |
| Deltoid Muscles | | | | |
| Latissimus Group | | | | |
| Biceps | | | | |
| Triceps | | | | |
| Forearm Muscles | | | | |
| Hand Muscles | | | | |
| Lower Extremity Strength | | | | |
| Hip Flexion Upward | | | | |
| Hip Flexion Downward | | | | |
| Hip Abduction | | | | |
| Hip Adduction | | | | |
| Knee Extension | | | | |
| Knee Flexion | | | | |
| Ankle Dorsiflexion (flex foot toward rear) | | | | |
| Ankle Plantarflexion (flex foot downward) | | | | |
| Toes | | | | |
| Additional comments: | | | | |
| Patient Name: | | | | |
| Examination performed by: Date: | | | | |

Source: Author

If time permits, extremity strength tests are best performed on deck due to limited space in most offshore chambers. However, if the chamber and all personnel are ready and it is apparent that Type II symptoms are presenting, it is not advisable to delay recompression to perform the extremity strength test. Most components of the test can be performed in the chamber.

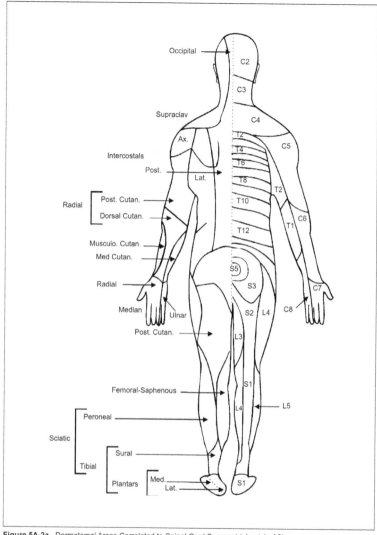

**Figure 5A-2a.** Dermatomal Areas Correlated to Spinal Cord Segment (sheet 1 of 2).

Source: *U.S. Navy Diving Manual Revision 7*

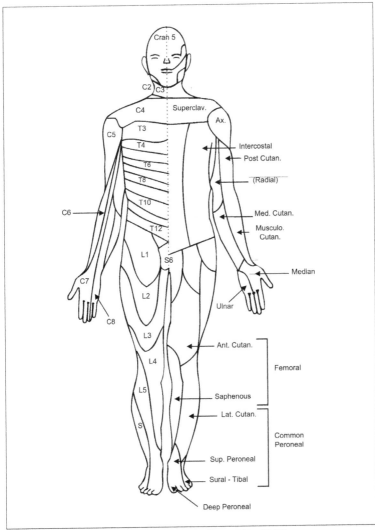

**Figure 5A-2b.** Dermatomal Areas Correlated to Spinal Cord Segment (sheet 2 of 2).

Source: *U.S. Navy Diving Manual Revision 7*

**Table 5A-2.** *Reflexes.*

| Test | Procedure |
|------|-----------|
| Biceps | The examiner holds the patient's elbow with the patient's hand resting on the examiner's forearm. The patient's elbow should be slightly bent and his arm relaxed. The examiner places his thumb on the patient's biceps tendon, located in the bend of the patient's elbow. The examiner taps his thumb with the percussion hammer, feeling for the patient's muscle to contract. |
| Triceps | The examiner supports the patient's arm at the biceps. The patient's arm hangs with the elbow bent. The examiner taps the back of the patient's arm just above the elbow with the percussion hammer, feeling for the muscle to contract. |
| Knee | The patient sits on a table or bench with his feet off the deck. The examiner taps the patient's knee just below the kneecap, on the tendon. The examiner looks for the contraction of the quadriceps (thigh muscle) and movement of the lower leg. |
| Ankle | The patient sits as above. The examiner places slight pressure on the patient's toes to stretch the Achilles' tendon, feeling for the toes to contract as the Achilles' tendon shortens (contracts). |

Source: *U.S. Navy Diving Manual Revision 7*

## RAPID NEURO EXAM (4 MINUTE NEURO)

The following pages contain the Rapid Neuro Exam used by the Canadian Navy. It is recommended by the Undersea & Hyperbaric Medical Society, and typically can be performed on deck while the chamber is being made ready. It can be performed in only 4 minutes, but all of the major indicators of neurological involvement are covered.

### Four-Minute Neuro

Patient's Name: _____

Place: _____    Date: _____

Time: _____

| HEAD AND NECK | Normal | Abnormal |
|---------------|--------|----------|
| Orientation *(time, person, place)* | _____ | _____ |
| Visual Acuity *(count fingers; ask about double vision)* | _____ | _____ |
| Visual Fields *(bring fingers from behind patient's head)* | _____ | _____ |
| Pupils equal and reactive to light | _____ | _____ |
| Eye movement *("H" pattern; nystagmus)* | _____ | _____ |
| Clench teeth *(check jaw muscles)* | _____ | _____ |
| Furrow brow | _____ | _____ |

Shut eyes tight
*(check muscles above and below eyes)* _____  _____

Check hearing/noises _____  _____

Smile or grimace _____  _____

Swallow _____  _____

Protrude tongue *(check for deviation to one side)* _____  _____

Shrug shoulders
*(apply force both shoulders; check resistance)* _____  _____

| **SENSATION** | **Normal** | **Abnormal** |
|---|---|---|
| Ask if any unusual sensation | _____ | _____ |

Sensation (draw fingernails from both hands simultaneously; inside and out, along length, and across opposing sides of the following)

Check sensation of:

| checks | _____ | _____ |
|---|---|---|
| forehead | _____ | _____ |
| lower jaw | _____ | _____ |
| arms | _____ | _____ |
| trunk | _____ | _____ |
| back | _____ | _____ |
| legs | _____ | _____ |
| Sensation same on both sides | _____ | _____ |

| **MOTOR FUNCTION** | **Normal** | **Abnormal** |
|---|---|---|
| Finger squeezes bilaterally | _____ | _____ |
| Thumbs up and down, resist pushing arms together and apart | _____ | _____ |

Flexion and extension:

| hip | _____ | _____ |
|---|---|---|
| knee | _____ | _____ |
| ankle | _____ | _____ |
| Plantar Reflex (Babinski) *(toes down = normal)* | _____ | _____ |

Source: Canadian Navy Fleet Diving Unit

# SECTION 15
## Chamber Operation, Care, and Maintenance

The deck decompression chamber is considered a piece of emergency equipment. Even if it is not used in daily diving operations, it is imperative to maintain it in a constant state of readiness. This applies to all aspects of the chamber: cleanliness, gas supplies and delivery systems, gauge calibration, pressure vessel integrity, testing, and certification.

### CLEANING

The two reasons we perform regular cleaning of a chamber are to maintain a healthy environment for the diver and for fire prevention. The chamber environment is usually damp, and mold will readily grow if the unit is not kept clean. Dust has been proven in the past to have been the cause of fires in oxygen-rich environments. Thorough and regular cleaning will keep the chamber a healthy and safe environment.

For chamber interior wash-down, the best product to use is tri-sodium phosphate (TSP) mixed in warm water, followed by a warm water rinse. If the chamber is not used daily, it must be washed down before use. If it is used daily, it should be washed down at least twice per week. View ports should be cleaned with water only. BIBS masks should be removed while washing the chamber, cleaned, inspected, and replaced. BIBS masks may be cleaned with isopropyl alcohol, a dettol-water solution, or commercially available BIBS wipes.

### CHAMBER OPERATION

It is recommended that a daily checklist be performed prior to each shift to ensure that the chamber is clean and ready and all systems are tested. A sample daily checklists are provided in this section.

The interior of the chamber is considered a foreign material exclusion (FME) zone. Only those materials and products approved for use in a hyperbaric environment may enter beyond the transfer lock manway.

FME can be a matter of life and death. For example, a butane cigarette lighter accidently dropped from a shirt pocket in the chamber will mean certain death for chamber occupants (and probably the operator) if it is not removed prior to pressurization. All personnel entering the chamber (even for maintenance and cleaning) must remove footwear, empty pockets, and remove any dirty clothing or coveralls. All mattresses, blankets, pillows, etc must be chamber safe. Clothing worn by occupants must be chamber safe (100% cotton).

The internal temperature of the chamber should be maintained between 70°F and 85°F. Temperatures above 85°F are too hot for the occupant to undergo treatment, therefore that is the maximum interior temperature you will want to allow at any time. Temperatures below 70°F will chill the occupant in longer exposures and affect the occupant's ability to off-gas at a proper rate. If the chamber is containerized, the A/C unit or heater should be in operation in time to have the interior temperature in the proper zone prior to occupants entering. If the chamber is not containerized, a cover should be erected to shield the unit from the sun. Ventilation will lower the internal temperature, and blankets or burlap laid over the outer shell and soaked with water will help as well. A climate-controlled sea-container or enclosure is preferable, and it will also make FME easier.

The breathing or treatment gas delivery pressure must be maintained at a level high enough to avoid excessive work-of-breathing for the occupant, while staying below the maximum for the BIBS system. The most commonly used BIBS are the Scott Pressure-Vac II. This system requires a delivery pressure between 110 and 125 psi. The operator should check the OEM specifications for other brands of BIBS masks. Once the delivery pressure is set, the free-flow adjustment (dial-a-breath) on the BIBS mask should be turned out until it free flows, then back a quarter turn until it just stops. To use BIBS deeper than 60 fsw, a back-pressure regulator must be installed on the overboard dump line (inside the penetrator). Using BIBS without this regulator deeper than 60 fsw puts the occupant on BIBS in danger.

It is important for the chamber operator to watch the occupant(s) during blow-down (pressurization of the chamber). If the occupant cannot equalize, the blow-down will have to stop. There is a contingency plan for this, known as the "Safe Way Out" provided for the US Navy Tables. The Safe Way Out is detailed in this handbook. (See Section 1: Using the *USN Revision 7* Decompression Tables.)

Foot traffic should be kept clear of the control panel of the chamber. During operations, only the personnel required to be present should be allowed in the area. The chamber operator must not allow himself or herself to become distracted. The depth (internal pressure) should be maintained with as little fluctuation as possible. The oxygen level of the chamber environment should be maintained in the 20-22% range. It should never be allowed to drop below 19% or climb above 25%.

Ventilation will control the oxygen level. Any dropping of internal pressure not caused by temperature change or ventilation should be noted, and if significant, will justify a pressure/leak test. Ventilation to remove $CO_2$ is not as critical in units equipped with a scrubber, unless the occupants are performing work such as CPR. Ventilation will be required in these cases and will obviously be required if running deep treatment tables on air. The ventilation rates are as follows: 3 scfm for each occupant at rest; and 6 scfm for each occupant performing strenuous activity (such as CPR). The formula to calculate flow rates for ventilation is as follows:

$$R = \frac{V \times 18}{T \times \frac{(P + 33)}{33}}$$

Where:
R = Chamber ventilation rate
V = Chamber volume in cubic feet
T = Time (in seconds) to change chamber pressure by 10 fsw
P = Chamber pressure (gauge) in feet seawater

Once the ventilation rate is established using the above formula, mark the valve positions. Ventilation is best performed by opening the inlet valve to the marked position and controlling the vent with the exhaust valve only. Once the required ventilation is performed, the two valves are shut simultaneously.

Travel rates are as defined by the table being used, but should the operator find that the travel rate is lagging, do not increase the travel rate toward the end of the travel period to "catch up." Adjust the time on the dive sheet to match the actual travel time. This applies not only to travel between stops but also on travel to surface from the final chamber stop.

The operator should monitor the occupant(s) regularly to ensure that all is well, watching for any signs of oxygen toxicity. It should be noted that a slight twitching of the lips and facial muscles is quite common when on BIBS at depth and should not be considered in itself to be a sign or symptom of oxygen toxicity.

Once the chamber has surfaced, the operator should have the occupants unplug the BIBS masks and remove them for cleaning. If any of the chamber bedding is damp, it should be removed for drying at this time as well. Chamber maintenance should follow a regular schedule. Daily maintenance should be performed at the start of the shift, whereas weekly can often be performed on a weather day. Most offshore operations are required to perform IMCA DO23 or DO24 audits, and most, if not all of the items on the six-monthly maintenance, will be addressed in these audits. The following checklists are provided for a pattern and will help ensure nothing is missed during maintenance.

| Daily Chamber Maintenance Checklist | |
|---|---|
| Chamber clean and free of odors | |
| Chamber free of unnecessary equipment | |
| Door seals inspected, in good condition and lightly lubricated with $O_2$ safe lube | |
| Primary air supply topped up and ready; regulators set | |
| Backup air supply topped up and ready; regulators set | |
| Chamber drain valves closed (and zip–tied) on both locks | |
| Gag valves open; overpressure relief valves visually inspected | |
| Supply and inlet valves function tested on both locks | |
| Exhaust valves function tested on both locks | |
| Gauges function tested, zero set, and comparison checked on both locks | |
| Medical oxygen and treatment gas supplies checked | |
| All BIBS function tested and cleaned | |
| Chamber communications function–tested | |
| Sound–powered phones function–tested | |
| Firefighting system or extinguisher checked | |
| Mattress, blankets, and pillows dry and in chamber | |
| Lighting system checked | |
| Waste bucket in chamber | |
| Chamber internal medical kit in chamber | |

| Weekly Chamber Maintenance Checklist | |
|---|---|
| Inner lock cleaned out and scrubbed down (with TSP or mild non–ionic detergent) | |
| Entrance lock cleaned out and scrubbed down | |
| Door dogs and hinges inspected, lubricated if required | |
| Chamber internal medical kit contents checked | |
| Chamber trauma kit contents checked | |
| Medical lock function–tested (including equalization gauges) | |
| Chamber lighting function–tested | |
| Chamber communications function tested | |
| Sound–powered phones function–tested | |
| Function test gag valves on overpressure relief valves | |

| Six Month and Annual Chamber Maintenance Checklist | |
|---|---|
| Check for in–date chamber gauge calibration (required twice per year) | |
| Pressure/Leak test (bi–annually or when chamber is relocated or viewports removed) | |
| Visually inspect condition of exterior paint – repaint as required | |
| Visually inspect condition of interior paint (chips or missing paint require re–painting) | |
| Visually inspect all chamber thru–hull penetrators | |
| Visually inspect all viewports | |
| Remove, clean, replace, and lubricate door seals | |
| Function–test all chamber systems including medical lock | |
| Verify that all components of both medical kits with a shelf life are in–date | |
| Verify that a copy of flowcharts and treatment tables are with the chamber | |

The following is the pressure/leak test procedure for deck decompression chambers as found in the *U.S. Navy Diving Manual*. The USN test is the universally accepted standard.

**Decompression Chamber Pressure/Leak Test**

| STEP | REQUIRED OPERATION |
|------|-------------------|
| 1 | Close the inner door of chamber, and pressurize inner lock to 100 fsw. Snoop all penetrators, welds, viewports, door seals, valves, fittings, and pipe joints. |
| 2 | Mark all leaks. Depressurize chamber and adjust, repair, or replace chamber components as necessary to eliminate leaks. |
| 3 | Repeat steps 1 and 2 above as necessary until all leaks are eliminated. |
| 4 | Pressurize chamber to 225 fsw and hold (adding air as required) for 5 minutes. Disregard small leaks (champagne bubbles) at this pressure. |
| 5 | Depressurize the chamber to 165 fsw. Hold for 1 hour (do not add air). If pressure drops below 145 fsw in 1 hour, locate and mark leaks. Depressurize the chamber and repair according to step 2. Repeat procedure until chamber pressure holds above 145 fsw. |
| 6 | Repeat steps 1 through 5 with the inner door open. Leak test only the outer lock of the chamber. |

**Notes:**

1. This pressure/leak test should be performed on the initial installation, when relocated, after any repairs, after view port replacement, and /or at two-year intervals.

2. When locating leaks, use only non-ionic detergent in potable water as a detection agent. Rinse viewports with clean water after leak testing.

3. If leaks are found on a weld, do not perform repairs in the field. Do not perform weld repairs on the chamber without the authorization of the equipment manager.

Below is a sample form that may be used to properly record the results of the chamber pressure/leak test.

The pressure/leak test is the perfect time to test the gauges by comparison (if they have not been recently calibrated). The form that follows will allow you to record the results of the comparison test. A copy of the completed form should stay near the chamber panel. Any significant deviation in gauge readings will obviously require changing gauges. Note: Gauges should not require tapping to achieve a correct reading; sticking gauges should be replaced at the earliest opportunity.

## Decompression Chamber Gauge Comparison Test

| TEST GAUGE READING | INNER LOCK GAUGE READING | OUTER LOCK GAUGE READING |
|---|---|---|
| 10 fsw | | |
| 20 fsw | | |
| 30 fsw | | |
| 40 fsw | | |
| 50 fsw | | |
| 60 fsw | | |
| 70 fsw | | |
| 80 fsw | | |
| 90 fsw | | |
| 100 fsw | | |
| 110 fsw | | |
| 120 fsw | | |
| 130 fsw | | |
| 140 fsw | | |
| 150 fsw | | |
| 160 fsw | | |
| 165 fsw | | |

Chamber serial number:

PVHO number:

Test Gauge serial no:                    I/L gauge serial no:

O/L gauge serial no:

Date:                                    Vessel and location:

Technician:                              Supervisor:

Comments:

## CHAMBER SAFETY GUIDELINES

- Never allow petroleum or any petroleum product to enter the chamber.

- Do not allow any flammable substances to enter the chamber.

- Do not use oil on oxygen or air fittings, valves, regulators, or gauges.

- Never permit the chamber to be used for gear storage or as a bunkhouse.

- Do not allow footwear to be worn inside the chamber.

- Do not permit diving suits of any kind to be worn in the chamber.

- Have all personnel in street clothes empty pockets before entering the entrance lock of the chamber.

- Do not allow cell phones or other electronics to enter the chamber.

- Check door seals and door dogs on a regular basis (daily).

- Do not allow doors to remain dogged after blow down.

- Maintain medical oxygen supply for BIBS system between 110-125 psig delivery pressure.

- Perform a checklist at the start of every shift as a chamber operator.

- When operating chamber, do not allow yourself to be distracted.

- Look in on the chamber occupant often, watching for symptoms of CNS oxygen toxicity.

- If the occupant cannot be viewed for any reason, employ an inside tender.

- If a single occupant is in the chamber for $O_2$ treatment or decompression, the mask must be held in place and the head harness not fastened.

- Do not perform repairs or modifications to the chamber unless you are qualified and authorized to do so.

- Always practice good chamber maintenance.

# SECTION 16
# Oxygen Safety

Oxygen, when combined with many other substances under pressure will promote very rapid burning and/or explosion. Many people are aware of this when it comes to petroleum or other products containing hydrocarbons. But common dust, if allowed to accumulate in an oxygen valve or hose, can burn or explode. Using the wrong type of hose to transport oxygen can also cause an explosion. Unfortunately, common sense is not enough when it comes to the safe use of high-pressure (HP) oxygen. What you don't know, can hurt you. By following these simple rules, you can avoid trouble:

- Any gas analyzed at 25% oxygen or above is treated the same as pure oxygen.

- Crack it first. Always "crack" the valve on oxygen cylinders before installing regulators or manifolds. This will help blow any foreign material out of the valve.

- Use the proper regulator. Oxygen regulators must be bagged and tagged "Oxygen Service–Oxygen Cleaned."

- Use the proper piping. HP oxygen should be routed through Tungum or 316 stainless piping, not normal stainless steel, brass, or copper. All piping and valves must be $O_2$ cleaned prior to use.

- Use the proper valves. High pressure oxygen valves must be needle valves. Never use ball valves on HP oxygen. LP valves should be needle valves as well, but ball valves are allowed for LP low-flow applications. If using ball valves, they should be marked "open slowly."

- Never use oil or grease on any oxygen line, valve, gauge, or fitting– high or low pressure.

- When working on oxygen systems, clean all wrenches and tools off with degreaser before you proceed with the work. Make absolutely sure oil and grease are cleaned off the tools.

- Never use oxygen regulators or hoses to transport any gas other than oxygen.

- Keep oxygen hoses to a minimum. Use hard pipe whenever possible.

- Only use certified "$O_2$ Safe" hose to transport oxygen. It should be "Synflex" or an equivalent.

- If oxygen equipment has been contaminated by hydrocarbons, do not use it until it has been $O_2$ cleaned and inspected.

- Use the "Bag and Tag" system. Once oxygen equipment has been inspected and found $O_2$ clean, keep it sealed in an airtight bag until use. All oxygen equipment should be stored in sealed bags when not in use, with a tag stating, "Oxygen Service–Oxygen Cleaned."

## OXYGEN CLEANING

Any and all components used in oxygen storage and delivery (from the cylinder to the mask) must be kept $O_2$ clean. As well, any breathing gas with an oxygen percentage 25% or higher is treated the same as pure, 100% oxygen. The intent of this section is not to teach proper oxygen cleaning but as a refresher for those who have been previously trained in oxygen cleaning.

In the past, oxygen cleaning was often done with dishwashing detergent and hot potable water. Now there are various products available for oxygen cleaning marketed under different names (Simple Green, Blue Gold, Biox). To establish the best product to use, talk to your local industrial gas supplier. They do more oxygen cleaning than you will ever have to do, and they know the products that are locally available. Before using these cleaners, carefully read the safety data sheets and find out what precautions you must take, if any, when using them. Remember: All breathing-gas systems must be flushed twice with potable water after cleaning and blown dry with clean, oil-free breathing gas.

Most cleaning products require any hard piping to be filled with the cleaning fluid and left to stand for one hour before it is purged, then flushed with potable water twice and purged again. With deck whips, hoses, and umbilicals, the cleaning fluid is usually left to stand for 10 minutes before flushing and purging. It is recommended that the directions for the cleaning product used be followed exactly as presented, staying as close as possible to the prescribed temperatures and times specified.

When preparing for Nitrox or in-water $O_2$ decompression operations, ensure that all components of the system are $O_2$ cleaned. This includes the storage cylinders, pigtails, king valves, regulators, high-pressure and low-pressure deck whips, panel plumbing, gauges, valves, umbilicals, diver's helmets, bailout bottles, contents gauges, test gauges, and bailout regulators. Typically, helmets and regulators are disassembled, cleaned in an ultrasonic wash, checked with black light, and re-assembled without lubricants. To inspect the equipment to ensure that it is $O_2$ clean, use ultraviolet (black) light. Most problem areas will show up easily under UV light. Oxygen cleaning should always be done in a sterile environment.

# SECTION 17:
# Nitrox Operations

In recent years, a new mode of diving has emerged called nitrox (represented as $N_2O_2$). Although it is sometimes called oxygen-enriched air, nitrox is in fact a mixed gas since it is not atmospheric air, and the breathing medium must be mixed prior to its use. The theory behind nitrox is to decrease the percentage of nitrogen in air, which maximizes no decompression bottom time and reduces the decompression time required after dives. This is accomplished either by removing nitrogen from or adding oxygen to breathing quality air, thereby reducing the partial pressure of the inert gas, nitrogen.

Varying mixes are used, from 75/25 to 60/40. 50/50 is used as a treatment gas in chambers. Nitrox is becoming more widely used in our industry, particularly in depths between 50 and 110 fsw. Nitrox is most useful in the range between 40 and 80 fsw. The advantages and disadvantages are as follows:

## Advantages of Nitrox
- Extended bottom times without decompression
- Reduced decompression required for longer dives
- Reduced residual nitrogen after dives
- Reduced risk of DCS
- Reduced nitrogen narcosis on the deeper end

## Disadvantages of Nitrox
- Increased risk of CNS oxygen toxicity
- Special equipment required for mixing
- Special cleaning required for equipment used
- Long dives can result in pulmonary oxygen toxicity
- More expensive than air diving
- Maximum depth of 110 fsw

Pressurized oxygen requires special safety measures, and any mixture with above 25% oxygen content is considered pure oxygen. The two mixtures most commonly used in commercial work are 60/40 (0–80 fsw) and 68/32 (80–110 fsw). Both of these mixes have more than 25% oxygen, so both require the same treatment and safety measures as 100% oxygen.

**All equipment used in nitrox diving operations must be oxygen cleaned. This includes cylinders, deck whips, panels, regulators, umbilicals, bailouts, and helmets. Failure to follow oxygen cleaning and safety guidelines may result in explosion and fire, causing injury or death.**

The oxygen in any given breathing mixture does not factor into decompression; it is the partial pressure of the inert gas that determines decompression based on bottom time at a given depth. To calculate the required decompression for a nitrox mixture, we find the depth on atmospheric air that has the same partial pressure of nitrogen (equivalent air depth) and follow the air diving table for that depth, whether it is a standard air or surface decompression table. For example, using a 68/32 mix on a dive to 63 fsw, the $ppN_2$ is 2.0 ATA, and using atmospheric air, the $ppN_2$ at 50 fsw is 2.0 ATA, so the equivalent air depth (EAD) is 50 fsw on a 32% dive to 63 fsw. The formula for calculating EAD is as follows:

$$EAD = \frac{(1 - O_2\%) \ (D + 33)}{0.79} - 33$$

Where:
EAD = Equivalent Air Depth
$O_2\%$ = the oxygen percentage of the gas blend expressed as a decimal
D = the depth (in fsw) of the diver breathing the gas blend

The table that follows allows for quick determination of the EAD without having to perform the calculations. The depth of the proposed dive is read on the far left column (blue), the row is followed across horizontally to line up with the oxygen percentage in the nitrox mix (read across the top in green), and the resulting number is the EAD. For example, a proposed dive will be to 66 fsw, using a 60/40 mix. The EAD for this dive will be 43 fsw, so decompression follows the USN 50 FSW Air Decompression Table.

A real concern in nitrox diving is the partial pressure of oxygen at depth. Because of the elevated oxygen percentages, the partial pressures are very high, particularly at the deeper depths for each mixture. The universally accepted cutoff for partial pressure of oxygen is 1.4 ATA. This is reflected on the EAD table: the lower right corner is in red, with no equivalent air depths given. When using nitrox, it is necessary to have an in-line oxygen analyzer on the panel and to be alert for signs of CNS oxygen toxicity when diving at the higher partial pressures.

**Equivalent Air Depth Table**

| Depth (fsw) | Oxygen Percentage in Breathing Media | | | | | | | | |
|---|---|---|---|---|---|---|---|---|---|
| | 32 | 34 | 36 | 38 | 40 | 42 | 44 | 46 | 48 |
| 20 | 13 | 12 | 10 | 9 | 8 | 6 | 5 | 4 | 2 |
| 22 | 15 | 13 | 12 | 11 | 9 | 8 | 6 | 5 | 4 |
| 24 | 17 | 15 | 14 | 12 | 11 | 9 | 8 | 6 | 5 |
| 26 | 18 | 17 | 15 | 14 | 12 | 11 | 9 | 8 | 6 |
| 28 | 20 | 18 | 17 | 15 | 14 | 12 | 11 | 9 | 8 |
| 30 | 22 | 20 | 18 | 17 | 15 | 14 | 12 | 11 | 9 |
| 32 | 23 | 22 | 20 | 18 | 17 | 15 | 14 | 12 | 10 |
| 34 | 25 | 23 | 22 | 20 | 18 | 17 | 15 | 13 | 12 |
| 36 | 27 | 25 | 23 | 22 | 20 | 18 | 16 | 15 | 13 |
| 38 | 29 | 27 | 25 | 23 | 21 | 20 | 18 | 16 | 14 |
| 40 | 30 | 28 | 27 | 25 | 23 | 21 | 19 | 17 | 16 |
| 42 | 32 | 30 | 28 | 26 | 24 | 23 | 21 | 19 | 17 |
| 44 | 34 | 32 | 30 | 28 | 26 | 24 | 22 | 20 | 18 |
| 46 | 35 | 33 | 31 | 29 | 27 | 25 | 23 | 21 | 19 |
| 48 | 37 | 35 | 33 | 31 | 29 | 27 | 25 | 23 | 21 |
| 50 | 39 | 37 | 35 | 33 | 30 | 28 | 26 | 24 | 22 |
| 52 | 41 | 38 | 36 | 34 | 32 | 30 | 28 | 26 | 23 |
| 54 | 42 | 40 | 38 | 36 | 33 | 31 | 29 | 27 | 25 |
| 56 | 44 | 42 | 40 | 37 | 35 | 33 | 31 | 28 | 26 |
| 58 | 46 | 43 | 41 | 39 | 37 | 34 | 32 | 30 | 27 |
| 60 | 47 | 45 | 43 | 40 | 38 | 36 | 33 | 31 | 29 |
| 62 | 49 | 47 | 44 | 42 | 40 | 37 | 35 | 32 | 30 |
| 64 | 51 | 48 | 46 | 44 | 41 | 39 | 36 | 34 | |
| 66 | 53 | 50 | 48 | 45 | 43 | 40 | 38 | 35 | |
| 68 | 54 | 52 | 49 | 47 | 44 | 42 | 39 | | |
| 70 | 56 | 53 | 51 | 48 | 46 | 43 | 40 | | |

| Depth (fsw) | Oxygen Percentage in Breathing Media | | | | | | | | |
|---|---|---|---|---|---|---|---|---|---|
| | 32 | 34 | 36 | 38 | 40 | 42 | 44 | 46 | 48 |
| 72 | 58 | 55 | 53 | 50 | 47 | 45 | | | |
| 74 | 60 | 57 | 54 | 51 | 49 | 46 | | | |
| 76 | 61 | 58 | 56 | 53 | 50 | 48 | | | |
| 78 | 63 | 60 | 57 | 54 | 52 | | | | |
| 80 | 65 | 62 | 59 | 56 | 53 | | | | |
| 82 | 66 | 63 | 61 | 58 | 55 | | | | |
| 84 | 68 | 65 | 62 | 59 | | | | | |
| 86 | 70 | 67 | 64 | 61 | | | | | |
| 88 | 72 | 68 | 65 | 62 | | | | | |
| 90 | 73 | 70 | 67 | | | | | | |
| 92 | 75 | 72 | 69 | | | | | | |
| 94 | 77 | 74 | 70 | | | | | | |
| 96 | 78 | 75 | | | | | | | |
| 98 | 80 | 77 | | | | | | | |
| 100 | 82 | 79 | | | | | | | |
| 102 | 84 | 80 | | | | | | | |
| 104 | 85 | | | | | | | | |
| 106 | 87 | | | | | | | | |
| 108 | 89 | | | | | | | | |
| 110 | 91 | | | | | | | | |
| 112 | | | | | | | | | |

Nitrox operations require special procedures and equipment. They are as follows:

- Oxygen analyzer on the panel for diver's breathing mixture
- Two independent supplies of nitrox for each working diver
- Diver's bailout to contain the same nitrox blend used for the dive
- Supply whips and panel plumbing oxygen cleaned
- Diver's umbilical and helmet oxygen cleaned
- Diver's bailout bottle and regulator oxygen cleaned

### Mixing Nitrox ($N_2O_2$)

Mixing $N_2O_2$ onsite is significantly cheaper than buying pre-packaged gas. There are a few methods of mixing nitrox: oil-less HP compressor with an oxygen injection system; oil-less HP compressor with a molecular sieve; LP compressor with a nitrox membrane; and high-pressure (HP) mixing using breathable compressed air and medical oxygen. HP mixing, also known as partial-pressure mixing, tends to be used most often offshore, and that is the method reviewed herein.

Oxygen must be handled with care during mixing, and only $O_2$ cleaned equipment can be used. When mixing gas in a cylinder (or even in a sat bell or chamber for oxygen makeup) often one gas will drop and the other rise, not mixing initially, but gradually mixing over time. This condition is known as stratification or layering. To avoid stratification in a sat system, saturation divers sometimes wave towels to help mix the gas. The larger the area over which the two gases are exposed to one another, the better they will mix. Cylinders or quads are laid down horizontally, which gives a greater area of exposure for the two gases to mix.

Blending takes time, so the nitrox is not used for at least 24 hours after mixing, and the oxygen percentage is tested before and during use with an oxygen analyzer. Mixing gas involves working with high-pressure gases. It also involves working with 100% oxygen under high pressure. Because of this, there are safety precautions that must be followed every time. These safety precautions are as follows:

- Never pump or attempt to compress oxygen other than with an industry-approved gas transfer pump, certified clean for oxygen service.

- Ensure all hoses and fittings used are oxygen clean and approved for oxygen transfer.

- Ensure that the cylinders or quads used to mix and store the mixture are oxygen clean.

- Always cascade the oxygen first, metering flow with the valve on the oxygen cylinder.

- When opening valves, stand to one side and look away.

- Wear all personal protective equipment when gas mixing.

- Test the breathing air source regularly with Draeger tubes for oil mist.

When starting to mix the gas, cascade the oxygen first. It is recommended that there be at least 200 psi of $N_2O_2$ or breathing air in the mixing quad before adding the oxygen. This helps to reduce the risk of adiabatic compression temperature increase, which can have disastrous consequences. Control the flow with a metering valve or the king valve on the oxygen quad and not the king valve on the mixing quad. Once the correct amount of oxygen has been cascaded, close the oxygen valve first, then the valve on the mixing quad. Then add breathing air as required to bring the mixing quad up to final pressure.

Keep the mix cylinders lying horizontal to avoid stratification, and do not use the mix for at least 24 hours. Once the mixing operation is complete, ensure that the nitrox cylinders are clearly marked for content, showing the percentage of nitrogen and oxygen (i.e., $N_2O_2$ 68/32) and the date and time it was blended. Variations of +2% in oxygen content are typically accepted. The following gas mixing sheet will provide the pressures required to blend the gases.

**Manual Gas Mixing Sheet**

| Initial Mix | $N_2O_2$ | PSI | PSI $O_2$ | PSI $N_2$ | PSI to add |
|---|---|---|---|---|---|
| | 1 | 2 | 3 | 4 | |
| | | | | | |
| | | | 11 | | 12 |
| | | | | | |
| | | | 10 | 9 | 13 |
| | | | | | |

| Desired Mix | 5 | 6 | 7 | 8 | |
|---|---|---|---|---|---|
| | | | | | |

This mixing sheet will aid in calculating exactly how much breathing air and how much medical oxygen to add (in psi) to end up with any given nitrox mixture. The steps below explain how to use the mixing sheet. Once the all of the steps have been followed, check the math, then follow the calculation check to ensure that all of the figures are correct.

## STEP-BY-STEP INSTRUCTIONS FOR GAS MIXING SHEET

| Box | Box Entry |
|---|---|
| 1. | Enter initial mix percentages (i.e.,60/40) |
| 2. | Enter psi of initial mix |
| 3. | Enter psi of $O_2$ in initial mix by multiplying psi from Box 2 by percentage and divide the answer by 10 |
| 4. | Enter psi of $N_2$ in initial mix by Box 3 from Box 2 |
| 5. | Enter desired mix, using percentages (i.e., 60/40) |
| 6. | Enter psi of desired mix |
| 7. | Enter psi of $O_2$ in desired mix by multiplying psi from Box 6 by the $O_2$ content and divide the answer by 100 |
| 8. | Enter psi of $N_2$ in desired mix by deducting Box 7 from Box 6 |
| 9. | Enter result of Box 8 minus Box 4 |
| 10. | Enter the result of Box 9 multiplied by 21 and divided by 79 |
| 11. | Enter the result of Box 7 less total of boxes 3 and 10 |
| 12. | Enter the result from Box 11 |
| 13. | Enter the sum of boxes 9 and 10 |

The figure in Box 12 is the amount of oxygen (pdi) to cascade into the mixture. The figure in Box 13 is the amount of breathing air (psi) to cascade into the mixture.

## CHECK THE FIGURES

Providing that the following are true, the gas mixture is correct:

a. Boxes 2, 12, and 13 equal Box 6

b. Boxes 3, 10, and 11 equal Box 7

c. Boxes 4 and 9 equal Box 8

After allowing the mix to settle for 24 hours, test the oxygen percentage with an oxygen analyzer. Always use an oxygen analyzer on the panel while running surface supplied nitrox. Oxygen analyzers are required to be accurate within 0.5% and typically are calibrated onsite using calibration gas.

**WARNING:** DO NOT EXCEED THE DEEPEST RECOMMENDED DEPTH FOR EACH NITROX MIX. DOING SO PUTS THE DIVER AT RISK FOR CNS OXYGEN TOXICITY OCCURING AT DEPTH, WITH A HIGH PROBABILITY OF FATAL RESULTS. ALWAYS CHECK THE PERCENTAGES BEFORE USING THE MIXTURE. ALWAYS USE AN OXYGEN ANALYZER WHEN USING MIXED GAS. ALWAYS HAVE THE SAME MIXTURE IN THE BAILOUT THAT IS RUNNING THROUGH THE PANEL.

### Oxygen Toxicity

Oxygen toxicity is a factor that must be considered with nitrox ($N_2O_2$). As a general rule, CNS oxygen toxicity is a threat to the diver any time the partial pressure of oxygen ($ppO_2$) approaches or exceeds 1.6 ATA. Breathing atmospheric air, the diver can exceed 218 fsw before this becomes an issue. By comparison, when breathing a 60/40 blend, the $ppO_2$ hits 1.6 ATA at 99 fsw and when breathing a 68/32 blend, the 1.6 ATA threshold is reached at 132 fsw. To reduce the risk, most commercial operations do not exceed 1.4 ATA on the in-water working portions of diving operations.

The included EAD table has a 1.4 ATA cut-off built in. Pulmonary oxygen toxicity is a more common problem with nitrox. Although it seldom results in death, pulmonary oxygen toxicity does damage the lungs, leading to a marked decrease in pulmonary function. Long duration dives (in excess of 300 minutes bottom time) should be avoided when the $ppO_2$ is above 1.0 ATA.

The effects of pulmonary toxicity are cumulative. In addition to that, some in the diving medical community now believe that repeated long exposures to high partial pressures of oxygen lead to disbaric osteo-necrosis (bone necrosis), which for years was assumed to be the result of exposure to high partial pressures of inert gas, nitrogen in particular. Long duration dives and multiple repetitive dives with high $ppO_2$ should be avoided in any case.

# SECTION 18
## Using the DCIEM Helium-Oxygen Tables

The DCIEM helium-oxygen tables were developed in the same manner as the air tables in that test subjects were monitored using the Doppler ultrasound bubble detector while testing the tables. The tables were designed using an 84/16 $HeO_2$ mixture, with a limit of 1.6 ATA on the partial pressure of oxygen in the normal range and a limit of 1.8 ATA in the exceptional exposure range. The tables can be used with any $HeO_2$ mixture with an $O_2$ percentage of 16 or above, provided that the $ppO_2$ at depth does not exceed 1.6 ATA for 30 minutes. The following tables are provided for $HeO_2$ operations:

- Table 6  Abort Table

- Table 7  In-Water Oxygen Decompression

- Table 8  Surface Decompression Using Oxygen

- Table 9  Emergency Decompression

The **Abort Table (Table 6)** is to be used for dives that do not achieve a maximum depth greater than 120 fsw. This table provides the ability to abort the dive using both no-decompression and decompression modes, depending on the bottom time. All decompression stops in the Abort Table are air stops. Any time the diver's depth exceeds 120 fsw, the In-Water O₂ Decompression or Surface Decompression Using Oxygen Table is used.

TABLE 6 DCIEM Helium–Oxygen Abort Table

| Depth (fsw) | Bottom Time (min) | Max Time to 1st Stop | STOP TIMES AT VARIOUS DEPTHS IN MINUTES Breathing Air | | | | | | | | Total Decomp Time (min) |
|---|---|---|---|---|---|---|---|---|---|---|---|
| | | | 80 | 70 | 60 | 50 | 40 | 30 | 20 | 10 | |
| 30 | 55 | 1 | | | | | | | | | 1 |
| 40 | 20 | 1 | | | | | | | | | 1 |
| | 30 | 1 | | | | | | | | 3 | 4 |
| | 40 | 1 | | | | | | | | 12 | 13 |
| 50 | 13 | 1 | | | | | | | | | 1 |
| | 20 | 1 | | | | | | | | 4 | 5 |
| | 30 | 1 | | | | | | | | 12 | 13 |
| 60 | 10 | 1 | | | | | | | | | 1 |
| | 20 | 1 | | | | | | | | 7 | 8 |
| | 25 | 1 | | | | | | | 2 | 13 | 16 |
| | 30 | 1 | | | | | | | 3 | 16 | 20 |
| 70 | 8 | 2 | | | | | | | | | 2 |
| | 12 | 1 | | | | | | | | 5 | 6 |
| | 20 | 1 | | | | | | | 3 | 11 | 15 |
| | 30 | 1 | | | | | | | 6 | 19 | 26 |
| 80 | 6 | 2 | | | | | | | | | 2 |
| | 10 | 2 | | | | | | | | 6 | 8 |
| | 15 | 1 | | | | | | | 3 | 7 | 11 |
| | 20 | 1 | | | | | | | 5 | 14 | 20 |
| | 25 | 1 | | | | | | | 7 | 18 | 26 |
| 90 | 5 | 2 | | | | | | | | | 2 |
| | 10 | 2 | | | | | | | | 8 | 10 |
| | 15 | 2 | | | | | | | 5 | 10 | 17 |
| | 20 | 1 | | | | | | 2 | 6 | 16 | 25 |
| 100 | 5 | 2 | | | | | | | | | 2 |
| | 10 | 2 | | | | | | | 3 | 7 | 12 |
| | 15 | 2 | | | | | | 2 | 5 | 13 | 22 |
| 110 | 5 | 2 | | | | | | | | | 2 |
| | 10 | 2 | | | | | | | 4 | 7 | 13 |
| | 15 | 2 | | | | | | 3 | 6 | 14 | 25 |
| 120 | 5 | 2 | | | | | | | | | 2 |
| | 10 | 2 | | | | | | | 6 | 7 | 15 |

The **In-Water Oxygen Decompression Table (Table 7)** is one of two options provided. Close examination of the in-water air stop times compared with the surface decompression table will indicate that all in-water air stops are identical in both tables. This allows the decision to be made to shift to surface decompression mode at any point during the dive.

**TABLE 7 DCIEM HeO₂ In–Water Oxygen Decompression**

| Depth (fsw) | Bottom Time (min) | Max Time to 1st Stop | STOP TIMES AT VARIOUS DEPTHS IN MINUTES | | | | | | | | | | | O₂ | Decomp Time (min) |
| --- | --- | --- | --- | --- | --- | --- | --- | --- | --- | --- | --- | --- | --- | --- | --- |
| | | | Breathing Air | | | | | | | | | | | | |
| | | | 140 | 130 | 120 | 110 | 100 | 90 | 80 | 70 | 60 | 50 | 40 | 30 | |
| 120 | 10 | 2 | | | | | | | | | | | | 7 | 10 |
| | 20 | 2 | | | | | | | | | | | 3 | 22 | 28 |
| | 30 | 2 | | | | | | | | | | 2 | 4 | 30* | 44 |
| | 40 | 2 | | | | | | | | | | 4 | 5 | 47* | 64 |
| | 50 | 1 | | | | | | | | | 2 | 4 | 7 | 60** | 85 |
| | 60 | 1 | | | | | | | | | 3 | 4 | 11 | 72** | 102 |
| | 70 | 1 | | | | | | | | | 3 | 7 | 13 | 82** | 117 |
| | 75 | 1 | | | | | | | | | 4 | 9 | 13 | 85** | 123 |
| | Exceptional Exposure: Emergency Use Only | | | | | | | | | | | | | | |
| | 80 | 1 | | | | | | | | | 4 | 11 | 13 | 89** | 129 |
| | 90 | 1 | | | | | | | | 1 | 4 | 14 | 18 | 90*** | 144 |
| | 100 | 1 | | | | | | | | 2 | 8 | 13 | 24 | 90*** | 154 |
| 130 | 10 | 2 | | | | | | | | | | | | 7 | 10 |
| | 20 | 2 | | | | | | | | | | 1 | 4 | 24 | 32 |
| | 30 | 2 | | | | | | | | | 1 | 3 | 4 | 31* | 47 |
| | 40 | 2 | | | | | | | | | 2 | 4 | 5 | 55* | 74 |
| | 50 | 2 | | | | | | | | | 3 | 5 | 9 | 67** | 97 |
| | 60 | 1 | | | | | | | | 1 | 4 | 6 | 12 | 79** | 114 |
| | 70 | 1 | | | | | | | | 2 | 8 | 13 | 24 | 88** | 129 |
| | Exceptional Exposure: Emergency Use Only | | | | | | | | | | | | | | |
| | 80 | 1 | | | | | | | | 3 | 4 | 13 | 17 | 90*** | 144 |
| | 90 | 1 | | | | | | | | 3 | 10 | 11 | 25 | 91*** | 157 |
| | 95 | 1 | | | | | | | | 4 | 11 | 11 | 28 | 92*** | 163 |

## TABLE 7 DCIEM HeO$_2$ In–Water Oxygen Decompression

| Depth (fsw) | Bottom Time (min) | Max Time to 1st Stop | 140 | 130 | 120 | 110 | 100 | 90 | 80 | 70 | 60 | 50 | 40 | O$_2$ 30 | Decomp Time (min) |
|---|---|---|---|---|---|---|---|---|---|---|---|---|---|---|---|
| | 10 | 2 | | | | | | | | | | | | 10 | 13 |
| | 15 | 2 | | | | | | | | | | | 3 | 20 | 26 |
| | 20 | 2 | | | | | | | | | | 3 | 3 | 26 | 35 |
| | 30 | 2 | | | | | | | | | 2 | 4 | 4 | 38* | 56 |
| | 40 | 2 | | | | | | | | 1 | 3 | 4 | 7 | 60** | 88 |
| | 50 | 2 | | | | | | | | 2 | 4 | 4 | 12 | 73** | 108 |
| 140 | 60 | 2 | | | | | | | | 3 | 4 | 9 | 12 | 85** | 126 |
| | 65 | 2 | | | | | | | | 3 | 4 | 11 | 13 | 90** | 134 |
| | Exceptional Exposure: Emergency Use Only |||||||||||||||
| | 70 | 1 | | | | | | | 1 | 3 | 5 | 12 | 14 | 90*** | 142 |
| | 80 | 1 | | | | | | | 1 | 4 | 9 | 11 | 24 | 91*** | 157 |
| | 90 | 1 | | | | | | | 2 | 4 | 12 | 15 | 28 | 94*** | 172 |
| | 10 | 2 | | | | | | | | | | | 1 | 13 | 17 |
| | 15 | 2 | | | | | | | | | | 2 | 3 | 22 | 30 |
| | 20 | 2 | | | | | | | | | 1 | 3 | 4 | 28 | 39 |
| | 25 | 2 | | | | | | | | | 2 | 4 | 4 | 31* | 49 |
| | 30 | 2 | | | | | | | | 1 | 3 | 4 | 4 | 46* | 66 |
| | 35 | 2 | | | | | | | | 2 | 3 | 4 | 6 | 58* | 81 |
| | 40 | 2 | | | | | | | | 2 | 4 | 4 | 9 | 63** | 95 |
| 150 | 45 | 2 | | | | | | | | 3 | 4 | 4 | 11 | 72** | 107 |
| | 50 | 2 | | | | | | | 1 | 3 | 4 | 6 | 12 | 80** | 119 |
| | 55 | 2 | | | | | | | 1 | 4 | 4 | 8 | 12 | 86** | 128 |
| | 60 | 2 | | | | | | | 2 | 3 | 4 | 11 | 13 | 90*** | 141 |
| | Exceptional Exposure: Emergency Use Only |||||||||||||||
| | 80 | 2 | | | | | | | 3 | 3 | 8 | 11 | 21 | 92*** | 156 |
| | 90 | 2 | | | | | | | 3 | 4 | 11 | 14 | 28 | 95*** | 173 |
| | 95 | 1 | | | | | | 1 | 3 | 7 | 10 | 17 | 30 | 96*** | 181 |

## TABLE 7 DCIEM HeO₂ In-Water Oxygen Decompression

| Depth (fsw) | Bottom Time (min) | Max Time to 1st Stop | STOP TIMES AT VARIOUS DEPTHS IN MINUTES Breathing Air | | | | | | | | | | | O₂ | Decomp Time (min) |
|---|---|---|---|---|---|---|---|---|---|---|---|---|---|---|---|
| | | | 140 | 130 | 120 | 110 | 100 | 90 | 80 | 70 | 60 | 50 | 40 | 30 | |
| 160 | 10 | 2 | | | | | | | | | | | 2 | 15 | 20 |
| | 15 | 2 | | | | | | | | | | 3 | 3 | 23 | 32 |
| | 20 | 2 | | | | | | | | | 2 | 3 | 4 | 30* | 42 |
| | 25 | 2 | | | | | | | | 1 | 3 | 3 | 4 | 36* | 55 |
| | 30 | 2 | | | | | | | | 2 | 3 | 4 | 5 | 52* | 74 |
| | 35 | 2 | | | | | | | | 3 | 3 | 5 | 7 | 60** | 91 |
| | 40 | 2 | | | | | | | 1 | 3 | 4 | 4 | 10 | 70** | 105 |
| | 45 | 2 | | | | | | | 2 | 3 | 4 | 6 | 11 | 79** | 118 |
| | 50 | 2 | | | | | | | 2 | 4 | 4 | 8 | 12 | 86** | 129 |
| | 55 | 2 | | | | | | | 3 | 3 | 5 | 10 | 13 | 90*** | 142 |
| | Exceptional Exposure: Emergency Use Only | | | | | | | | | | | | | | |
| | 60 | 2 | | | | | | 1 | 3 | 3 | 7 | 10 | 15 | 91*** | 148 |
| | 70 | 2 | | | | | | 2 | 3 | 4 | 10 | 11 | 27 | 95*** | 170 |
| | 80 | 2 | | | | | | 2 | 4 | 8 | 9 | 19 | 31 | 98*** | 189 |
| 170 | 10 | 2 | | | | | | | | | | | 3 | 16 | 23 |
| | 15 | 2 | | | | | | | | | 1 | 3 | 4 | 25 | 36 |
| | 20 | 2 | | | | | | | | 1 | 2 | 4 | 4 | 30* | 49 |
| | 25 | 2 | | | | | | | | 2 | 3 | 4 | 4 | 43* | 64 |
| | 30 | 2 | | | | | | | 1 | 3 | 3 | 4 | 6 | 59* | 84 |
| | 35 | 2 | | | | | | | 2 | 3 | 3 | 4 | 9 | 66** | 100 |
| | 40 | 2 | | | | | | | 3 | 3 | 3 | 6 | 10 | 76** | 114 |
| | 45 | 2 | | | | | | 1 | 3 | 3 | 4 | 7 | 12 | 84** | 127 |
| | 50 | 2 | | | | | | 1 | 3 | 3 | 5 | 9 | 13 | 90*** | 142 |
| | Exceptional Exposure: Emergency Use Only | | | | | | | | | | | | | | |
| | 55 | 2 | | | | | | 2 | 3 | 3 | 7 | 10 | 15 | 91*** | 149 |
| | 60 | 2 | | | | | | 2 | 3 | 4 | 8 | 11 | 21 | 94*** | 161 |
| | 65 | 2 | | | | | | 3 | 3 | 5 | 9 | 11 | 28 | 96*** | 173 |
| | 70 | 2 | | | | | | 3 | 4 | 6 | 10 | 15 | 30 | 97*** | 183 |
| | 75 | 2 | | | | | 1 | 3 | 3 | 9 | 9 | 21 | 33 | 98*** | 195 |

## TABLE 7 DCIEM HeO₂ In−Water Oxygen Decompression

| Depth (fsw) | Bottom Time (min) | Max Time to 1st Stop | STOP TIMES AT VARIOUS DEPTHS IN MINUTES — Breathing Air | | | | | | | | | | | O₂ | Decomp Time (min) |
|---|---|---|---|---|---|---|---|---|---|---|---|---|---|---|---|---|
| | | | 140 | 130 | 120 | 110 | 100 | 90 | 80 | 70 | 60 | 50 | 40 | 30 | |
| 180 | 5 | 3 | | | | | | | | | | | | 6 | 10 |
| | 10 | 3 | | | | | | | | | | 1 | 3 | 18 | 26 |
| | 15 | 2 | | | | | | | | | 2 | 3 | 4 | 27 | 39 |
| | 20 | 2 | | | | | | | | 2 | 3 | 3 | 4 | 32* | 52 |
| | 25 | 2 | | | | | | | 1 | 3 | 3 | 4 | 3 | 50* | 72 |
| | 30 | 2 | | | | | | | 2 | 3 | 3 | 4 | 8 | 60** | 93 |
| | 35 | 2 | | | | | | 1 | 2 | 3 | 4 | 4 | 10 | 72** | 109 |
| | 40 | 2 | | | | | | 2 | 2 | 3 | 4 | 7 | 11 | 82** | 124 |
| | 45 | 2 | | | | | | 2 | 3 | 3 | 4 | 9 | 12 | 90*** | 136 |
| | 50 | 2 | | | | | | 3 | 3 | 3 | 6 | 10 | 15 | 90*** | 148 |
| *Exceptional Exposure: Emergency Use Only* | | | | | | | | | | | | | | | |
| | 55 | 2 | | | | | 1 | 3 | 3 | 4 | 7 | 11 | 20 | 94*** | 161 |
| | 60 | 2 | | | | | 1 | 3 | 3 | 5 | 9 | 11 | 28 | 96*** | 174 |
| | 65 | 2 | | | | | 2 | 3 | 3 | 7 | 9 | 16 | 31 | 98*** | 187 |
| | 70 | 2 | | | | | 2 | 3 | 4 | 8 | 10 | 21 | 35 | 99*** | 200 |
| 190 | 5 | 3 | | | | | | | | | | | | 6 | 10 |
| | 10 | 3 | | | | | | | | | | 2 | 3 | 19 | 28 |
| | 15 | 3 | | | | | | | | | 3 | 3 | 4 | 28 | 42 |
| | 20 | 2 | | | | | | | 1 | 2 | 3 | 3 | 4 | 35* | 56 |
| | 25 | 2 | | | | | | | 2 | 3 | 3 | 3 | 6 | 55* | 80 |
| | 30 | 2 | | | | | | 1 | 3 | 2 | 4 | 3 | 9 | 65** | 100 |
| | 35 | 2 | | | | | | 2 | 3 | 3 | 3 | 6 | 10 | 77** | 117 |
| | 40 | 2 | | | | | 1 | 2 | 3 | 3 | 3 | 9 | 11 | 87** | 132 |
| | 45 | 2 | | | | | 1 | 3 | 3 | 3 | 6 | 9 | 14 | 90*** | 147 |
| *Exceptional Exposure: Emergency Use Only* | | | | | | | | | | | | | | | |
| | 50 | 2 | | | | | 2 | 2 | 3 | 4 | 8 | 9 | 19 | 94*** | 159 |
| | 55 | 2 | | | | | 2 | 3 | 3 | 5 | 9 | 11 | 26 | 97*** | 174 |
| | 60 | 2 | | | | | 2 | 3 | 3 | 7 | 9 | 15 | 32 | 98*** | 188 |
| | 65 | 2 | | | | 1 | 2 | 3 | 4 | 8 | 10 | 21 | 36 | 99*** | 202 |

## TABLE 7 DCIEM HeO₂ In–Water Oxygen Decompression

| Depth (fsw) | Bottom Time (min) | Max Time to 1st Stop | 140 | 130 | 120 | 110 | 100 | 90 | 80 | 70 | 60 | 50 | 40 | O₂ 30 | Decomp Time (min) |
|---|---|---|---|---|---|---|---|---|---|---|---|---|---|---|---|
| 200 | 5 | 3 | | | | | | | | | | | | 6 | 10 |
| | 10 | 3 | | | | | | | | | | 2 | 4 | 20 | 30 |
| | 15 | 3 | | | | | | | | 1 | 3 | 3 | 4 | 30* | 45 |
| | 20 | 2 | | | | | | | 2 | 2 | 3 | 4 | 3 | 41* | 63 |
| | 25 | 2 | | | | | | 1 | 2 | 3 | 3 | 3 | 7 | 60** | 92 |
| | 30 | 2 | | | | | | 2 | 3 | 3 | 3 | 4 | 10 | 71** | 109 |
| | 35 | 2 | | | | | 1 | 2 | 3 | 3 | 3 | 8 | 10 | 82** | 125 |
| | 40 | 2 | | | | | 2 | 2 | 3 | 3 | 5 | 9 | 12 | 90*** | 144 |
| | 45 | 2 | | | | | 2 | 3 | 3 | 3 | 7 | 10 | 16 | 93*** | 155 |
| Exceptional Exposure: Emergency Use Only | | | | | | | | | | | | | | | |
| | 50 | 2 | | | | 1 | 2 | 3 | 3 | 5 | 8 | 10 | 25 | 96*** | 171 |
| | 55 | 2 | | | | 1 | 3 | 3 | 3 | 6 | 9 | 13 | 32 | 99*** | 187 |
| | 60 | 2 | | | | 2 | 2 | 3 | 4 | 8 | 9 | 21 | 36 | 100*** | 203 |
| 210 | 5 | 3 | | | | | | | | | | | | 7 | 11 |
| | 10 | 3 | | | | | | | | | 1 | 3 | 3 | 22 | 33 |
| | 15 | 3 | | | | | | | | 2 | 3 | 3 | 4 | 30* | 51 |
| | 20 | 3 | | | | | | | 2 | 3 | 3 | 3 | 4 | 47* | 71 |
| | 25 | 2 | | | | | | 2 | 2 | 3 | 4 | 2 | 9 | 60** | 95 |
| | 30 | 2 | | | | | | 1 | 2 | 3 | 3 | 6 | 10 | 75** | 116 |
| | 35 | 2 | | | | | 2 | 2 | 3 | 3 | 4 | 8 | 12 | 87** | 134 |
| | 40 | 2 | | | | | 1 | 2 | 3 | 3 | 6 | 9 | 15 | 90*** | 150 |
| Exceptional Exposure: Emergency Use Only | | | | | | | | | | | | | | | |
| | 45 | 2 | | | | 2 | 2 | 3 | 3 | 4 | 7 | 11 | 21 | 96*** | 167 |
| | 50 | 2 | | | | 2 | 2 | 3 | 4 | 5 | 9 | 12 | 30 | 98*** | 183 |
| | 55 | 2 | | | | 3 | 2 | 3 | 4 | 7 | 9 | 19 | 37 | 99*** | 201 |

Note: "STOP TIMES AT VARIOUS DEPTHS IN MINUTES" (depths 140–40 = Breathing Air; depth 30 = O₂).

TABLE 7 DCIEM HeO₂ In–Water Oxygen Decompression

| Depth (fsw) | Bottom Time (min) | Max Time to 1st Stop | STOP TIMES AT VARIOUS DEPTHS IN MINUTES Breathing Air | | | | | | | | | | | O₂ | Decomp Time (min) |
|---|---|---|---|---|---|---|---|---|---|---|---|---|---|---|---|
| | | | 140 | 130 | 120 | 110 | 100 | 90 | 80 | 70 | 60 | 50 | 40 | 30 | |
| | 5 | 4 | | | | | | | | | | | | 7 | 12 |
| | 10 | 3 | | | | | | | | | 2 | 2 | 4 | 23 | 35 |
| | 15 | 3 | | | | | | | 1 | 2 | 3 | 3 | 4 | 30* | 52 |
| | 20 | 3 | | | | | | 1 | 3 | 2 | 3 | 3 | 5 | 52* | 78 |
| | 25 | 2 | | | | | 1 | 2 | 3 | 2 | 3 | 4 | 9 | 66** | 103 |
| | 30 | 2 | | | | | 2 | 2 | 3 | 3 | 3 | 7 | 10 | 80** | 123 |
| 220 | 35 | 2 | | | | 1 | 2 | 3 | 3 | 3 | 4 | 9 | 13 | 90*** | 146 |
| | 40 | 2 | | | | 2 | 2 | 3 | 3 | 3 | 7 | 10 | 18 | 94*** | 160 |
| | Exceptional Exposure: Emergency Use Only | | | | | | | | | | | | | | |
| | 50 | 2 | | | 1 | 2 | 2 | 3 | 3 | 5 | 8 | 11 | 27 | 98*** | 178 |
| | 55 | 2 | | | 1 | 2 | 3 | 3 | 3 | 7 | 9 | 16 | 35 | 100*** | 197 |
| | 60 | 2 | | | 2 | 2 | 3 | 3 | 5 | 7 | 10 | 24 | 41 | 101*** | 216 |
| | 5 | 4 | | | | | | | | | | | | 8 | 13 |
| | 10 | 3 | | | | | | | | | 2 | 3 | 4 | 24 | 37 |
| | 15 | 3 | | | | | | | 2 | 2 | 3 | 3 | 3 | 33* | 55 |
| | 20 | 3 | | | | | | 2 | 2 | 3 | 3 | 3 | 6 | 57* | 85 |
| | 25 | 3 | | | | | 2 | 2 | 3 | 3 | 2 | 5 | 9 | 71** | 111 |
| 230 | 30 | 2 | | | | 1 | 2 | 3 | 2 | 3 | 3 | 8 | 11 | 85** | 131 |
| | 35 | 2 | | | | 2 | 2 | 3 | 3 | 2 | 7 | 8 | 15 | 90*** | 150 |
| | Exceptional Exposure: Emergency Use Only | | | | | | | | | | | | | | |
| | 40 | 2 | | | 1 | 2 | 3 | 2 | 3 | 4 | 8 | 10 | 22 | 97*** | 170 |
| | 45 | 2 | | | 2 | 2 | 2 | 3 | 3 | 7 | 8 | 13 | 33 | 99*** | 190 |
| | 50 | 2 | | | 2 | 3 | 2 | 3 | 5 | 7 | 9 | 21 | 40 | 100*** | 210 |

## TABLE 7 DCIEM HeO₂ In–Water Oxygen Decompression

| Depth (fsw) | Bottom Time (min) | Max Time to 1st Stop | STOP TIMES AT VARIOUS DEPTHS IN MINUTES | | | | | | | | | | | | Decomp Time (min) |
|---|---|---|---|---|---|---|---|---|---|---|---|---|---|---|---|
| | | | Breathing Air | | | | | | | | | | | O₂ | |
| | | | 140 | 130 | 120 | 110 | 100 | 90 | 80 | 70 | 60 | 50 | 40 | 30 | |
| 240 | 5 | 4 | | | | | | | | | | | | 8 | 13 |
| | 10 | 3 | | | | | | | | 1 | 2 | 3 | 4 | 25 | 39 |
| | 15 | 3 | | | | | | 1 | 2 | 2 | 3 | 3 | 3 | 36* | 59 |
| | 20 | 3 | | | | | 1 | 2 | 2 | 3 | 3 | 3 | 7 | 60** | 95 |
| | 25 | 3 | | | | 1 | 2 | 2 | 3 | 3 | 2 | 6 | 10 | 75** | 118 |
| | 30 | 3 | | | | 2 | 2 | 3 | 2 | 3 | 4 | 9 | 12 | 89** | 140 |
| | 35 | 2 | | | 1 | 2 | 3 | 2 | 3 | 3 | 7 | 9 | 18 | 93*** | 159 |
| | *Exceptional Exposure: Emergency Use Only* | | | | | | | | | | | | | | |
| | 40 | 2 | | | 2 | 2 | 3 | 2 | 3 | 5 | 8 | 12 | 27 | 98*** | 180 |
| | 45 | 2 | | 1 | 2 | 2 | 3 | 3 | 3 | 7 | 9 | 17 | 38 | 100*** | 203 |
| 250 | 10 | 3 | | | | | | | | 1 | 3 | 3 | 4 | 26 | 41 |
| | 15 | 3 | | | | | | 1 | 2 | 3 | 3 | 3 | 3 | 40* | 64 |
| | 20 | 3 | | | | | 2 | 2 | 2 | 3 | 3 | 3 | 8 | 61** | 98 |
| | 25 | 3 | | | | 2 | 2 | 2 | 3 | 2 | 3 | 7 | 10 | 80** | 125 |
| | 30 | 3 | | | 1 | 2 | 2 | 3 | 3 | 2 | 6 | 8 | 14 | 90*** | 150 |
| | 35 | 2 | | 1 | 1 | 2 | 3 | 2 | 3 | 4 | 7 | 10 | 22 | 96*** | 169 |
| | *Exceptional Exposure: Emergency Use Only* | | | | | | | | | | | | | | |
| | 40 | 2 | | 1 | 2 | 2 | 3 | 3 | 2 | 7 | 8 | 13 | 34 | 99*** | 192 |
| | 45 | 2 | | 2 | 2 | 2 | 3 | 2 | 6 | 7 | 9 | 22 | 41 | 101*** | 215 |

**TABLE 7 DCIEM HeO₂ In–Water Oxygen Decompression**

| Depth (fsw) | Bottom Time (min) | Max Time to 1st Stop | STOP TIMES AT VARIOUS DEPTHS IN MINUTES — Breathing Air | | | | | | | | | | | O₂ | Decomp Time (min) |
|---|---|---|---|---|---|---|---|---|---|---|---|---|---|---|---|
| | | | 140 | 130 | 120 | 110 | 100 | 90 | 80 | 70 | 60 | 50 | 40 | 30 | |
| 260 | 10 | 4 | | | | | | | | 2 | 2 | 3 | 4 | 28 | 44 |
| | 15 | 3 | | | | | | 2 | 2 | 3 | 3 | 3 | 3 | 45* | 70 |
| | 20 | 3 | | | | 1 | 2 | 2 | 2 | 3 | 3 | 3 | 9 | 65** | 104 |
| | 25 | 3 | | | 1 | 2 | 2 | 2 | 3 | 2 | 3 | 8 | 11 | 84** | 132 |
| | 30 | 3 | | 1 | 1 | 2 | 2 | 3 | 2 | 3 | 7 | 8 | 16 | 91*** | 155 |
| | Exceptional Exposure: Emergency Use Only | | | | | | | | | | | | | | |
| | 35 | 3 | | 1 | 2 | 2 | 3 | 2 | 3 | 5 | 7 | 12 | 26 | 98*** | 180 |
| | 40 | 2 | 1 | 1 | 2 | 3 | 2 | 3 | 4 | 6 | 9 | 16 | 39 | 100*** | 204 |
| 270 | 10 | 4 | | | | | | | | 1 | 2 | 2 | 3 | 29 | 46 |
| | 15 | 3 | | | | | 1 | 2 | 2 | 3 | 3 | 2 | 5 | 49* | 76 |
| | 20 | 3 | | | | 2 | 2 | 2 | 2 | 3 | 2 | 4 | 9 | 70** | 111 |
| | 25 | 3 | | | 2 | 2 | 2 | 2 | 3 | 2 | 4 | 8 | 12 | 88** | 139 |
| | 30 | 3 | | 1 | 2 | 2 | 2 | 3 | 2 | 4 | 7 | 9 | 18 | 94*** | 163 |
| | Exceptional Exposure: Emergency Use Only | | | | | | | | | | | | | | |
| | 35 | 3 | 1 | 1 | 2 | 2 | 3 | 2 | 3 | 6 | 8 | 13 | 31 | 99*** | 190 |
| | 40 | 3 | 2 | 1 | 2 | 2 | 3 | 2 | 5 | 7 | 10 | 20 | 42 | 101*** | 216 |

## TABLE 7 DCIEM $HeO_2$ In–Water Oxygen Decompression

| Depth (fsw) | Bottom Time (min) | Max Time to 1st Stop | 160 | 150 | 140 | 130 | 120 | 110 | 100 | 90 | 80 | 70 | 60 | 50 | 40 | $O_2$ 30 | Decomp Time (min) |
|---|---|---|---|---|---|---|---|---|---|---|---|---|---|---|---|---|---|
| 280 | 10 | 4 | | | | | | | | | 1 | 2 | 3 | 3 | 3 | 30* | 52 |
| | 15 | 3 | | | | | | | 2 | 2 | 2 | 2 | 3 | 3 | 6 | 53* | 82 |
| | 20 | 3 | | | | | | | 1 | 2 | 2 | 2 | 2 | 6 | 9 | 74** | 117 |
| | 25 | 3 | | | | 1 | 2 | 2 | 2 | 2 | 3 | 2 | 5 | 8 | 13 | 90*** | 149 |
| | Exceptional Exposure: Emergency Use Only | | | | | | | | | | | | | | | | |
| | 30 | 3 | | | 1 | 1 | 2 | 2 | 2 | 3 | 2 | 5 | 7 | 10 | 22 | 96*** | 172 |
| | 35 | 3 | | | 2 | 1 | 2 | 2 | 3 | 2 | 4 | 6 | 8 | 15 | 36 | 100*** | 200 |
| | 40 | 3 | | 1 | 1 | 2 | 2 | 3 | 2 | 3 | 6 | 7 | 11 | 24 | 44 | 103*** | 228 |
| 290 | 10 | 4 | | | | | | | | | 2 | 2 | 3 | 3 | 3 | 30* | 53 |
| | 15 | 3 | | | | | | 1 | 1 | 2 | 3 | 2 | 3 | 3 | 6 | 57* | 87 |
| | 20 | 3 | | | | | | 2 | 1 | 2 | 2 | 2 | 3 | 7 | 9 | 78** | 123 |
| | 25 | 3 | | | | 2 | 1 | 2 | 2 | 3 | 2 | 3 | 6 | 8 | 15 | 90*** | 153 |
| | Exceptional Exposure: Emergency Use Only | | | | | | | | | | | | | | | | |
| | 30 | 3 | | | 1 | 2 | 2 | 2 | 2 | 3 | 2 | 5 | 8 | 11 | 26 | 98*** | 181 |
| | 35 | 3 | | 1 | 1 | 2 | 2 | 2 | 3 | 2 | 5 | 6 | 9 | 18 | 40 | 101*** | 211 |
| 300 | 10 | 4 | | | | | | | | 1 | 2 | 2 | 2 | 4 | 3 | 30* | 54 |
| | 15 | 4 | | | | | | 1 | 2 | 2 | 2 | 3 | 2 | 4 | 7 | 60** | 98 |
| | 20 | 3 | | | | 1 | 1 | 2 | 2 | 2 | 3 | 2 | 3 | 7 | 11 | 81** | 129 |
| | 25 | 3 | | | 1 | 1 | 2 | 2 | 2 | 3 | 2 | 3 | 7 | 8 | 17 | 92*** | 159 |
| | Exceptional Exposure: Emergency Use Only | | | | | | | | | | | | | | | | |
| | 30 | 3 | | | 1 | 1 | 2 | 2 | 2 | 2 | 3 | 6 | 8 | 13 | 31 | 99*** | 191 |
| | 35 | 3 | | 2 | 1 | 2 | 2 | 2 | 2 | 3 | 5 | 7 | 10 | 22 | 42 | 103*** | 222 |
| 310 | Exceptional Exposure: Emergency Use Only | | | | | | | | | | | | | | | | |
| | 10 | 4 | | | | | | | | 1 | 2 | 2 | 3 | 3 | 3 | 31* | 55 |
| | 15 | 4 | | | | | | 2 | 2 | 2 | 2 | 3 | 2 | 3 | 9 | 60** | 100 |
| | 20 | 3 | | | | 1 | 2 | 2 | 2 | 2 | 2 | 3 | 3 | 8 | 11 | 85** | 135 |
| | 25 | 3 | | | 2 | 1 | 2 | 2 | 2 | 2 | 3 | 3 | 7 | 10 | 19 | 94*** | 166 |
| | 30 | 3 | | 1 | 2 | 2 | 2 | 2 | 2 | 2 | 4 | 6 | 8 | 15 | 35 | 101*** | 201 |
| | 35 | 3 | 1 | 1 | 2 | 2 | 2 | 2 | 2 | 3 | 6 | 7 | 12 | 26 | 44 | 104*** | 233 |

## TABLE 7 DCIEM HeO₂ In–Water Oxygen Decompression

| Depth (fsw) | Bottom Time (min) | Max Time to 1st Stop | STOP TIMES AT VARIOUS DEPTHS IN MINUTES Breathing Air | | | | | | | | | | | | | | O₂ 30 | Decomp Time (min) |
|---|---|---|---|---|---|---|---|---|---|---|---|---|---|---|---|---|---|---|
| | | | 160 | 150 | 140 | 130 | 120 | 110 | 100 | 90 | 80 | 70 | 60 | 50 | 40 | | |
| **320** | Exceptional Exposure: Emergency Use Only | | | | | | | | | | | | | | | | | |
| | 10 | 4 | | | | | | | | 2 | 2 | 2 | 3 | 3 | 3 | 34* | 59 |
| | 15 | 4 | | | | | | 1 | 2 | 1 | 2 | 3 | 2 | 3 | 3 | 9 | 63** | 104 |
| | 20 | 3 | | | 1 | 1 | 2 | 2 | 2 | 2 | 2 | 3 | 4 | 8 | 12 | 88** | 141 |
| | 25 | 3 | | 1 | 1 | 2 | 2 | 2 | 2 | 2 | 2 | 5 | 7 | 10 | 23 | 96*** | 174 |
| | 30 | 3 | 1 | 1 | 2 | 2 | 1 | 3 | 2 | 2 | 4 | 7 | 9 | 17 | 39 | 102*** | 211 |
| **330** | Exceptional Exposure: Emergency Use Only | | | | | | | | | | | | | | | | | |
| | 10 | 4 | | | | | | | | 2 | 2 | 2 | 3 | 3 | 3 | 36* | 61 |
| | 15 | 4 | | | | | | 2 | 1 | 2 | 2 | 2 | 3 | 2 | 5 | 9 | 67** | 110 |
| | 20 | 4 | | | 1 | 2 | 1 | 2 | 2 | 3 | 2 | 2 | 5 | 8 | 13 | 90*** | 151 |
| | 25 | 3 | | 2 | 1 | 2 | 1 | 2 | 3 | 2 | 2 | 6 | 7 | 11 | 27 | 98*** | 183 |
| | 30 | 3 | 1 | 2 | 1 | 2 | 2 | 2 | 2 | 2 | 6 | 6 | 10 | 20 | 42 | 102*** | 219 |

The **Surface Decompression Using Oxygen Table (Table 8)** is provided to allow shortening of the diver's in-water time. The procedure for Table 8 is very similar to that for Table 3 in the air tables. The difference is that the final stop before leaving the water (30 fsw) is an oxygen breathing stop. The similarities are the 7-minute surface interval, the 40-foot chamber stop depth, and 30/5 oxygen/air breathing cycles.

TABLE 8  DCIEM HeO₂ Surface Decompression Using Oxygen

| Depth (fsw) | Bottom Time (min) | Max Time to 1st Stop | 160 | 150 | 140 | 130 | 120 | 110 | 100 | 90 | 80 | 70 | 60 | 50 | 40 | O₂ 30 | Surface Interval | DDC O₂ 40 | Decomp Time (min) |
|---|---|---|---|---|---|---|---|---|---|---|---|---|---|---|---|---|---|---|---|
| **120** | 20 | 2 | | | | | | | | | | | | | 3 | 2 | | 21 | 36 |
| | 30 | 2 | | | | | | | | | | | | 2 | 4 | 4 | | 30* | 54 |
| | 40 | 2 | | | | | | | | | | | | 4 | 5 | 8 | | 50* | 81 |
| | 50 | 1 | | | | | | | | | | | 2 | 4 | 7 | 11 | | 60** | 103 |
| | 60 | 1 | | | | | | | | | | | 3 | 4 | 11 | 12 | | 71** | 120 |
| | 70 | 1 | | | | | | | | | | | 3 | 7 | 13 | 19 | Time from leaving 30 fsw water stop to 40 fsw in chamber not to exceed 7 minutes. | 73** | 134 |
| | 75 | 1 | | | | | | | | | | | 4 | 9 | 13 | 29 | | 71** | 145 |
| Exceptional Exposure: For Emergency Use Only |
| | 80 | 1 | | | | | | | | | | | 4 | 11 | 13 | 30* | | 71** | 153 |
| | 90 | 1 | | | | | | | | | | 1 | 4 | 14 | 18 | 35* | | 74** | 170 |
| | 100 | 1 | | | | | | | | | | 2 | 8 | 13 | 24 | 36* | | 76** | 183 |
| **130** | 15 | 2 | | | | | | | | | | | | | 2 | 2 | | 17 | 31 |
| | 20 | 2 | | | | | | | | | | | | 1 | 4 | 2 | | 23 | 40 |
| | 30 | 2 | | | | | | | | | | | 1 | 3 | 4 | 6 | | 35* | 63 |
| | 40 | 2 | | | | | | | | | | | 2 | 4 | 5 | 10 | | 56* | 91 |
| | 50 | 2 | | | | | | | | | | | 3 | 5 | 9 | 11 | | 67** | 114 |
| | 60 | 1 | | | | | | | | | | 1 | 4 | 6 | 12 | 16 | | 74** | 132 |
| | 70 | 1 | | | | | | | | | | 2 | 4 | 10 | 13 | 30* | | 73** | 151 |
| Exceptional Exposure: For Emergency Use Only |
| | 80 | 1 | | | | | | | | | | 3 | 4 | 13 | 17 | 30* | | 77** | 168 |
| | 90 | 1 | | | | | | | | | | 3 | 10 | 11 | 25 | 37* | | 76** | 186 |
| | 95 | 1 | | | | | | | | | | 4 | 11 | 11 | 28 | 38* | | 77** | 193 |

## TABLE 8 DCIEM $HeO_2$ Surface Decompression Using Oxygen

| Depth (fsw) | Bottom Time (min) | Max Time to 1st Stop | STOP TIMES AT VARIOUS DEPTHS IN MINUTES | | | | | | | | | | | | | | | | [illegible] |
|---|---|---|---|---|---|---|---|---|---|---|---|---|---|---|---|---|---|---|---|
| | | | In–Water Stops | | | | | | | | | | | | | | Surface Interval | DDC $O_2$ | |
| | | | Breathing Air | | | | | | | | | | | | | $O_2$ | | | |
| | | | 160 | 150 | 140 | 130 | 120 | 110 | 100 | 90 | 80 | 70 | 60 | 50 | 40 | 30 | | 40 | |
| 140 | 15 | 2 | | | | | | | | | | | | | 3 | 2 | Time from leaving 30f sw water stop to 40f sw in chamber not to exceed 7 minutes. | 19 | [illegible] |
| | 20 | 2 | | | | | | | | | | | | 3 | 3 | 3 | | 25 | [illegible] |
| | 30 | 2 | | | | | | | | | | | 2 | 4 | 4 | 8 | | 41* | [illegible] |
| | 40 | 2 | | | | | | | | | | 1 | 3 | 4 | 7 | 10 | | 60** | [illegible] |
| | 50 | 2 | | | | | | | | | | 2 | 4 | 4 | 12 | 12 | | 73** | [illegible] |
| | 60 | 2 | | | | | | | | | | 3 | 4 | 9 | 12 | 27 | | 74** | [illegible] |
| | 65 | 2 | | | | | | | | | | 3 | 4 | 11 | 13 | 30* | | 73** | [illegible] |
| Exceptional Exposure: For Emergency Use Only | | | | | | | | | | | | | | | | | | | |
| | 70 | 1 | | | | | | | | | 1 | 3 | 5 | 12 | 14 | 30* | | 77** | [illegible] |
| | 80 | 1 | | | | | | | | | 1 | 4 | 9 | 11 | 24 | 37* | | 77** | [illegible] |
| | 90 | 1 | | | | | | | | | 2 | 4 | 12 | 15 | 28 | 39* | | 78** | [illegible] |
| 150 | 10 | 2 | | | | | | | | | | | | | 1 | 2 | | 12 | [illegible] |
| | 15 | 2 | | | | | | | | | | | | 2 | 3 | 2 | | 21 | [illegible] |
| | 20 | 2 | | | | | | | | | | | 1 | 3 | 4 | 2 | | 29 | [illegible] |
| | 25 | 2 | | | | | | | | | | | 2 | 4 | 4 | 6 | | 34* | [illegible] |
| | 30 | 2 | | | | | | | | | | 1 | 3 | 4 | 4 | 9 | | 48* | [illegible] |
| | 35 | 2 | | | | | | | | | | 2 | 3 | 4 | 6 | 10 | | 60** | [illegible] |
| | 40 | 2 | | | | | | | | | | 2 | 4 | 4 | 9 | 11 | | 64** | [illegible] |
| | 45 | 2 | | | | | | | | | | 3 | 4 | 4 | 11 | 12 | | 72** | [illegible] |
| | 50 | 2 | | | | | | | | | 1 | 3 | 4 | 6 | 12 | 15 | | 76** | [illegible] |
| | 55 | 2 | | | | | | | | | 1 | 4 | 4 | 8 | 12 | 27 | | 75** | [illegible] |
| | 60 | 2 | | | | | | | | | 2 | 3 | 4 | 11 | 13 | 30* | | 74** | [illegible] |
| Exceptional Exposure: For Emergency Use Only | | | | | | | | | | | | | | | | | | | |
| | 70 | 2 | | | | | | | | | 3 | 3 | 8 | 11 | 21 | 37* | | 77** | [illegible] |
| | 80 | 2 | | | | | | | | | 3 | 4 | 11 | 14 | 28 | 39* | | 79** | [illegible] |
| | 85 | 2 | | | | | | | | 1 | 3 | 7 | 10 | 17 | 30 | 40* | | 79** | [illegible] |

## TABLE 8  DCIEM HeO Surface Decompression Using Oxygen

| Depth (fsw) | Bottom Time (min) | Max Time to 1st Stop | 160 | 150 | 140 | 130 | 120 | 110 | 100 | 90 | 80 | 70 | 60 | 50 | 40 | O₂ 30 | Surface Interval | DDC O₂ 40 | Decomp Time (min) |
|---|---|---|---|---|---|---|---|---|---|---|---|---|---|---|---|---|---|---|---|
| | | | | | | | | | Breathing Air | | | | | | | | | | |
| 160 | 10 | 2 | | | | | | | | | | | | | 2 | 2 | | 14 | 28 |
| | 15 | 2 | | | | | | | | | | | | 3 | 3 | 2 | | 23 | 41 |
| | 20 | 2 | | | | | | | | | | | 2 | 3 | 4 | 3 | | 30* | 57 |
| | 25 | 2 | | | | | | | | | | 1 | 3 | 3 | 4 | 8 | | 39* | 73 |
| | 30 | 2 | | | | | | | | | | 2 | 3 | 4 | 5 | 9 | | 54* | 92 |
| | 35 | 2 | | | | | | | | | | 3 | 3 | 5 | 7 | 10 | | 61** | 109 |
| | 40 | 2 | | | | | | | | | 1 | 3 | 4 | 4 | 10 | 12 | | 70** | 124 |
| | 45 | 2 | | | | | | | | | 2 | 3 | 4 | 6 | 11 | 13 | | 78** | 137 |
| | 50 | 2 | | | | | | | | | 2 | 4 | 4 | 8 | 12 | 26 | | 76** | 152 |
| | 55 | 2 | | | | | | | | | 3 | 3 | 5 | 10 | 13 | 30* | | 75** | 164 |
| | Exceptional Exposure: For Emergency Use Only | | | | | | | | | | | | | | | | Time from leaving 30f sw water stop to 40 fsw in chamber not to exceed 7 minutes. | | |
| | 60 | 2 | | | | | | | | 1 | 3 | 3 | 7 | 10 | 15 | 32* | | 78** | 173 |
| | 70 | 2 | | | | | | | | 2 | 3 | 4 | 10 | 11 | 27 | 39* | | 79** | 199 |
| | 80 | 2 | | | | | | | | 2 | 4 | 8 | 9 | 19 | 31 | 40* | | 81** | 218 |
| 170 | 10 | 2 | | | | | | | | | | | | | 3 | 2 | | 15 | 30 |
| | 15 | 2 | | | | | | | | | | | 1 | 3 | 4 | 2 | | 25 | 45 |
| | 20 | 2 | | | | | | | | | | 1 | 2 | 4 | 4 | 5 | | 30* | 61 |
| | 25 | 2 | | | | | | | | | | 2 | 3 | 4 | 4 | 8 | | 46* | 82 |
| | 30 | 2 | | | | | | | | | 1 | 3 | 3 | 4 | 6 | 10 | | 60** | 102 |
| | 35 | 2 | | | | | | | | | 2 | 3 | 3 | 4 | 9 | 11 | | 67** | 119 |
| | 40 | 2 | | | | | | | | | 3 | 3 | 3 | 6 | 10 | 13 | | 75** | 133 |
| | 45 | 2 | | | | | | | | 1 | 3 | 3 | 4 | 7 | 12 | 25 | | 76** | 151 |
| | 50 | 2 | | | | | | | | 1 | 3 | 3 | 5 | 9 | 13 | 30* | | 75** | 164 |
| | Exceptional Exposure: For Emergency Use Only | | | | | | | | | | | | | | | | | | |
| | 55 | 2 | | | | | | | | 2 | 3 | 3 | 7 | 10 | 15 | 31* | | 79** | 175 |
| | 60 | 2 | | | | | | | | 2 | 3 | 4 | 8 | 11 | 21 | 38* | | 79** | 191 |
| | 65 | 2 | | | | | | | | 3 | 3 | 5 | 9 | 11 | 28 | 39* | | 80** | 203 |
| | 70 | 2 | | | | | | | | 3 | 4 | 6 | 10 | 15 | 30 | 40* | | 81** | 214 |
| | 75 | 2 | | | | | | | 1 | 3 | 3 | 9 | 9 | 21 | 33 | 40* | | 82** | 225 |

# TABLE 8  DCIEM HeO Surface Decompression Using Oxygen

| Depth (fsw) | Bottom Time (min) | Max Time to 1st Stop | STOP TIMES — In-Water Stops Breathing Air 160 | 150 | 140 | 130 | 120 | 110 | 100 | 90 | 80 | 70 | 60 | 50 | 40 | O2 30 | Surface Interval | DDC O2 40 | Decomp Time (min) |
|---|---|---|---|---|---|---|---|---|---|---|---|---|---|---|---|---|---|---|---|
| 180 | 10 | 3 | | | | | | | | | | | | | 1 | 3 | 2 | | 16 | 32 |
| | 15 | 2 | | | | | | | | | | | 2 | 3 | 4 | 2 | | 27 | 48 |
| | 20 | 2 | | | | | | | | | | 2 | 3 | 3 | 4 | 6 | | 34* | 67 |
| | 25 | 2 | | | | | | | | | 1 | 3 | 3 | 4 | 3 | 10 | | 51* | 90 |
| | 30 | 2 | | | | | | | | | 2 | 3 | 3 | 4 | 8 | 10 | | 61** | 111 |
| | 35 | 2 | | | | | | | | 1 | 2 | 3 | 4 | 4 | 10 | 12 | | 72** | 128 |
| | 40 | 2 | | | | | | | | 2 | 2 | 3 | 4 | 7 | 11 | 21 | | 77** | 147 |
| | 45 | 2 | | | | | | | | 2 | 3 | 3 | 4 | 9 | 12 | 30* | | 76** | 159 |

**Exceptional Exposure: For Emergency Use Only**

| Depth (fsw) | Bottom Time (min) | Max Time to 1st Stop | 160 | 150 | 140 | 130 | 120 | 110 | 100 | 90 | 80 | 70 | 60 | 50 | 40 | O2 30 | Surface Interval | DDC O2 40 | Decomp Time (min) |
|---|---|---|---|---|---|---|---|---|---|---|---|---|---|---|---|---|---|---|---|
| 180 | 50 | 2 | | | | | | | | 3 | 3 | 3 | 6 | 10 | 15 | 30* | | 80** | 175 |
| | 55 | 2 | | | | | | | 1 | 3 | 3 | 4 | 7 | 11 | 20 | 39* | | 78** | 191 |
| | 60 | 2 | | | | | | | 1 | 3 | 3 | 5 | 9 | 11 | 28 | 39* | | 80** | 204 |
| | 65 | 2 | | | | | | | 2 | 3 | 3 | 7 | 9 | 16 | 31 | 40* | | 82** | 218 |
| | 70 | 2 | | | | | | | 2 | 3 | 4 | 8 | 10 | 21 | 35 | 39* | | 84** | 231 |

| Depth (fsw) | Bottom Time (min) | Max Time to 1st Stop | 160 | 150 | 140 | 130 | 120 | 110 | 100 | 90 | 80 | 70 | 60 | 50 | 40 | O2 30 | Surface Interval | DDC O2 40 | Decomp Time (min) |
|---|---|---|---|---|---|---|---|---|---|---|---|---|---|---|---|---|---|---|---|
| 190 | 10 | 3 | | | | | | | | | | | | 2 | 3 | 2 | | 18 | 36 |
| | 15 | 3 | | | | | | | | | | 3 | 3 | 4 | 2 | | 29 | 51 |
| | 20 | 2 | | | | | | | | | 1 | 2 | 3 | 3 | 4 | 7 | | 39* | 74 |
| | 25 | 2 | | | | | | | | | 2 | 3 | 3 | 3 | 6 | 10 | | 56* | 98 |
| | 30 | 2 | | | | | | | | 1 | 3 | 2 | 4 | 3 | 9 | 11 | | 66** | 119 |
| | 35 | 2 | | | | | | | | 2 | 3 | 3 | 3 | 6 | 10 | 13 | | 77** | 137 |
| | 40 | 2 | | | | | | | 1 | 2 | 3 | 3 | 3 | 9 | 11 | 27 | | 76** | 155 |
| | 45 | 2 | | | | | | | 1 | 3 | 3 | 3 | 6 | 9 | 14 | 30* | | 78** | 172 |
| | 50 | 2 | | | | | | | 2 | 2 | 3 | 4 | 8 | 9 | 19 | 38* | | 79** | 189 |

**Exceptional Exposure: For Emergency Use Only**

| Depth (fsw) | Bottom Time (min) | Max Time to 1st Stop | 160 | 150 | 140 | 130 | 120 | 110 | 100 | 90 | 80 | 70 | 60 | 50 | 40 | O2 30 | Surface Interval | DDC O2 40 | Decomp Time (min) |
|---|---|---|---|---|---|---|---|---|---|---|---|---|---|---|---|---|---|---|---|
| 190 | 55 | 2 | | | | | | | 2 | 3 | 3 | 5 | 9 | 11 | 26 | 40* | | 80** | 204 |
| | 60 | 2 | | | | | | | 3 | 3 | 3 | 7 | 9 | 15 | 32 | 40* | | 82** | 219 |
| | 65 | 2 | | | | | | 1 | 2 | 3 | 4 | 8 | 10 | 21 | 36 | 39* | | 85** | 234 |

Surface Interval: Time from leaving 30 fsw water stop to 40 fsw in chamber not to exceed 7 minutes.

## TABLE 8  DCIEM HeO Surface Decompression Using Oxygen

In-Water Stops are breathing air (columns 160–40 fsw). O2 stop is at 30 fsw. Surface Interval note (spanning all rows): "Time from leaving 30 fsw water stop to 40 fsw in chamber not to exceed 7 minutes." DDC O2 is at 40 fsw.

| Depth (fsw) | Bottom Time (min) | Max Time to 1st Stop | 160 | 150 | 140 | 130 | 120 | 110 | 100 | 90 | 80 | 70 | 60 | 50 | 40 | O2 30 | DDC O2 40 | Decomp Time (min) |
|---|---|---|---|---|---|---|---|---|---|---|---|---|---|---|---|---|---|---|
| 200 | 10 | 3 | | | | | | | | | | | | 2 | 4 | 2 | 19 | 38 |
| | 15 | 3 | | | | | | | | | | 1 | 3 | 3 | 4 | 3 | 30* | 59 |
| | 20 | 2 | | | | | | | | | 2 | 2 | 3 | 4 | 3 | 8 | 45* | 82 |
| | 25 | 2 | | | | | | | | 1 | 2 | 3 | 3 | 3 | 7 | 10 | 60** | 109 |
| | 30 | 2 | | | | | | | | 2 | 3 | 3 | 3 | 4 | 10 | 12 | 70** | 127 |
| | 35 | 2 | | | | | | | 1 | 2 | 3 | 3 | 3 | 8 | 10 | 22 | 77** | 149 |
| | 40 | 2 | | | | | | | 2 | 2 | 3 | 3 | 5 | 9 | 12 | 30* | 76** | 167 |
| | 45 | 2 | | | | | | | 2 | 3 | 3 | 3 | 7 | 10 | 16 | 37* | 79** | 185 |
| — Exceptional Exposure: For Emergency Use Only | | | | | | | | | | | | | | | | | | |
| 200 | 50 | 2 | | | | | | 1 | 2 | 3 | 3 | 5 | 8 | 10 | 25 | 39* | 81** | 202 |
| | 55 | 2 | | | | | | 1 | 3 | 3 | 3 | 6 | 9 | 13 | 32 | 40* | 83** | 218 |
| | 60 | 2 | | | | | | 2 | 2 | 3 | 4 | 8 | 9 | 21 | 36 | 40* | 84** | 234 |
| 210 | 10 | 3 | | | | | | | | | | | 1 | 3 | 3 | 2 | 21 | 41 |
| | 15 | 3 | | | | | | | | | | 2 | 3 | 3 | 4 | 4 | 30* | 62 |
| | 20 | 3 | | | | | | | | | 2 | 3 | 3 | 3 | 4 | 9 | 49* | 88 |
| | 25 | 2 | | | | | | | | 2 | 2 | 3 | 3 | 4 | 9 | 10 | 62** | 114 |
| | 30 | 2 | | | | | | | 1 | 2 | 3 | 3 | 3 | 6 | 10 | 13 | 75** | 136 |
| | 35 | 2 | | | | | | | 2 | 2 | 3 | 3 | 4 | 8 | 12 | 26 | 78** | 158 |
| | 40 | 2 | | | | | | 1 | 2 | 3 | 3 | 3 | 6 | 9 | 15 | 34* | 80** | 181 |
| — Exceptional Exposure: For Emergency Use Only | | | | | | | | | | | | | | | | | | |
| 210 | 45 | 2 | | | | | | 2 | 2 | 3 | 3 | 4 | 7 | 11 | 21 | 39* | 80** | 197 |
| | 50 | 2 | | | | | | 2 | 2 | 3 | 4 | 5 | 9 | 12 | 30 | 40* | 82** | 214 |
| | 55 | 2 | | | | | | 3 | 2 | 3 | 4 | 7 | 9 | 19 | 37 | 39* | 85** | 233 |

## TABLE 8  DCIEM HeO Surface Decompression Using Oxygen

| Depth (fsw) | Bottom Time (min) | Max Time to 1st Stop | STOP TIMES AT VARIOUS DEPTHS IN MINUTES 160 | 150 | 140 | 130 | 120 | 110 | 100 | 90 | 80 | 70 | 60 | 50 | 40 | O2 30 | Surface Interval | DDC O2 40 | Decomp Time (min) |
|---|---|---|---|---|---|---|---|---|---|---|---|---|---|---|---|---|---|---|---|
| 220 | 10 | 3 | | | | | | | | | | | 2 | 2 | 4 | 2 | | 22 | 43 |
| | 15 | 3 | | | | | | | | | 1 | 2 | 3 | 3 | 4 | 5 | | 32* | 66 |
| | 20 | 3 | | | | | | | | 1 | 3 | 2 | 3 | 3 | 5 | 10 | | 53* | 95 |
| | 25 | 2 | | | | | | | 1 | 2 | 3 | 2 | 3 | 4 | 9 | 11 | | 67** | 122 |
| | 30 | 2 | | | | | | | 2 | 2 | 3 | 3 | 3 | 7 | 10 | 19 | | 79** | 148 |
| | 35 | 2 | | | | | | 1 | 2 | 3 | 3 | 3 | 4 | 9 | 13 | 30* | | 78** | 166 |
| | 40 | 2 | | | | | | 2 | 2 | 3 | 3 | 3 | 7 | 10 | 18 | 37* | | 80** | 190 |
| Exceptional Exposure: For Emergency Use Only | | | | | | | | | | | | | | | | | | | |
| | 45 | 2 | | | | | 1 | 2 | 2 | 3 | 3 | 5 | 8 | 11 | 27 | 40* | | 82** | 209 |
| | 50 | 2 | | | | | 1 | 2 | 3 | 3 | 3 | 7 | 9 | 16 | 35 | 40* | | 84** | 228 |
| | 55 | 2 | | | | | 2 | 2 | 3 | 3 | 5 | 7 | 10 | 24 | 41 | 39* | | 88** | 249 |
| 230 | 10 | 3 | | | | | | | | | | | 2 | 3 | 4 | 2 | | 24 | 46 |
| | 15 | 3 | | | | | | | | | 2 | 2 | 3 | 3 | 3 | 7 | | 34* | 70 |
| | 20 | 3 | | | | | | | | 2 | 2 | 3 | 3 | 3 | 6 | 10 | | 58* | 103 |
| | 25 | 3 | | | | | | | 2 | 2 | 3 | 3 | 2 | 5 | 9 | 12 | | 71** | 129 |
| | 30 | 2 | | | | | | 1 | 2 | 3 | 2 | 3 | 3 | 8 | 11 | 23 | | 79** | 155 |
| | 35 | 2 | | | | | | 2 | 2 | 3 | 3 | 2 | 7 | 8 | 15 | 34* | | 80** | 181 |
| Exceptional Exposure: For Emergency Use Only | | | | | | | | | | | | | | | | | | | |
| | 40 | 2 | | | | | 1 | 2 | 3 | 2 | 3 | 4 | 8 | 10 | 22 | 39* | | 81** | 200 |
| | 45 | 2 | | | | | 2 | 2 | 2 | 3 | 3 | 7 | 8 | 13 | 33 | 40* | | 84** | 222 |
| | 50 | 2 | | | | | 2 | 3 | 2 | 3 | 5 | 7 | 9 | 21 | 40 | 39* | | 87** | 243 |
| 240 | 10 | 3 | | | | | | | | | | 1 | 2 | 3 | 4 | 2 | | 25 | 48 |
| | 15 | 3 | | | | | | | | 1 | 2 | 2 | 3 | 3 | 3 | 8 | | 38* | 76 |
| | 20 | 3 | | | | | | | 1 | 2 | 2 | 3 | 3 | 3 | 7 | 10 | | 60** | 112 |
| | 25 | 3 | | | | | | 1 | 2 | 2 | 3 | 3 | 2 | 6 | 10 | 13 | | 75** | 137 |
| | 30 | 3 | | | | | | 2 | 2 | 3 | 2 | 3 | 4 | 9 | 12 | 27 | | 79** | 163 |
| | 35 | 2 | | | | | 1 | 2 | 3 | 2 | 3 | 3 | 7 | 9 | 18 | 36* | | 81** | 190 |
| Exceptional Exposure: For Emergency Use Only | | | | | | | | | | | | | | | | | | | |
| | 40 | 2 | | | | | 2 | 2 | 3 | 2 | 3 | 5 | 8 | 12 | 27 | 40* | | 82** | 211 |
| | 45 | 2 | | | | 1 | 2 | 2 | 3 | 3 | 3 | 7 | 9 | 17 | 38 | 39* | | 87** | 236 |

Surface Interval: Time from leaving 30 fsw water stop to 40 fsw in chamber not to exceed 7 minutes.

## TABLE 8  DCIEM HeO Surface Decompression Using Oxygen

| Depth (fsw) | Bottom Time (min) | Max Time to 1st Stop | 160 | 150 | 140 | 130 | 120 | 110 | 100 | 90 | 80 | 70 | 60 | 50 | 40 | O₂ 30 | Surface Interval | DDC O₂ 40 | Decomp Time (min) |
|---|---|---|---|---|---|---|---|---|---|---|---|---|---|---|---|---|---|---|---|
| **250** | 10 | 3 | | | | | | | | | | 1 | 3 | 3 | 4 | 2 | | 27 | 51 |
| | 15 | 3 | | | | | | | | 1 | 2 | 3 | 3 | 3 | 3 | 9 | | 42* | 82 |
| | 20 | 3 | | | | | | | 2 | 2 | 2 | 3 | 3 | 3 | 8 | 11 | | 62** | 117 |
| | 25 | 3 | | | | | | 2 | 2 | 2 | 3 | 2 | 3 | 7 | 10 | 18 | | 80** | 150 |
| | 30 | 3 | | | | | 1 | 2 | 2 | 3 | 3 | 2 | 6 | 8 | 14 | 31* | | 81** | 178 |
| | 35 | 2 | | | | 1 | 1 | 2 | 3 | 2 | 3 | 4 | 7 | 10 | 22 | 38* | | 82** | 200 |
| Exceptional Exposure: For Emergency Use Only ||||||||||||||||||| |
| | 40 | 2 | | | | 1 | 2 | 2 | 3 | 3 | 2 | 7 | 8 | 13 | 34 | 39* | | 85** | 224 |
| | 45 | 2 | | | | 2 | 2 | 2 | 3 | 2 | 6 | 7 | 9 | 22 | 41 | 39* | | 89** | 249 |
| **260** | 10 | 4 | | | | | | | | | 2 | 2 | 3 | 4 | 2 | | 29 | 53 |
| | 15 | 3 | | | | | | | | 2 | 2 | 3 | 3 | 3 | 3 | 9 | | 47* | 88 |
| | 20 | 3 | | | | | | 1 | 2 | 2 | 2 | 3 | 3 | 3 | 9 | 11 | | 66* | 123 |
| | 25 | 3 | | | | | 1 | 2 | 2 | 2 | 3 | 2 | 3 | 8 | 11 | 21 | | 80* | 156 |
| | 30 | 3 | | | | 1 | 1 | 2 | 2 | 3 | 2 | 3 | 7 | 8 | 16 | 34* | | 81* | 185 |
| Exceptional Exposure: For Emergency Use Only ||||||||||||||||||| |
| | 35 | 3 | | | | 1 | 2 | 2 | 3 | 2 | 3 | 5 | 7 | 12 | 26 | 39* | | 83** | 210 |
| | 40 | 2 | | | 1 | 1 | 2 | 3 | 2 | 3 | 4 | 6 | 9 | 16 | 39 | 39* | | 87** | 237 |
| **270** | 10 | 4 | | | | | | | | 1 | 2 | 2 | 3 | 4 | 2 | | 30* | 60 |
| | 15 | 3 | | | | | | | 1 | 2 | 2 | 3 | 3 | 2 | 5 | 9 | | 52* | 95 |
| | 20 | 3 | | | | | | 2 | 2 | 2 | 2 | 3 | 3 | 4 | 9 | 12 | | 70** | 130 |
| | 25 | 3 | | | | | 2 | 2 | 2 | 2 | 3 | 2 | 4 | 8 | 12 | 25 | | 80** | 163 |
| | 30 | 3 | | | | 1 | 2 | 2 | 2 | 3 | 2 | 4 | 7 | 9 | 18 | 36* | | 82** | 194 |
| Exceptional Exposure: For Emergency Use Only ||||||||||||||||||| |
| | 35 | 3 | | | 1 | 1 | 2 | 2 | 3 | 2 | 3 | 6 | 8 | 13 | 31 | 39* | | 85** | 221 |
| | 40 | 3 | | | 2 | 1 | 2 | 2 | 3 | 2 | 5 | 7 | 10 | 20 | 42 | 39* | | 89** | 249 |

*Surface Interval column note (vertical):* Time from leaving 30 fsw water stop to 40 fsw in chamber not to exceed 7 minutes.

Columns 160–40 are In-Water Stops, Breathing Air. Column 30 is O₂. Column 40 (right) is DDC O₂.

## TABLE 8  DCIEM HeO Surface Decompression Using Oxygen

| Depth (fsw) | Bottom Time (min) | Max Time to 1st Stop | 160 | 150 | 140 | 130 | 120 | 110 | 100 | 90 | 80 | 70 | 60 | 50 | 40 | O2 30 | Surface Interval | DDC O2 40 | Decomp Time (min) |
|---|---|---|---|---|---|---|---|---|---|---|---|---|---|---|---|---|---|---|---|
| 280 | 10 | 4 | | | | | | | | | 1 | 2 | 3 | 3 | 3 | 4 | | 30* | 58 |
| | 15 | 3 | | | | | | | 2 | 2 | 2 | 2 | 3 | 3 | 6 | 9 | | 56* | 101 |
| | 20 | 3 | | | | | 1 | 2 | 2 | 2 | 2 | 3 | 2 | 6 | 9 | 13 | | 73** | 136 |
| | 25 | 3 | | | | 1 | 2 | 2 | 2 | 2 | 3 | 2 | 5 | 8 | 13 | 28 | | 81** | 170 |
| | Exceptional Exposure: For Emergency Use Only | | | | | | | | | | | | | | | | | | |
| | 30 | 3 | | | 1 | 1 | 2 | 2 | 2 | 3 | 2 | 5 | 7 | 10 | 22 | 38* | | 83** | 204 |
| | 35 | 3 | | | 2 | 1 | 2 | 2 | 3 | 2 | 4 | 6 | 8 | 15 | 36 | 39* | | 87** | 233 |
| | 40 | 3 | | 1 | 1 | 2 | 2 | 3 | 2 | 3 | 6 | 7 | 11 | 24 | 44 | 39* | | 90*** | 265 |
| 290 | 10 | 4 | | | | | | | | | 2 | 2 | 3 | 3 | 3 | 4 | | 30* | 64 |
| | 15 | 3 | | | | | | 1 | 1 | 2 | 3 | 2 | 3 | 3 | 6 | 10 | | 59* | 106 |
| | 20 | 3 | | | | 2 | 1 | 2 | 2 | 3 | 2 | 3 | 6 | 8 | 15 | 17 | | 79** | 148 |
| | 25 | 3 | | | | 2 | 1 | 2 | 2 | 3 | 2 | 3 | 6 | 8 | 15 | 31* | | 82** | 183 |
| | Exceptional Exposure: For Emergency Use Only | | | | | | | | | | | | | | | | | | |
| | 30 | 3 | | | 1 | 2 | 2 | 2 | 2 | 3 | 2 | 5 | 8 | 11 | 26 | 39* | | 84** | 213 |
| | 35 | 3 | | 1 | 1 | 2 | 2 | 2 | 3 | 2 | 5 | 6 | 9 | 18 | 40 | 39* | | 89** | 245 |
| 300 | 10 | 4 | | | | | | | | 1 | 2 | 2 | 2 | 4 | 3 | 5 | | 30* | 66 |
| | 15 | 4 | | | | | | 1 | 2 | 2 | 2 | 3 | 2 | 4 | 7 | 10 | | 60** | 114 |
| | 20 | 3 | | | | 1 | 1 | 2 | 2 | 2 | 3 | 2 | 3 | 7 | 11 | 18 | | 81** | 154 |
| | 25 | 3 | | | 1 | 1 | 2 | 2 | 2 | 3 | 2 | 3 | 7 | 8 | 17 | 34* | | 82** | 190 |
| | Exceptional Exposure: For Emergency Use Only | | | | | | | | | | | | | | | | | | |
| | 30 | 3 | | 1 | 1 | 2 | 2 | 2 | 2 | 2 | 3 | 6 | 8 | 13 | 31 | 39* | | 85** | 223 |
| | 35 | 3 | | 2 | 1 | 2 | 2 | 2 | 2 | 3 | 5 | 7 | 10 | 22 | 42 | 39* | | 90*** | 255 |

The In-Water Stops (columns 160–40) are breathing air; the 30 column is the O2 stop.

Surface Interval: Time from leaving 30 fsw water stop to 40 fsw in chamber not to exceed 7 minutes.

## TABLE 8  DCIEM HeO Surface Decompression Using Oxygen

Surface Interval note (vertical in original): Time from leaving 30 fsw water stop to 40 fsw in chamber not to exceed 7 minutes.

| Depth (fsw) | Bottom Time (min) | Max Time to 1st Stop | \[Breathing Air\] 160 | 150 | 140 | 130 | 120 | 110 | 100 | 90 | 80 | 70 | 60 | 50 | 40 | O₂ 30 | DDC O₂ 40 | Decomp Time (min) |
|---|---|---|---|---|---|---|---|---|---|---|---|---|---|---|---|---|---|---|
| **310** | Exceptional Exposure: For Emergency Use Only | | | | | | | | | | | | | | | | | |
| 310 | 10 | 4 |  |  |  |  |  |  |  | 1 | 2 | 2 | 3 | 3 | 3 | 6 | 32* | 69 |
| 310 | 15 | 4 |  |  |  |  |  | 2 | 2 | 2 | 2 | 3 | 2 | 3 | 9 | 10 | 62** | 119 |
| 310 | 20 | 3 |  |  |  | 1 | 2 | 2 | 2 | 2 | 2 | 3 | 3 | 8 | 11 | 21 | 82** | 160 |
| 310 | 25 | 3 |  |  | 2 | 1 | 2 | 2 | 2 | 2 | 3 | 3 | 7 | 10 | 19 | 36* | 83** | 198 |
| 310 | 30 | 3 |  | 1 | 2 | 2 | 2 | 2 | 2 | 2 | 4 | 6 | 8 | 15 | 35 | 39* | 87** | 233 |
| 310 | 35 | 3 | 1 | 1 | 2 | 2 | 2 | 2 | 2 | 3 | 6 | 7 | 12 | 26 | 44 | 39* | 90*** | 270 |
| **320** | Exceptional Exposure: For Emergency Use Only | | | | | | | | | | | | | | | | | |
| 320 | 10 | 4 |  |  |  |  |  |  |  | 2 | 2 | 2 | 3 | 3 | 3 | 7 | 35* | 74 |
| 320 | 15 | 4 |  |  |  |  | 1 | 2 | 1 | 2 | 3 | 2 | 3 | 3 | 9 | 11 | 64** | 123 |
| 320 | 20 | 3 |  |  | 1 | 1 | 2 | 2 | 2 | 2 | 2 | 3 | 4 | 8 | 12 | 24 | 82** | 166 |
| 320 | 25 | 3 |  | 1 | 1 | 2 | 2 | 2 | 2 | 2 | 2 | 5 | 7 | 10 | 23 | 37* | 84** | 206 |
| 320 | 30 | 3 | 1 | 1 | 2 | 2 | 1 | 3 | 2 | 2 | 4 | 7 | 9 | 17 | 39 | 39* | 89** | 244 |
| **330** | Exceptional Exposure: For Emergency Use Only | | | | | | | | | | | | | | | | | |
| 330 | 10 | 4 |  |  |  |  |  |  |  | 2 | 2 | 2 | 3 | 3 | 3 | 7 | 38* | 77 |
| 330 | 15 | 4 |  |  |  | 2 | 1 | 2 | 2 | 2 | 3 | 2 | 2 | 5 | 9 | 11 | 68** | 129 |
| 330 | 20 | 4 |  |  |  | 1 | 2 | 1 | 2 | 3 | 2 | 2 | 5 | 8 | 13 | 27 | 82** | 171 |
| 330 | 25 | 3 |  | 2 | 1 | 2 | 1 | 2 | 3 | 2 | 2 | 6 | 7 | 11 | 27 | 38* | 85** | 215 |
| 330 | 30 | 3 | 1 | 2 | 1 | 2 | 2 | 2 | 2 | 6 | 6 | 10 | 20 | 42 | 39* | | 90*** | 253 |

The **Emergency Decompression Table (Table 9)** is provided for use in the case of a loss of oxygen or for oxygen toxicity. This table offers three options: in-water air decompression, surface decompression using oxygen, and surface decompression using air. The in-water air decompression option has water stops at 20 and 10 fsw, where the oxygen decompression table finishes at 30 fsw. The surface decompression using oxygen option starts at completion of the 30 fsw air stop, and the chamber stops are at 40 fsw. The surface decompression using air option also starts at completion of the 30 fsw air stop and has chamber stops at 40, 30, 20, and 10 fsw.

Table 9 DCIEM HeO₂ Emergency Decompression

| Depth (fsw) | Bottom Time (min) | In–Water Air 30 | 20 | 10 | Decomp Time | Surface Interval | O₂ 40 | Decomp Time | Surface Interval | Air 40 | 30 | 20 | 10 | Decomp Time |
|---|---|---|---|---|---|---|---|---|---|---|---|---|---|---|
| 120 | 20 | 4 | 7 | 21 | 37 | | 21 | 38 | | 3 | 4 | 7 | 21 | 51 |
| | 30 | 8 | 16 | 35 | 67 | | 30* | 58 | | 4 | 8 | 16 | 35 | 86 |
| | 40 | 16 | 18 | 65 | 110 | | 50* | 89 | | 5 | 16 | 18 | 65 | 138 |
| | 50 | 22 | 27 | 82 | 145 | | 60** | 114 | | 7 | 22 | 27 | 82 | 181 |
| | 60 | 24 | 44 | 86 | 173 | | 71** | 132 | | 11 | 24 | 44 | 86 | 215 |
| | 70 | 38 | 57 | 85 | 204 | | 73** | 153 | | 13 | 38 | 57 | 85 | 262 |
| | 75 | 58 | 60 | 85 | 230 | | 71** | 174 | | 13 | 58 | 60 | 85 | 308 |
| | 80 | 65 | 63 | 85 | 242 | | 71** | 183 | | 13 | 65 | 63 | 85 | 327 |
| | 90 | 75 | 65 | 87 | 265 | | 74** | 205 | | 18 | 75 | 65 | 87 | 365 |
| | 100 | 77 | 65 | 88 | 278 | | 76** | 219 | | 24 | 77 | 65 | 88 | 386 |
| 130 | 15 | 4 | 5 | 18 | 31 | | 17 | 33 | | 2 | 4 | 5 | 18 | 44 |
| | 20 | 4 | 9 | 22 | 42 | | 23 | 42 | | 4 | 4 | 9 | 22 | 57 |
| | 30 | 12 | 15 | 45 | 82 | | 35* | 69 | | 4 | 12 | 15 | 45 | 105 |
| | 40 | 20 | 21 | 74 | 128 | | 56* | 101 | | 5 | 20 | 21 | 74 | 160 |
| | 50 | 22 | 37 | 85 | 163 | | 67** | 125 | | 9 | 22 | 37 | 85 | 201 |
| | 60 | 32 | 55 | 86 | 197 | | 74** | 148 | | 12 | 32 | 55 | 86 | 248 |
| | 70 | 60 | 63 | 87 | 240 | | 73** | 181 | | 13 | 60 | 63 | 87 | 320 |
| | 80 | 65 | 65 | 88 | 256 | | 77** | 198 | | 17 | 65 | 65 | 88 | 345 |
| | 90 | 79 | 64 | 90 | 283 | | 76** | 223 | | 25 | 79 | 64 | 90 | 394 |
| | 95 | 81 | 65 | 90 | 291 | | 77** | 231 | | 28 | 81 | 65 | 90 | 407 |

*Rotated notes within columns:* Water stops 40 fsw and deeper from in-water O₂ or Sur–D–O₂ tables (Table 7 or 8). Time from leaving 30 fsw in–water to 40 fsw in–chamber not to exceed 7 min. Time from leaving 30 fsw in–water to 40 fsw in–chamber not to exceed 7 min.

## Table 9 DCIEM HeO₂ Emergency Decompression

| Depth (fsw) | Bottom Time (min) | | In-Water | | | | | Deck Decompression Chamber | | | | | | | | |
|---|---|---|---|---|---|---|---|---|---|---|---|---|---|---|---|---|
| | | | Air | | | Decomp Time | Surface Interval | O₂ | Decomp Time | Surface Interval | | Air | | | | Decomp Time |
| | | | 30 | 20 | 10 | | | 40 | | | 40 | 30 | 20 | 10 | |
| 140 | 15 | | 4 | 5 | 20 | 34 | | 19 | 36 | | 3 | 4 | 5 | 20 | 48 |
| | 20 | | 6 | 11 | 24 | 49 | | 25 | 47 | | 3 | 6 | 11 | 24 | 65 |
| | 30 | | 16 | 17 | 55 | 100 | | 41* | 82 | | 4 | 16 | 17 | 55 | 127 |
| | 40 | | 20 | 26 | 82 | 145 | | 60** | 114 | | 7 | 20 | 26 | 82 | 179 |
| | 50 | | 24 | 48 | 86 | 182 | | 73** | 138 | | 12 | 24 | 48 | 86 | 225 |
| | 60 | Water stops 40 fsw and deeper from in-water O₂ or Sur-D-O₂ tables (Table 7 or 8) | 54 | 62 | 87 | 233 | Time from leaving 30 fsw in-water to 40 fsw in-chamber not to exceed 7 min. | 74** | 175 | Time from leaving 30 fsw in-water to 40 fsw in-chamber not to exceed 7 min. | 12 | 54 | 62 | 87 | 305 |
| | 65 | | 65 | 65 | 87 | 250 | | 73** | 188 | | 13 | 65 | 65 | 87 | 334 |
| | 70 | | 65 | 65 | 89 | 255 | | 77** | 196 | | 14 | 65 | 65 | 89 | 341 |
| | 80 | | 79 | 65 | 91 | 285 | | 77** | 224 | | 24 | 79 | 65 | 91 | 395 |
| | 90 | | 83 | 65 | 93 | 303 | | 78** | 241 | | 28 | 83 | 65 | 93 | 421 |
| 150 | 10 | | 4 | 5 | 13 | 25 | | 12 | 27 | | 1 | 4 | 5 | 13 | 37 |
| | 15 | | 4 | 7 | 20 | 38 | | 21 | 40 | | 3 | 4 | 7 | 20 | 52 |
| | 20 | | 4 | 12 | 28 | 54 | | 29 | 51 | | 4 | 4 | 12 | 28 | 69 |
| | 25 | | 12 | 15 | 45 | 84 | | 34* | 71 | | 4 | 12 | 15 | 45 | 107 |
| | 30 | | 18 | 18 | 65 | 115 | | 48* | 93 | | 4 | 18 | 18 | 65 | 144 |
| | 35 | | 20 | 25 | 78 | 140 | | 60** | 110 | | 6 | 20 | 25 | 78 | 173 |
| | 40 | | 22 | 34 | 85 | 162 | | 64** | 125 | | 9 | 22 | 34 | 85 | 200 |
| | 45 | | 24 | 46 | 87 | 181 | | 72** | 138 | | 11 | 24 | 46 | 87 | 223 |
| | 50 | | 30 | 56 | 87 | 201 | | 76** | 151 | | 12 | 30 | 56 | 87 | 250 |
| | 55 | | 54 | 63 | 87 | 235 | | 75** | 177 | | 12 | 54 | 63 | 87 | 308 |
| | 60 | | 65 | 65 | 89 | 254 | | 74** | 191 | | 13 | 65 | 65 | 89 | 339 |
| | 70 | | 79 | 65 | 91 | 283 | | 77** | 221 | | 21 | 79 | 65 | 91 | 389 |
| | 80 | | 83 | 65 | 94 | 304 | | 79** | 241 | | 28 | 83 | 65 | 94 | 422 |
| | 85 | | 85 | 66 | 95 | 315 | | 79** | 251 | | 30 | 85 | 66 | 95 | 437 |

## Table 9 DCIEM $HeO_2$ Emergency Decompression

| Depth (fsw) | Bottom Time (min) | | In-Water | | | | Deck Decompression Chamber | | | | | | | | |
|---|---|---|---|---|---|---|---|---|---|---|---|---|---|---|---|
| | | | Air | | | Decomp Time | Surface Interval | $O_2$ | Decomp Time | Surface Interval | Air | | | | Decomp Time |
| | | | 30 | 20 | 10 | | | 40 | | | 40 | 30 | 20 | 10 | |
| 160 | 10 | Water stops 40 fsw and deeper from in-water $O_2$ or Sur-D-$O_2$ tables (Table 7 or 8) | 4 | 5 | 15 | 28 | Time from leaving 30 fsw in-water to 40 fsw in-chamber not to exceed 7 min. | 14 | 30 | Time from leaving 30 fsw in-water to 40 fsw in-chamber not to exceed 7 min. | 2 | 4 | 5 | 15 | 41 |
| | 15 | | 4 | 9 | 21 | 42 | | 23 | 43 | | 3 | 4 | 9 | 21 | 56 |
| | 20 | | 6 | 14 | 32 | 63 | | 30* | 60 | | 4 | 6 | 14 | 32 | 80 |
| | 25 | | 16 | 16 | 54 | 99 | | 39* | 81 | | 4 | 16 | 16 | 54 | 126 |
| | 30 | | 18 | 21 | 73 | 128 | | 54* | 101 | | 5 | 18 | 21 | 73 | 158 |
| | 35 | | 20 | 30 | 84 | 154 | | 61** | 119 | | 7 | 20 | 30 | 84 | 188 |
| | 40 | | 24 | 43 | 87 | 178 | | 70** | 136 | | 10 | 24 | 43 | 87 | 219 |
| | 45 | | 26 | 55 | 87 | 196 | | 78** | 150 | | 11 | 26 | 55 | 87 | 240 |
| | 50 | | 52 | 63 | 88 | 235 | | 76** | 178 | | 12 | 52 | 63 | 88 | 306 |
| | 55 | | 65 | 65 | 89 | 255 | | 75** | 194 | | 13 | 65 | 65 | 89 | 340 |
| | | | | | | | | | | | | | | | |
| | 60 | | 69 | 66 | 90 | 266 | | 78** | 205 | | 15 | 69 | 66 | 90 | 357 |
| | 70 | | 83 | 66 | 94 | 302 | | 79** | 238 | | 27 | 83 | 66 | 94 | 418 |
| | 80 | | 85 | 66 | 98 | 324 | | 81** | 258 | | 31 | 85 | 66 | 98 | 447 |
| | | | | | | | | | | | | | | | |
| 170 | 10 | | 4 | 5 | 16 | 31 | | 15 | 32 | | 3 | 4 | 5 | 16 | 45 |
| | 15 | | 4 | 10 | 23 | 47 | | 25 | 47 | | 4 | 4 | 10 | 23 | 62 |
| | 20 | | 10 | 14 | 40 | 77 | | 30* | 66 | | 4 | 10 | 14 | 40 | 98 |
| | 25 | | 16 | 17 | 63 | 111 | | 46* | 90 | | 4 | 16 | 17 | 63 | 138 |
| | 30 | | 20 | 26 | 79 | 144 | | 60** | 112 | | 6 | 20 | 26 | 79 | 177 |
| | 35 | | 22 | 38 | 86 | 169 | | 67** | 130 | | 9 | 22 | 38 | 86 | 207 |
| | 40 | | 26 | 52 | 87 | 192 | | 75** | 146 | | 10 | 26 | 52 | 87 | 235 |
| | 45 | | 50 | 62 | 88 | 232 | | 76** | 176 | | 12 | 50 | 62 | 88 | 301 |
| | 50 | | 65 | 65 | 90 | 256 | | 75** | 194 | | 13 | 65 | 65 | 90 | 341 |
| | | | | | | | | | | | | | | | |
| | 55 | | 67 | 66 | 91 | 266 | | 79** | 206 | | 15 | 67 | 66 | 91 | 355 |
| | 60 | | 81 | 66 | 93 | 291 | | 79** | 229 | | 21 | 81 | 66 | 93 | 400 |
| | 65 | | 83 | 66 | 95 | 305 | | 80** | 242 | | 28 | 83 | 66 | 95 | 423 |
| | 70 | | 85 | 66 | 97 | 318 | | 81** | 254 | | 30 | 85 | 66 | 97 | 440 |
| | 75 | | 85 | 67 | 100 | 333 | | 82** | 265 | | 33 | 85 | 67 | 100 | 458 |

## Table 9 DCIEM HeO₂ Emergency Decompression

| Depth (fsw) | Bottom Time (min) | In-Water Air 30 | Air 20 | Air 10 | In-Water Decomp Time | Surface Interval | DDC O₂ 40 | DDC Decomp Time | Surface Interval | DDC Air 40 | Air 30 | Air 20 | Air 10 | DDC Decomp Time |
|---|---|---|---|---|---|---|---|---|---|---|---|---|---|---|
| 180 | 10 | 4 | 5 | 17 | 33 | | 16 | 34 | | 3 | 4 | 5 | 17 | 47 |
| | 15 | 4 | 11 | 26 | 52 | | 27 | 50 | | 4 | 4 | 11 | 26 | 67 |
| | 20 | 12 | 15 | 47 | 88 | | 34* | 73 | | 4 | 12 | 15 | 47 | 111 |
| | 25 | 20 | 20 | 71 | 127 | | 51* | 100 | | 3 | 20 | 20 | 71 | 157 |
| | 30 | 20 | 31 | 83 | 156 | | 61** | 121 | | 8 | 20 | 31 | 83 | 191 |
| | 35 | 24 | 46 | 87 | 183 | | 72** | 140 | | 10 | 24 | 46 | 87 | 224 |
| | 40 | 42 | 59 | 88 | 220 | | 77** | 168 | | 11 | 42 | 59 | 88 | 280 |
| | 45 | 60 | 65 | 90 | 250 | | 76** | 189 | | 12 | 60 | 65 | 90 | 329 |
| | 50 | 65 | 66 | 92 | 265 | | 80** | 205 | | 15 | 65 | 66 | 92 | 352 |
| | 55 | 83 | 66 | 94 | 294 | | 78** | 230 | | 20 | 83 | 66 | 94 | 404 |
| | 60 | 83 | 66 | 96 | 307 | | 80** | 243 | | 28 | 83 | 66 | 96 | 425 |
| | 65 | 85 | 67 | 99 | 324 | | 82** | 258 | | 31 | 85 | 67 | 99 | 447 |
| | 70 | 83 | 68 | 101 | 337 | | 84** | 270 | | 35 | 83 | 68 | 101 | 462 |
| 190 | 10 | 4 | 4 | 19 | 35 | | 18 | 38 | | 3 | 4 | 4 | 19 | 49 |
| | 15 | 4 | 13 | 28 | 58 | | 29 | 53 | | 4 | 4 | 13 | 28 | 72 |
| | 20 | 14 | 16 | 55 | 100 | | 39* | 81 | | 4 | 14 | 16 | 55 | 125 |
| | 25 | 20 | 23 | 77 | 139 | | 56* | 108 | | 6 | 20 | 23 | 77 | 172 |
| | 30 | 22 | 38 | 86 | 170 | | 66** | 130 | | 9 | 22 | 38 | 86 | 208 |
| | 35 | 26 | 54 | 88 | 197 | | 77** | 150 | | 10 | 26 | 54 | 88 | 240 |
| | 40 | 54 | 63 | 90 | 241 | | 76** | 182 | | 11 | 54 | 63 | 90 | 313 |
| | 45 | 65 | 66 | 92 | 264 | | 78** | 202 | | 14 | 65 | 66 | 92 | 350 |
| | 50 | 81 | 67 | 93 | 290 | | 79** | 227 | | 19 | 81 | 67 | 93 | 397 |
| | 55 | 85 | 67 | 96 | 309 | | 80** | 244 | | 26 | 85 | 67 | 96 | 427 |
| | 60 | 85 | 67 | 100 | 326 | | 82** | 259 | | 32 | 85 | 67 | 100 | 450 |
| | 65 | 83 | 68 | 103 | 341 | | 85** | 273 | | 36 | 83 | 68 | 103 | 467 |

In-Water Air column note: Water stops 40 fsw and deeper from in-water O₂ or Sur-D-O₂ tables (Table 7 or 8)

Surface Interval note: Time from leaving 30 fsw in-water to 40 fsw in-chamber not to exceed 7 min.

## Table 9 DCIEM HeO₂ Emergency Decompression

| Depth (fsw) | Bottom Time (min) | In-Water Air 30 | 20 | 10 | Decomp Time | Surface Interval | O₂ 40 | Decomp Time | Surface Interval | Air 40 | 30 | 20 | 10 | Decomp Time |
|---|---|---|---|---|---|---|---|---|---|---|---|---|---|---|
| 200 | 10 | 4 | 4 | 20 | 37 | | 19 | 40 | | 4 | 4 | 4 | 20 | 52 |
| | 15 | 6 | 14 | 32 | 66 | | 30* | 62 | | 4 | 6 | 14 | 32 | 82 |
| | 20 | 16 | 17 | 62 | 111 | | 45* | 90 | | 3 | 16 | 17 | 62 | 137 |
| | 25 | 20 | 28 | 81 | 150 | | 60** | 119 | | 7 | 20 | 28 | 81 | 184 |
| | 30 | 24 | 45 | 88 | 184 | | 70** | 139 | | 10 | 24 | 45 | 88 | 225 |
| | 35 | 44 | 59 | 89 | 224 | | 77** | 171 | | 10 | 44 | 59 | 89 | 285 |
| | 40 | 65 | 65 | 91 | 259 | | 76** | 197 | | 12 | 65 | 65 | 91 | 343 |
| | 45 | 79 | 67 | 93 | 285 | | 79** | 222 | | 16 | 79 | 67 | 93 | 387 |
| | 50 | 83 | 67 | 96 | 305 | | 81** | 241 | | 25 | 83 | 67 | 96 | 420 |
| | 55 | 85 | 68 | 99 | 324 | | 83** | 258 | | 32 | 85 | 68 | 99 | 448 |
| | 60 | 85 | 69 | 103 | 344 | | 84** | 274 | | 36 | 85 | 69 | 103 | 472 |
| 210 | 10 | 4 | 6 | 20 | 40 | | 21 | 43 | | 3 | 4 | 6 | 20 | 54 |
| | 15 | 8 | 14 | 38 | 75 | | 30* | 66 | | 4 | 8 | 14 | 38 | 94 |
| | 20 | 18 | 19 | 68 | 123 | | 49* | 97 | | 4 | 18 | 19 | 68 | 152 |
| | 25 | 20 | 34 | 84 | 162 | | 62** | 124 | | 9 | 20 | 34 | 84 | 198 |
| | 30 | 26 | 52 | 88 | 196 | | 75** | 149 | | 10 | 26 | 52 | 88 | 239 |
| | 35 | 52 | 63 | 90 | 241 | | 78** | 184 | | 12 | 52 | 63 | 90 | 312 |
| | 40 | 73 | 66 | 93 | 276 | | 80** | 215 | | 15 | 73 | 66 | 93 | 371 |
| | 45 | 83 | 67 | 96 | 301 | | 80** | 236 | | 21 | 83 | 67 | 96 | 412 |
| | 50 | 85 | 67 | 100 | 321 | | 82** | 254 | | 30 | 85 | 67 | 100 | 443 |
| | 55 | 83 | 69 | 103 | 341 | | 85** | 272 | | 37 | 83 | 69 | 103 | 468 |

Water stops 40 fsw and deeper from in-water. O₂ or Sur-D-O₂ tables (Table 7 or 8)

Surface Interval (In-Water): Time from leaving 30 fsw in-water to 40 fsw in-chamber not to exceed 7 min.

Surface Interval (Deck Decompression Chamber): Time from leaving 30 fsw in-water to 40 fsw in-chamber not to exceed 7 min.

## Table 9 DCIEM HeO₂ Emergency Decompression

| Depth (fsw) | Bottom Time (min) | In-Water Air 30 | 20 | 10 | Decomp Time | Surface Interval | O₂ 40 | Decomp Time | Surface Interval | Air 40 | 30 | 20 | 10 | Decomp Time |
|---|---|---|---|---|---|---|---|---|---|---|---|---|---|---|
| 220 | 10 | 4 | 8 | 21 | 44 | | 22 | 45 | | 4 | 4 | 8 | 21 | 59 |
| | 15 | 10 | 14 | 44 | 84 | | 32* | 71 | | 4 | 10 | 14 | 44 | 105 |
| | 20 | 20 | 22 | 74 | 136 | | 53* | 105 | | 5 | 20 | 22 | 74 | 168 |
| | 25 | 22 | 40 | 86 | 174 | | 67** | 133 | | 9 | 22 | 40 | 86 | 212 |
| | 30 | 38 | 57 | 89 | 216 | | 79** | 167 | | 10 | 38 | 57 | 89 | 271 |
| | 35 | 60 | 65 | 92 | 257 | | 78** | 196 | | 13 | 60 | 65 | 92 | 337 |
| | 40 | 79 | 67 | 95 | 291 | | 80** | 227 | | 18 | 79 | 67 | 95 | 395 |
| | 45 | 85 | 67 | 99 | 315 | | 82** | 249 | | 27 | 85 | 67 | 99 | 434 |
| | 50 | 85 | 68 | 103 | 337 | | 84** | 268 | | 35 | 85 | 68 | 103 | 464 |
| | 55 | 83 | 70 | 107 | 359 | | 88** | 288 | | 41 | 83 | 70 | 107 | 490 |
| 230 | 10 | 4 | 9 | 22 | 47 | | 24 | 48 | | 4 | 4 | 9 | 22 | 62 |
| | 15 | 14 | 15 | 50 | 95 | | 34* | 77 | | 3 | 14 | 15 | 50 | 119 |
| | 20 | 20 | 25 | 79 | 146 | | 58* | 113 | | 6 | 20 | 25 | 79 | 179 |
| | 25 | 24 | 46 | 88 | 187 | | 71** | 141 | | 9 | 24 | 46 | 88 | 226 |
| | 30 | 46 | 61 | 91 | 233 | | 79** | 178 | | 11 | 46 | 61 | 91 | 297 |
| | 35 | 73 | 66 | 94 | 277 | | 80** | 215 | | 15 | 73 | 66 | 94 | 372 |
| | 40 | 83 | 67 | 97 | 304 | | 81** | 239 | | 22 | 83 | 67 | 97 | 416 |
| | 45 | 85 | 69 | 101 | 330 | | 84** | 262 | | 33 | 85 | 69 | 101 | 455 |
| | 50 | 83 | 70 | 106 | 353 | | 87** | 282 | | 40 | 83 | 70 | 106 | 483 |

In-Water note: Water stops 40 fsw and deeper from in-water O₂ or Sur-D–O₂ tables (Table 7 or 8)

Surface Interval note: Time from leaving 30 fsw in-water to 40 fsw in-chamber not to exceed 7 min.

## Table 9 DCIEM HeO₂ Emergency Decompression

| Depth (fsw) | Bottom Time (min) | In-Water Air 30 | In-Water Air 20 | In-Water Air 10 | Decomp Time | Surface Interval | O₂ 40 | Decomp Time | Surface Interval | Air 40 | Air 30 | Air 20 | Air 10 | Decomp Time |
|---|---|---|---|---|---|---|---|---|---|---|---|---|---|---|
| 240 | 10 | 4 | 10 | 24 | 51 | | 25 | 50 | | 4 | 4 | 10 | 24 | 66 |
| | 15 | 16 | 16 | 56 | 105 | | 38* | 84 | | 3 | 16 | 16 | 56 | 131 |
| | 20 | 20 | 29 | 82 | 155 | | 60** | 122 | | 7 | 20 | 29 | 82 | 189 |
| | 25 | 26 | 52 | 89 | 199 | | 75** | 150 | | 10 | 26 | 52 | 89 | 241 |
| | 30 | 54 | 64 | 92 | 250 | | 79** | 190 | | 12 | 54 | 64 | 92 | 323 |
| | 35 | 77 | 67 | 95 | 289 | | 81** | 226 | | 18 | 77 | 67 | 95 | 391 |
| | 40 | 85 | 68 | 99 | 318 | | 82** | 251 | | 27 | 85 | 68 | 99 | 437 |
| | 45 | 83 | 70 | 105 | 345 | | 87** | 275 | | 38 | 83 | 70 | 105 | 473 |
| 250 | 10 | 4 | 11 | 26 | 55 | | 27 | 53 | | 4 | 4 | 11 | 26 | 70 |
| | 15 | 18 | 17 | 62 | 115 | | 42* | 91 | | 3 | 18 | 17 | 62 | 143 |
| | 20 | 22 | 34 | 85 | 167 | | 62** | 128 | | 8 | 22 | 34 | 85 | 204 |
| | 25 | 36 | 57 | 89 | 216 | | 80** | 168 | | 10 | 36 | 57 | 89 | 269 |
| | 30 | 67 | 65 | 94 | 270 | | 81** | 209 | | 14 | 67 | 65 | 94 | 357 |
| | 35 | 81 | 67 | 98 | 303 | | 82** | 239 | | 22 | 81 | 67 | 98 | 413 |
| | 40 | 83 | 69 | 102 | 331 | | 85** | 263 | | 34 | 83 | 69 | 102 | 455 |
| | 45 | 83 | 71 | 108 | 360 | | 89** | 288 | | 41 | 83 | 71 | 108 | 491 |
| 260 | 10 | 4 | 12 | 27 | 58 | | 29 | 55 | | 4 | 4 | 12 | 27 | 73 |
| | 15 | 18 | 19 | 67 | 123 | | 47* | 97 | | 3 | 18 | 19 | 67 | 151 |
| | 20 | 22 | 39 | 87 | 176 | | 66** | 134 | | 9 | 22 | 39 | 87 | 214 |
| | 25 | 42 | 61 | 91 | 231 | | 80** | 177 | | 11 | 42 | 61 | 91 | 291 |
| | 30 | 73 | 67 | 95 | 283 | | 81** | 219 | | 16 | 73 | 67 | 95 | 378 |
| | 35 | 83 | 68 | 100 | 317 | | 83** | 249 | | 26 | 83 | 68 | 100 | 433 |
| | 40 | 83 | 70 | 106 | 347 | | 87** | 276 | | 39 | 83 | 70 | 106 | 476 |

In-Water Surface Interval column: Water stops 40 fsw and deeper from in-water O₂ or Sur–D–O₂ tables (Table 7 or 8)

Deck Decompression Chamber Surface Interval columns: Time from leaving 30 fsw in-water to 40 fsw in-chamber not to exceed 7 min.

## Table 9 DCIEM HeO₂ Emergency Decompression

| Depth (fsw) | Bottom Time (min) | In-Water Air 30 | In-Water Air 20 | In-Water Air 10 | In-Water Decomp Time | Surface Interval | DDC O₂ 40 | DDC Decomp Time | Surface Interval | DDC Air 40 | DDC Air 30 | DDC Air 20 | DDC Air 10 | DDC Decomp Time |
|---|---|---|---|---|---|---|---|---|---|---|---|---|---|---|
| 270 | 10 | 4 | 13 | 30 | 63 | | 30* | 62 | | 4 | 4 | 13 | 30 | 78 |
| | 15 | 18 | 21 | 72 | 132 | | 52* | 104 | | 5 | 18 | 21 | 72 | 162 |
| | 20 | 24 | 46 | 88 | 188 | | 70** | 142 | | 9 | 24 | 46 | 88 | 228 |
| | 25 | 50 | 63 | 92 | 245 | | 80** | 188 | | 12 | 50 | 63 | 92 | 314 |
| | 30 | 77 | 67 | 97 | 294 | | 82** | 230 | | 18 | 77 | 67 | 97 | 396 |
| | 35 | 83 | 69 | 102 | 329 | | 85** | 260 | | 31 | 83 | 69 | 102 | 450 |
| | 40 | 83 | 71 | 109 | 362 | | 89** | 288 | | 42 | 83 | 71 | 109 | 494 |
| 280 | 10 | 8 | 14 | 33 | 71 | | 30* | 62 | | 3 | 8 | 14 | 33 | 89 |
| | 15 | 18 | 24 | 76 | 141 | | 56* | 110 | | 6 | 18 | 24 | 76 | 172 |
| | 20 | 26 | 51 | 89 | 198 | | 73** | 149 | | 9 | 26 | 51 | 89 | 240 |
| | 25 | 56 | 65 | 93 | 257 | | 81** | 198 | | 13 | 56 | 65 | 93 | 333 |
| | 30 | 81 | 67 | 99 | 307 | | 83** | 242 | | 22 | 81 | 67 | 99 | 417 |
| | 35 | 83 | 70 | 105 | 342 | | 87*** | 272 | | 36 | 83 | 70 | 105 | 468 |
| | 40 | 83 | 73 | 112 | 377 | | 90*** | 304 | | 44 | 83 | 73 | 112 | 511 |
| 290 | 10 | 8 | 14 | 37 | 76 | | 30* | 68 | | 3 | 8 | 14 | 37 | 94 |
| | 15 | 20 | 26 | 80 | 150 | | 59* | 116 | | 6 | 20 | 26 | 80 | 183 |
| | 20 | 34 | 54 | 90 | 212 | | 79** | 165 | | 9 | 34 | 54 | 90 | 262 |
| | 25 | 67 | 66 | 95 | 275 | | 82** | 214 | | 15 | 67 | 66 | 95 | 364 |
| | 30 | 83 | 68 | 101 | 319 | | 84** | 252 | | 26 | 83 | 68 | 101 | 435 |
| | 35 | 83 | 71 | 108 | 356 | | 89** | 284 | | 40 | 83 | 71 | 108 | 486 |

Note (In-Water column): Water stops 40 fsw and deeper from in-water O₂ or Sur–D–O₂ tables (Table 7 or 8)

Note (Surface Interval columns): Time from leaving 30 fsw in-water to 40 fsw in-chamber not to exceed 7 min.

Table 9 DCIEM HeO₂ Emergency Decompression

| Depth (fsw) | Bottom Time (min) | In-Water Air 30 | 20 | 10 | Decomp Time | Surface Interval | O₂ 40 | Decomp Time | Surface Interval | Air 40 | 30 | 20 | 10 | Decomp Time |
|---|---|---|---|---|---|---|---|---|---|---|---|---|---|---|
| 300 | 10 | 10 | 15 | 41 | 84 | | 30* | 71 | | 3 | 10 | 15 | 41 | 104 |
| | 15 | 20 | 30 | 82 | 159 | | 60** | 124 | | 7 | 20 | 30 | 82 | 193 |
| | 20 | 36 | 58 | 91 | 222 | | 81** | 172 | | 11 | 36 | 58 | 91 | 276 |
| | 25 | 73 | 67 | 96 | 287 | | 82** | 224 | | 17 | 73 | 67 | 96 | 384 |
| | 30 | 83 | 69 | 104 | 332 | | 85** | 262 | | 31 | 83 | 69 | 104 | 453 |
| | 35 | 83 | 72 | 111 | 369 | | 90*** | 294 | | 42 | 83 | 72 | 111 | 501 |
| 310 | 10 | 12 | 14 | 46 | 90 | | 32* | 75 | | 3 | 12 | 14 | 46 | 112 |
| | 15 | 20 | 34 | 85 | 168 | | 62** | 129 | | 9 | 20 | 34 | 85 | 204 |
| | 20 | 42 | 61 | 92 | 234 | | 82** | 181 | | 11 | 42 | 61 | 92 | 294 |
| | 25 | 77 | 67 | 99 | 299 | | 83** | 234 | | 19 | 77 | 67 | 99 | 402 |
| | 30 | 83 | 70 | 106 | 343 | | 87** | 272 | | 35 | 83 | 70 | 106 | 468 |
| | 35 | 83 | 74 | 113 | 383 | | 90*** | 309 | | 44 | 83 | 74 | 113 | 517 |
| 320 | 10 | 14 | 15 | 51 | 99 | | 35* | 81 | | 3 | 14 | 15 | 51 | 123 |
| | 15 | 22 | 38 | 86 | 176 | | 64** | 134 | | 9 | 22 | 38 | 86 | 214 |
| | 20 | 48 | 63 | 93 | 246 | | 82** | 190 | | 12 | 48 | 63 | 93 | 313 |
| | 25 | 79 | 68 | 100 | 309 | | 84** | 243 | | 23 | 79 | 68 | 100 | 418 |
| | 30 | 83 | 72 | 108 | 356 | | 89** | 283 | | 39 | 83 | 72 | 108 | 485 |
| 330 | 10 | 14 | 16 | 54 | 103 | | 38* | 84 | | 3 | 14 | 16 | 54 | 127 |
| | 15 | 22 | 42 | 88 | 184 | | 68** | 140 | | 9 | 22 | 42 | 88 | 222 |
| | 20 | 54 | 65 | 94 | 258 | | 82** | 198 | | 13 | 54 | 65 | 94 | 313 |
| | 25 | 81 | 69 | 102 | 321 | | 85** | 253 | | 27 | 81 | 69 | 102 | 436 |
| | 30 | 83 | 72 | 111 | 367 | | 90*** | 292 | | 42 | 83 | 72 | 111 | 499 |

*In-Water:* Water stops 40 fsw and deeper from in-water O₂ or Sur-D-O₂ tables (Table 7 or 8)

*Surface Interval:* Time from leaving 30 fsw in-water to 40 fsw in-chamber not to exceed 7 min.

**NOTICE:** Helium-oxygen dives should never be performed using only a down-line. The use of an enclosed stage or wet bell complete with on-board emergency gas supply is **strongly recommended**. On-board emergency gas supply should include (clearly marked) HeO₂ and air for decompression. Helium-oxygen dives must never be performed without a chamber onsite.

## GENERAL PROCEDURE FOR USING HELIUM-OXYGEN TABLES

The HeO$_2$ mixture is breathed for the entire duration of the dive, from when the diver leaves surface until he/she reaches the first decompression stop, when a gas change to air is performed. All in-water decompression stops up to the 30 fsw stop are performed on air. Once the diver reaches 30 fsw, another gas change to oxygen is performed. At this point, the diver can complete decompression in-water on oxygen or have a shortened O$_2$ water stop and decompress in the chamber on oxygen. Either way, the ascent from 30 fsw to surface is performed while breathing oxygen.

As with the air tables, the exceptional exposure portion is intended for emergency use only, and planned dives within the exceptional exposure range are not recommended. The depth cut off for normal diving is 300 fsw, with dives deeper than this point being considered exceptional exposure. The time cut-off for normal diving is a total in-water time of 3 hours 30 minutes or a bottom time of 25 minutes at 300 fsw. Any bottom times exceeding these parameters are considered exceptional exposure dives.

**Descent Rate:** The maximum rate of travel from surface to bottom is 60 fpm (feet seawater per minute).

**Ascent Rate:** As in the air tables, the ascent rate is 60 + 10 fpm from bottom to the first stop, the same between stops, and from the last stop to the surface.

**Bottom Time:** As in the air tables, bottom time is reckoned as beginning when the diver leaves surface until the diver leaves bottom, rounded up to the next full minute.

**Depth:** The deepest depth the diver achieves during the dive, measured by pneumofathometer with the correction factor added in. Readings for maximum depth should be taken with the pneumo hose at the diver's ankle.

**Stop Time:** Decompression stop time includes travel time from the previous stop in all cases except the first stop due to the gas change and the

30 fsw stop due to the gas change. In these two instances, stop time begins when the diver is confirmed on the new gas.

**Gas Change (Gas Switching):** Gas changes from helium-oxygen to air or vice versa are confirmed by voice change in the diver. For gas changes from air to oxygen, once the $O_2$ analyzer on the panel reads above 95%, allow an additional 20 seconds of flushing to confirm. (Medical oxygen often analyzes at slightly below 100%.)

**Surface Interval for Surface Decompression:** The surface interval for $HeO_2$ surface decompression begins when the diver leaves the 30 fsw stop and ends when the diver is confirmed on oxygen at 40 fsw in the chamber. The maximum surface interval allowed is 7 minutes.

**Oxygen Breathing:** As with the air tables, the maximum time to have divers breathing oxygen is 30 minutes without a 5-minute air break. This applies to both in-water oxygen and chamber oxygen. When using in-water oxygen, the helmet is not flushed at the start of the air break or at the resumption of oxygen breathing. Air breaks are not included in stop times (in-water or chamber), but they are included in the total decompression time.

**Delays in Ascent to First Stop:** Any delay of more than 30 seconds in reaching the first stop is added to the bottom time of the dive, and the appropriate decompression schedule is selected on the table.

**Delays in Ascent Between Stops:** A delay in leaving an air stop is considered decompression time, and the time of delay can be subtracted from the next shallower stop. This does not apply to the 30 fsw oxygen stop. This stop is not to be shortened due to delays at deeper stops.

**Missed First Stop:** If the first stop is passed on ascent, change to air and remain at the second stop for the combined times of the first and second stops. This only applies to missing the first stop and not subsequent stops. If more than one stop is missed, see Omitted Decompression under Emergency Procedures in this section.

**Flying after Helium-Oxygen Dives:** Rules for flying after diving are different with helium-oxygen than they are for air. They are as follows:

- No decompression helium-oxygen dives require a surface interval of 12 hours before flying.

- Decompression HeO$_2$ dives with total dive time less than or equal to 2 hours require a surface interval of 24 hours before flying.

- Decompression HeO$_2$ dives where the total dive time is greater than 2 hours require a surface interval of 48 hours before flying.

## EMERGENCY PROCEDURES
### Maximum Surface Interval Exceeded or Omitted Decompression
In the event that the 7-minute surface interval (SI) is exceeded but the chamber has started pressurization prior to :06::20 and reaches 40 fsw prior to :10::00 and divers are asymptomatic, double the delay time rounded to the next whole minute, adding it to the decompression required for the 40 fsw chamber stop.

If the SI is exceeded or decompression is omitted and the total time of decompression remaining is less than 30 minutes, commence a Treatment Table 5. If the total decompression time remaining is 30 minutes or more, commence Treatment Table 6.

### Minor Symptoms of Oxygen Toxicity
If minor symptoms (no convulsions) of O$_2$ toxicity occur on the in-water O$_2$ stop, switch to air, ventilate, and wait for all symptoms to subside. Wait an additional 15 minutes, and choose one of the following:

- Resume O$_2$ decompression at the point of interruption.

- If in-water O$_2$ requirements for Table 8 have been met, perform Sur-D-O$_2$ using Table 8.

- Subtract 30 fsw air/O$_2$ time from 30 fsw and shallower stops and decompress using Table 9.

If oxygen breathing is resumed and toxicity symptoms recur, switch to air and decompress using Table 9.

If minor symptoms occur in the chamber, subtract completed 40 fsw Air/$O_2$ time from 40 fsw and shallower stops and decompress in the chamber using Table 9.

### Oxygen Convulsions and Serious Symptoms of Toxicity

Immediately switch to air and ventilate. Stabilize the diver (do not change diver's depth while convulsing).

- **In-Water:** Once symptoms have completely subsided, if in-water $O_2$ requirements for Table 8 have been met, surface diver and decompress in chamber on Table 8. Otherwise follow Table 9. Diver must be surfaced carefully to reduce risk of embolism. If any uncertainty exists as to whether diver may have an arterial gas embolism, treat as such.

- **In Chamber:** Switch to Table 9. Air/$O_2$ time at 40 fsw in the chamber counts as good time and is subtracted from the 40 fsw and shallower stops on Table 9.

### Loss of Oxygen In-Water

In the event of a loss of oxygen on the in-water oxygen stop, immediately switch the diver to air. If $O_2$ can be reestablished within 15 minutes, resume decompression at the point of interruption. If oxygen cannot be restored, the following options may be used:

1. If the in-water $O_2$ requirements of Table 8 have been met, decompress in chamber on Table 8.

2. Complete the 30 fsw stop requirements for Table 9, and switch to Sur-D-$O_2$ (Table 8).

3. Complete decompression in-water using Table 9. Air/$O_2$ time may be subtracted from 30 fsw and shallower stops on Table 9.

## Loss of Oxygen in Chamber

If oxygen can be restored within 15 minutes, resume decompression at the point of interruption. Time on air is considered "dead time." If oxygen cannot be restored within 15 minutes, enter Table 9 at 40 fsw. Air/O$_2$ time at 40 fsw in the chamber may be subtracted from the 40 fsw and shallower stops on Table 9.

## Loss of Gas at Depth

The following procedures are to be followed for loss of gas at depth:

a. **Lost HeO$_2$:** In the event the diver loses heliox, the diver switches to bailout, returns to the stage (bell), and plugs into the on-board gas supply. Abort the dive, bring diver to first stop, and change to air.

b. **Lost Air:** In the event the diver loses air, he switches to bailout (HeO$_2$) and plugs into the on-board air supply (stage or bell mount). Continue decompression at the point of interruption. If unable to access on-board air, continue decompression on helium-oxygen in accordance with Table 7. If at all possible, shift the diver to air prior to the 30 fsw O$_2$ stop. Upon surfacing, if diver is asymptomatic, initiate Treatment Table 5. If diver is symptomatic, treat for decompression sickness as symptoms dictate.

c. **Unable to Switch to Air at First Stop:** If unable to switch to air at the first water stop, keep the diver on HeO$_2$ for up to 5 minutes. Once air is restored or on-board air is plugged in, resume decompression at the point of interruption. If unable to restore surface air or unable to access on-board air, continue decompression on helium-oxygen. Restore air if possible, prior to arrival at 30 fsw O$_2$ stop. Upon surfacing, if diver is asymptomatic, initiate Treatment Table 5. If diver is symptomatic, treat for decompression sickness as symptoms dictate.

d. **Unable to Switch to Oxygen at 30 fsw Stop:** If unable to switch to oxygen, decompress according to Table 9. If oxygen is available to the chamber, Table 8 may be used after the completion of the 30 fsw air stop on Table 9.

## Symptoms of DCS During Surface Interval

Occasionally when performing Sur-D-$O_2$ dives, signs and symptoms of decompression sickness will present during the surface interval. Typically, these will be mild symptoms and will occur late in the surface interval. If the symptoms have completely resolved by the time the diver is confirmed on oxygen at 40 fsw in the chamber, decompress as indicated in the selected schedule on Table 8. If the symptoms have not completely resolved by the time the diver is confirmed on oxygen at 40 fsw, press the diver to 60 fsw and initiate a Treatment Table 6.

# SECTION 19
# Emergency Medical Care (First Aid)

First aid is classically defined as the immediate, temporary assistance provided to a victim of injury or illness before the services of emergency medical personnel or a physician can be obtained. The purpose of first aid is to prevent further injury or worsening of the victim's condition. When an accident occurs, the proper response can mean the difference between life and death, temporary or permanent disability, and short- or long-term hospitalization.

In the diving environment, due to time delays inherent in the distances from medical treatment and medical facilities, the classic definition of first aid is frequently obscured by circumstances. It is for this reason that everyone involved in diving operations should have more than just an understanding of the basics of first aid. All divers should complete a comprehensive first aid and cardiopulmonary resuscitation course as offered by St. John Ambulance, the National Safety Council First Aid Institute, or the local branch of Red Cross. More appropriately, at least one diver per crew per shift should be trained and certified as a diver medical technician.

## MEDICAL EMERGENCY RESPONSE PLAN
Every commercial diving operation should have a medical emergency response plan (MERP). Offshore, copies of this plan are kept on the bridge of the vessel, the diving superintendent's office, and in dive control. On smaller jobs (inland and coastal) it will be kept with the diving manual. Typically, it is a printed document with an accompanying laminated flowchart, which has the following information: onsite location of medical equipment and supplies; names of designated on-board medical response personnel for each shift; names and contact information for on-call hyperbaric physician; contact information for patient transport, such as med-evac vessels or aircraft; contact details for on-call medical facility or hospital; and for smaller projects, the location of the nearest chamber.

## MEDICAL EQUIPMENT

Most diving operations worldwide are performed according to IMCA D014—The International Code of Practice for Offshore Diving, most often referred to as the IMCA Guideline. IMCA has a diving medical advisory committee (DMAC), which consists of hyperbaric physicians from around the world. DMAC advises the diving contractors on diver's health issues, diver's medical fitness, treatment techniques and emergency medical equipment (DMAC-diving.org). The medical kits used offshore are the DMAC trauma kit and the DMAC chamber internal medical kit. The contents list for the DMAC medical kits (DMAC 15) is updated often, with the current list in DMAC 15 Revision 4. A copy of the list may be found in Section 12: Diving Medicine.

## BASIC PRINCIPLES OF EMERGENCY
### Medical Care

The first step in administering first aid is to evaluate the victim's condition quickly and accurately and to elect an appropriate course of action. This evaluation must be done systematically, quickly, and comprehensively. In caring for the victim of a medical or trauma emergency, there are several steps involved in immediate assessment and intervention. Too often these have been viewed as separate components. In reality, assessment and care constitute a continuum.

**Accident Scene Safety:** The first concern of any rescue operation is scene safety. When rescuers jump head first into a situation without any concern for their own safety, they often become additional victims, drawing more resources and thereby failing to contribute to the rescue. The scene may never be completely safe, but steps can be taken to mitigate the risk. On diving operations, rescuers need to pay attention to the sea state and current, unsecured deck gear or loads, areas with poor air quality, or any other threat to the safety of the rescuer.

**Primary Assessment:** Once immediate threats to safety have been addressed, the victim can be tended. First, establish responsiveness. If the victim is responsive, even minimally, he/she obviously has a pulse and is breathing. At this point, there exists an emergent condition and help should be summoned. Depending on the location, this could be calling the coast guard or radio the medic on the ship. Designate someone to do this task, and check for a pulse. This may require rapid removal/cutting of the exposure suit, even if it is that expensive drysuit. If there is no pulse, the treatment is simple—chest compressions. Meanwhile, another rescuer should be getting the AED and preparing the oxygen kit to assist ventilations.

**Secondary Assessment:** Once immediate threats to a victim's life have been corrected or eliminated, a more comprehensive examination is carried out. In a trauma victim, this is a thorough head-to-toe evaluation of all body parts and systems. In a medical emergency, the secondary survey may be more focused on those body parts and systems that have the greatest likelihood of being involved based on the victim's chief complaint. It is possible that during the secondary survey, the rescuer may identify problems that, if left unchecked, might develop into life-threatening circumstances. During this phase of the care continuum, additional treatment and stabilization may be provided beyond that initiated during the initial assessment. Never should an assessment delay transport by Medevac to an appropriate medical facility. Although generally not viewed as a part of out-of-hospital emergency medical care, it is possible that even though the rescuer is not a medical professional, he/she may be called upon to deliver definitive care in the diving setting.

**Infection Control:** It is important to eliminate direct contact with the casualty's blood or other bodily fluids, mucous membranes, wounds, or burns. The tools that rescuers should employ to protect themselves include the following:

- Good quality, disposable latex, nitrile, or vinyl gloves. Fit is not as critical as protection. If gloves are too big, that shouldn't be a problem. But, if gloves are too small, there is the risk of having the gloves tear when being applied or during use, an event that must be avoided at all costs.

- A pocket mask with a one-way valve should it be necessary to provide artificial ventilation to the victim using the mouth and lungs as the means for restoring or supplementing the victim's breathing.

- Eye protection in the form of eyeglasses that are wide enough to prevent fluids from becoming splashed in the eyes. More appropriately, medical kits used in the diving environment should contain inexpensive goggles designed for emergency medical care. As a last resort, in the diving environment, the rescuer might even employ a dive mask for this purpose, though it is likely to be cumbersome.

- A disposable, medical face mask will prevent the inhalation of infectious organisms in airborne droplets. Though in the marine setting the rescuer is unlikely to encounter such situations, there are certain infections for which a face mask may also be appropriately put on the victim as well as the rescuer—coronaviruses, meningitis, and tuberculosis, for example.

Each of these items is relatively inexpensive and should be a part of a personal kit or the medical kit carried on board every boat. First aiders and diver medics should monitor the WHO and CDC websites for the infectious diseases trending and precautions should be appropriate for the current situation.

## A DETAILED LOOK: THE PRIMARY SURVEY

If the body loses its ability to take in oxygen and release carbon dioxide through the respiratory system or can no longer move life-sustaining oxygen through the circulatory system, then tissues, organs, and eventually, the person will die. Likewise, if there is no detectable circulation, the patient may die. The main purpose of the primary assessment is the establishment and/or maintenance of an adequate airway to ensure that the victim is breathing and that adequate circulation is present. These are the first steps to take in basic life support (BSL), also known to many as cardiopulmonary resuscitation (CPR). In 2010, the American Heart

Association (AHA) changed the "ABC's" (airway, breathing, circulation) to "CAB" (compressions, airway, breathing) based on clinical- and evidence-based research. The first step is to determine whether the victim has simply fainted. Assuming there are no signs/symptoms of injury to suggest spinal trauma, roll the victim into a face-up position on a firm surface like the deck of a boat or the firm sand on a beach. Gently shake the victim and shout, "Are you OK?" Should trauma be a possibility, spinal stabilization must be considered. In such cases, do not shake the victim but simply tap on the victim's shoulder firmly and shout. If the victim has simply fainted, the victim will usually regain consciousness immediately or soon after lying down. If the victim does not respond or regain consciousness, ask bystanders to notify whatever emergency medical services are available. If the victim regains consciousness and is breathing adequately, then continue to the initial assessment, again provided that no life-threatening bleeding is present. At this point, the rescuer should perform a scan of the victim looking for breathing and other signs of life. Rescuers trained in BLS for the health care provider (HCP) are trained to check for a pulse. If not trained in this procedure, proceed directly to compressions if no signs of life are present. The action, once known as "look-listen-feel," has been removed from the BLS algorithm. By performing CAB, the first step has been taken in the performance of BLS. CAB is broken down into the following steps:

**Compressions:** As soon as it has been determined that the patient is unresponsive and not breathing, chest compressions must be administered. Without spontaneous heartbeat, the oxygen being supplied through the lungs cannot reach the body's tissues and organs. According to the *2010 AHA Guidelines*, begin with 30 chest compressions, followed with two breaths. Chest compressions should be started immediately if there is no breathing or if there is only agonal breathing, which are very slow, gasping-type breaths. If trained, such as in BLS for the HCP, a pulse may be checked. However, if there is any question that a pulse may be absent, or if one is not sure they feel a pulse, chest compressions should be started immediately. Chest compressions should be done at a rate of at least 100 per minute and at least 2" in depth.

**Airway:** To open the victim's airway, use the head-tilt, chin-lift method which puts a hand (the one closest to the victim's head) on the victim's forehead, while two or three fingers of the other hand are placed under the bony portion of the victim's jaw. By lifting with the fingers under the jaw and, at the same time, pressing gently on the victim's forehead, the head is tilted back into a hyper-extended position. This lifts the tongue and keeps it from blocking the airway of the victim. Sometimes, opening the airway is enough to start the victim breathing spontaneously. Ensure that the victim is conscious enough to maintain his/her own airway or manually open the airway to make certain it is maintained.

If it is suspected that the victim may have sustained a spinal injury, then the technique used for opening the airway is called the "jaw thrust maneuver." This process is accomplished by taking both thumbs and placing them pointing downward on the large bones under the victim's eyes—the cheek bones. With the thumbs in this position, the rescuer should be able to get his/her fingers behind the victim's jaw at the point where the rescuer can feel the bend in the lower jaw or mandible. With the thumbs and fingers in this position and using the opposing forces of the thumb against the fingers, the rescuer will be able to move the jaw forward. This will lift the tongue off the back of the throat and establish an open airway. All of this must be done without any manipulation of the spine, which must be maintained in a neutral position.

**Breathing:** Once an adequate airway has been established, then breathing must be evaluated and either restored or aided. If the victim is not breathing, initiate ventilations according to the agency you were trained by, which in most cases is one breath every 3-5 seconds if giving rescue breaths only, or 2 breaths per 30 chest compressions if performing CPR. Use an oxygen-powered positive pressure valve or a bag-valve mask connected to an oxygen source. If neither of these are available, perform mouth-to-mask ventilations. Ideally, all victims should receive supplemental oxygen as part of breathing restoration, but this is particularly true when dealing with a diving emergency.

After each ventilation, allow the victim to passively exhale. To ventilate the patient, use a pocket mask, tru-fit mask, or other oral-nasal type mask. To seal the mask on the victim's face, make the OK sign to demonstrate the preferred hand position for the hand grasping the mask device. The thumb and index finger circle the port through which the rescuer ventilates the victim while the remaining fingers are used to assist in maintaining the seal of the mask over the victim's face.

The circular device appearing above the thumb and index finger is the one-way valve incorporated in the mask, which prevents the victim's exhaled air or other expired or regurgitated matter from entering the caregiver's mouth or airway. Use of these one-way valves is consistent with the concept of self-protection when providing care to a victim. The oral-nasal mask is placed over the victim's mouth and nose, with the opening of the breathing tube directly over the victim's mouth. The fingers of the right hand are used to lift the jaw, while the left hand is on the forehead. Even with the pocket mask device, the head-tilt chin-lift technique must be utilized to maintain an open airway. With the left and right hands in proper position, the caregiver ventilates the victim for 1.5 to 2 seconds per ventilation and allows the victim to exhale passively between breaths. Using peripheral vision, the caregiver can also monitor chest rise with each ventilation to be certain that the breaths are properly entering the victim's lungs. If chest rise is not observed during efforts to ventilate, the head-tilt, chin-lift maneuver should be repeated, since the airway may be blocked by the victim's tongue or other anatomic structures. If such repositioning does not result in successful ventilation of the victim, then there may be an airway obstruction that cannot be corrected simply by repositioning. In these cases, the foreign body airway obstruction technique learned in formal CPR training should be employed.

Next, it is vital to determine if there is life-threatening bleeding; if such bleeding is found, it must be stopped. Once it has been observed that a conscious victim can speak clearly and seems to be properly oriented to his/her surroundings and there is no obvious life-threatening bleeding, the primary assessment has been completed.

## Emergency Airway Management and Artificial Ventilation

It is most desirable to have the victim's airway maintenance supplemented by using an oropharyngeal airway if, as a part of the life support provided, artificial ventilations are required. Ventilations may be provided using mouth-to-mask ventilation, or more preferably, ventilation utilizing a manually-triggered, oxygen-powered, positive-pressure demand valve or a bag-valve mask connected to an oxygen source.

If the victim is breathing, then a decision must be made whether the breathing is adequate or if some supplemental ventilation is required.

Most victims of serious illness or injury will be breathing relatively rapidly. In some cases, this is a positive finding, but if the victim is breathing too rapidly, there may not be enough air moving in and out of the lungs with each breath. In such cases, the breathing must be managed.

Using a watch, count the number of breaths the victim takes during 15 seconds. Multiply that by four to determine the number of times the victim is breathing each minute.

If the victim is breathing at a rate of less than 10 breaths per minute and is symptomatic, supplementing respirations may be required.

## Adult One Rescuer CPR

Artificial ventilation is done by mouth-to-mouth resuscitation or utilizing a supplemental device as described previously, while artificial circulation is done by external cardiac massage. Together, they are called CPR.

Every diver should complete a CPR course from a recognized training agency. Some of those include the local Red Cross, American Heart

Association, St. John Ambulance, or an Offshore Petroleum Industry Training Organization (OPITO)- approved first aid training organization.

CPR is aimed at supplying the victim's body with oxygen and ridding the body of excess carbon dioxide. The purpose of CPR may also include the establishment and maintenance of the victim's circulation until more advanced life support can be initiated or until normal breathing and heartbeat are restored. Once begun, CPR is continued until relieved by emergency medical personnel or until the rescuer is unable to continue.

For the sake of simplicity, this discussion deals exclusively with one rescuer CPR. In the event that CPR is required for an extended period of time, other divers can continue one rescuer CPR should the rescuer become overly fatigued. If two people are properly trained, two rescuer CPR may be utilized.

If trained in BLS, check the victim's pulse, otherwise assess respirations as previously described and begin chest compressions as instructed by your BLS course. Do this by sliding two fingertips gently into the groove-like indentation between the trachea (windpipe) and the large muscle (sternocleidomastoid) running down the side of the victim's neck. If the heart is beating adequately, a pulse may be felt in a major artery found in this anatomic landmark—the carotid artery.

Take 5-10 seconds to detect the victim's pulse before going any further. The 5-10 second delay serves two purposes. First, it may take a few seconds to discern a weak pulse. Second, if the victim's heart is beating extremely slowly, but still beating spontaneously, it may take that long to feel more than one pulse beat. This would be particularly true in cases of severe hypothermia and certain depressant drug overdose. If there is a pulse, then the victim's heart is still beating, and chest compressions are not needed. However, if the victim is still not breathing, then give the victim rescue breaths at a rate of one breath every 5 seconds (8-10 breaths per minute).

Check the pulse every few minutes to be certain the victim's heart is still beating. It is generally believed that, in an adult, the presence of a pulse in the carotid artery is consistent with a blood pressure adequate to keep the brain sufficiently per fused. In a sense, if a pulse is present, the victim has blood pressure sufficient to sustain life.

If no pulse is felt, then the victim's heart is probably not beating, or it is not beating adequately. Another possibility is that the victim's heart is not beating in an organized fashion and may require defibrillation. In any event, chest compressions are necessary. Initiate chest compressions along with ventilations. Expose the victim's chest, if it is not already bared. Place the heel of the other hand, which is closest to the victim's head, on the lower half of the sternum, with the other hand placed on top of the first. It helps to interlock your fingers to avoid putting pressure on the ribs. Compress the sternum at a rate of at least 100 compressions per minute. Each compression should be at least 2" in depth.

After compressing the victim's chest for 30 strokes, ventilate the victim 2 more times and then continue alternating 30 chest compressions with two ventilations. After five cycles of compressions and ventilations, recheck the pulse. If the pulse has returned, stop chest compressions but continue artificial ventilations as needed. If there has been no return of pulse, then the victim should be ventilated and chest compressions and artificial ventilation should continue in the same 30:2 configuration.

CPR is continued in this manner until the victim begins to breathe spontaneously or if the rescuer is too weak to continue, is relieved by someone else who knows how to do cardiopulmonary resuscitation, or the victim is placed in the care of emergency medical personnel.

### Early Defibrillation

It is now evident that CPR by itself may not be adequate to save lives in cardiac arrest. The 1992 National Conference on Cardiopulmonary Resuscitation (CPR) and Emergency Cardiac Care (ECC) concluded that there was the need for more widespread use of early defibrillation intervention. While basic CPR prolongs the life of the victim for a few minutes, most victims of sudden cardiac arrest will not ultimately survive unless there is further intervention. An automated external defibrillator (AED) should be kept on site at all commercial diving operations.

Sudden death secondary to cardiac disease is a leading cause of death in the United States. Estimates are that if all the links in what is called the "chain of survival" are intact, upward of 49% of all victims of sudden cardiac death might survive to discharge. This contrasts to rather dismal survival to discharge rates that occur at present in the United States with the system as it exists in most parts of the country. The critical links in the chain of survival include the following:

- early recognition of the problem and mobilization of the EMS response

- early CPR intervention

- early defibrillation

- early advanced cardiac life support

A diver trained in CPR can be instrumental in performing the key functions in the first three links in the chain, i.e. call for help, CAB, and defibrillation (*2010 AHA Guidelines*).

Some heart rhythm abnormalities can be corrected by administering an electric (direct current [DC] shock to the heart muscle. One of these abnormal rhythms is known as ventricular fibrillation. When the heart is in ventricular fibrillation, the heart quivers without pumping any blood. It is estimated that the majority (80–90%) of adults with sudden cardiac arrest not due to chest trauma are suffering from ventricular fibrillation when the initial electrocardiogram reading is obtained. (Information from *2010 AHA Guidelines*.)

Almost all survivors of ventricular fibrillation have received early defibrillation. Survival dramatically falls if the first defibrillation effort is not delivered within 8-10 minutes of the initial arrest. The emphasis on early defibrillation is so great that the implication of the 2010 report is that, optimally, automated external defibrillators should be available to deal with sudden cardiac death.

The AED is a medical device that not only analyzes a victim's cardiac rhythm but also guides the rescuer through the steps to deliver the potentially lifesaving shock. Automated external defibrillators sold today are described as semi-automatic in their method of operation. The semi-automatic defibrillator analyzes the cardiac rhythm and determines if a shock is warranted. The shock cannot be delivered without some physical action by the rescuer. The material below, very briefly, shows the steps in the utilization of one such device. As with most material in this section, it is important to recognize that the brief presentation here does not constitute training but simply provides material to supplement appropriate training by the agencies previously cited.

AEDs are remarkable devices in that they not only analyze cardiac rhythms but also provide voice prompts to the caregiver. For example, some of the "spoken" computer-generated commands that may be heard from the automated defibrillator's speaker include the following: "stand clear," "analyzing," "charging," "press to shock," "check pulse," "start CPR," "stop CPR," "check victim," etc.

As in basic CPR described above, the victim is checked for responsiveness, breathing, and pulse. In the nonbreathing and pulse-less victim, ensure that someone has activated the EMS system and, at the same time, have someone bring the automatic defibrillator to the victim and place it beside the victim. If there is more than a momentary delay until the automated defibrillator is deployed, perform basic CPR and, if possible, the victim's breathing should be supported with supplemental oxygen.

The automated defibrillator, due to its sophisticated computer technology, is typically not the sort of device that a diver will purchase for himself. However, it has largely been established as a standard of care that should be present, along with adequate oxygen and oxygen delivery devices, on dive support vessels, offshore construction vessels, and smaller dive vessels.

## Stopping Life-Threatening Bleeding

Once the presence of a pulse and the patient airway and breathing have been ensured, the last phase of the primary assessment/intervention is control of any visible, life-threatening, or severe bleeding.

It is unusual that any external bleeding will require care beyond direct pressure to the site of the bleeding and, if the injury is to an extremity, lifting it above the level of the heart. It is important, particularly when bleeding is present, to be cognizant of the infection risks and take the steps necessary for protection. Remove the disposable gloves from their packaging and put gloves on before proceeding.

Provided there is time, a sterile dressing should be removed from its packaging in a manner that the sterility of the dressing is maintained to the maximum extent.

The sterile dressing should be firmly held against the wound with a gloved hand and, if the wound is in an extremity, the extremity should be lifted above the level of the victim's heart. The force of gravity working against the movement of blood will, in a small part, contribute to the slowing of the rate of bleeding.

If direct pressure with the dressing substantially slows but does not entirely stop the bleeding, do not remove the dressing. Instead, apply another dressing on top of the blood-soaked dressing and continue this process until the soaking of the dressings subsides or until it is determined that more aggressive methods must be employed to stop the bleeding.

**Pressure Points**

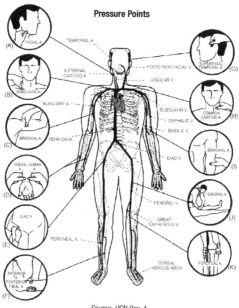

Source: *USN Rev. 4*

If direct pressure and elevation do not significantly reduce the rate of the flow of blood, then it may be necessary to use alternative means to stop the bleeding. If the uncontrolled bleeding is in the upper arm, pressure should be applied to the brachial artery, found on the inside of the upper arm. Apply pressure where there is a pulse. This will compress the artery against the bone of the upper arm.

The pressure point to use for bleeding in the leg is the femoral artery. Feel along the crease in the groin on the inside of the upper leg to find a pulse. Use the heel of one hand to compress the artery against the bone.

A tourniquet is the absolute last resort in an effort to control bleeding from an extremity. The "litmus test" applied to the use of the tourniquet is when the risk of the loss of a portion of the limb is an acceptable trade-off for the stopping of the bleeding that cannot be stopped by any other means.

A three- to four-inch band of cloth makes a good tourniquet. This is usually a triangular bandage folded into what is known as a cravat. The cravat should be placed between the victim's heart and the wound, about one inch above the wound. The cravat is wrapped around the extremity and an overhand knot is tied in the cravat to hold it in place.

A stout stick is needed, or on a boat, a wrench is usually readily available, at least 6 inches in length. Place it over the overhand knot and then tie it in place with a square knot. Twist the stick in circles until the bleeding stops. Once the bleeding has stopped, take another cravat and use it to tie the stick in place.

Remember, the tourniquet is a last-ditch effort to stop bleeding that cannot be stopped by direct pressure, elevation, or the use of pressure points. There are also several commercially manufactured tourniquets on the market. Be certain that the direct pressure and elevation method or pressure on an arterial pressure point have been given adequate time before deciding to apply a tourniquet.

**Applying a Tourniquet**

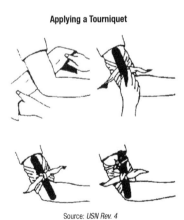

Source: *USN Rev. 4*

If the tourniquet is used as other than a short-term, stop-gap measure, take a marking device of some kind and write the initials "TQ" on the victim's forehead as well as the time the tourniquet was applied. Finally, in preparing the victim for transport, never allow the tourniquet to be covered since it may be missed or accidentally dislodged. Keeping the tourniquet in sight will make all those involved in the care or handling of the victim aware of the tourniquet's presence.

### Managing the Victim with Suspected Spinal Injury

Always consider the possibility that in-water trauma may have caused injury to the victim's spinal cord. Some mechanisms of possible spinal injury include the victim hitting his/her head on the bottom of a boat, being struck by a crane load, being struck by boat or watercraft, or a victim thrown around uncontrollably in the surf. These examples presume a spinal cord injury has taken place, and inappropriate management of the victim may lead to further and permanently disabling injury.

The part of the spinal cord that is most frequently injured in such accidents is the cervical spine, the section of the spinal column in the neck. The most critical aspect of managing such victims is maintaining the cervical spine in a neutral inline position. This means that a rescuer should try to keep the victim's neck in a position that approximates the normal position that the neck is in when the victim is standing upright with the head looking straight forward.

When moving a victim in the water, manual support to keep the head in that position is supplemented by the buoyant effect of the water. In essence, the water can provide some of the splinting effect necessary. In the water, cradle the victim's head between your forearms while stabilizing the head relative to the spine by placing your hands on the victim's torso. It is impossible to stabilize the cervical spine by holding only the head while floating in the water. It is important that the rescuer get assistance in managing such a victim immediately, since maintaining a victim in this position, while keeping the body aligned, is extremely difficult to do alone.

In wading water, the victim needs to be towed with one arm being utilized to stabilize the spine itself, while the other hand is used to maintain the head in a neutral position. Again, assistance of other trained individuals or bystanders should be enlisted as soon as possible. If the victim is otherwise stable, he/she should be maintained in the water until additional assistance arrives with appropriate equipment for removing the victim from the water and replacing the manual stabilization technique being employed.

Removing such a victim from the water to a boat is always a difficult process. After getting the maximum amount of help, stabilize the victim onto a backboard or basket litter (Stokes litter). Firmly tie the Stokes litter down in the LARS basket at water level and winch it up onboard. If the diving operation is not using a LARS, use the vessel's hydraulic crane to lift the Stokes Litter onboard using the lifting slings provided with the Stokes litter.

## A COMPLETE VICTIM ASSESSMENT: THE SECONDARY SURVEY
### The Head-To-Toe Examination
Initiate the secondary survey after completing primary victim care, having identified and managed those problems that might be life-threatening. The secondary survey by first responders in the field should never delay formal Medevac transport to an emergency department. If Medevac has not arrived and time permits, proceed with the secondary survey.

In the process of this further evaluation, a rescuer reevaluates the victim to be certain that no potentially life-threatening problems were missed during primary victim care. The rescuer is also identifying those problems that may not be life-threatening but should be managed, or at the very least, noted at the conclusion of the secondary survey. During this integrated process, the rescuer will also interview the victim to learn any significant facts regarding the victim's medical history and exactly what brought on the problem.

For a victim suffering an illness, the secondary survey may take on a slightly different pattern than for the victim suffering from injury (trauma). The trauma victim requires a complete head-to-toe check, while in illness-emergency surveys, a rescuer will generally focus on those parts of the body about which the victim is complaining. In order not to confuse the issue, this discussion will explain the secondary survey as it relates to a trauma victim. To use these techniques on an illness victim, simply use those procedures that would apply to the part of the body about which the victim is complaining. In both injury and illness, the medical history interview that is described in the next section is essentially the same.

The eyes and hands are the tools every rescuer will need to conduct a secondary survey. Visualization and recognition of abnormalities, as well as touching the victim, are the primary methods used by every caregiver, including physicians.

The secondary survey is performed from head to toe. Particularly in the case of a trauma victim, it is necessary to remove all unnecessary body covering so that the victim's body surfaces can be seen and touched. In all cases, this is done with discretion and concern for the victim's emotional and physical welfare. If it is necessary to remove a woman's clothing, for example, be careful to cover her breasts with a sheet or towel in the interest of modesty. The same sensitivity applies when the genital area of either sex is exposed.

If a wetsuit must be removed, start by cutting at the neck of the suit down the sleeve. Removal of coverings to expose the victim begins at the upper body since there is greater risk to the victim from injuries to the neck, chest, and abdomen than from injuries to the lower extremities. As much as possible, cut apparel at or near the seams so that the wetsuit or garment may possibly be repaired later. However, never jeopardize the victim for the sake of a garment. As garments are removed, constantly scan the victim's exposed body for signs of injury.

Rather than exposing a little of the victim and assessing, it will keep the process more organized and less likely to miss something important to expose the victim all at once. Then return to the victim's head to begin the thorough head-to-toe evaluation.

Remember that by this point, primary victim care has been completed and the rescuer can be relatively confident that all obvious life-threatening injuries have been identified and treated.

Using proper personal protective equipment, begin the secondary assessment of the victim by gently palpating (feeling) the victim's scalp and noting any deformities or places where fluid that may be blood is present. External bleeding hidden by the hair will be evident from the appearance of blood on the gloved fingers. Note any reaction the victim may have to being touched that appears to indicate feeling pain. Examine the ears for any bleeding or discharge.

Next, slide both hands to the back of the victim's neck to feel for any noticeable deformities and any indication that pain is present. If it appears that an injury mechanism may have caused injury to the spine, or if neck pain response is elicited, stabilize the neck. Enlist the assistance of another caregiver or a bystander to hold the victim's head in a neutral position. Additionally, if the victim is conscious and oriented, caution the victim that it is important that no head movement take place since it might lead to further injury.

Using your hand, cover one of the victim's eyes. While doing so, watch the pupil (black, central portion of the eye) to observe if it dilated (got larger) while it was shaded. If it did not, it may indicate some serious problems either to the eye itself or the brain. When the hand shading the eye is removed, the pupil should constrict (get smaller). This procedure should be repeated with the other eye. Again, failure of the pupil to react in this fashion is a sign of possible abnormality and should be noted.

Move the fingers down to the prominent bones under the eyes and press gently. Feel for deformity and watch the victim for a response to pain when these bones are pressed. While doing this segment of the assessment, also examine the nostrils for the discharge of blood-like fluid. Do one side of the victim's face and then the other, so as to specifically identify an area where an injury has occurred.

The victim's mouth should be opened either voluntarily or by the rescuer. Note any pain when the victim's mouth is opened and examine the inside of mouth for any debris, broken teeth, blood clots, etc. If any loose or foreign matter is noticed, carefully remove it with your fingers. Be careful not to push such material deeper into the victim's airway, and do not reach too far back into the victim's throat to remove the object or vomiting may be stimulated.

Examine the front portion of the neck visually for open wounds or signs of injury, such as abrasions or discoloration. The entire neck should be gently palpated with the fingertips, particularly in diving accidents. If little "blister pack" bubbles are felt under the skin or noises that sound like Rice Krispies® are heard when pressing on the tissues, it probably indicates the presence of subcutaneous emphysema. This indicates the presence of free air bubbles under the skin and is usually found in severe lung injuries where air has actually escaped from the lungs and chest cavity and has migrated under the skin to the neck region.

A visual scan of the skin over the collarbone (clavicle) is performed to identify injuries or discoloration, usually bruising, consistent with injury. Use fingers to press gently along the length of each collarbone, the most commonly fractured bone in the body. By checking these bones and others separately rather than using both hands and doing them simultaneously, the rescuer only has to elicit a painful response from the victim once, since it is evident when palpating a victim unilaterally which side the injury is on. If both bones are palpated at the same time and the victim is not completely lucid, a painful response may be difficult to isolate relative to location without repeating the stimulation that caused pain.

Reexamine the chest. Remember that it was visually scanned at the time the garments were removed. If any open wounds are noted that look like they are through the chest wall or are bubbling, have someone place a gloved hand over the wound to prevent further passage of air in and out. Later, after the examination is complete, the bystander's hand can be replaced with some form of dressing which will prevent air from entering the chest. The Asherman Chest Seal®, developed by a U.S. Navy SEAL, is a device specifically designed for rapid treatment of such chest injuries.

Use one hand to stabilize the chest on the side opposite the section of the chest that will be palpated. Use fingers to feel for each rib that can be palpated. In finding a rib, pressure should be applied and the rib evaluated for stability. Does it feel loose or are there pieces of a broken rib rubbing against neighboring, damaged bone? This process is repeated for every rib that can be felt, and then is done in exactly the same fashion on the other side. In addition to feeling for lack of stability as described above, also watch for a painful response from the victim.

Imagine that there are two lines drawn on the front of the victim's body. One of these lines goes from the chin down the middle of the body through the belly button. These two imaginary lines subdivide the victim's abdomen into four quadrants. First visually scan the abdomen for signs of injury, and then palpate each of these four quadrants separately, noting if it is hard, is stiffened by the victim when pressed upon, or causes a painful response from the victim when pressed on. Each quadrant of the abdomen is palpated separately. Mentally note the findings. Other than managing any open wounds found on the abdomen, the rescuer's only role in this phase of the assessment is to identify anything abnormal.

When reporting the findings to emergency medical services personnel, describe in which of the four areas of the abdomen the findings were present. Going back to the imaginary lines from above, the abdomen is separated into four quadrants described as the right upper quadrant (RUQ), left upper quadrant (LUQ), right lower quadrant (RLQ), and left lower quadrant (LLQ). Left and right in this regard, as in all other descriptions relative to left and right on a victim, refer to the victim's right and left.

Though it will not do anything different to a victim knowing what may be injured or ailing in a particular quadrant, it may be of interest to know the major abdominal organs found in each of the four quadrants. The major organs of the RUQ are the liver and the gall bladder. The LUQ contains the stomach and the spleen. The appendix is found in the RLQ. Small and large intestine can be found in both of the lower quadrants, with the major structure in the LLQ being the terminal segments of the large intestine. The urinary bladder is located in the middle of the bottom of the abdomen as is a woman's uterus. The female reproductive organs and ovaries are found in both the RLQ and the LLQ.

Now place both palms on the "wings" of the pelvis (anatomically described as the superior iliac crests). With hands in this position, push them toward each other and "squeeze" the pelvis toward the middle of the victim's body, noting any feeling of instability or any painful response.

If the above evaluation did not elicit any response from the victim, shift position slightly so that your body is over the victim's pelvis, and shift hand position slightly. With the hands in this position, push on both sides of the pelvis simultaneously. Again, try to note any instability of the pelvis and any painful response on the part of the victim.

Visually examine each leg, looking for any obvious deformity of the legs and joints, unevenness in size (indicating swelling), open wounds, abrasions, or bruising. With both hands, palpate the entire length of each leg separately. This palpation should be fairly deep since the objective is to feel for the bones underneath. One must at least press deeply enough to stimulate a painful response to pressure from the victim if injury is present.

After completing the visual and manual evaluation of each leg, use one hand to stabilize the bottom of the leg and, if the victim is conscious, ask the victim to wiggle their toes on the leg being held. Then stroke the foot with fingertips and ask the victim if that touch was felt. This procedure is then repeated on the opposite leg. This method is used to determine if the nerves to the leg are functioning properly from a sensory standpoint and whether or not the victim is capable of voluntarily moving the lower extremities.

Now evaluate the victim's arms. As with all other parts of the body, the first step is to visually scan the arms for obvious deformities or injuries. Next, in a fashion similar to the procedure used with the legs, the bones of the arms are palpated, checking one arm at a time.

Finally, the arm is stabilized with one hand in a fashion similar to the procedure described with the leg above. Ask the victim to wiggle his fingers first, then stroke the hand with your fingers and ask the victim if the touch can be felt. This procedure is performed on both arms. Similar to the steps used for the legs, this procedure determines if the nerve pathways to and from the arms are intact.

When reaching the victim's wrist, feel for the presence of a radial pulse. This pulse is found on the underside of the arm at the same side of the wrist where the thumb is on the hand. If a pulse is present, it is a pretty good sign that the victim's blood pressure is probably not dangerously low. If a watch is available, count the pulse beats in 15 seconds. Taking that number and multiplying by four will yield the victim's heart rate for one minute. Alternatively, count the pulses for 30 seconds and double the result. If no pulse is felt at the wrist on either arm, the rescuer needs to consider the possibility that the victim is very ill due to what is called shock. If that is the case, oxygen needs to be administered as soon as possible, as well as measures taken to conserve the victim's body heat.

If there are no injuries to the lower extremities and no head injury, it may be appropriate to elevate the lower extremities. This allows gravity to assist with the shifting of some of the victim's blood from the legs to the body core. If the victim complains of increased discomfort in the head or the victim finds it more difficult to breathe with the legs in this position, then the victim should be maintained in a flat position.

In this section, an attempt has been made to concentrate on recognition and management of problems, but it is necessary to briefly examine the concept of shock. The technical definition of shock is inadequate tissue perfusion. This means that the circulatory system is incapable of delivering adequate oxygen and nutrients to the tissues, most significantly the vital organs. At the same time, potentially toxic byproducts of the body's metabolism are no longer being removed adequately. The grave results of this process, without appropriate recognition and intervention, may be death to tissues, organs, or in the most extreme cases, the victim. The simplest means of identifying impending or present shock is observable in the physical appearance of the victim along with an increased heart rate. A drop in blood pressure is also a significant sign of shock but may only occur later.

The body's natural defenses against shock will cause the victim to appear pale and skin will feel cool to the touch. At the same time, the victim's skin surface will usually be extremely moist (often described as clammy). Without further understanding of the complex details of shock, rescuers need to recognize that a victim who is pale, cool, clammy, and has either a weak or absent pulse at the wrist may be in very grave condition. This victim needs immediate, aggressive care which, for the most part, is beyond the scope of the basic caregiver. The principal steps to take when shock is suspected include the following:

- Keep the victim lying down.

- Prevent the loss of body heat, and make sure the victim is dry to limit evaporative heat loss.

- Administer oxygen to the victim as soon as these signs of shock are recognized.

In these situations, the pulse should be felt at the neck in the same fashion used during primary victim care and the heart rate determined by counting those pulses for 15 or 30 seconds and multiplying as described earlier.

Now, observe the rise and fall of the victim's chest, and count the number of respirations in 15 or 30 seconds. Multiply in the same way as with the pulse to assess the victim's breathing rate.

The last step in the secondary assessment or survey is to record the findings. On a smaller vessel like an SRP boat, it may be difficult but use the back of a dive sheet, if necessary, or a cellphone - just get it recorded. On a larger vessel or an inland project, pen and paper will be easier to find.

The information is recorded from head to toe with all injuries noted. The presence or absence of motor control and feeling in the four limbs is recorded. Finally, the presence or absence of a radial pulse is noted, along with the heart rate and breathing rate. Also, in this part of the note-taking process, record observations relative to "what happened" to cause the victim's condition.

## Taking the Necessary History

Aside from the immediate medical or injury problems (medically referred to as acute conditions), it is also important for all medical caregivers to know something about the victim's medical history that might have some relevance to the current problem. If, during the secondary survey, problems have been identified that require treatment quickly, then the performing of the medical history interview can be delayed until those conditions are cared for. Some examples of problems that might need immediate attention include the following:

- Airway or breathing deterioration
- Failure of victim's overall condition, consistent with shock
- Wounds that need to have bleeding stopped and dressings applied
- Injuries to the bones or joints that need to be splinted

- Diving illnesses that need the immediate administration of oxygen

- Marine life injuries that need immediate treatment in order to relieve significant victim discomfort

Failing any of the problems listed above, the victim history-taking interview should follow immediately after recording the findings from the primary and secondary assessments.

First, explain to the victim that it is important to learn something about the victim's medical history, so those caring for the victim will have important medical details available when making treatment decisions. We use a mnemonic to easily learn the necessary components of the complete medical history—SAMPLE. Each letter represents a vital component of the victim's medical history:

**S** - Signs and symptoms

**A** - Allergies

**M** - Medications

**P** - Past illnesses or injuries; past medical history

**L** - Last meal or last oral intake

**E** - Events leading up to the injury or illness

As part of the medical history interview, have the victim describe his/her symptoms. In the victim's own words, if pain is present, what does it feel like? Does anything make the pain worse or better? How long has the pain been present and has its intensity changed during that period? Does the pain remain in one place or does it seem to radiate or travel to other parts of the body? Have the patient rate the pain on a scale of 0 to 10, with 10 being the worst pain possible.

All information learned during this part of the interview should be recorded in the same fashion as the findings during the primary and secondary assessment and subsequently related to medical care personnel who assume responsibility for the victim. Signs and symptoms include the patient's chief complaint, or what is described to you as the problem, then any additional information about what is ailing the viction is included here. This will include location and severity of pain. Allergies are important as some acute allergic reactions, called anaphylactic responses, may trigger breathing difficulties and may also lead to the victim slipping into a severe shock state. Sometimes, people have such reactions from the consumption of certain seafood. At other times, stinging insects may precipitate allergic reactions in people. In the marine setting, though quite rare, true anaphylactic reactions have been observed after a victim has sustained a marine life sting. If the victim does have an allergic history from bites and stings or past allergic reactions to certain foods, it is important to monitor the victim's condition closely. Be on the alert for breathing difficulties or severe deterioration of the victim, since this may be the early signs of a major crisis.

A rescuer is not expected to know what certain medications do, but victims can usually tell why he/she may be taking certain medications. If a victim says he/she is taking "water" or "pressure" pills, the victim may have a history of heart or high blood pressure problems, which may have caused the present medical emergency. If the victim takes "sugar" pills or medication for "sugar," suspect diabetes. People with seizure disorders should not be cleared for diving. Typically, persons with epilepsy may take medications such as Dilantin®, Tegretol®, or phenobarbital. A more extensive discussion of medications is unnecessary for the basic caregiver, but any time a victim is taking prescription medications, it may indicate that there is a disease process which caused the victim's difficulty or contributed to it. Divers who have trouble clearing their ears while diving sometimes use decongestants. These medications have a finite effect which may wear off while diving. This can carry a "rebound effect," which may contribute to a diving-related injury.

When discussing past illnesses with a victim, concentrate on major illnesses that might cause or contribute to a victim's difficulties or precipitate a victim becoming unstable enough to sustain injury. In the diving and marine environment, the illnesses that may lead to serious problems include heart disease, respiratory diseases (including asthma), high blood pressure (hypertension), diabetes, and seizure disorders.

What a victim has ingested orally may be a cause of a victim's difficulty. In the marine setting, ingestion of certain marine life can lead to various illnesses. Dehydration has been implicated as a contributing factor to diving injuries. Question a diving injury victim relative to adequate non-alcoholic fluid intake during the prior 24 hours. Alcohol or other drugs of abuse may be contributors to a victim's injuries. Query the victim relative to the use of alcohol or drugs during the period of time coincident with the injury or illness. Low blood sugar (hypoglycemia) may be a cause of instability in both diabetics and nondiabetics alike. Determine whether the victim has eaten within a reasonable period of time prior to the illness or injury. Basically, information relative to any ingestion that may have contributed to the problem should be noted and reported to the medical care professionals who assume the victim's care.

Perhaps the most significant part of the medical history interview has to do with the events which led up to the injury or illness. In the simplest terms, this is the "what happened" part of the interview. In diving accidents, it is important to learn the dive profile, not that it influences treatment, but to avoid a repeat of the problem. The diving equipment the victim was using should be kept together in one place, just in case investigators require it for inspection. In the case of non - diving related trauma, it is significant to ask the victim if everything was normal before the injury. The information to elicit here is whether the injury was purely an accident or if there was some medical problem that precipitated the victim hurting himself/herself. In the case of injuries, it may be useful to learn what caused the accident resulting in the trauma in order to prevent future similar accidents. As far as possible, record in the victim's own words regarding what took place before an accident. If the problem is medical, have the victim describe what was taking place before the symptoms of the problem were first noticed. Specifically, what activity was the victim involved in? Was the victim at rest or performing a specific strenuous activity? What had the victim been doing in the hours immediately preceding the onset of illness? Did the victim notice any unusual feelings during those hours that were not quite normal, but did not seem too severe?

## ELECTROCUTION

Electrocution may result from the careless handling, poor design, or poor maintenance of power equipment such as welding and cutting equipment or electric underwater lights. All electrical equipment used underwater should be well insulated. In addition, divers should be properly insulated from any possible source of electrical current. Another source of electrocution and electrical burns is lightning.

Prevention of electrocution from lightning is simply a matter of divers not permitting themselves to remain out in the open, particularly on a small open boat, when there is obviously the threat of lightning from thunderstorms. The IMCA Guideline recommends ceasing diving operations at the first sign of an electrical storm. When seeking shelter from storms, it is important to avoid places and structures where one might reasonably expect lightning to strike (i.e. under a crane boom or in structures that stand alone on an open deck).

Although it is extremely unlikely a diver will be electrocuted, it could well happen to deck crew. Victims often are not able to separate themselves from the source of the shock. Before intervening, the rescuer must first be certain that he/she, too, is not being exposed to an electrocution hazard. When attempting to separate the electrocution victim from the source of the electricity, make certain that a nonconducting material is used to facilitate the separation. Nonmetallic poles and long pieces of dry lumber (like a wooden oar) are objects that might be found in the diving environment suitable for separating the victim from an electrical source. If an electrical extension cord is involved, it might be most effective to find the plug and disconnect the cord.

**Signs and Symptoms of Electrocution:**

- Unconsciousness

- Seizures

- Cardiopulmonary arrest

- Burns (Electrical burns rarely appear as severe as the actual tissue damage that has occurred.)

The victim, if unresponsive after being separated from the electrical source and ensuring the scene is safe, must have a primary assessment performed and may likely require CPR. Since many electrocutions place the victim into ventricular fibrillation, rapid deployment of the AED is a prudent action. Even when an electrocution victim seems normal after the event, evaluation at a medical care institution is required. Potentially lethal side effects of electrical injury include heart dysrhythmias, kidney abnormalities and failure, and methemoglobinemia, a severe and life-threatening condition that is precipitated by the unseen breakdown of tissues following serious injury.

## WOUNDS

Open wounds, most often lacerations, are frequently encountered in the marine environment. The primary concern is always to stop all of the bleeding and to prevent any further contamination of the wound.

Since blood will undoubtedly be present, caregivers must don disposable gloves for protection. Dressing packages should be opened in a manner that will minimize contamination of the dressing.

Place the dressing over the victim's wound and apply pressure until all bleeding has stopped. Bleeding extremities are also elevated while direct pressure is applied. Both pressure and gravity are used to slow bleeding. If the bleeding continues and soaks through the first dressing applied, apply an additional dressing on top of the first. This process of adding dressings continues until the bleeding stops with blood-soaked dressings remaining in place.

With the bleeding stopped, apply a self-conforming bandage to hold the dressing in place. The first step in this process is to utilize some technique to keep the bandage from "spinning" around the victim's wound as it is applied. By wrapping one corner of the end of the bandage and "locking" it under the first wrap of the bandage, the conforming bandage can be stabilized on any body part.

Most bandaging techniques employ the open spiral/closed spiral technique. The open spiral is wrapping the bandage so that the dressing is held in place but is not overlapped sequentially. That will be executed during the closed spiral phase. When holding a roll of conforming bandage, it is held in such a way that the additional material is released from "under" the bandage roll rather than from the "top." This method makes it a bit easier to maintain appropriate tension on the bandage as well as make it less likely that the bandage will "get away."

After securing the dressing in place with the open spiral, wrap the bandage in the opposite direction utilizing the closed spiral technique. In this wrapping of the bandage, each wrap overlaps the previous wrap so that the dressing is completely covered by the bandage.

When applying a bandage to a victim, several options are available at the end of the procedure to secure the bandage in place. One simple approach is to tape the bandage in place. The bandage may also be split along its length with an overhand knot tied in the resulting "tails" and these tail pieces being used to tie the bandage in place by encircling the extremity and tying a square knot. Another common technique, which helps create a pressure dressing, is to create a loop in the bandaging material at the end of the bandaging process. The bandage is then taken back in the opposite direction until it can be passed through the loop. Secure the dressing using an overhand knot tied in the bandage. Be certain that the knot is not made so tight that the circulation is impaired. A finger should fit under the tied part of the bandage without too much effort.

After the bandage is tied, trim excess bandaging material from the ends so that these pieces will not become entangled in anything and compromise the management of the victim. With the dressing tied in place by the bandaging method chosen, periodically touch the victim's hand or foot, depending upon the extremity bandaged, to make sure it remains as warm as the opposite extremity and monitor the skin color as well. If there is any abnormality, there is a possibility the bandage has impaired the victim's circulation or swelling has caused such impairment. The bandage should be untied and retied more loosely.

If treating smaller wounds and unable to get the victim to medical assistance immediately, the small wounds may be washed with soap and water and then dressed in the same manner as above. The only difference is that there will not be any substantial bleeding that needs to be stopped.

## BURNS

When one is exposed to boats, there are many sources of heat that may cause burns. Manifolds, stuffing boxes, generators, compressors, and gas or alcohol stoves are just a few of the heat sources that may cause such burns. Burns can be particularly insidious injuries leading to infection, severe scarring, and partial disability of the burned area. There are three generally accepted classifications of burns with which you should have some familiarity:

- **Superficial or first-degree burns:** Classified as a burn involving only the epidermis and often referred to as superficial burns, they redden the skin but initially cause no other damage. Treat such burns by immersing the effected body part in cool water to stop the burn. The objective is to reduce the temperature of the affected tissues to limit the damage and reduce the victim's discomfort. If on board a boat and looking for some immediate relief for minor burns, Burn Gel® or other similar products can be used. This is a gel material that may be spread on minor burns, but most significantly, it contains 2% Lidocaine HCl, a topical anesthetic.

- **Partial thickness or second-degree burns:** Classified as a burn involving the epidermis and the dermis, but not penetrating the dermis, these are sometimes called partial thickness burns. They are more severe than first-degree burns as there is more extensive tissue damage. Blistering is a strong indication of a second-degree burn. For small burns of this classification, the same type of treatment as for first-degree burns may be initially utilized. This should be followed with the application of sterile dressings or specialized burn dressings, discussed below. Though blisters may not be attractive, care should be taken to keep the blisters intact since they are a natural "bandage" covering injured tissue below and protecting from infection.

- **Full thickness or third-degree burns:** Classified as a full-thickness burn with all layers of the skin receiving damage, they are sometimes confused with second-degree burns. A strong indicator are areas that are dry and white or even charred black. The patient may complain of severe pain or no pain at all, which indicates severe nerve damage (although there will usually be pain around the periphery of the third-degree burn). Third-degree burns may involve permanent nerve damage, respiratory arrest, and other major complications and victims should be transported immediately to a medical facility.

There has been a tendency among first aid providers over the years to want to put something on burns. A very simple rule is "don't". Most topical substances that are commonly used do nothing to enhance healing, and most are suspended in material which has limited bacteriostatic strength but can act as a "glue" for particulate matter that may come into contact with the victim. Also, since all serious burns should be assessed medically, these substances will have to be removed by medical personnel so that the burn may be appropriately evaluated and treated.

All but the most minor superficial burns should be evaluated at a hospital emergency department. In addition, there are several types of burn situations that need to be treated in hospitals designated as burn centers. Local emergency medical services personnel should be aware which facilities are designated burn centers. If there is any doubt, the victim should be transported to the nearest trauma center. Those burn injuries which require such special attention include the following:

- Partial thickness burns covering more than 15% of body surface area

- Full-thickness burns covering more than 5% of body surface area

- Any significant burns involving the hands, face, feet, or genital area

- Any high-voltage electrical burns

- Any inhalation or airway burns

- Any chemical burns from chemicals that may continue to destroy tissues

- Any burns which occurred with associated significant other injuries

There are several methods for determining the percentage of the body surface area burned. However, the simplest procedure is a method of estimation based on the surface area of the victim's palm. As a rough estimating tool, each "palm" is equal to 1% of the victim's body surface. Visually estimate the surface area of the victim's palm and then make an estimate as to how many of those palm surface areas would cover the burned area. So, if the estimate is that 10 of the victim's palms might cover the burned area that would equal a 10% burn. Another common method is the rule of nines. For this method, each full arm is 9%, the front of each leg is 9%, and the back of each leg is 9%. The upper front torso is 9% as well as the lower front torso (abdominal area), with the corresponding back area each being another 9%. The head is the final 9% bringing the total of these 11 areas to 99%. The pubic area is the final 1%.

## FRACTURES AND SPRAINS

"Slip and fall" injuries are a problem, particularly when wet boat decks come into play. Detailed diagnosis of bone and joint injuries typically are left to trained medical personnel. All a rescuer really needs to do is to recognize that there has been an injury that may involve the bones and joints.

If a victim has suffered a falling or twisting injury and complains of severe pain in a bone or joint, the initial presumption should be that injury has taken place. Swelling and discoloration may confirm such injuries. Injuries like this need to be evaluated by a medical professional, preferably in a hospital emergency room. Even if there is no fracture present, there may be significant injury to the tissues surrounding a joint and the injury needs to be managed as a fracture.

Principles of bone and joint injury management are universal in that the primary objective is to immobilize the bones and joints immediately above and immediately below the site of the injury. The ankle is a commonly injured joint in the marine environment. Typically, the onboard clinic or hospital has aluminum splints of various sizes for each body joint.

The forearm bones are commonly fractured either by falls or having heavy objects falling upon them. Managing such an injury ideally requires the assistance of a bystander or another caregiver during the initial stages so that any additional movement of the injured extremity is minimized. The victim's upper arm, elbow, wrist, and hand are stabilized manually first. Due to the interconnections between the hand and the arm, it is important to be certain that the hand is immobilized. This will prevent unnecessary pain and further injury to the victim. The hand should be immobilized in what is described as the position of function. One of the simplest methods of doing this is by placing a roll of self-conforming bandage gently into the victim's grip while the support of the arm is manually maintained.

Another caregiver or bystander can manage the manual support of the injured extremity while the rescuer shapes a SAM® splint to the victim's arm. The SAM® splint was developed by orthopedic surgeon Sam Scheinberg and is an ideal device for the marine environment, since it is essentially impervious to the environment, light in weight, and when rolled up takes up very little space. This splint can also be reused and is suitable for bone and joint injuries of the arm as well as wrist, shoulder, and, when two splints are used together, can be used to splint the leg or ankle. The splint is secured in place using a self-conforming bandage in the same manner as discussed in wound management.

For upper extremity injuries, the splint is only the first part of care and the arm should be further supported and immobilized using a sling and swathe. To prepare a sling for the victim, tie an overhand knot in the point of the triangular bandage that will be used as the splint. If a triangular bandage is laid out flat, two "long arms" and one "short arm" will be noticed. The knot should be tied at the very end of the short arm. The knot will help to form the "cup" at the victim's elbow when the sling is applied. When applying the sling to the victim, take the portion of the triangular bandage closest to the victim's body and pass it around the side of the neck on the same side as the injury. The other end of the triangular bandage, the portion which is on the outside of the victim's arm, is passed over the shoulder opposite the victim's injured arm. The sling is tied behind the victim's neck with a square knot, but the knot should rest to the side of the neck in the interest of the victim's comfort. As a final safeguard, take another triangular bandage and bring it over the outside of the upper arm and tie it off under the victim's opposite arm. This is described as the swathe and yields a full immobilization of the injured arm. With slight modifications, this same sling and swathe technique is useful for the management of upper arm, shoulder, and collar bone injuries.

## POSSIBLE MEDICAL PROBLEMS

Though most people encountered on a diving operation are generally healthy, it is possible that on board a boat, divers may be exposed to certain medical emergencies. None of these will be discussed in great detail, but some thoughts are offered relative to the initial management of some illnesses that may be encountered.

## Respiratory Emergencies

The simplest way to classify respiratory problems is those victims breathing too fast, those breathing too slowly, or those whose breathing is impaired due to some internal obstruction.

## Hyperventilation

Breathing too fast (tachypnea) may be a natural response to injuries or to blood loss and need not be treated. Instead, deal with the underlying problems in a manner previously discussed. Tachypnea may also be a result of diabetes or other metabolic emergencies and needs the attention of medical professionals, as it may be a sign of a very serious medical condition.

However, the hyperventilation syndrome can be a problem. By definition, hyperventilation means increased ventilation which depletes blood $CO_2$ below 35 to 38 mm Hg. This may lead to an imbalance of respiratory gases in the body that need to maintain a relatively delicate balance. It is usually precipitated from some emotional response, but once started, appears to be self-sustaining and beyond the voluntary control of the victim.

The victim will usually breathe from 35 to 50 times per minute and may complain of numbness and tingling around the mouth and nose. The victim is anxious and appears to be suffering from air hunger and may also exhibit cramping of the hands and forearms.

Management of this type of hyperventilation is directed at getting the victim's respiratory gases back into balance. Take two immediate actions:

1. Continue to reassure the victim that everything is OK, and that the victim needs to concentrate on trying to slow his/her breathing.

2. Using either a paper bag or an oxygen mask not connected to any oxygen, have the victim re-breathe his/her own exhaled air. This

will increase the level of carbon dioxide in the blood, the gas that has been depleted via hyperventilation, and brings the respiratory rate back under control.

If the victim's breathing does not quickly come under control, the victim needs to be treated by more advanced emergency medical personnel.

### Inadequate Breathing (Hypoventilation)

This type of problem can be the result of a disease process, extreme weakness, or some injuries that cause the victim to limit chest wall movement. In any case, the problem leads to an inadequate volume of gas being exchanged each minute, with too little oxygen being taken into the system, and too little carbon dioxide being exhaled.

The rescuer may notice the problem by observing a very slow breathing rate of less than 10 breaths per minute. Very shallow breathing or cyanosis (a bluish color change seen in the nail beds and around the lips) may be present. Any of these findings should be treated by administering oxygen and providing ventilatory support to the victim in the manner discussed previously.

### Obstructive Problems

Diseases such as chronic bronchitis, emphysema, and asthma all result in some degree of blockage or impairment of normal gas exchange. If a victim has one of these diseases and such a person is in respiratory difficulty and in obvious distress, oxygen should be administered and supplementary ventilation should be considered. Such victims are almost always more comfortable if maintained in a sitting position. These are emergencies that need to be transferred immediately to the emergency medical services system for care.

### Cardiovascular Emergencies

In the course of discussing primary victim care, the procedures to follow in the event of cardiac arrest were examined. Even if the condition being treated is essentially self-limiting, like angina, the victim needs to be transferred to the emergency medical services system for ongoing care and ultimate disposition. It has been recognized that one of the leading causes of unnecessary deaths from heart disease occurs because of delay in reaching appropriate care. Do not contribute to the problem.

Certain chronic cardiac problems, the most common of which is called chronic or congestive heart failure, will usually involve a victim in respiratory distress and needing appropriate care, along with immediate transfer to the emergency medical services system. Other heart conditions usually present with a victim having any one of the following signs and symptoms:

- Chest pain (This pain will usually be described by the victim as crushing or squeezing and will not be relieved by any change of position or with breathing.)

- Respiratory distress

- Nausea or vomiting

- Unusual fatigue

- Skin color and quality that may be shock-like as previously described or cyanotic

Angina is a condition where a victim usually has the chest pain precipitated by either physical or emotional stress. The pain of angina is brought on by inadequate blood flow to the heart muscle and might be compared to a cramp of the heart muscle. However, it is often difficult to distinguish the pain of angina from that of a more serious cardiac problem. The rescuer should take several steps if initially it appears that angina is the victim's problem:

1. Calm and reassure the victim and keep the victim in a position in which they are most comfortable, often a sitting position.

2. Administer oxygen to the victim.

3. If the victim has medication for angina, assist the victim in taking the medication. If the medication is nitroglycerin in tablet form, wear disposable gloves when handling the medication, since it can be absorbed through the skin and give the caregiver a severe headache.

4. Give an adult aspirin to the patient if not allergic.

Very often, the symptoms of the angina will quickly disappear when the victim has been calmed, oxygen has been administered, and the victim's own medication has been taken. If the victim's pain and discomfort does not quickly subside, it must be presumed that angina is not the problem but that the victim is having an acute myocardial infarction (heart attack) and may be in imminent threat of death. Treatment for the heart attack victim is essentially the same as that for the angina victim at the basic level, except that the victim must be cautioned not to assist in his/her movements in any way, and thus allow you to move the victim at all times. If the victim is in a tight-fitting wetsuit or similar garment, these restricting garments must be loosened in order to allow the victim to breathe with as little effort as possible. The AED should be immediately accessible, in the event the victim becomes unresponsive.

### Stroke (Cerebro-Vascular Accident)

Strokes are usually precipitated by either a blockage of a blood vessel leading to the brain or a rupture of a vessel in the brain. Most often, victims of these problems have a history of high blood pressure. On occasion, a stroke may occur, as in the case of heart attacks, without any prior medical history or warning. A victim suffering from a stroke will exhibit one or more of the following signs and symptoms:

- Headache (sometimes described as the worst headache the victim has ever had)

- Visual disturbances (the victim will tell the caregiver that their vision is distorted or that they are blind in one or both eyes)

- Abnormalities of speech

- Inability to move one side of the body or weakness or loss of feeling to one side of the body

- Memory loss or disorientation

- Seizures

- Loss of consciousness

With recognition of any of these signs or symptoms, activate emergency medical service resources. The following immediate care must be given to the victim:

- The victim's breathing status needs to be monitored since stroke victims sometimes have difficulty protecting their own airway. If any difficulty is noticed, position the victim in a way that breathing is unobstructed.

- Keep the victim calm and reassured. If the victim is still responsive, place them in a position in which they are most comfortable with constant attention to their airway. The recovery position is recommended.

- Administer oxygen.

- Make sure that the victim's body temperature is maintained and that no additional body heat will be lost.

- If the victim is unresponsive, place the victim on his/her side in such a way that any saliva or vomit will tend to drain out of the mouth rather than being inhaled.

This care and vigilant monitoring should continue until the victim is transferred to emergency medical services personnel.


### Convulsions (Seizure)

Seizures may be simply described as a short-circuit in the victim's brain which may result in involuntary action of an isolated segment of the victim's body. Generalized motor seizures or convulsions are a major medical emergency and require intervention beyond the basic level. Contact local emergency medical services personnel. With a seizing victim, certain essential care must be performed while awaiting the arrival of emergency care personnel:

- Do not try to restrain the victim in any way.

- Move any objects away from the victim that might cause injury.

- Make sure that the victim's airway is maintained. This is particularly important after the active seizing stops. Most seizures are followed by a period of unconsciousness, and it is during that period that the airway may become impaired. Position the victim in a manner similar to the unconscious stroke victim.

- After the active seizure, do not try to arouse the victim if they seem to be sleeping. This is a natural aftermath to a major seizure.

Take notes relative to the progression of the seizure (what part of the body it started in) and the duration of the active seizing. This information, along with any other known medical history, should be given to emergency medical services personnel upon their arrival.

## CONCLUSION

The first aider must remember that his/her mission is to save life and do no harm. Although the first aider's job is typically finished upon arrival of emergency medical help, as previously mentioned, the more information the first aider can provide to medical personnel when the casualty is handed over, the better. This sometimes will require designating a helper to take notes, particularly if there is more than one casualty. Typically, on a commercial diving operation, a thorough report is made of any incident and always when first aid is rendered. Notes should be made while the incident is still fresh in the mind of the first aider.

# A NOTE FROM THE AUTHOR

Men have strived to work underwater for as long as they have worked on the water. Ports in the Roman Empire employed divers to retrieve cargo lost overboard over two thousand years ago. The Greeks had sponge divers, the Japanese and Arabs had pearl divers, but all of the early divers had one common problem—their bottom time was limited to one breath. In the early 1800s, the Deane brothers and Augustus Siebe created helmets that allowed the diver to breathe air from the surface, and they ushered in a new era of working underwater. Since the mid 1930s, deep diving has been performed using mixed gas, and since it was first used in 1965, saturation diving has become very common. The advances in both technique and equipment within the past 50 years alone are truly remarkable.

One would think an industry able to trace its roots back that far would be developed to a point that an accident would be a rare thing and a fatality would be unheard of. Unfortunately, that is far from the case. Too many accidents occur in this industry that should not happen. Every year there are divers killed for lack of a bailout, killed because machinery is not locked out, killed by differential pressure, killed by improper rigging, and killed while burning unvented tanks. The list continues. Every one of these accidents has one thing in common: **they have happened before and should not happen again**. We are not learning by our mistakes.

Every diver has must realize that if you can "flange up" a spool piece or install hydra-tights quicker than anyone else on the crew, it will not matter to your family when they are burying you. Life does not have instant replay. If the job you are on is not being run safely, speak up or walk away. It is better to be unemployed and alive than to be a dead "yes man." Working safely does not cost—it pays.

It is my sincere wish that every diver using this handbook will make a conscious decision to operate safely, to refuse to work in unsafe conditions, and that every last one will enjoy a long retirement. Too many never had the chance. Visit the Divers Association International page, or the Stop Commercial Diver Deaths page on Facebook, and the Divers Association section of the forums at www.longstreath.com. Ask your questions or have your say. Together our voices will be heard.

I wish to thank my friend CPO1 Charles Trombley who recently retired as Chief Diver, Fleet Diving Unit Atlantic, Canadian Navy, for taking the time and the patience to provide the technical editing. I am truly honored to have a man of his caliber edit my work. Also, I wish to thank my friend John Carl Roat for providing information and encouragement to me. I appreciate the good folks at Best Publishing Company who made this possible once again.

# ABOUT THE AUTHOR

Hal Lomax came from a family of commercial fishermen and had a love for the sea since he was a small boy. He decided on his career at age 5, when his great-uncle, a long-time diver, set a Morse copper helmet over his head. By the age of 10, he was on the fishing boats on weekends with his uncles and grandfather. Before the age of 16, he worked deep sea on the salvage tugs. In the mid-1970s, he worked as a diver, training on the job under ex-military divers as there were no schools yet established in Canada.

He went on to work for many different outfits over the years: on inland hydro dams and power plants, coastal construction and demolition projects, and on offshore salvage, construction, and oil field work. He ran his own diving business for a couple of decades and operated his own school for a time, where he wrote all of the course material and texts. In 2006, Hal went back to work offshore as a free-lance supervisor. He is a founding member of the Divers Association International and currently sits on the board of directors as board member for Canada. Since he hung up his helmet at the end of 2007, Hal works in various locations around the world as a diving superintendent and supervisor.

Hal has written several articles for *Underwater Magazine* and is the author of the *Commercial Diver Training Manual, 6th Edition*, also published by Best Publishing Company.

Hal Lomax
Past

Hal Lomax
Present

Printed in the USA
CPSIA information can be obtained
at www.ICGtesting.com
CBHW061101161223
2510CB00019B/4